Early
ANDERSON COUNTY
SOUTH CAROLINA

Newspapers, Marriages
and Obituaries

1841-1882

By:

Tom C. Wilkinson

Please direct all correspondence and orders to:

www.southernhistoricalpress.com
or
SOUTHERN HISTORICAL PRESS, Inc.
PO BOX 1267
375 West Broad Street
Greenville, SC   29601
southernhistoricalpress@gmail.com

ISBN #0-89308-103-5

EARLY ANDERSON COUNTY, SOUTH CAROLINA

NEWSPAPERS

Abstracted by Tom C. Wilkinson of the city of Greenville, South
Caroline.

The first paper is "The Highland Sentinel" published at Calhoun,
Anderson District, South Carolina.

The second paper is "The Anderson Gazette" published at the town
of Anderson, South Carolina. The last article is dated 24
February, 1848.

The third paper is "The Anderson Intelligencer" beginning with
4 September 1860. Some issues are missing: from 28 March 1861
to 27 July 1865. From that date until 19 December 1878, the
issues were fairly complete. Some issues were torn or difficult
to read, so there are some notices with gaps. Started July
1882 to October 12, 1882.

"The Highland Sentinel", Calhoun, Anderson District, S. C.

Issue of:
Thursday, November 5, 1840:
Obituary - Margaret Naomi Smith, daughter of Rev. Wiley C.
Smith, age 2 yrs and 3 mos. on Wednesday the 29th ult.

"The Anderson Gazette", Anderson Court House, South Carolina.

Issue of:
Thursday, January 14, 1841:
Married: On Thursday evening the 7th instant by the Rev. Wm.
P. Martin, Mr. Richard W. Grubbs to Miss Elizabeth Clement,
daughter of Hugh and Mary Clement, all of this District.

Obituary: Departed this life at his residence near Calhoun,
on Sunday morning the 3d inst., from Dropsey, after a protracted and painful attack, John Poor, Sen'r. in the 67th year of
his age. The deceased was one of the first settlers of this
district. He had resided upon the same premises through life,
and by industry, prudence, and economy, had succeeded in laying
up a goodly portion of this worlds goods. He had long been
known and respected, as a kind neighbor and devoted friend, and
was perhaps more distinguished than nine tenths of mankind for
his kind, hospitable, and generous nature. He had never attached
himself to any church, but died rejoicing in the hope of a
blessed immortality, beyond the grave. He has left behind him
a numerous train of relations, and friends, to mourn his loss,
but who drive much consolation, by knowing that, "what is their
loss, is his eternal gain".

Issue of:
Thursday, January 21, 1841:
Married: On Thursday the 7th of January by Halbert Acker, Esq.,
Mr. Benjamin Satterfield to Miss Susan Gaines, all of Anderson
District.

1

Issue of:
Thursday, February 4, 1841:
Married: On Tuesday evening the 2nd inst. by Halbert Acker,
Esq., Mr Strother Watkins to Miss Kiziah Nixon all of this
District.

Issue of:
Thursday, February 11, 1841:
Married: On Tuesday evening the 2d of Feb. by the Rev. W. P.
Martin of Abbeville District, Mr. William Ellison to Miss
Abigail C. Perit, daughter of Mary and Alfred Perit, Esq., all
of Lawrence District.

Issue of:
Thursday, February 18, 1841:
Married: On Thursday evening the 4th inst., by the Rev. San-
ford Vandiver, Mr. James Pleasant Gray of Abbeville, to Miss
Mary Ann Frances, eldest daughter of Col. John McFall of
Anderson District.

Married: On the 4th inst. by the Rev. John Vandiver, Mr.
Andrew Tate to Miss Susan Elizabeth Shirley, daughter of
Jonathan Shirley, all of this District.

Issue of:
Thursday, March 11, 1841:
Married: On Sunday evening, the 27th of February, by the Rev.
Wm. Magee, Mr. Caleb B. Holland to Miss Elizabeth Cox, all of
Anderson District.

Married: On Wednesday the 3d inst., by the Rev. Wm. Magee,
Mr. Andrew Jackson Wakefield of Abbeville to Miss Emaline
Elizabeth McGee of Anderson District.

Married: On Thursday evening the 4th inst. by the Rev. Wm.
Magee, Mr. Alfred E. Reed to Miss Elizabeth Acker all of this
District.

Issue of:
Thursday, March 25, 1841:
Married: On Thursday the 18th inst. by the Rev. W. Magee, Mr.
Thomas W. Davis to Miss Sarah Kay all of this District.

Issue of:
Thursday, April 22, 1841:
Married: On Tuesday evening the 13th inst. by the Rev. William
Magee, Mr. John R. Worthington to Miss Frances E. Magee.

Married: On Tuesday evening the 13th inst. by the Rev. William
Magee, Mr. William C. Armstrong to Miss Nancy E. Magee both
daughters of Mr. Burrel Magee. of this District.

Married: On Sunday evening, the 18th inst., by the Rev. William
Magee, Mr. Henry Mattox to Miss Matilda M. Braswell all of this
District.

Issue of:
Thursday, April 29, 1841:
Married: On the 28th of March by the Rev. W. P. Martin, Mr.
Thomas Taylor to the widow Permelia Jones, all of Laurens Dist.

2

Issue of:
Thursday, May 27, 1841:
Married: On Wednesday evening the 19th inst. by the Rev. W. P.
Martin, Mr. John P. Harrison of Cokesbury, to Miss Hulda
Lawson, daughter of Bluford and Sarah Lawson all of Abbeville
District

Issue of:
Thursday, June 3, 1841:
Married: At Summerville, on Tuesday evening the 25th ultimo,
by the Rev. Thomas Hutchins, of Charleston, S. C., Mr. James
H. Anderson to Miss Mary M. Adams, all of Hamburg, S. C.

Married: On Thursday evening the 27th ultimo, by the Rev. W.
Magee, Mr. Anderson Braswell to Miss Mary Ann Hunt, daughter of
Mr. William Hunt, all of Anderson District.

Issue of:
Thursday, July 1, 1841:
Obituary: Another Revolutionary Soldier Gone. Died at the
residence of Reuben Day in Pickens District, on the 30th of
last May, Mr. William Day, one of the patriots of the revolution in the 88th year of his age, after a severe and painful
illness, which he bore with christian resignation. He has
left four children and a large circle of friends to mourn his
loss.

Issue of:
Thursday, August 19, 1841:
Death: Death by Lightning. Mr. William Durham of this District had two children instantly killed by lightning during a
storm of wind and rain, on Friday the 6th inst. The electric
fluid descended down the chimney to the hearth, where his son
about ten, and his daughter, twelve years old, received the
fatal shock. This should serve as an admonition to persons,
to keep as distant as possible from chimneys, during a thunder
cloud, as lightning will attach to the tallest object near its
place of descent.

Issue of:
Friday, September 17, 1841:
Obituary: Died at his place on Tuesday night, the 7th inst.
Mrs. Frances Broyles, consort of Maj. Aaron Broyles, in the
seventy second year of her age. The deceased had for several
years complained at times of a difficulty which she experienced
in breathing, supposed to originate from dropsey of the chest;
but had not for some months past, until within a few days of
her death, made the least complaint, and apparently enjoyed
better health, than she had done for years. Some three or four
days previous to the fatal night, which terminated her earthly
existence, she at times felt returning symptoms of the disease,
but on that evening was apparently stouter than usual; she
[eat] a healthy supper, and retired to rest at 9 o'clock in
excellent health and spirits, and was aft day light the next
morning found lying in the same position as when she dropped to
sleep, a lifeless corpse. Her spirit had left its clayey
tenement; she had "sweetly slept her life away" without a
moments pain; a struggle, or a groan. Thus has death been
stalking in our midst, and has borne away a venerable matron,
whose piety, and many virtues rendered her an ornament to her
sex, and to human nature, Mrs. Broyles up to the day of her

3

death, an uncommon stout woman, and although rising three score and ten years, was almost as active and sprightly as a girl. She possessed an extra ordinary intellect for a female and her whole energy was devoted to the happiness of her race. But few women have ever lived or died so universally and deservedly beloved by all who knew them. Blessed in the possession of an amply supply of the things of this world, her kind and generous nature rendered her a mother to the poor and afflicted, within the whole bounds of her acquaintance. To administer to the wants of the needy, and relieve the sufferings of the afflicted, seemed to be her only earthly desire, and with the ample means to do good, which God had placed in her store, so successful was she in this Heavenly calling, that her loss to the whole community is irreparable. She had many years been a pious and exemplary member of the Baptist Church, devout follower of the christian Religion; therefore the only consolation which is left to her numerous friends and relatives; knowing that her loss to them can never be supplied on earth, is the pleasing recollection that their loss is her eternal gain. They feel that she now occupies an exalted seat in the realms of eternal glory, free from all the trials, vexations, and sufferings of the sulunary world. She has entered upon the enjoyment of eternal happiness, and has left many bright and glorious examples for their imitation.

Issue of:
Friday, September 17, 1841:
Obituary: On the 24th of August last, Mrs. Mary Crayton, aged 68 years the 14th of April last. The deceased had been the mother of eight children, most of whom had fallen into the grave in advance of her; she has however left a long train of relatives, and friends to mourn her loss. Mrs. Crayton was much distinguished for [her] amiable disposition, and many private virtues, and may be said to have been in some respects a mother to the whole community. She has died beloved and regretted by all who knew her and although she never had made an open profession of Religion she enjoyed a confident hope of meeting her children who had gone before her, in a better world, there to enjoy eternal life.

Issue of:
Friday, October 1, 1841:
Married: In Cobb County, Georgia on the 8th ult. by the Rev. Mr. Oslin, Dr. O. P. Skelton, formerly of this District, to Mrs. T. Caroline Griffis, daughter of Dr. J. B. Randall.

Issue of:
Friday, October 8, 1841:
Married: On the 12th inst. by the Rev. A. Rice, Mr. Abner H. Magee, to Miss Ann Melvina, daughter of Zachariah Hall, Esq. all of Anderson District.

Issue of:
Friday, October 29, 1841:
Married: On Thursday evening the 21st inst. by the Rev. Wm. Magee, Mr. Andrew J. Brock to Miss Elizabeth Ann Kay, all of this District.

Issue of:
Friday, November 19, 1841:
Married: On Thursday the 11th inst. by the Rev. Wm. Magee, Mr.

William Mitchell of Abbeville District to Miss Hultam Kay of Anderson District.

Married: On the 7th inst. by J. T. Whitfield, Esq., Mr. Moses Anderson, to Miss Adaline, daughter of Amos Voyles, all of Anderson District.

Issue of:
Friday, December 24, 1841:
Married: On Tuesday the 14th inst. by the Rev. M. Gambrell, Mr. Griffin Brazeal of Anderson District to Miss Eliza, daughter of Bailey Barton, Esq. of Pickens District.

Issue of:
Friday, January 7, 1842:
Funeral Notice: The friends and relatives of John Cooly, deceased, are informed that the Rev. Sanford Vandiver, will preach his funeral on the first Sunday in February at Big Creek Meeting House; and on the same day, the Rev. Mr. King, will preach his daughters funeral at the same place.

Married: On Tuesday the 22nd ult. by Rev. W. Magee, Mr. Stephen Hanes to Miss Laura Ann Martin both of this District.

Married: By the Rev. W. Magee, on Thursday the 23rd ult, Mr. Joel Smith to Miss Elizabeth Brock of this District.

Married: [On the same evening] by Rev. W. Magee, Mr. John Ruff of this District to Miss Jane Caroline Bell, of Abbeville District.

Obituary: Died in the village on the 8th day of December last, Mrs. Caroline Webb, consort of Elijah Webb, Esq. in the 34th year of her age.

Issue of:
Friday, January 14, 1842:
Married: On the 9th inst. by the Rev. Sanford Vandiver, Mr. Andrew Jackson Gibson to Miss Mary, daughter of Mr. Lewis Whitfield, of this District.

Married: On Wednesday evening the 12th inst., by the Rev. Wm. Magee, Mr. Wm. B. Gibson of this village, to Miss Elizabeth Vandiver, of this District.

Issue of:
Friday, January 21, 1842:
Married: On Thursday evening the 13th inst. by the Rev. Codor Gantt, Mr. Henry Millford of Abbeville District, to Miss Elizabeth Brackenridge of this District.

Married: On Wednesday evening the 19th inst. by the Rev. A. Rice, Mr. John C. Griffin to Miss Martha Ann, daughter of Mr. Richard Prince, all of this Village.

Issue of:
Friday, January 28, 1842:
Married: On Thursday the 20th inst. by the Rev. Wm. Magee, Mr. Joshua Burton of Abbeville District to Miss Louisa Jane, youngest daughter of Mr. Levi Clinkscales, of Anderson District.

Married: On Thursday evening the 20th inst. by the Rev. Mr.
Hembree, Mr. James G. Bowen to Miss Drucilla Hembree, all of
Anderson District.

Married: On Thursday the 20th inst. by the Rev. David Simmons,
Mr. C. P. Bruce to Miss Elizabeth, daughter of Mr. James R.
Fant, all of this District.

Issue of:
Friday, February 4, 1842:
Married: On Tuesday evening, 27th ult. by the Rev. W. P.
Arnold, Wm. McIntosh, Esq., of Elberton, Georgia to Miss. M.
L. Allen of Elbert County, Georgia.

Married: On Tuesday evening, 27th ult. by the Rev. W. P.
Arnold, Mr. Henry J. Sanders of Anderson District, S. C. to
Miss Sarah H. Tucker, of Elbert County, Georgia.

Issue of:
Friday, February 18, 1842:
Married: On Thursday the 27th of January by Jesse S. Magee,
Esq., Mr. Thomas A. Minton to Miss Nancy Ann, daughter of Mr.
Samuel Baldwin of Pickens.

Married: On Thursday the 10th inst. by the Rev. Z. W. Barnes,
the Rev. John H. Zimmerman, of Abbeville to Miss Louisa Jane,
daughter of Capt. Robert B. Norris of Anderson District.

Issue of:
Friday, March 4, 1842:
Married: On Wednesday evening the 2d inst. by the Rev. S.
Fant, Mr. John M. Langston to Miss Mary Addeline Gray, all of
this Village.

Issue of:
Friday, March 11, 1842:
Married: On Thursday evening the 3d inst. by the Rev. A. Rice,
Mr. H. Rice Clinkscales to Miss Mary Ann, daughter of Capt.
Robert B. Norris, all of Anderson District.

Issue of:
Married: On Wednesday evening the 16th inst. by the Rev. Wm.
Carlyle, Mr. Wm. J. Broom, to Miss Mary Ann Drennan, of this
Village.

Married: In Spartanburg District, on South Tyger River, on
the 1st inst., by the Rev. David Humphries, Rev. Wm. Harrison,
of Anderson District, S. C., to Miss Henrietta, daughter of
Maj. James Anderson.

Issue of:
Friday, March 25, 1842:
Suicide: Remarkable Instance of Suicide- "Capt. James Pettit,
residing near McNair in Polk County, Tennessee, commited suicide on the 16th of February, by blowing his brains out with
a rifle. [Long details follow]

Issue of:
Friday, April 29, 1842:
Obituary: Died, in this Village on Tuesday the 26th of April

of Chronic Bronchitis, Mr. S. W. Catlin, aged between twenty eight and thirty years. He was a native of Vermont and a printer by trade.

<u>Issue of</u>:
Friday, May 27, 1842:
Married: On the 10th inst. by the Rev. Richard Phillips, Dr. Major J. Lewis of Cumming, Forsyth County, Georgia, formerly of Rock Mills, Anderson District, So. Carolina to Miss Evelina Jane, daughter of Thomas Leneir, Esq. of Gwinnette County, Ga.

<u>Issue of</u>:
Friday, June 10, 1842:
Married: In the vicinity of this Village on Thursday evening the 2d inst. by the Rev. S. Fant, Mr. Abner A. Mitchell, to Miss Eliza E. Moore, all of this district.

<u>Issue of</u>:
Friday, July 22, 1842:
Obituary: Died on the 4th of July, Mrs. Mary Ann Webb of Henry County, Georgia, wife of Charles Webb, deceased, of this District, aged near seventy years.

<u>Issue of</u>:
Friday, August 19, 1842:
Married: On Thursday the 11th inst. by the Rev. Wm. Magee, Mr. Hyram Nelson, of Greenville District, to Miss Tabitha Cox, of this District.

<u>Issue of</u>:
Friday, September 16, 1842:
Married: On Sunday the 11th inst. by Andrew Todd, Esq., Mr. James Jerret to Miss Margaret, daughter of the Rev. Phillip Elrod, all of this District.

Married: On the 14th inst. by the Rev. W. Magee, Mr. William A. White, to Miss Eliza Jane Cox, all of this District.

<u>Issue of</u>:
Friday, September 30, 1842:
Married: On the 15th inst., by the Rev. Wilson Ashley, Mr. John [M. or G.] Branyon to Miss Rosannah, daughter of Reuben Kay.

<u>Issue of</u>:
Friday, October 7, 1842:
Married: On Thursday evening the 15th inst. by the Rev. William Magee, Mr. Samuel Dean, to Miss Mary H., daughter of Mr. Moses Dean, all of this District.

Married: On Thursday the 29th inst., by the Rev. William Magee, Mr. Redmon G. Wyatt to Miss Nellie Ann Seawright, all of this district.

<u>Issue of</u>:
Friday, October 14, 1842:
Married: On Sunday evening the 9th inst., by the Rev. Wm. Magee, Mr. N. H. Ertzberger of New York, to Miss Gracy Kay, of this District.

Issue of:
Friday, October 28, 1842:
Married: On Tuesday evening the 18th inst., by the Rev. J. W.
Bohannon, Mr. Henry Parker to Miss Caroline George, all of
this Village.

Married: On the 19th inst. by the Rev. Sanford Vandiver, Mr.
Thomas Guest to Miss MA[?]ima Ausbourn, all of Pickens District.

Issue of:
Friday, December 9, 1842:
Married: On Thursday the 1st of December by the Rev. Wm.
Magee, Mr. Aaron Davis of this District, to Miss Margaret
Morrison, of Abbeville Dist.

Issue of:
Friday, December 16, 1842:
Married: On Tuesday evening the 13th December by the Rev. Wm.
Magee, Mr. George Soward, to Miss Sarah Ann Lowe, both of this
District.

Issue of:
Friday, December 23, 1842:
Obituary: Died of Scaratina Anginosa, on the 13th inst.,
Rebekah Jane, child of Dr. Wm. and Mary Anderson, age two years
and nearly six months.

Issue of:
Friday, January 6, 1843:
Obituary: Died in this village on Tuesday morning the 27th
of December last, Mr. Nathaniel Jeffers, aged about sixty years.
Mr. Jeffers was one of the first settlers of our village.

Married: On Thursday the 22nd of December by the Rev. Wm.
Magee, Mr. Thomas Yeargan to Miss Elizabeth Harris, all of this
District.

Married: On Thursday the 22nd of December by the Rev. A.
Williams, Mr. Samuel M. Pyles to Miss Nancy A., daughter of
Ezekiel Razor, all of Abbeville District.

Married: On Thursday the 22nd of December by James Gilmer,
Esq., [of Anderson District] Mr. Zadok Skelton to Mrs. Sarah
Fuller, all of Pickens District.

Married: On the 7th of December, at Providence Church in
Pickens District, by the Rev. W. C. Smith, the Rev. J. S.
Antly of Orangeburg, to Miss Mahala K. A., daughter of Rev.
David Gambrell of this District.

Married: On Thursday the 15th December by the Rev. W. C.
Smith, Mr. Elbert Burriss to Miss Matilda Jane, daughter of
Zachariah Hall, Esq., all of this District.

Married: On Friday the 30th of December by the Rev. W. C.
Smith, Mr. Allison Langston to Miss Adaline Vandiver, all of
this District.

Issue of:
Friday, January 20, 1843:
Married: On Thursday evening the 12th inst. by the Rev. David

Humphries, Mr. B. F. Crayton, to Miss M. E., daughter of Capt.
John P. Benson, all of this village.

Married: On Sunday evening the 15th inst. by the Rev. W.
Magee, Mr. Welbourn Keaton to Miss Mahala, daughter of W.
Acker, Esq., all of this District.

Issue of:
Friday, February 3, 1843:
Obituary: Departed this life on 21st ult. at his residence in
Abbeville District, Capt. James Calhoun in 64th year of his
age. (Was a brother of Hon. John C. Calhoun... [followed by
lengthy writeup]

Married: On Thursday evening the 26th ult. by the Rev. R.
King, Mr. Jonathan N. Smith, to Miss Serena Kay, all of this
District.

Issue of:
Friday, February 10, 1843:
Married: On Wednesday evening the 8th inst. by the Rev. A.
Rice, Mr. James R. Tow?rs to Miss Ann Melvina, daughter of the
Rev. Wm. Magee, all of this District.

Married: On the 2d inst. by the Rev. S. Vandiver, Mr. Pressley
Lindar to Miss __cy Ousborn, all of Pickens District.

Issue of:
Friday, February 24, 1843:
Married: On Tuesday evening the 14th inst. by the Rev. Wm.
Magee, Mr. James Gambrell, of Anderson, to Miss Susan Acker
Tarrant, of Greenville District.

Married: On Wednesday evening the 15th inst. by the Rev. A.
Rice, Mr. John Wesley Carpenter to Miss Nancy Brown, all of
this District.

Married: On Thursday evening the 16th inst. by the Rev. M.
Gambrell, Mr. Gambrell Breazeal to Miss Sarah Ann Harkins, all
of this District.

Issue of:
Friday, March 3, 1843:
Obituary: Died at her residence near Calhoun, on the 23rd of
February ult., of Cancer, Mrs. Edney Brown, wife of Dr. G. R.
Brown, in the 43d year of her age.

Issue of:
Friday, March 17, 1843:
Married: On the 9th inst., by the Rev. Wm. Magee, Mr. Perry
C. Ware to Miss Adaline P. Gaines, all of Abbeville District.

Issue of:
Friday, April 14, 1843:
Obituary: Died, at her residence in this District, on the 14th
of March last, Mrs. Ann Dupre Gaillard, consort of Doct. Charles
L. Gaillard, aged about 28 years.

Issue of:
Friday, April 21, 1843:
Married: In Greenville Village, on Tuesday evening the 18th

inst. by the Rev. C. C. Pinckney, Mr. George M. Chapline of
Mercer County, Kentucky, to Miss Wilhelmine B. Chick, of the
former place.

Issue of:
Friday, June 9, 1843:
Married: On Sunday the 4th inst. by A. Todd, Esq., Mr. Jesse
Brown to Miss Caroline Embers, both of Anderson District.

Issue of:
Friday, June 23, 1843:
Obituary: Departed this life in the Village of Anderson on
Monday evening the 19th inst., of inflamation of the stomach,
Mrs. Martha Ann Griffin, in the 19th year of her age, consort of
John C. Griffin and second daughter of Richard Prince, Esq.,
late of this District.

Issue of:
Friday, June 30, 1843:
Obituary: Died of a lingering Consumption at the Martin
Springs, Spartanburg District, S. C. on the 31st of May 1843,
Mr. Marcus Motes, in the 34th year of his age. The deceased
was born and raised in Laurens District, S. C. and for a short
period of his life, was a resident and merchant of Anderson
Village. In November, 1840, he married Miss Elizabeth L.,
eldest daughter of Mr. Moses Dean of Anderson District.
Lengthy writeup follows.]

Death: Also, in Laurens District, S. C. on the 13th of June
of inflamation of the brain, Sarah Narcissa, only child of Mr.
Marcus and Mrs. Elizabeth L. Motes, aged 5 months and 11 days.

Issue of:
Friday, July 14, 1843:
Married: On the 6th inst. by the Rev. A. Rice, Mr. Wm. Tucker
of Anderson District to Miss Sarah Boyd of Abbeville District,
the 4th wife for Mr. Tucker.

Issue of:
Friday, July 28, 1843:
Married: On Sunday the 13th inst. by Z. Hall, Esq., Miss
Sarah Taylor to Mr. Hiram Uldrake, all of this District.

Issue of:
Friday, August 11, 1843:
Married: On Thursday evening the 3d inst. by James Gilmer, Esq.
Mr. Andrew Pickens to Miss Sarah Ann Poole, all of this
District.

Issue of:
Friday, August 18, 1843:
Suicide: Rev. Matthew Gambrell hung himself the previous
night.

Married: On Sunday evening the 30th July by Zachariah Hall,
Esq., Mr. John Taylor to Miss Caroline Sligh, all of this
District.

Issue of:
Friday, September 8, 1843:
Married: On Sunday evening the 3d inst., by the Rev. W. Magee,

Mr. Henry Cobb to Miss Amanda, daughter of Mr. Enos Brock, all of this District.

Issue of:
Friday, September 22, 1843
Married: On Thursday evening the 15th inst. by the Rev. J. W. Bohannon, Mr. D. L. Whitaker to Miss Clarissa Prevett, all of this Village.

Issue of:
Married: On Thursday evening the 14th inst., by the Rev. W. Magee, Mr. J. B. Lewis to Miss Mary, youngest daughter of John Gambrell, all of this District.

Married: On Thursday the 21st inst., by Halbert Acker, Esq., Mr. Joseph Field to Miss Lucinda Caroline Brasswell, all of this District.

Issue of:
Friday, October 6, 1843:
Obituary: Departed this life on the 24th ultimo, John Randolph, eldest son of Mr. John M. Keys, of this District, aged four years and eleven months.

Married: On Wednesday the 27th ult., by A. Todd, Esq., Mr. Nathan Yerger to Miss Martha Ann Harris, all of this District.

Married: On Thursday evening the 5th inst., by the Rev. W. Magee, Mr. J. W. Simpson to Miss Susan C., daughter of the Rev. S. Vandiver, all of this District.

Issue of:
Friday, October 13, 1843:
Married: On Monday the 27th ult., by Robert M. Brown, Esq., Mr. Joseph B. Reid of this District. to Miss Barsheby Ayres of Georgia.

Married: On Monday evening the 9th inst. by the Rev. J. W. Bohannon, Mr. H. G. Whitaker to Miss Sarah Ann Millwee, all of this District.

Issue of:
Saturday, November 18, 1843:
Married: On Thursday evening last at Cedar Grove, by the Rev. Hugh Dickson, Col. James L. Orr, of Anderson, to Miss Mary Jane, second daughter of Dr. Samuel Marshall of Abbeville.

Issue of:
Saturday, December 2, 1843:
Obituary: Died at the residence of his mother in Pendleton on the evening of the 25th ult., Mr. Jacob W. Warley.

Obituary: Died at his residence in Tallahatchie County, Miss. after an illness of six weeks, Thomas J. Calhoun, a native of Abbeville District, S. C., but for many years a resident of Mississippi.

Obituary: Died of Appolexy [sic] in Columbia on the 7th ult., Joseph Black, Esq., a soldier of the Revolution, and for upwards of thirty years, a Representative in the state Legislature, from Abbeville District.

Issue of:
Obituary: Died on Thursday morning the 30th ult., Mr. Benjamin Clement, a native of Virginia, but for upwards of half a century an esteemed citizen of this District.

Obituary: On Thursday the 30th ult, Mr. Hezekiah Wakefield, at the Temple of Health in Abbeville District. He has left a numerous family to mourn his loss. He was an honest man, the noblest work of God.

Married: On Sunday the 8th of October, by James Gilmer, Esq., Mr. David McConnel to Miss Rosean Malinda, youngest daughter of Mr. James Conwill, all of Anderson District.

Married: On Thursday evening 7th inst. by the Rev. W. Magee, Mr. Theodore Baker to Miss Amandaline Davis, all of Abbeville District.

Issue of:
Saturday, December 16, 1843:
Married: On Thursday evening the 14th inst. by the Rev. T. Crawford, Mr. Lewis C. Clinkscales to Miss Elizabeth Pratt, all of Abbeville District.

Issue of:
Saturday, December 23, 1843:
Married: On Tuesday evening the 19th inst., by the Rev. Wm. Magee, Mr. Anderson Brock to Miss Caroline Cox, all of this District.

Issue of:
Saturday, January 6, 1844:
Obituary: Departed this life on Friday evening the 29th ult., James Lawrence, only son of Dr. W. H. and Jane S. Calhoun, in the fourth year of his age.

Obituary: Died, on Saturday, 23d December, ult., William Joseph, eldest son of Mr. and Mrs. Rignal Groves, age five years.

Married: On Thursday, 19th December ult., by the Rev. Henry Tyler, Mr. Joel Dyer, to Miss Nancy Caldwell, all of Anderson District.

Married: On Thursday 21st December, by the Rev. Henry Tyler, Mr. Lewis W. Stowers, to Miss Catherine, youngest daughter of Wm. Dooly, Esq. all of Elbert County, Georgia.

Married: On Thursday evening, the 4th inst. by the Rev. S. Fant, Mr. Francis Johnson of Union District, to Miss Rebecca Morris, of this District.

Married: On Thursday evening, the 4th inst. by the Rev. J. W. Bohannon, Mr. D. H. Drennan to Miss Malinda H. Millwee, all of this District.

Issue of:
Saturday, January 13, 1844:
Married: On Thursday the 4th inst. by A. Todd, Esq., Mr. Robert Simpson to Miss Mary Irena Whitman, all of Anderson District.

12

Married: On Thursday evening 11th inst. by the Rev. W. Magee,
Mr. H. O. Harris to Miss Priscilla C. Herndon all of this
District.

Issue of:
Saturday, January 20, 1844:
Married: On Thursday evening, 11th inst., by the Rev. D.
Humphreys, Capt. Moses Haslet to Miss Milly Tilly.

Issue of:
Saturday, January 27, 1844:
Married: On Tuesday the 26th inst. by the Rev. J. E. Manning,
Mr. B. F. Duncan to Miss Tabitha Smith, all of Anderson District.

Issue of:
Saturday, February 3, 1844:
Married: On Tuesday evening the 30th ultimo, by the Rev. W.
Dickerson, Mr. Joseph Moore to Miss Phebe Wilson, all of this
District.

Married: On Thursday evening last, by the Rev. Wm. Magee, Mr.
J. K. Valentine, to Miss Hester McPherson, all of this District.

Issue of:
Saturday, February 10, 1844:
Married: On Sunday evening the 4th inst. by Robert M. Brown,
Esq., Mr. Jesse Dyer to Miss Eliza Bobo, all of Franklin County,
Georgia.

Issue of:
Saturday, February 17, 1844:
Married: On Friday evening the 26th January by the Rev. D.
Humprheys, Mr. Hosea P. Hays to Miss Mary Howie, all of Ander-
son District.

Married: On Wednesday evening the 31st January, by the Rev.
D. Humphreys, Dr. George R. Brown to Miss Louisa Horton, all
of this District.

Married: On Tuesday evening the 13th inst. by the Rev. Wm.
Magee, Capt. Ira G. Morehead of this District, to Miss Susan,
daughter of Jos. Young, of Pickens District.

Issue of:
Saturday, February 24, 1844:
Married: On Thursday evening the 15th inst. by the Rev. D.
Humphreys, Mr. Hiram Gentry to Miss Jane Caldwell, all of
Anderson District.

Married: On Thursday evening the 22nd inst. by the Rev. Wm.
Magee, Mr. Nimrod Kay to Miss Darkus McCoy, all of this
District.

Issue of:
Saturday, March 2, 1844:
Married: On Thursday the 22nd ult. by the Rev. A. Acker, Dr.
Jas. H. Ware of Laurens District. to Miss Margaret, only
daughter of Col. H. G. Johnson, of Greenville District.

Issue of:
Saturday, March 9, 1844:

Murder: John Jones, living in lower part of Greenville County in the neighborhood of Col. Brockman, was murdered by his negro boy, Peter, on Monday last.

Married: On Tuesday the 16th of January by the Rev. D. Simmons, Mr. O. P. Fant of Anderson District, to Miss McGee of Pickens District, S. C.

Obituary: Died, of Apoplexy, at his residence at Due West Corner in Abbeville District, Mr. George Brownlee, in the 63d year of his age.

Issue of:
Saturday, March 23, 1844:
Married: On Tuesday the 19th inst. by A. D. Gray, Esq., Mr. Robert McCown to Miss Clara Ann Hall, all of Anderson District.

Married: On Tuesday evening the 19th inst. by the Rev. W. Magee, Mr. Franklin Cobb to Miss Jane Pickel, all of this District.

Married: By the Rev. W. Magee at Anderson Court House on Thursday evening the 21st inst., Mr. Alfred Holt to Miss Harriet P. Thomason.

Obituary: Died on Wednesday the 20th inst. at his residence in this District after a protracted illness, C. I. E. B. Moore.

Issue of:
Friday, April 12, 1844:
Married: On Tuesday evening the 9th inst. by the Rev. Wm. Carlisle, Capt. Archibald Todd to Miss Jane McAllister, all of this District.

Issue of:
Friday, April 19, 1844:
Married: On Thursday evening the 29th of March by Robert Brown, Esq., Mr . S. Ward to Miss Francis League, all of this District.

Obituary: Died in the Village of Anderson on the 1st inst., Mrs. Mary Prince, wife of Mr. C. J. Prince, formerly of Charleston, though for the last eleven years a resident of this village.

Issue of:
Friday, April 26, 1844:
Married: On the 14th inst. by Robert Griffin, Esq., Mr. Albert Calhoun to Miss Elvira Carwile, all of Greenwood.

Married: After a long and protracted engagement which they bore with christian fortitude, at last consumated by marriage, on the 18th inst. by the Rev. W. P. Hill, Mr. John Williams Cheatham, to Miss Nancy, eldest daughter of Hardyman Clark, Esq. all of this District.

Obituary: James Stuart, Sr., a citizen of this District, was killed on Tuesday morning 16th inst., by a waggon wheel, passing over his body, loaded with a heavy stock of timber, which he was carrying to a sawmill. He survived the accident only a few hours, which were spent in the most earnest suplication to heaven for mercy; although he had long been a proffessor of

the christian religion, he feared that he had not been zealous
enough in the service of his devine master. He was upwards of
80 years of age, and was remarkably stout and active for so
advanced an age. He was buried by the side of his father,
who, when he died, had attained his 96th year, and by his father
in-law, who died at the advanced age of 116 years. [Followed by
poetry]

Obituary: Departed this life on Sunday the 13th inst., Joseph
M. Major, of this district, after a short illness, which he bore
with fortitude, in the full triumph of a christian faith. He
has left an interesting family to mourn his melancholy decease.

Issue of:
Friday, May 17, 1844:
Married: On Sunday the 4th inst. by Robert M. Brown, Esq.,
Mr. R. R. Timmons to Miss Nancy Dyer.

Married: On Sunday the 4th inst. by Robert M. Brown, Esq., Mr.
Nathan Sanders, to Miss Amey Dyer, all of Franklin County,
Georgia.

Issue of:
Friday, May 31, 1844:
Obituary: Death of Judge Baylis J. Earle [Lengthy]

Obituary: We are again called upon to record an affective
bereavement in the death of Mrs. Cinderilla Darcus Amanda
Keys, the late wife of Mr. Robert A. Keys, of this neighborhood, and daughter of Mr. John E. Norris, who departed this
life on Monday the 13th inst. the fond and interesting mother
of two little children, and an infant of a few days, the kind
and confiding wife of a devoted husband, to whom she had been
married but little more than four years-the affectionate and
beloved daughter of an endeared family-the estimable and
respected member of a large circle of friends and neighbors-
the meek, consistent and exemplary member of the Presbyterian
Church at Anderson C. H., with which she had been suddenly
torn from these various relations and having nearly attained
her 22nd year, in the bloom of life, consigned to the silent
grave.
Those who survive her know that it is so, but it is hard to
realize as truth. Even when called a few weeks before at the
same Churchyard to yield up an esteemed friend whose death
had been antcipated for weeks and months, the like thought
forced itself upon us. But in the instance we now record a
knowledge of her illness was accompanied with the announcement of her death to many. The bright prospect of a blessed
immortality, revealed by faith is alone calculated to wipe
away the tear of sorrow and bind up the broken heart. What
consolation may we not derive from the words of the text used
on the occasion in a sermon addressed to a large circle of
weeping mourners, "Blessed are the death who die in the Lord."

Issue of:
Friday, June 7, 1844:
Married: On Thursday evening the 30th ult. by the Rev. Samuel
Gibson, Charles J. Elford, Esq. to Miss Sarah A. Sloan, all of
Greenville.

Issue of:
Friday, June 14, 1844:
Married: On Thursday evening the 23d ult., by the Rev. Mr. Hill,
Dr. Samuel S. Marshall, to Miss Ann. E., only daughter of Dr.
Barrett, all of Abbeville District.

Obituary: Died at his residence in the Village of Anderson,
on Friday evening the 7th inst., after a painful and protracted illness, Mr. William Waller, in the 62nd year of his age.
He was born in Durham, England, and emigrated to the city of
Charleston in 1811, where he resided until 1837, when he left
the city, with the hope of regaining his health which had
become greatly impaired by an asthmatic affection. It was the
happy fortune of the deceased to endear himself to all the
various circles in which he moved. In his intercourse with
the world, he was frank, generous and manly; with a heart which
never turned from the afflicted if its benevolence and charity
could alleviate suffering and sorrow; and when he had done a
good deed he was impressed with the consciousness of a rich
reward, if not on earth, in the courts of glory. He had been
for 38 years an exemplary member of the Episcopal Church, and
his career through life was adorned with all the graces and
virtues which beautify the Christian character. The Sabbath
before his decease, was spent with the people of God in religious devotions; and when he gave full expression to his
feelings, it was done in the belief, that the hour was near at
hand when he must bid adieu to time and enter upon eternity,
with the confident hope of meeting his christian brethren in
Heaven; nor did this hope fail him in the trying hour of death-
when sinking into its icy embrace he manifested great calmness
and resignation in viewing the termination of his earthly
course strengthened by the consciousness, that he was going to
a home eternal and in the skies where the wicked cease from
troubling and the weary are at rest. He has left a wife, four
daughters and one son; an affectionate family to deplore their
melancholy and grievous bereavement. His body was interred in
the yard of the Presbyterian Church, and the funeral services
performed in presence of a large cocourse of the citizens of
our Village and its vicinity. Let the living imitate the
virtues of the dead.

Issue of:
Friday, June 21, 1844:
Married: On Thursday evening the 13th inst. by the Rev. Charles
P. Dean, Mr. Harvey Trippe, to Miss Mary Gilstrap, all of this
District.

Obituary: "In the midst of life we are in Death" Died, of
Peritoneal inflamation, at 2 o'clock on Friday morning the 14th
inst., Mrs. Sarah Ann Breazeale, consort of Mr. Gambrell
Breazeale, and only daughter of Hugh and Martha Harkins of this
District, in the 19th year of her age. It is painful to record
the death of the good and virtuous,even when aged and infirm,
but when called to perform the same sad duty of one who had
just entered the genial spring of youth; surrounded with all
the conforts earth could afford, and the most flattering
prospect of many years sojourn in the land, the solace of
declining parents, the joyous partner of a doating husband,
the loving mother of an only infant, and the central attraction
of a large circle of relatives and friends, our tongue refuses

16

to give utterance to our feelings - the heart sickens at contemplating the vanity of all things earthly, and we are made
to exlain in the language of Holy Writ great indeed are the
"mysteries of Godliness." Such are the reflections suggested
in recurring to the melancholy demise of Mrs. Breazeale. She
had just passed the 18th year of her age, and being blest with
a vigorous Constitution, had scarcely ever realized what it
was to be sick, until confined to the fatal bed, from which her
spirit took its eternal flight to another, and it is confidently hoped, better world. But sixteen months had elapsed
since she became the partner of a kind and affectionate husband, and but five weeks had she been the mother of a promising infant. The Idol of the husbands heart is gone; an
"aching void" is there created that this world can never fully
fill; the infant has lost a mother, yet, if spared may arrive
to manhood, may go down to old age, but is destined, never to
know a mothers love, or profit by a mothers counsels-the
parents are deprived of the society of an only daughter (and
only child save one) in whom their affections were so completely
wrapt up, that without her, this world would seem, "a dreary
waste, a howling wilderness of woe" but for the consolation of
knowing that the "Lord gave and the Lord has taken away" for
purposes of his own glory-a large circle of friends mourn the
loss of one who from the generosity of her nature, the amiable-
ness of her dispostion, and the sweetness of her temper,
was bound to them by the strongest ties of attachment and society mourns the loss of one of its most valuable members. The
only consolation for all of these, is to be found in the confident belief, that "their loss is her eternal gain." Mrs.
Breazeale had never made a public profession of Religion, but
a day or two before her decease, she gave her friends the
strongest possible assurance of her acceptance with God. She
expressed confidently her reconciliation with the Father, and
her entire willingness to go at his command. She gave directions as to the precise disposition-which she wished made of
her body-where it should be laid and the manner in which it
should be interred. These instructions were followed, and
the finite now sleeps; where may it rest in peace till the
morning of the resurrection, when re-united with the infinite
and thus made perfect, May it enter into the relms of eternal
glory, "Blessed are the dead that die in the Lord, for their
works do floow them"

Issue of:
Friday, June 28, 1844:
Married: On Thursday the 20th inst. by the Rev. Wm. Potter,
Dr. C. L. Gaillard to Miss Elizabeth M. Dart, all of this
District.

Obituary: Departed this life on Thursday 20th inst., Mrs.
Elizabeth Jolly, age about 90 years; she was indeed "old and
well stricken in years", and had been long and patiently waiting for the time to come, when her feeble body should be consigned to its mother dust, and her immortal spirit wing its
way to the bosom of her saviour. She had seen many privations
in life-being the mother of a family of small children during
the Revolutionary War, and her husband being in the service of
his country. She had to provide for the wants of her little
ones, and was often robbed of her little all and driven to
the swamps by ruthless bands of tories. She had for many
years been an exemplary member of the Baptist Church and by her

orderly walk and conversation, she evinced to all that her
"treasure was not of this world," but that she had a "home not
made with hands eternal and in the Heavens." "Blessed are the
dead that die in the Lord."

Issue of:
Friday, July 5, 1844:
Obituary: Died on the 24th of June, Turner Richardson, infant
son and only child of Peter and Malvina McPhail, age 4 months
and 19 days, "suffer little children to come unto me, and forbid them not, for such is the Kingdom of Heaven."

Obituary: Departed this life on the 29th ult., after a painful
illness of three years continuance, Mrs. Rebecca Humphries,
wife of the Rev. David Humphries, and daughter of S. Cunningham, Esq., in the 39th year of her age. During this long period
many efforts were made to arrest the progress of the disease.
Change of air, scenery were tried, mineral springs resorted
to-aid was sought from the combined skill of able Physicians.
At times we were encouraged to believe, that ultimate success
would crown these exertions. But death ever steady to its
purpose continued to pursue its victim, thro' all the lanes
and avenues of life - Though his advanced quard for a time
appeared to be defeated, the attack was again and again renewed,
till life itself was drawn out to a mere thread, and that body
once healthy and vigorous was reduced to a skeleton. It was
amazing the amount of suffering she patiently endured for the
last few weeks of her life. For the last ten weeks she appeared to have been sitting upon the utmost crag of time, beyond
which lies death and eternity; and undismayed looked death in
the face. The force of disease sometimes so excited the mind
as to cause it to wander-she at times lamented that she could
not control it, and for a moment feared she was unprepared to
grapple with the King of terrors - But when the mind returned
from fever, and again resumed its proper balance she expressed
her entire confidence in the merits of a Saviour, so as to
expel all fear. She disclaimed all personal merit. She said
she was in the hands of her Heavenly Master, and she was
willing to be disposed of at his pleasure. She felt a deep
sense of gratitude to this numerous friends for all their
kind sympathies with her in her affliction, and to those who
trimmed the midnight lamp around her wasting form, and dying
couch. When at times attempting to describe her feelings and
views in the near prospect of death, she remarked that she
had no language that could describe them so well as the
language used in that beautiful hymn, 431 of the General
Assembly's Collection, beginning:
        "When language and disease invade,
            This tumbling house of clay:
        'Tis sweet to look beyond my pains,
            and long to fly away," etc.
She reminded her husband of his responsible station he occupied
and urged him most solemnly to fidelity to God, to the Churches
of his charge, and to his own family. She was not unmindful
of the eternal interests of her children, and at suitable times
tried deeply to impress their young minds with the importance
of being prepared for that solemn change that awaited them.
Although death has deprived a husband of his greatest source
of earthly comfort, and seven children of a fond mother, of a
mothers care, counsel and prayers; and a large circle of

relatives and neighbors of a faithful friend; we have the consolation to believe it could not deprive the deceased of an
interest in that inheritance which is incorruptable, undefiled,
and fadeth not away. (The Charleston Observer will please copy)

Issue of:
Friday, July 12, 1844:
Obituary: Died in this neighborhood on the 3d inst., Mrs. P.
A. H. Archer, wife of Wm. M. Archer and daughter of Mr. John
E. Norris, after a short illness - aged 24 years. Her death,
though an event upon which she looked with quiet composure
and calm, submission is another mysterious dispensation of
Providence which has very deeply impressed the minds of our
whole community. Her last visit to the Presbyterian Church in
this village, of which she was a consistent member, was but a
few weeks before her death, to mingle her tears at the grave of
a younger sister, who had been suddenly stricken down in the
midst of youth and health. It is but a just tribute to our
departed friend, to record that in the various relations she
sustained in life, and in all her intercourse, she was kind,
social and exemplary. Her end was such as might be expected
from her life. Early impressed in her sickness that she was
soon to follow her sainted sister, with a strong confidence
that he in whom she had for years placed her confidence, would
sustain her in this last great conflict, her greatest burthen
was the condition in which she was leaving her devoted husband
and four small children the youngest an infant but a few days
old. These ties according to a course of nature are hard to
sever, but faith points to God and yields to his sovereingnty
with resignation and assurance. This too was her lot. How
sweet the consolation, now that the earth has closed over this
devoted wife, fond mother and beloved daughter and sister, to
remember how peacefully she sunk to rest in the arms of a much
loved Saviour, to await the arriving of her aged parents, her
afflicted husband and orphan children when they will no more
know the pangs of seperation.

Issue of:
Friday, July 26, 1844:
Married: On Thursday evening the 23d inst., by Zachariah Hall,
Esq., Mr. Henry Goodwyn to Miss Elizabeth Ann Stephens, all of
this District.

Issue of:
Friday, August 9, 1844:
[Front Page] "Murders in Darlington District" - Two murders
have occurred in Darlington District, Vincent Sims murdered by
three brothers Lewis James and John McLendon.
Mr. Hazeltine killed by his own negroes below Mars Bluff.
[Negroes were man and wife.]

Married: On Thursday evening the 25th ult. by the Rev. W. C.
Smith, Mr. Thomas C. Gower of Greenville District to Miss Jane
J., second daughter of W. A. Williams of this District.

Married on Thursday evening the 1st inst. by the Rev. Wm.
Magee, Mr. John Todd to Miss Sarah Jane Sherrill, all of this
District.

Married: On the 16th of May by Robert B. Brown, Esq., Mr. D.
Bobo to Miss Nancy Daren.

Married: On the 16th of June by Robert B. Brown, Esq., Mr. Levi H. Brown to Miss Mary Ann Browning.

Married: On the 1st inst. by Robert B. Brown, Esq., Mr. John Bolling to Miss Elizabeth Bridges.

Married: On Thursday evening the 1st inst. by Zachariah Hall, Esq., Mr. John Lathum to Miss Sarah Hall, all of this District.

Issue of:
Friday, August 16, 1844:
Obituary: Departed this life on the 31st ult., William Henry, youngest son of Jesse R. and Elizabeth Smith, aged 3 years, 5 months and 5 days. "Suffer little children to come unto me, and forbid them not, for such is the Kingdom of Heaven."

Issue of:
Friday, August 23, 1844:
Married: On the morning of the 7th instant by the Rev. Edwin Cater, in Newberry Village, Chancellor J. Johnston to Miss Amelia, daughter of the late David DeWalt.

Married: On Tuesday evening the 20th inst. by the Rev. David Humphries, Mr. James Brownlee of Abbeville, to Miss Caroline Creswell, of Anderson.

Issue of:
Friday, August 30, 1844:
Married: On Wednesday evening the 21st instant by the Rev. Wm. Magee, Mr. Abner Cox to Miss Milly, daughter of Elijah Wyatt, all of this District.

Obituary: Died on the 21st instant, after a few days illness, at the residence of her husband, Mrs. Eliza E. Brown, consort of Mr. Sidi H. Brown. The gentleness of her manners, and the amiability of her disposition, attached her to a numerous circle of friends who are left to unite their sympathies with her afflicted husband and her orphan children.

Issue of:
Friday, September 20, 1844:
Obituary: Died on Monday night the 19th of August last, Mrs. Francis B. Shirley, wife of Thomas Shirley, in the 28th year of her age. The deceased had been at times, for more than a year, laboring under a disease of the chest, thought to be dropsy, but for three months previous to her demise, was apparently much improved in health. She retired to bed on Monday night to all appearance in good health, and at day break the next morning was discovered by her husband a corpse at his side. Her spirit had left this clayey tenement, and as confidently hoped had took its flight to realms of eternal bliss. In all the relations of wife, mother, neighbor, friend and Christian, being a devoted member of the Baptist Church, Mrs. Shirley was admired by all who knew her, and her death has created a void in the neighborhood that the world can never fill. She has left a widowed mother, an affectionate husband, three small children and numerous friends and relatives to mour her irreparable loss - but they weep not as those who have no hope. They confidently believe that she was called to obey the summons of her Lord and Master. "Come unto me ye blessed of my father, inherit the Kingdom prepared for you from the foundation of the world."

Obituary: Died on the 6th of September, after an illness of
fifteen minutes, Peter K. Thomson, a native of Anderson District
S. C., Student of Erskine College, and member of Senior Class.
Under circumstances most solemn, and awfully impressive, the
friends and relatives of the deceased have been called upon to
mour his early departure. The many noble and amiable features
in his character, his engaging manners, his quick and penetrating intellect, have endured him to an extensive circle of
acquaintances. Few have had more flattering and encouraging
prospects. Possessed of a strong and vigorous constituion,
blessed with parental tenderness and affection, and well
trained under the assidious labors of beloved instructors, he
bid fair to become an ornament to his country and a blessing
to his day and generation. But alas! how changed? The fondest
hopes have been blasted, the most cheering prospects have
been obscured by clouds of sorrow and gloom. Almost on the very
eve of bidding farewell to his "Alma Mater", our beloved friend
has been snatched away by the hand of death. The morn of that
eventful day saw him arise as healthy and vigorous as ever;
at the sound of the College bell he was seen with his accustomed
elasticity of steps, repairing to the Chapel to offer up with
his beloved companions, a morning sacrifice to the Father of
mercies. None then could have predicted the melancholy fate
which awaited him. No marks of disease could any where be
traced. A more than ordinary flow of spirits animated his
always expressive countenance. But before that same morning
sun, which had arisen upon him with its accustomed splendor set
beneath the western horizon, our lamented friend lay a pale
and lifeless corpse, his spirit had winged its way to God who
gave it existence. At the early death of one so amiable, so
promising and intelligent - sorrow has filled every heart. His
affectionate parents have been called to mourn over a son, of
whom they might well have been proud. His beloved instructors,
his dear class mates and fellow students have given away to
grief, for one of whose worth, they held so exalted an opinion.
Well may his country unite with the host of mourners, for him,
had his life been spared, she would have remembered him among
her benefactors. But an inscratable [sic] Providence has seen
fit to remove him; let be therefore, bow at his soverign
pleasure, and say "Thy will be done."

Issue of:
Friday, October 4, 1844:
Married: On Tuesday evening the 24th ult., by the Rev. D.
Simmons, Mr. Sam C. Reeder to Miss Rebecca Messer, all of
Pickens District.

Married: On Thursday evening the 26th ult. by the Rev. Mr.
Davis, Mr. William Oliver Gray to Miss Lodosky Adeline, daughter
of John Mars, Esq. all of Abbeville.

Issue of:
Friday, October 11, 1844:
Married: On Sunday the 6th inst. by R. M. Brown, Esq., Mr.
Paschal Bailey, to Miss Nancy Bennet, all of Georgia.

Married: On Thursday evening the 26th ult. by A. Todd, Esq.,
Mr. Thomas Howel to Miss Elmina, daughter of Wm. T. Elrod, all
of Anderson District.

Married: On Thursday evening the 19th ult. by the same [A. Todd
Esq.] Mr. Andrew Latham to Miss Mary Ann Elizabeth, daughter of
Daniel Stephens, all of Anderson District.

Married: On Sunday the 6th inst. by A. Todd, Esq., Mr. Fenton
J. Hall to Miss Merena Duncan, all of Anderson District.

Obituary: Died on Tuesday the 8th instant Anderson C. H. of
Scarlet Fever, Miss Jane Moore of Abbeville. The fatal disease
that terminated her earthly career fastened upon the system
on Friday night and at 9 o'clock Tuesdy morning she was no more.
She was a student in the Female Academy at his place and had
been in our midst but two short months in which time she attached herself warmly to her companions.

Issue of:
Friday, October 18, 1844:
Married: At Anderson C. H. on Thursday morning the 17th inst.
by the Rev. D. Humphries, Col. Joel W. Miller of Spartanburg
to Miss Martha Elvira, daughter of Christopher Orr, Esq.

Married: On Tuesday evening the 15th inst. by the Rev. D.
Humphries, William Howie to Miss Eliza McLin, all of this
District.

Married: On Thursday evening the 10th inst. by the Rev. W.
Magee, Mr. Dudley C. Howard to Miss Elizabeth Jane Porter, all
of this District.

Married: On Wednesday evening the 16th inst. by the Rev. W.
Magee, Mr. Fleetwood Rice to Mrs. Elizabeth L. Motes, of this
District.

Obituary: Died at Due West Corner, of Inflamation of the brain,
on the 5th of June last, Francis George, son of Rev. J. N.and
E. J. Young, in the second year of his age.

Obituary: Departed this life at Due West Corner on the 23d of
Sept. last of Pulmonic Consumption, Elizabeth Jane, wife of
Rev. J. N. Young, leaving one child, an infant son to feel
her loss. The deceased was a native of the State of Ohio, in
which she continued to reside until the Fall of 1841. She had
early devoted herself to the service of God, by a public profession of religion, which through her short but useful life
she adorned by a godly walk and conversation. During her protracted ill health which commenced with an attack of measles
in March of 1843, she manifested Christian meekness and
resignation. When compelled by the rapid progress of disease
to be absent from the services of the sanctuary, the Bible
was her source of comfort. So strong was her trust in the
merits of the atonement that death was disarmed of its terrors.
But for the thought of the helpless infant which she was about
to leave, she would have been "willing rather to be absent
from the body and to be present with the Lord." After the
death of her first born to whom she was bound by no ordinary
tie she frequently remarked that now she felt an interest that
she had not before in heaven, since her dear son was there.
Her many vitues and becoming deportment gained for her even
among strangers many friends.

Friday, October 25, 1844:
Married: On Thursday evening 7th inst. by the Rev. W. Magee, Mr. Elihu P. Saunders, to Miss Harriet E. Mitchell, all of this District.

Issue of:
Friday, November 8, 1844:
Married: On Wednesday evening the 23d ult. by the Rev. G. W. Moore, Capt. P. J. Coates, to Miss Ann, daughter of Capt. Wm. Sanders, all of this District.

Married: On Thursday evening the 24th ult. by the Rev. W. Magee, Mr. Tyre Y. Martin, to Miss Sally Rasor, both of Abbeville District.

Married: On Sunday evening the 27th ult. by the Rev. W. Magee, Mr. James Williamson, of Alabama, to Miss Susan Cox, of this District.

Married: On Sunday evening the 27th ult. by Wm. Kay, Esq., Mr. Coker, to Susan Gray, all of this District.

Married: On Thursday evening the 31st ultimo, by the Rev. W. Magee, Mr. James H. Wiles, to Miss Ursley Louiza Hall, all of this District.

Married: On Tuesday the 29th ult. by A. Todd, Esq., Mr. Blalock, to Miss Jane Elrod, both of this District.

Married: On Sunday evening the 3d inst., by the Rev. S. Vandiver, Mr. Bartler Lanier to Miss Delphia C. Orsborn, all of Pickens District.

Obituary: Departed this life on Monday the 21st ultimo, Mrs. Harriet C. Magee, consort of Mr. John Magee, of confirmed consumption, after an illness of several months. She was taken from the bosom of an affectionate and loving husband and ten children, and a large train of connexion to mourn her loss. Yet they sorrow not as those who have no hope - she died as she lived, in peace with her God, and with all mankind. She had been an exemplary member of the Baptist Church for upward of twenty three years. During her protracted illness she retained a sound mind, and often expressed herself as being perfectly willing to be absent from this body of clay, and to be present with her Lord and Saviour where her afflictions and toils should end.

Issue of:
Friday, September 26, 1845:
Married: On Tuesday evening the 23rd inst. by the Rev. J. C. Chalmers, Mr. A. M. Holland, of Pickens C. H., to Miss Margaret E., daughter of Wm. Sherard, Esq., of this District.

Issue of:
Friday, October 10, 1845:
Married: On Thursday evening, 2d inst. by the Rev. A. Rice, Mr. John Magee, of this District, to Mrs. Lucy C. Thornton, of Elbert Co., Ga.

Married: On Tuesday evening the 7th inst. by the Rev. W. Magee, Mr. Nimrod S. Mitchell to Miss Elizabeth L. Toler, all of this District.

Married: On Tuesday evening the 7th inst. by H. Hammond, Esq., Mr. James Cain to Miss Matilda Yeargan, all of this District.

Issue of:
Friday, October 24, 1845:
Married: On Tuesday evening, 7th inst. by A. D. Gray, Mr. Blackman Burton, to Miss Sarah Ann McAllister, all of this District.

Issue of:
Friday, October 31, 1845:
Married: On Tuesday morning, 21st inst. by the Rev. J. C. Chalmers, Rev. J. N. Young, Professor of Mathmatics in Erskine College, to Miss E. F. Strong of Anderson District.

Issue of:
Friday, November 7, 1845:
Married: On Tuesday evening, 4th inst. by the Rev. J. Hill-house, Rev. D. Humphreys of Anderson to Miss Mary M., daughter of Dr. Wm. Hunter, dec'd. of Pickens.

Married: On the 15th ult. by the Rev. Mr. Murn, Mr. John H. Gray to Miss Sarah M. Harrison, all of Lowndes County, Miss.

Issue of:
Friday, November 14, 1845:
Obituary: Departed this life on Saturday morning the 25th October 1845, at his residence in Atala [sic] County, Missi-ssippi, Maj. James G. Clark, in the Forty Eighth year of his age. The deceased was a native of Anderson District, South Caroline, and removed to Mississippi in the year 1836. The writer of this Obituary has been for many years, intimately acquainted with the deceased and can truly say, that he was a consistent and zealous member of the Methodist E. Church for more than twenty years, a great part of which time, he acted as a Class leader to the general satisfaction of his brethen and the community at large in which he lived. He was a great friend to Sabbath schools, nothing gave him more pleasure than to be engaged in instructing youth in the ways of piety and virtue. He was a kind father, a good master, and highly esteemed neighbor. Ministers of every order, always found his house an asylum, and often made it their home. Indeed, his heart was always open,and his hand ever extended to relieve suffering humanity, Long! long! will his immediate neighbors and friends recollect his acts of kindness. He bore his last long sickness, (which was at first billious fever and chills, but eventually terminated in an inflation of the lungs,) with Christian fortitude. He was sensible of the near approach of death, and was often heard to praise God for Redeeming Grace and Dying Love. A few days before his death, at his request, the Sacrament of the Lords supper was administered to him and those of his family who are members of the church, by a Minis-ter who was in attendance. He has left an affectionate wife, seven children and many friends, to mourn his loss; but blessed by God, they mourn not as those who have no hope, but are well assured that their loss is his Eternal gain. "Blessed are the death which die in the Lord, yea saith the Spirit,

they shall rest from their labors, and their works do follow
them." M. W.

Issue of:
Friday, November 21, 1845:
Married: On Thursday evening, 13th inst. by the Rev. Wm. Magee,
Mr. Wm. Magee, Jr. of Anderson District, to Miss Emily P.
Thornton, of Elbert County, Ga.

Married: On Tuesday evening, 18th inst. by the Rev. A. Rice,
Dr. C. C. Hammond to Miss Mary Elizabeth, eldest daughter of
Dr. G. R. Brown, all of this District.

Issue of:
Friday, December 5, 1845:
Obituary: The Friends and acquaintances of Dr. O. R. Broyles,
Maj. John T. Broyles, and the relatives generally of Maj. Aaron
Broyles, are invited to attend the funeral of the latter, from
his late residence, at the Baptist Church at Calhoun, on the
Second Sabbath of December, instant. December 4, 1845.

Issue of:
Friday, December 12, 1845:
Married: On Thursday evening, 4th inst., by the Rev. Alexander
Acker, Mr. William H. Acker to Miss Mary E. Hammond, all of
this District.

Married: On Tuesday evening 9th inst., by the Rev. T. L.
McBryde, Mr. W. S. Todd to Miss Adelia C., eldest daughter
of Col. Herbert Hammond, all of this District.

Issue of:
Friday, December 19, 1845:
Married: On Thursday evening, 4th inst., by the Rev. Willis
Dickerson, Mr. William Jones, to Miss Mary Ann, daughter of
Mrs. Sarah Hunnicutt, all of this District.

Issue of:
Friday, December 26, 1845:
Married: On Thursday evening, 11th inst., by the Rev. D.
Humphreys, Mr. Thomas C. Wilkes to Miss Martha, youngest
daughter of A. McElroy, Esq., all of this District.

Married: On Thursday evening, 18th inst. by the Rev. W.
Magee, Mr. Major Morehead to Miss Rebecca Jane Smith, all of
this District.

Married: On Thursday evening, 18th inst. by the Rev. A. Rice,
Maj. J. L. Padgett to Mrs. Hester Guyton, all of this District.

Issue of:
Friday, January 9, 1846:
Married: On Thursday evening, 18th ult. by the Rev. Wm. Carlisle,
Mr. James Mills, of Laurens District, to Miss Catherine J.,
daughter of A. Simpson, Esq., all of this District.

Married: On Tuesday evening, 23rd ultimo, by the Rev. J. C.
Chalmers, Wm. A. Lewis, Esq., of Rock Mills, S. C. to Miss
Eleanor J., their daughter of John Gordon, Esq., of Elbert
County, Georgia.

Married: On Thursday evening, 25th ult., by Rev. J. L. Crumley,
Mr. R. A. Keys to Miss Sarah, second daughter of Mr. E. Brazeale, all of this District.

Married: On Thursday evening, 31st ult. by the Rev. D. Humphreys, Mr. Wm. Caldwell to Miss Jane Campbell, all of this
District.

Issue of:
Friday, January 16, 1846:
Married: On Thursday evening, 8th inst. by the Rev. A. Acker,
Mr. John C. Griffin of this Village, to Miss Frances E., eldest
daughter of H. Acker, Esq., of Queensborough.

Issue of:
Friday, January 30, 1846:
Obituary: Departed this life on the 17th inst., Benjamin J.
McFall, aged twenty four years, two months and twelve days.
Deprived of a religious education he never made a profession
of the Christian Religion, but was remarkably sober and moral
in his deportment, and was very early the subject of religious
impressions, which he kept secret, till after he was confined
to his bed; his long and severe affliction, he bore with great
fortitude and without murmuring. A few hours before his death,
he professed to have received forgiveness for his sins, saying
he was ready to die. - that he freely forgave all his enemies,
and exhorted the Physician who attended him, and others, to
meet him in heaven.

Married: On Thursday evening, 22nd inst., by James Gilmer, Esq.,
Mr. Davis, of Gwinnet County, Ga., to Miss Amanda, daughter of
Mr. Sam. McGee of this District.

Married: On Tuesday evening, 27th inst. by the Rev. Wm. Magee,
Mr. William M. Cooly to Miss Hemutel, daughter of Mr. E.
Pepper, all of this District.

Issue of:
Friday, February 6, 1846:
Married: On the 26th ult. by the Rev. D. Humphreys, Mr. Charles
Williford to Miss Elizabeth Skelton, all of this District.

Obituary: Departed this life, after a lingering illness of
eight years, at the residence of her father in this District,
on the 26th ult. Eleanor Caroline, daughter of Henry Cobb, Esq.,
in the eighteenth year of her age.

Issue of:
Friday, February 13, 1846:
Obituary: Departed this life on Friday, the 6th inst., James
Seawright, in the 55th year of his age. He was sitting on a
chair conversing, and apparently in good health as usual, when
he dropped from his seat and instantly expired. The deceased
had been some time previous laboring under something like
dropsy of the chest, but for some little time past seemingly got
well of that. He left behind an amiable wife and three children,
together with numerous friends and relatives, to mourn his
loss. He was an affectionate husband, an indulgent parent and
master, and a kind and obliging neighbor. His loss to his
family and friends can never be made up, but we trust that
their loss is his eternal gain. We do not know that the

deceased ever made a public profession of religion, yet he was
an exemplary, and one that always delighted to hear of the
advancement of the cause of Christ.

Issue of:
Friday, March 6, 1846:
Obituary: Died on Sunday evening, the 1st inst. at her father's
residence, Mary Mariah, daughter of Halbert and Elizabeth Acker,
aged thirteen years and ten months.

Issue of:
Friday, March 13, 1846:
Married: On Thursday evening, 5th inst. by Rev. T. L. McBride,
Mr. Henry Steele to Miss Elizabeth R., eldest daughter of Mr.
James Todd all of this District.

Married: On the 8th inst., by David Taylor, Esq., Mr. John
Simpson to Miss Mary Crenshaw, all of Pickens District.

Issue of:
Friday, March 27, 1846:
Married: On Sunday evening, the 22nd inst., by Elijah Webb,
Esq., Mr. Calvin Hunnicut to Miss Cealy Risner, all of Ander-
son District.

Obituary: Departed this life, at his residence in Anderson
District, Mr. James Erskine, in the 89th year of his age, after
an illness of six weeks. Mr. Erskine was for many years a
consistent member of the Presbyterian Church at Broadway.
During his confinement his sufferings were indescribably great,
but his resignation and patience were likewise great. He felt
that he was entirely in the hands of his kind and Heavenly
Father, to whom he long looked, in whom he had long trusted.
God, reconciled through the death of the Lord Jesus Christ,
was the rock on which all his hopes rested for a happy fu-
turity. He is no more - but his friends mourn not like those
who have no hope. "Blessed are the dead who die in the Lord,
yea saith the spirit, for they rest from their labors and their
labors do follow them."

Issue of:
Friday, April 3, 1846:
Married: On Tuesday the 31st ult. by the Rev. W. Magee, Mr.
Stephen Shirley to Miss Sarah, youngest daughter of James
Major, Esq., all of this District.

Issue of:
Friday, April 10, 1846:
Married: On Sunday evening, the 5th inst. by the Rev. B. F.
Mauldin, Mr. Osborne Mauldin of Pickens District, to Miss
Harriet Elizabeth Balentine, of this District.

Obituary: Died, at his residence in this District, on Sunday
morning the 5th inst., Mr. Chester Kingsley, aged Forty Eight
years, lacking five days. Mr. Kingsley was born in Lucerne
County, Pennsylvania, on the 10th April 1798. He was raised,
educated and learned the trade of house joiner and cabinet-
maker, chiefly in the State of Connecticut. He removed to
South Carolina in the year 1820, and settled at, or near
Gentsville in Abbeville District, where, after prosecuting his
trade for some three or four years profitably, he entered into

the mercantile business which he followed most successfully
till the year 1836, when he married a young and accomplished
wife, daughter of Major Cain Broyles, of Tennessee, and settled
himself permanently on his farm near Craytonville in this District, where he has since proven himself a farmer indeed, in
the fullest acception of term. In every business of life,
Mr. Kingsley seemed to possess a talent commensurate with its
importance, and by dint of a perseverance peculiar to Northern
men who come south, he managed to accumlate a very handsome
fortune. He enjoyed in a high degree the respect and confidence of all who knew him; in 1840 he was honored by his fellow
citizens of Anderson District, with a seat in the popular branch
of the State Legislature, where he made a useful and acceptable
member. In June last Mr. Kingsley had the misfortune to lose
his wife suddenly, in the midst of rosy health; with a constitution previously impaired, he was unable to withstand the
shock. Grief, deep and poignant, took possession of his soul,
and has since preyed upon him, insomuch that he could not be
comforted, and gradually declined in health and strength, till
death removed his troubled spirit, and permitted it to soar
away and meet his beloved wife, as we have reason to hope, in
the realms of Glory. He told the writer a short time before
his death, that his comfort in this world, even with health,
was blasted and gone, that his only joy was in a pleasing hope
of sins forgiven, and a seat of peace and comfort prepared for
him, beside his sainted wife, at the right hand of God in Heaven.
He has left three lovely little orphan children, to mourn the
loss of a kind father, in a little less than nine months from
the death of their loving and still remembered mother. Mr.
Kingsley was indeed a most affectionate husband and father,
a kind master, a devoted friend and neighbor, and in his death,
the District lost one of its best citizens. He had no blood
relatives in the State, but a large circle of friends are left
to mourn his loss to them.

Issue of:
Friday, May 1, 1846:
Married: On Thursday eveing, 22nd ult. by the Rev. W. P.
Martin, Mr. Elisha Williamson of Laurens District, to Miss
Elmina Mattison, of this District.

Issue of:
Friday, May 22, 1846:
Married: On Thursday, 7th inst. by the Rev. W. Magee, Mr.
William Jones to Miss Mary Sullivan, all of this District.

Issue of:
Friday, May 29, 1846:
Married: On Tuesday, 19th inst. by the Rev. W. C. Smith, Mr .
Moses Chamblee to Miss M. S. Hall, all of this District.

Obituary: Departed this life on the 21st inst. in this
District, John H. Drennan, aged 35 years, after lingering three
years with consumption, during which time he suffered much;
leaving a desolate companion and three small children to realize
the sad bereavement and mourn the loss of a kind husband and
an affectionate father. Mr. Drennan had never connected himself with any religious denomination, his bad health being
the only reason. He professed to be reconciled to God, through
the merits of Christ his Saviour, and manifested a strong

desire to be absent from the body and present with the Lord. A short time before his decease, he conversed satisfactorily to all who heard him, on the subject of death, and his hope and trust in God, through a crucified Saviour; commiting himself and weeping family to the mercy and favor of their Heavenly Father. May his widow and fatherless children share in the sympathies, prayers and kindness of the humane and liberal.

Issue of:
Friday, June 5, 1846:
Married: On the 21st ultimo by the Rev. David Humphreys, Mr. Joel J. Cunningham to Miss Rebecca S., eldest daughter of Capt. J. P. Benson, all of Anderson Village.

Issue of:
Friday, July 3, 1846:
Married: On Thursday evening, 25th ult. by the Rev. Robert King, Mr. W. M. Kay to Miss Sarah A., only daughter of Mr. James Campbell, all of this District.

Issue of:
Obituary: Departed this life on the 29th of June, Samuel Cunningham, Esq., in the eighty-second year of his age, after a protracted illness of five weeks, occasioned by dropsy of the chest. He was born and raised in Laurens District, S. C., where he maintained the character of an honest man and a good citizen. He represented that District in the State Legislature from 1812 to 1817. He has resided in Anderson District for the last ten years, during which period he has devoted his time to the interests of his farm, and to the quiet enjoyment of his family and friends. Though not inclined to mingle such in society, yet he secured to himself a number of warm friends, who were kind to him while living and lament him when dead. He united with the Presbyterian Church in 1829. The evening of the day on which he joined himself with the Church, he took up the cross and acted as the high point of his own household ever afterwards, till prevented by feebleness and disease. His views of the great scheme of Devine mercy were very clear; he had a deep sense of his own isnfulness and weakness, and a strong confidence in the efficacy of the Atonement - there he rested firmly and comfortably all his hopes of devine acceptance, and death was robbed of all its terrors. During his protracted illness, it was refreshing to hear him conversing of experimental piety, and speaking of the manifold goodness of God to him through a long life. At the commencement of his affliction he examined carefully the grounds of his hope, and after being satisfied he was resting on the true foundation, the promise of God afforded him an unfailing source of comfort, that enable him to hear with great composure of mind his bodily sufferings which were at times very excruciating. He often remarked that his sufferings were not to be compared with those of the blessed Jesus. On one occasion, when he was thought to be dying, the friends were assembled, and his grandchildren standing before him, countenance manifested intense anxiety to say something; at length he said in a low tone "Oh, if I had strength of talk," but was unable to proceed. At times when contemplating the joys of the celestial world, it would so kindle his desires and affections, he would say, "If I had strength of describe the happiness I feel." On another occasion, when he evidently thought his sufferings were coming to a close, he reached out his trembling hand and

took the writer of this article by the arm, and drawing his ear down to his lips, in a low whisper he said, "I think I shall soon be in Heaven." In fact, for several weeks he appeared to walk on the confines of the celestial world, and to enjoy a foretaste of that happiness enjoyed by those who are constantly drinking of the pure River of water of life that flows through the midst of the Paradise of God. "Let me die the death of the Righteous, and let my last end be like this."

Issue of:
Friday, July 17, 1846:
Obituary: Died at the Residence of their father, Michael Magee, in this District, on the 5th inst., at half past 3 o'clock in the morning, Assenith Elvira Magee, born July 14, 1839, also, on the same day, at 20 minutes past 12 o'clock, in the evening, Mary Elizabeth Lucinda Magee, born May 14th, 1832, aged 14 years and nearly 2 months. They were both lovely children. Mary made a profession of Religion at the age of 10 years and from that time until the day of her death lived the life of a consistent Christian; she was admired for her meekness and humility of manners - never was there a more kind affectionate daughter and sister. About two years before she died, she said to the writer, "If it is the will of God that I should die, I have hope that I shall be happy - all my trust is in Christ." To her father she said, whilst she clasped him with her little arms, "Father, I love you best of all, but I love my saviour more than you." On the next day at 10 o'clock, they were both deposited side by side in the same tomb, where their bodies will rest in sweet repose until the mourn of the resurrection, whilst their happy souls have returned to God who gave them. Their grave was literally bathed with the tears of their affec- tionate parents, brothers and numerous relatives and friends that attended on the mournful occasion. Their disease was thought to be billous congestive fever; though some difference of opinion exists on the subject. They were confined about two weeks. A. R.

Issue of:
Friday, July 24, 1846:
Married: On Thursday evening, 16th inst., by Rev. David Humphreys, Capt. Samuel M. Wilkes, to Miss Louisa C. H., daughter of Elijah Webb, Esq. all of this place.

Issue of:
Friday, August 7, 1846:
Married: On Sunday evening the 19th ult. by Andrew Todd, Esq., Mr. Elijah Hatcher to Miss Sarah Howard, all of this District.

Obituary: Died at his residence in this District on the 2nd inst., William Smith, Sen., in the eighty second year of his age. The deceased was a native of Ireland, and at an early period of life emigrated to his country, and settled in the District of Ninety-Six, and there continued during the eventful struggle for independence. Although quite a boy at this time, he had a faithful recollection of the thrilling incidents and trying viscisitudes of war and torture to which the inhabi- tants of this section were exposed during the prevalence of a rancorous partisan warfare. A love of liberty had been early and deeply implanted from witnessing the ruffian deportment and savage atrocities of the marauding parties with which this District was infested - He ever afterwards manifested a most

ardent devotion to liberty, and when the sun of life was fast
setting, when recounting the tragic events of this dark period
in our history, his countenance kindled with the effulgence of
better days, and he seemed to forget the infirmities and dec...
of age under the soul stirring influence of a reminisense of
the wanton and ruthless barbarities perpetrated by the gallows -
branded villains who figured in old Ninety-Six District. By
his death, another link in the fast shortening chain of living
memory which connects the present with the past, is severed.
He was among the number of pioneers in the settlement of this
District, having removed to it about the year 1783, and continued
to reside in it up to the period of his death. The deceased
was an individual of plain and unobtrusive manners. Pleased
with retirement, and his own humble pursuits, he seldom left
his homestead. He had been for the last five years of his life
a consistent and pious member of the Associate Reformed Church.
He has left an aged wife and a number of children and relatives
to lament his death - yet with the comforting conviction that
their loss was his eternal gain.

Issue of:
Friday, August 21, 1846:
Obituary: Departed this life on the 29th July last, of Typhoid
Fever, at her home, Haywood County, West Tenn., Mrs. Ann
Melvina, consort of Abner H. Magee, Jr., aged about 22 years,
leaving a companion and two small children, together with a
large circle of relatives to mourn their loss. Their grief,
however, is mixed with joy as she gave satisfactory evidence
while living, that she was prepared for a better world than
this. Few perhaps ever spent their days more to the comfort
and consolation of their friends, than she did - her disposition was amiable and unassurring always rendering every one
pleasant in her company. Her life was strickly moral; and the
last six or seven years she devoted to her blessed saviour,
having professed the religion of her master, she loved and
served him, - and as she approached the end of her journey,
her attachment grew stronger and stronger, until she quietly
breathed her last, and fell into the arms of her blessed Lord.
May this dispensation of God's providence be sanctified to the
good and everlasting happiness of all who may survive her. S.M.

Issue of:
Friday, September 11, 1846:
Married: On Sunday morning the 6th inst., by the Rev. W. Magee,
Mr. Asbury Brooks, to Miss Laura Herring.

Married: On Tuesday evening the 8th inst., by the Rev. W.
Magee, Mr. J. H. Wright, to Miss Assenath May.

Married: On Tuesday evening the 8th inst., by the Rev. W.
Magee, Mr. John Sayler, Jun., to Miss Elizabeth May. All of
this District.

Obituary: Departed this life, August 31st, 1846, in this
District, Jas. Brown in the eighty ninth year of his age. He
was an active soldier in the Revolution; having been attached
to the command of Sumter, he was with him in most of his
principle battles, and shared with that ceteran and brave
officer the dangers and hardships of that period. He removed
to this District many years ago, and maintained an honest name

through life. A widow and two children survive him. A few days after, on the 3d September (inst.) in the same house, the father of his widow, Amariah Felton, also died, at the advanced age of ninety-five years.

Issue of:
Friday, September 25, 1846:
Married: On Thursday evening the 17th inst., by the Rev. A. Williams, Mr. E. W. Seawright to Miss Mary R. Pyles, all of Abbeville District.

Married: On Thursday evening the 17th inst., by the Rev. W. Magee, Mr. James Cox to Miss Duranda Cobb, all of this District.

Married: On Tuesday evening, 23d inst., by The Rev. D. Humphreys, Mr. Wm. W. Anderson of Spartanburg, to Miss Jane Cauble of Greenville.

Issue of:
Friday, September 25, 1846:
Obituary: Died at his residence in this District, on Thursday the 17th instant, the Rev. John Vandiver, aged 72 years. He had suffered greatly with sickness at intervals since 1844, at which time he became feeble to take his wonted exercise. The malady with which he was afflicted continued to prey on his constitution with increasing severity till about five weeks ago, when he was confined to his bed,and complained of severe misery in every part of his body, which continued to increase till his Spirit took its flight. The deceased was a devout follower of the meek and lowly Jesus, having attached himself to the Christian Church in early life, and for the last fifteen years of his life, was assiduously - devoted to proclaiming the Gospel of Christ. He left a widow and nine children besides an extensive circle of relatives and friends to imitate his virtues while living, and sorrow over his death. "But they sorrow not as those who have no hope."

Issue of:
Friday, October 2, 1846
Married: On Sunday evening the 20th ult., by the Rev. J. Burris, Mr. Jasper Hembree to Miss Louisa Dickson, all of this District.

Issue of:
Friday, October 9, 1846:
Obituary: Died at the residence of William Jolly, in Pickens District, on the 2d ult., Mrs. Sarah J. Branyan, consort of the late Thomas Branyan, of Abbeville District, aged 63 years. She had gone to visit her daughter, Mrs. Jolly, and while there, experienced an attack of billious fever, and though she received every attention which filial affection could bestow, the decease terminated her existence in the house of her daughter, after an illness of eighteen days.

Obituary: Died at his residence in Abbeville District, on the 24th ult., Thomas Branyan, in the 68th year of his age, after a short and severe attack of billious fever. Mr. and Mrs. Branyan supported the character of affectionate parents and kind neighbors. Called to their exit in a few days of each other, they seemed indeed to be "one flesh", and the affliction is doubly severe to their family of eight children and a large circle of friends. "All that live must die, passing through nature to eternity."

Issue of:
Friday, October 23, 1846:
Married: On Tuesday evening, 20th inst., by the Rev. W. Carlisle, Mr. Thomas H. Anderson of Christ Church Parish, to Miss Eugenia R. C., eldest daughter of Dr. Wm. Norris, deceased, of this District.

Issue of:
Friday, November 6, 1846:
Married: On Thursday the 15th ult., by the Rev. W. C. Smith, Mr. George Connell of Georgia, to Miss Sarah Field, of this District.

Married: On the 28th ult. by the Rev'd Henry Tyler, the Rev. Henry Cosper, of Georgia to Miss Malissa Raney, of this District.

Issue of:
Friday, November 13, 1846:
Married: On Sunday the 8th inst. by the Rev. James Hembree, Mr. Anderson Hix to Miss Hepzibah Bowen, all of this District.

Issue of:
Friday, December 4, 1846:
Married: On Tuesday evening the 1st inst. by Mr. H. Vandiver, Mr. Jesse Broome, to Miss Sarah E. McCoy, all of this District.

Issue of:
Friday, December 25, 1846:
Obituary: Died on Sunday morning, 29th ult., of Scarlet Fever, Martha Susan, only child of John A. and Susan C. Simpson, formerly of this District, but now of Tippah County, Mississippi, aged 2 years 2 months and 14 days. Their numerous relatives and friends will deeply sympathize with the bereaved parents, on account of the death of this interesting child. One of earth loveliest flowers has been thus transplanted into a more genial clime, there to flourish and bloom and live forever in a state of blessed immortality. S. H. B.

Issue of:
Friday, January 8, 1847:
Married: On the 22nd ult. by the Rev. A. Rice, Mr. Benjamin H. Shirley of Abbeville, to Miss Lucinda C., daughter of Capt. H. Brock, of Anderson District.

Married: On Thursday evening 24th ult., by James Gilmer, Esq., Mr. Henry H. Scudday, to Miss Sarah Ann, eldest daughter of Mr. Hugh Gregg, all of Anderson District.

Married: On the 31st ult., by the Rev. David Humphreys, Mr. P. K. Norris, to Miss Caroline, daughter of Capt. Wm. Sanders, all of Anderson District.

Obituary: Died on Sunday morning, 20th of December last, at the residence of her father in this District, Miss Catherine, youngest daughter of Wm. R. and Sarah Nelson, aged 21 years. By this event her relatives and friends are called to mourn

the departure of one who was dear to them in the various
relations of Daughter, Sister and Friend. She is gone-
her trials and troubles are over; she needs not now the hand
of affection to smooth her pillow nor the voice of consolation
to cheer her in the loneliness of the sick room. The subject
of this notice was afflicted for several years, and so complicated was her disease that it completely baffled the skill
of her physicians, so as to create in the minds of her friends
the certain anticipation of her dissolution, even months before her death. Alas, how swift do the shafts of death speed
their fatal errand. She whose youthful frame once gave some
appearance of activity and usefulness, is ushered in the
meredian of her days beyond the pale of earthly influences
and earthly associations; but while natural affection prompts
the sorrowing tear, and would fain recall to its bosom the one
who so recently tabernacled in the fashion of humanity, the
voice of lamentation is hushed by the consoling hope that what
is their loss is her unspeakable and eternal gain. Our departed
friend had been a consistent member of the Presbyterian Church
for several years, and that she was in the happy possession of
the "Pearl of great price" was manifested in all her deportment. Her bodily suffering was intense, yet she bore it all
with almost unexampled patience and Christian resignation.
It is enough for us to say that she lived and died the death of
the righteous, whose end is peace. To the aged parents, brothers and sisters, this afflictive dispensation is heavy; but
God has done it, and may he of his infinite mercy grant them
grace and resignation to say, with the once afflicted Job,
The Lord gave and the Lord hath taken away, and blessed be the
name of the Lord."

Issue of:
Friday, January 15, 1847:
Married: On Thursday the 7th inst. by the Rev. Amaziah Rice,
Mr. James Belcher, of Abbeville District, to Miss Nancy Elvira,
eldest daughter of Daniel Brown, Esq., of this Village.

Issue of:
Friday, January 22, 1847:
Married: On Wednesday the 6th inst., by the Rev. R. King, Mr.
W. L. Davis to Miss Caroline Duncan.

Married: On Tuesday the 12th inst., by the Rev. R. King, Mr.
B. H. Irby to Miss Amanda Irby.

Married: On Sunday the 17th inst. by the Rev. W. C. Smith,
Mr. B. Davis to Miss Jane Padgett.

Issue of:
Friday, February 5, 1847:
Married: On the evening of the 12th ult., by the Rev. A.
Rice, Capt. John B. Graham, formerly of this Village, now of
Lumpkin County, Georgia. to Miss Nancy Lavina, daughter of Mr.
John McDavid, of Greenville District.

Married: Early on Sunday morning 31st ult., by the Rev. W.
C. Smith, Mr. Enoch M. Fant, to Miss Margaret Ann Hall, all of
Anderson District.

Obituary: Died in this village on the 28th ult., after 7

days confinement, Mr. Jonathan Sawyer, in the 79th year of his age, Mr. Sawyer was a native of Westminster, Mass., but for many years past a respectable inhabitant of this village. He has left in this place, an aged companion to lament the loss of an affectionate husband, and an only son in the State of New York, a kind parent. "An honest man is the noblest work of God."

Obituary: Died in this village on Thursday the 28th ult., in the 25th year of his age, Mr. Ibsan Clinkscales, after an illness, (with occasional intervals), of five months continuance, which he bore with christian fortitude. To write out all that could be said in favor of this young man, would far exceed the bounds of an ordinary notice of this kind. Suffice it to say, that in all the relations of son, brother, and friend, he was excelled by none; he was the main stay and solace of his widowed mother, the kind and affectionate brother and truly it may be said of him, his virtues were many, his faults few. He was a consistent christian, having professed Christ, he adorned that profession. What was remarkable in his character, was, although he had many friends, it is not known to the writer that he ever had an enemy. "The memory of the just is blessed." A. R.

Issue of:
Friday, January 29, 1847:
Married: On Tuesday the 19th inst., by the Rev. R. King, Mr. J. W. Rogers to Miss Dicy Owen, all of this District.

Married: At Pickens C. H., on Tuesday evening, 19th inst., by the Rev. J. L. Kennedy, Mr. Jas. George to Miss Mary Telford.

Issue of:
Friday, February 12, 1847:
Married: On Tuesday evening, the 2d inst., by the Rev. Wiley C. Smith, Mr. Thomas King to Miss Jane Fant, all of Anderson District.

Issue of:
Friday, February 19, 1847
Married: On Wednesday evening, the 10th inst., by the Rev. D. Simmons, Mr.C. C. Langston of this Village, to Miss Ann Field Fant, of this District.

Married: On Thursday evening, the 11th inst., by the Rev. D. Simmons, Mr. James R. Bruce to Miss Elizabeth, daughter of John Cox, all of Anderson District.

Obituary: Emily Overby, second daughter of Mrs. Elizabeth Jackson, near this Village, departed this life on Thursday the 11th inst., after an illness of a few days, borne with great patience, in the thirteenth year of her age. Though spared only to commence life, she lived long enough to have learned the great end for which she was created. She was kind, meek and affectionate through life, and at the approach of death, of which she seemed the first to be satisfied, was calm, composed and confident of her interest and acceptance through a Saviour's blood. Her admonitions of her death-bed were solemn and impressive, and will be long remembered, with her many virtues, by her friends and relatives. Shortly before her death she indicated the place for her burial and the religious services she desired, as well as her grave as on some subsequent day. A large concourse of friends and relatives followed, with their tears, this interesting young female to her grave the day after her death. On Saturday next at 11 o'clock, a suitable funeral sermon is expected to be preached in the Presbyterian Church.

Issue of:
Friday, March 5, 1847:
Married: On Sunday morning, 21 st ultimo, by the Rev. B. F. Mauldin, Mr. S. Mauldin to Miss M. Shaw, all of Laurens District.

Married: On Thursday evening, 25th ult., by the Rev. B. F. Mauldin, Mr. E. W. Brazeal to Miss Elizabeth, eldest daughter of Capt. W. Cox, all of this District.

Married: On Thursday evening, 25th ult., by the Rev. A. Rice, Mr. R. M'Cadams to Miss Eliza Ann, only daughter of Robert Hall, all of Abbeville District.

Married: On Tuesday evening, 2d inst., in the Methodist Church this Village, by the Rev. W. G. Mullinax, Dr. Charles L. Gaillard to Miss Aletha L. Creswell, all of this District.

Obituary: Departed this life on Sunday evening the 21st ult., in the 24th year of her age, Miss Mary Elizabeth, daughter of Whit Smith, of this District, after an illness of fifteen weeks, which she bore with Christian patience. She had been an exemplary member of the Baptist Church for the last five years of her life, and during her illness gave ample testimony of her acceptance with God. As a daughter and sister she was kind and affectionate, and as a Christian meek and charitable.

Issue of:
Married: On Thursday evening, 4th inst., by the Rev. W. Carlisle, Mr. W. P. Todd to Miss Elizabeth, eldest daughter of Mr. John Carpenter, all of this district.

Issue of:
Friday, March 26, 1847:
Married: On the 16th inst., by the Rev. R. King, Mr. Greenlee Glasby to Miss Susan Lewis, daughter of Mr. Brooks Lewis, all of Anderson District.

Married: On Thursday evening the 18th inst., by the Rev. D. Simmons, Mr. Jefferson Allen, of Illinois, to Miss Mary Ward of Pickens District, S. C.

Issue of:
Friday, April 16, 1847:
Married: On Thursday, 1st inst., by the Rev. A. Rice, Capt. P. Tucker to Miss Lycenia C., daughter of Mr. David Hall, all of this District.

Married: On Thursday 8th inst., by the Rev. A. Rice, R. F. Wyatt, Esq., of this Village, to Miss Nancy O., daughter of John Rasor, dec'd., of Abbeville District.

Issue of:
Friday, April 23, 1847:

36

Married: In this District, on the 15th instant, by Elder
Robert King, Mr. John Rodgers, of Tuscaloosa, Ala., to Miss
Anna, eldest daughter of Jeremiah Rogers of this District.

Obituary: Died on Sunday morning the 18th instant, at Townville, in Anderson District, S. C., Rev. Sanford Vandiver, in
the sixtieth year of his age. He had been the subject of
severe affliction, caused by a derangement of his nervous
system, since the month of December 1845. Under the impression that exercise would be beneficial, he visited his daughter, Mrs. Brown, at Townville near his own residence, in
October 1846. While there, his disease became more violent,
and prevented his return home. The deceased made a public
profession of religion by attaching himself to the Baptist
Church, in the Seventeenth year of his age, and shortly thereafter he entered on the ministry, in which he continued zea-
lously to labor till prostrated by the affliction which snatched him away. To his numerous friends, many of whom reside
at a distance, the writer, who was a witness of the dying
scene, offers the consolation that he died in the full assurance of being happy beyond the grave. In the last hours of
his life, he spoke often and with great composure of his
speedy dissolution - expressed his readiness to meet death -
made his sundry arrangements as to the particulars of his
burial, and when the grim messenger arrived, he resigned his
spirit cheefully and without a struggle.

Issue of:
Friday, April 30, 1847:
Obituary: Died at her residence near this village on the 26th
inst., after an illness of three days, Mrs. Jane Rice, relect
of Mr. Hezekiah Rice, Jun., dec'd., in the 40th year of her
age. The subject of this short obituary embraced the christian religion when very young and united herself to the
Presbyterian Church, and constituted one of its most exemplary
members. Her sphere of usefullness having been confined almost
exclusively to the family circle, and at farthest to the
immediate neighborhood in which she resided, her amiable
qualities and christian virtue were known and appreciated
only by her most intimate acquaintances. A little more than
eleven years ago, after becoming the mother of five interesting
children, she was bereft of a kind and affectionate husband
by the hand of death. The care and management of a young and
helpless family and its affairs then devolved solely upon her,
which, to one naturally of a reserved and timid disposition
and delicate constitution, was no easy task. It was, indeed,
consoling to the relatives and friends of the deceased, to
witness the many manifestations she gave, in her last moments,
of her prospects of a blessed immortality beyond the grave; and
while her children and friends were weeping around, her sainted
spirit took its departure on angels' wings to the climes of
bliss and its former clay tenement gently fell asleep, to wake
no more till the morning of the resurrection.

Issue of:
Friday, May 7, 1847:
Married: On the 29th ult., by the Rev. David Humphreys, Mr.
Linsay A. Baker, to Miss Elizabeth Jane, eldest daughter of
Mr. Allen V. Brooks, all of this village.

Issue of:
Thursday, May 27, 1847:
Married: On the 20th inst., by the Rever'd A. Rice, Mr. Daniel
J. Barnett, of Spartanburg, to Miss Rachel L., daughter of
Henry Cobb, Esq., of Anderson District.

Issue of:
Thursday, July 22, 1847:
Married: On Tuesday evening, 13, inst., at West Union, Pickens
District, by the Rev. B. F. Mauldin, Joseph Brown, Esq., of
Canton, Georgia, to Miss Elizabeth, daughter of Col. Joseph
Grisham of the latter place.

Issue of:
Thursday, August 26, 1847:
Obituary: Died at his residence in this District on Tuesday
the 10th ult., Capt. John J. (Jasper) Robinson, in the 34th
year of his age, after nine days confinement, indeed he had
for some 3 weeks been complaining very much, but after confined
his suffering was severe, which he bore with unusual resignation,
never heard to murmur or repine. To write out all that could
be said about Capt. Robinson would far exceed an ordinary
notice of this kind; suffice it to say, that he was highly
esteemed by his neighbors, as such he was kind and obliging;
and a manly firmness was a marked trait in his character, in
all his transactions and business he was high-minded and honorable, in fact he was universally esteemed by all who knew
him, he was a kind husband and father, and an indulgent
master; left behind a wife and . . . children, together with
many relations and friends, to mourn his loss, although his
loss to his family and friends is irreparable, we trust their
loss may be his eternal gain; he was an honest man, the noblest
work of God. R. N. W.

Issue of:
Thursday, September 2, 1847:
Obituary: Departed this life on Saturday morning 7th ult.,
in this District, Mr. Henry A. Carpenter, in the 24th year of
his age. He was afflicted about two and a half years with
that formidable disease, consumption, which terminated his
existence. During all his illness he retained a remarkable
cheerfulness and submission to his approaching dissolution.
In the Fall of 1841, at Ebenezer Camp Meeting, he professed to
experience a change of heart; and shortly after his conversion
he joined the M. E. Church, in which he lived the remainder
of his life, a consistent member and follower of Christ, for
this was verified in the last days of his life. And but a few
hours before he died, he shouted and praised God, and prayed
even when the grim monster had laid his cold hand upon him.
His dying request was for all his friends and relations to meet
him in Heaven, for he said he was going there. Thus it has
pleased Providence to cut him down in the morning of life,
leaving his relations and friends to mourn their loss; yet
there remaineth a consolation that 'Robed in righteousness,
arrayed for Heaven, How fair in life he stood. - How lovely in
the hour of death his Cap?'

Married: On 31st ult., by the Rev. David Humphries, Dr. Michael
Anderson, of Spartanburg, to Miss Margaret Creswell of Anderson District.

Issue of:
Thursday, September 9, 1847:
Married: On 2d inst., by the Rev. Robert King, Mr. Alfred
Lewis, to Miss Clarissa Brewer, all of Anderson District.

Issue of:
Thursday, Sept. 30, 1847:
Obituary: Died, on Saturday September 4th, between the hours
of 11 and 12 at night, in the vicinity of Sandy Springs Camp
Ground, Mrs. Louise Caroline Morris, daughter of Isaac B. Hays
and consort of Richard M. Morris; aged 30 years, 1 month and
13 days. From her earliest years she was a serious, steady
girl. In June or July 1840, she became more concerned about
her future state, and attached herself to the Methodist Episcopal Church, at Ebenezer. She was esteemed an orderly member
of society, was an affectionate relative, an agreeable companion, a kind mother, and a peaceful neighbor. In her last
illness she was mostly confined to her bed between three and
four weeks. Her diease was suppose to be Miliary (sic)
fever, bro't on by improper exposure. Most of the time
during the three last weeks, she had an abiding sense of the
Divine presence resting with her; and frequently was constrained
to shout the high praises of the Lord of Glory. She at all
times expressed an entire resignation to the Divine will; and
in fervent prayer committed her three little children to His
kind care and keeping - then closed the scene in peace, and
has no doubt gone to join with the General Assembly and Church
of the first born, whose names are written in Heaven.

Issue of:
Thursday, October 7, 1847:
Married: On 30th ult., by Rev. David Duncan, Mr. Noel Strick-
land, to Miss Priscella Duncan, all of this District.

Issue of:
Thursday, October 14, 1847:
Married: In this Village, on Tuesday the 12th inst., by
Elijah Webb, Esq., Mr. Hugh McCearley, to Miss Sarah Dobbins,
all of this District.

Married: On Tuesday evening, the 7th inst., by Elijah Webb,
Esq., Mr. John H. Jones to Miss Mariah Louise Dean, daughter of
Mr. Moses Dean; and on the same evening, Mr. Andrew M. Norris,
to Miss Mary Elizabeth, daughter of William Steele, Esq.,
all of this District.

Issue of:
Thursday, October 21, 1847:
Married: On Wednesday evening, the 13th inst., by Elijah Webb,
Esq., Mr. James Kirby of Elbert County, Georgia, to Miss Mary
Ann Hays, of Anderson District.

Married: On the 10th inst., by the Rever'd Robert King, Mr.
D. O. Watkins, to Miss N. A. McCallister, all of this District.

Issue of:
Thursday, October 28, 1847:
Married: On Thursday the 14th inst., by the Rev. W. C. Smith,
Mr. W. K. Gary, of Georgia, to Miss Jane, daughter of Mr.
John McCown, of this District.

Issue of:
Obituary: Died on the morning of the 1st inst., after a painful
illness of two weeks, which he bore with patience and Chirstian
resignation, Mr. Asa Clinkscales, in the 45th year of his age.
Mr. Clinkscales was born and raised in this District - he was
a man of good mind, and well cultivated. In all the relations
of Father, Husband, Brother and Friend, he was unsurpassed.
He was one of those rare instances of character, that rise
above suspician. Of good and sound mind, his opinion and
judgement was relied on in all matters as worthy of the highest
consideration. Whatever he attempted to do, he always regarded as being worthy of being well done; and in all matters
of business, he was a pattern of neatness and order. But what
is above all, he was a Christian. In the fall of 1841, he
publicly professed his Saviour, and attached himself to the
Baptist Church at Anderson C. H., of which he lived and died a
worthy member; he has also served for several years as Clerk
of the Saluda Association. In his last illness, he always
expressed himself as having no fears, and only regretted to
leave his dear companion and little children; when told the
Lord would take care of them, he said, "Yes, he has taken
care of me." One of his excellencies was, always regard the
feelings of all; so careful was he in this respect, that the
writer of this, although long acquainted, and intimately so
for many years, has no recollection of a single instance, of
ever hearing him utter a word calculated to give pain to any
one. His words were always well ordered; as a Church Member,
his judgment and opinion was second to none. When he spoke,
he was always listened to. If he had an enemy on Earth, the
writer has no knowledge of the fact. "How insearchable are
thy ways O! God, to thy will be bow." Brother Clinkscales
has left a wife and six sons, with an aged father and many
other relatives and friends to mourn his loss; "but they sorrow
not as those who have no hope." A. R.   Nov. 2, 1847

Issue of:
Thursday, November 11, 1847:
Married: On Tuesday the 9th instant, by the Rev. Robert King,
Mr. Kennon Breazeal, to Miss Elizabeth Fretwell, both of
Anderson District.

Issue of:
Thursday, November 18, 1847:
Married: On the 4th inst., by the Rev. H. M. Barton, Mr. W.
M. Maret, of Pickens District, to Miss Mary, daughter of the
Rev. D. Simmons, of Anderson District.

Married: On the 11th inst., by the Rev. Robert King, Mr. J.
N. Smith, to Miss Drusilla, daughter of Mr. Henry Jolley, both
of this District.

Married: On the 14th inst., by the Rev. Robert King, Mr.
Richardson Elrod, to Miss Sarah E. Martin, both of Anderson
District.

Issue of:
Thursday, December 2, 1847:
Obituary: Died on Sunday evening the 28th of November, after
a painful and protracted illness, Mr. C. B. Webb, of this
District, in the 36th year of his age. The subject of this
notice has left a disconsolate widow and six small children,

besides many relatives and friends to mourn his early loss.
He was an affectionate husband, a kind and indulgent father,
and an esteemed and worthy citizen. Some twelve years previous
to his death he attached himself to the Baptist Church, in which
he lived an exemplary and pious life, and evinced a spirit
of Christian fortitude and quiet resignation in his last illness, to the decree of Him "whom to serve, is life eternal,"
and expired in full confidence of enjoying a never ending
and blissful immortality, in the high court of Heaven.

Married: On the 30th November, by the Rev. R. King, Mr.
Beverley W. Rogers to Miss Mary E. Owens, all of Anderson
Distirct.

Issue of:
Thursday, December 9, 1847:
Married: On the 2nd inst., by the Rev. W. C. Smith, Mr. E. M.
Burford, of Forsyth County, Georgia, to Miss Susan Brown, of
this District.

Married: On Sunday evening the 5th inst., by James McLeskey,
Esq., Mr. Andrew J. Bussy to Miss Susannah Betterton, all of
this District.

Issue of:
Thursday, December 16, 1847:
Obituary: Died in Anderson Village, November 23rd, 1847,
Dorothy Ann Brooks, in the sixteenth year of her age. Like
most young people, she spent her girlhood days negligent of
her soul's best interests, putting far off her dying day -
but while the bloom of youth was yet on her cheek, she was
seized by the rude hand of disease, and although her Physician
tried his utmost skill, she sunk under its force into an early
grave. Although in health she had put off her return to
God yet when laid on a sick bed she "thought on her ways and
turned her feet into the testimonies of the Lord," and after
several days and nights of sorrow on account of her want of
preparation to meet her Judge, she found peace in believing,
and gave to those around her testimony that the Religion of
Jesus has power to "make a dying bed feel soft as downy pillows
are." And full of the hope of immortality she breathed her
last without a struggle or a groan. J. M. C.

Issue of:
Thursday, December 23, 1847:
Married: On the 21st inst., by the Rev. Robert King, Mr.
David A. Geer, to Miss Lisena Evaline Drennan, both of this
District.

Married: On the 21st inst., by the Rev. David Humphreys, Dr.
J. P. Hillhouse, of Pickens District, to Miss Harriet D.
Foster of Greenville District.

Issue of:
Thursday, January 6, 1848:
Married: On the 22nd ult., by the Rev. R. King, Mr. Benjamin
F. Irby to Miss Ruthy M. Rogers, both of this District.

Married: On the 23rd ult. by the Rev. R. King, Mr. Drury
Hopkins, of Greenville District, to Miss Catherine R., daughter
of Mr. Charles Irby, of this District.

Married: On the 30th ult., by the Rev. R. King, Mr. Matthew
Gambrell, to Miss Ruth, daughter of Mr. E. Murphy, both of this
District.

Issue of:
Thursday, January 13, 1848:
Married: [On date not legible] by the Rev. H. Tyler of Georgia,
Capt. C. H. Speers of Franklin Co., Ga. to Miss Adaline Terrill,
of Pickens District, So. Carolina.

Obituary: Died at the residence of Neal Johnson, in Elbert
County, Ga. on the night of the 5th inst., Mr. Samuel G. Earle,
of Anderson District, S. C., in the 59th year of his age. The
very sudden and unexpected death of this gentleman, has cast
a deep and melancholy gloom over our District. The loss of
such a man, though great, is not confined to his immediate
family, and relatives; the whole community in which he lived
feels most sensibly the sad bereavement. He was a man of great
energy, uniform cheerfulness, and such vivacity. He possessed
a bold, independent mind, distinguished for its correct
judgement, a retentive memory, improved by a liberal education,
and close habitual industry, a generous heart, tempered by
Christian faith and charity; which combined, could but make a
character of eminent usefulness. In few instances have time
and talents been so diligently and usefully employed. As a
husband, father, brother, a friend and neighbor, what he was,
their bleeding hearts can tell, who were connected with him
in these interesting relations, who knew his kind and cheerful
temper, his frank and generous disposition, his universal
benevolence and his activity, in every good work. And however,
much, we may wonder at the mysterious providence, which has
removed from us such a man, so suddenly, deprived, in his last
moments, of the soothing attention of family and friends; yet
there is consolation in the thought: "When faith and patience,
hope and love,/ Have made us meet for Heaven above;/ How
blest the privlege to rise,/ Snatched in a moment to the
skies/ Unconscious to reign our breath,/ Nor taste the bitterness of death."

Issue of:
Thursday, January 20, 1848:
Married: At Orriville, on Thursday evening the 30th of December
last, by the Rev. J. L. Kennedy, Mr. Gustavus J. Orr, to Miss
Eliza Caroline, eldest daughter of Doctor William and Mary D.
Anderson.

Obituary: Died at his residence in this District, on the 29th
ult., Mr. Jeremiah W. Rogers, in the 57th year of his age.
The deceased was an honest, industrious man, a kind and indulgent husband and parent, and a good neighbor. He has left
a wife and five children, with many relatives to mourn his loss.

Issue of:
Thursday, January 27, 1848:
Married: On 20th inst., by the Rev. A. Rice, Mr. Robert H.
Ranson, to Miss Mary E. Rice, both of Anderson District.

Issue of:
Thursday, February 3, 1848:
Married: On the 20th ult., by the Rev. W. C. Smith, Mr. William

Ducksworth, to Miss Frances, eldest daughter of Mr. Griffin Brazeale, both of Anderson District.

Obituary: Died, on the 24th ult., Mrs. Rebecca, consort of Mr. Elijah Webb. The deceased was subjected to a protracted and painful illness, occasioned by consumption, in the latter stages of which, her sufferings are indescribable. Yet she bore them with that patience, forebearance, and resignation, which characterize the true christian, and in her last moments manifested a rare degree of faith in her acceptance with God, and longed to be with him at rest. In her death, is the loss of an affectionate wife, a kind and tender parent, a devoted and generous friend, and a useful and exemplary christian; and truly may we say of her, "Multis illa bonis flebilis accidit"

Issue of:
Thursday, February 10, 1848:
Obituary: Died, on January 27th, Mrs. Frances U. Branyon, wife of Mr. Tho. F. Branyon of Abbeville District, and daughter of Mr. and Mrs. John Herron, of Anderson District. To an amiable disposition, good sense, and a well informed mind, she united a firm religious hope. During the past summer, she became a member of the Presybterian Church, by a public profession of her faith in Christ. She had a remarkable presentiment of her approaching disolution. On the morning of the 21st, while in good health, she informed her husband that her end was near; that she was fully ready, for she had made her peace with God; and requested her companion not to grieve for her loss. On that day at 12 o'clock she was sent to her father's to visit her mother and young sister - languishing on a sick bed, where she remained till the morning of the 25th. Her health then was never better. On that morning she set out to return home, and was attacked of her journey with the illness that terminated her life in little more than two days. During the short period of her severe suffering, she preserved a remarkable cheerful-ness and resignation, repeated the former conversation with her husband to a female friend; and renewed her exhortation to her consort not to grieve for her loss. She retained her reason to the last and died at 6 o'clock on the evening of the 27th in the 20th year of her age.

Issue of:
Thursday, February 17, 1848:
Married: On Wednesday evening the 9th inst., by the Rev. A. Rice, Mr. Samuel J. Emerson, to Miss Nancy Louise Magee, all of Anderson District.

Married: On Thursday evening the 10th inst., by the Rev. W. P. Martin, Mr. Jesse P. Magee, to Miss Lucinda Elvira Emerson, daughter of James Emerson, all of Anderson District.

Funeral Honors: to 1st Serg't B. F. Mattison
Issue of:
Thursday, February 24, 1848:
Obituary: Another Revolutionary Soldier Gone - Departed this life, on Sunday evening 13th inst., Capt. David Sadler, in the 86th year of his age. He was a native of Pennsylvania, while in his youth, his parents emigrated to York District in this State, where he grew up to manhood. During the period of the Revolutionary war, he was frequently in the services of his

country. He was in a number of hard fought battles; and among
them Hick's defeat in York district. Here with a comparatively
small force they attacked the British and Tories, killing a
number, taking some prisoners, driving the others from the
battle ground, and retaking some of their own men who had been
previously taken prisoners by the enemy. He possessed a bold,
independent, venturesome spirit, which often exposed him to
danger; from which he made some hair-breadth escapes. On one
occasion when returning home from the army on parole, he met
a number of armed tories. He was near them before he saw the
. . . determined to march boldly up to them as they came . . .
the road. Assuming as much as possible, a fearless, independent countenance; and occasionally looking back, as if a part
of his company were approaching just behind, when in fact there
were none of his own men in many miles of him. The tories took
the alarm, gave him the road, and he passed on unmolested. On
another occasion, he and a companion of like spirit determined
to harrass a British fort. They selected a placed at conven-
ient distance, determined to fire on them every time a head was
seen above the wall. And the British returned the compliment
every time they got sight of them. They concealed themselves
while loading their muskets behind a large rock, but was more
exposed to the firing of the enemy while in the act of firing
themselves. They kept up the fire alternately, but seeing a
number of heads above the wall, they hurried to see who could
get ready first for the next man; his companion was ready a few
seconds in advance of him - while he had seated himself to
draw sight upon the heads above the wall, a ball from a british
musket took him in the forehead, and as he himself stood near
to occupy the same spot, the moment the other would leave - the
blood flew warm in his face from the death wound of his friend.
He was only separated from death by the space of a few seconds.
Again, while he and another soldier were searching for a tory
prisoner who had escaped from them, they came upon him at night,
in a house where there were more than three dozen tories with
their arms stacked around the walls of the house. They ordered
someone to get them a rope, which they refused, and threatened
in turn. Nothing daunted at the sight of their muskets or their
numbers, ordered them again to get a rope; the order not being
promptly obeyed, drew a pistol and struck over the head, and
ordered him to bring the rope instantly - the order was obeyed
and the prisoner tied and led before their eyes in triumph.
Nothing but that fearless spirit that led them into danger, now
extricated them from it. The tories must have supposed an
army was near, or they would not have been as reckless on danger.
He was a stranger to the fear of gun powder. It was not so in
his first engagement. The sight of the enemy at first gave him
the trembles - he felt some fears that he might be killed, but
having escaped the first battle unhurt, he though he might
escape danger altogether; he therefore gave himself but little
uneasiness on that subject during the remainder of the war.
After the conclusion of peace, he continued to live in York
District, where he married Eliza Britton, a daughter of Col.
Britton who was a distinguished officer of the Revolution. By
her he had ten children, six daughters and four sons, all of
whom he lived to see married and comfortably settled. And all
of them orderly members of the Presbyterian Church. From his
own statement, he remained thoughtless on the subject of
religion till after the termination of the war. During the
great revival of religion that overspread a large portion of
the Presbyterian churches in the States of North and South

Caroline, he became awakened and deeply
salvation. After he was enabled to put
Saviour's blood, he united with the Presoyte.
Soon after, he was elected a ruling elder, and l1veu
to adorn the office. More than thirty years ago, he an. .11s
family removed to this District and settled near Robert's
church, and became united with it. He was elected to the
eldership in that church, and continued to act as one of its
officers till enfeebled by age. As a member and officer of the
church, he manifested great moral courage. If a duty was
clearly presented, he never stopped to enquire what people
would think if he performed it, but attempted its performance.
When it became necessary to commence a process against an
offending member, if it was enjoined on him to communicate
with the offending person, and enquire if the reports were
true; he never asked to be excused because the duty was an
unpleasant one; but promptly complied and generally in such
a way as not to give offence. He was as little disturbed by
"the fear of man that bringeth a snare," as with the fear of
gunpowder. He was ready by his prayers and contributions to
aid all the benevolent enterprizes of the Church. The last
twelve months of his life, he was in almost daily expectation of
the approach of death. The love of the world was perhaps
never his besetting sin; but the later years of his life he
acted towards the world as a child weaned of its mother. Long
before his death he had so arranged his temporal matters, as
to unburden his own mind from its cares. When a christian
friend would call to see him, after hours conversation on
experimental peity, the interests of the soul and eternity,
if the crops, the markets, or the war was introduced, he would
request them to stop and read the bible, and explain it to
him or spend the time in such a way as would promote his
spiritual edification. He had a deep sense of his own weakness and unworthiness. He cherished no hopes but such as
were based upon a Saviour's blood. He prayed often and
fervently to God for preparation for his approaching end.
When he had forgotten everything else, even his own children,
he had not forgotten the Saviour - he had not forgotten to
offer up prayer to God through Christ for his mercies. He had
no fear of death, but was anxious for its approach. At
length, the powers of nature gave way, and "he entered into
that rest that remaineth for the people of God."

"The Anderson Intelligencer", Anderson Court House, South
Caroline.
Issue of:
Tuesday, September 4, 1860:
Married: On last Thursday evening in the Presbyterian Church,
Spartanburg by the Rev. Edwin Cater, the Pastor, A. T. Gaines,
Esq., Editor of the Caroline Spartan, to Miss Anna Hamilton,
all of that place.

Obituary: It is with feelings of the most profound regret
that we are called to record the death of Dr. Maxfield C.
Cobb who died at Belton on the 4th of August, in the 26th year
of his age, after a painful illness of eleven days. The
deceased graduated at Philadelphia in the spring of 1858,
since which time he has been diligently engaged in the practice of his profession in and around Belton, with his unusual
success - at all times willingly devoting his time and talent

to grapple with the ravages of disease, and to alleviate the
sufferings of his fellow beings. Few young men can boast of
fairer prospects and more warm hearted friends than Dr. Cobb,
but alas! he is no more. The full destroyer, the great
enemy of the human race, has torn him from all earthly hopes
and earthly endearments, and him in the cold and silent grave,
where we are hastening. Young man, reflect that though you
be healthy, vigorous, and prosperous as was the deceased,
still amid all this, death will soon visit you like it did him.
The Doctor leaves an aged and beloved father, with numerous
brothers and sisters to ever mourn their irreparable loss.
The country has lost one of its most noble and generous hearted
citizens, and the medical fraternity an intelligent, devoted
and high minded member.

Issue of:
Thursday, October 4, 1860:
Married: On Sunday last, by F. A. Hoke, Esq., Mr. William N.
Watson to Miss Martha C. Garrett, all of this District.

Obituary: Departed, this Life, on Friday the 21st ult., in
Anderson District, Mrs. Nancy Fields, consort of Horatio
Fields, and daughter of Moses and Rebecca Pressley. She was
born in Abbeville District in the year 1790, and married in
the year 1818. She was a kind, affectionate and dutiful
wife, attending, loving and indigent [sic] mother, and ...
husband and weeping friends to mourn her death. She joined
the Baptist Church. . . ago, and has ever since lived a consistent member thereof. Adorning her profession of religion
by a pious walk and godly conversation, sharing largely the
affection, and confidence of her brethen, and the high esteem
of all who knew her. Those who knew her best loved her most.
And calmly and quietly at life's last hour, she feel sweetly
asleep in the arms of that Saviour whom she loved and had so
much delighted to serve, and has doubtless gone home to the
land of rest that remaineth to the people of God, to live
forever amidst the glory of that world of unfading joys and
unalloyed bliss. Her husband, children and friends can say
of a truth "our loss is her eternal gain", and though she can
never return to us, We can go to her.

Obituary: Died, at the residence of her father-in-law, in
Anderson District, S. C., on the 27th ultimo, Mrs. Sallie S.
Cox, daughter of William and Amelia Mahaffey, of Laurens
District, in the 20th year of her age. We occasionally meet
with persons who seem too pure, too angelic, for this sinful
world; and when such are called away we say of them, they
were too good for earth. Such a person was the deceased. In
early life were seen developing - all three virtues which
adorn women. She was blest with beauty, intelligence and true
benevolence, to which was added unquestionable piety. In
the morning of her life - in the bloom of youth, she showed
her wisdom in first seeking the kingdom of God and his
righteousness. About two years ago, after professing faith in
Christ, she was buried with Him by baptism; from which time
till her death, she walked in newness of life, a consistent
member of the Baptist Church. On the 6th of last June she was
married to Mr. William Stanton Cox, a gentleman in every
respect worthy of such a wife as she proved herself to be.
New Tendrils daily clasped the affections of her husband, as
he daily became more acquainted with her surpassing virtues.
But a few short months had passed, when this happy couple

46

were called to part. The Master called - the happy bride must
go and leave her husband. But, blessed be God, she was ready
for the call; those who saw her die, experienced a scene of
rejoicing as well as weeping. When told by her husband that
she could not recover, she said to him, "I must die and leave
you." "Why is it that we must part so soon?" She then exclaimed "Not my will, O, Lord; but thine be done. I know -
yes, I know it - that I am going to Heaven. I'll meet my dear
mother there." Then embracing her husband, she said, "And
I'll meet your mother there, too." It seemed that her dying
hour was a foretaste of heavenly bliss. To be fully convinced
that she was in her right mind, the writer asked her if she
knew him; to which she replied, "Certainly I do, and I'll meet
you in Heaven." The dying scene was so affecting that one
standing by exclaimed, "Behold a saint die." Before she
expired, she offered up a beautiful prayer, that God would
have mercy on all present, and on mourning sinners, that they
might be prepared to meet her in Heaven. Then telling her
husband and sisters to meet her in Heaven she calmly fell
asleep in Jesus. Of a truth, "we all do fade away as a leaf."
Thus has faded away one of the fairest and loveliest of our
race. Her life on earth was short but she fought a good fight.
She died at her post. She was faithful until death and is now
in Heaven wearing the crown of life, and bearing palms of
victory in her hands. Husband, no longer weep for they bride/
Father, sisters, brothers dry your tears/ With the dear lost
one you shall abide/ If Heaven be your choice, when Christ
appears.

Issue of:
Thursday, October 18, 1860:
Married: On Tuesday evening, 2nd inst., by Rev. C. McKendree
Smith, at the residence of the bride's father, Mr. Vann La
Boon to Miss Delilah, daughter of Mr. Joseph L. and Margaret
Byrum, all of this District.

Issue of:
Thursday, October 25, 1860:
Married: On the 18th inst., at the Presbyterian Church,
Pendleton, by Rev. T. L. McBryde, R. J. Smith, Esq., and Sallie
E., eldest daughter of J. W. Cohn, all of this District.
** Issue of Thursday, November 1, 1860 - see Page 251
Issue of:
Thursday, November 29, 1860:
Married: On Tuesday evening, 30th ult., by Kelly Sullivan,
Esq., Mr. Robert A. Every and Miss Ellen Pettigrew, all of
Anderson District.

Married: On the 1st inst., by Rev. L. W. Stephens, E. P.
Edwards, Esq., and Miss G. H. Willis, both of Elbert, [county?]
Georgia.

Married: On the 20th inst., by Rev. J. D. Millhouse, Col. D.
C. Templeton and Miss M. Addie Day, all of Laurens District.

Married: On Thursday, the 1st of November, by the Rev. D.
Humphreys, Mr. David Sadler, of Anderson District, to Miss
Virginia Spear, of Florida.

Obituary: Death By Drowning. We learn with regret that
Thomas J. Geer, of this District, met a sad fate on Friday last,

by accidental drowning. He started from his home, before daylight, for the millpond, a short distance thence, for the
purpose of shooting duck. He was found a few hours afterward,
in the embrace of death. We forebear giving particulars, for
fear of adding an additional pang to his bereaved family. He
was about 25 years of age, and has left a wife and child to
mourn his sudden demise. They have our sympathies and this
sad affliction of Providence.

Obituary: Homicide - We learn that on Friday night last a
man named Thomas Harrison was shot at Pendleton by Francisco
Tischessero, better known in this section by the cognomen of
"Sancho." The ball entered head of deceased behind the right
ear, proving fatal almost instantly. Various reports are in
circulation regarding this affair, but as the case will
undergo judicial investigation, we think it prudent to give
none of them. The accused delivered himself up to the proper
authorities, and was remanded to the Sheriff of this District
the same night on which this unfortuante occurence took place.

Issue of:
Thursday, December 6, 1860:
Tribute - of respect to Archibald Todd, dec'd by Anderson
Division, No. 20, S. of T.

Issue of:
Thursday, December 13, 1860:
Article from Greenville newspaper: Mr. J. P. Poole hit a Mr.
E. O. Jacobs in the head with his pistol after both had fired
several shots in from of the Court House. Mr. Jacobs died
Friday night from the wounds.

Issue of:
Thursday, January 10, 1861:
Married: On the 20th ult., by Rev. J. C. Williams, Mr. William
King, of Henry County, Va., to Miss Mary J. Young, daughter of
the Rev. V. Young, of Abbeville District.

Issue of:
Thursday, January 17, 1861:
Married: On the 20th of December, by Rev. Samuel Green,
Charles F. Hoke, of Williamston, to Miss M. Lou Austin, of
Greenville.

Executed: Frederick Leach, who was sentenced at the Fall
Term of our Court, for the murder of Hampton Cobb, was hung on
Friday last in the suburbs of our town. As usual, there was
a large attendance of people in the village on that day.

Issue of:
Thursday, February 21, 1861:
Obituary: Died, on the 6th inst., at the plantation of her
brother, Rev. Benjamin Cropp, in Alabama, Mrs. Sarah C. Heche-
nin, widow of the late William J. Huguenin, Esq. of Beaufort
District, of this State, aged 64 years.

Issue of:
Thursday, February 28, 1861:
Married: On the 29th inst., by the Rev. W. E. Walters, Mr.
James H. (illegible) to Miss Martha J. Reagan, all of this
District.

Married: On the 2nd January, by the Rev. ___ (Illegible),
Elias E. Whitner of Anderson, S. C. to Miss Emma A. Williams,
of Bel Air, Florida.

Issue of:
Thursday, March 14, 1861:
Married: On the 15th of January last, by Rev. James H. Sullivan, of Fayette Co., Alabama, Mr. William G. Stow, of said
county, to Miss Sarah H. Warmack, of Tuscaloosa, Alabama.

Married: On the 14th of February, by Rev. Wm. L. Jones, Mr.
Francis M. Black to Miss Samantha A. Blakeney, all of
Fayette Co., Alabama.

Issue of:
Thursday, March 28, 1861:
Married: On the 14th ult., by the Rev. David Humphreys, Mr.
Benjamin Franklin Taylor to Miss Martha Jane Prince, both of
this District.

Obituary: William Maxwell Martin, son of William and Margaret
Martin, died on the 21st of February last, in the city of
Columbia, S. C., in the twenty fourth year of his age. He
was a young man of rare endowments. His immediate ancestry,
in the paternal line, were from Mecklenburg County, N. C.
His great grandfather, besides other Revolutionary services,
commanded a company at Kings Mountain; in the maternal line,
from Dumfrieshire, Scotland. The Bard, who has immortalized
the Shire, was not his superior as a poet, at his age. In
some respects they were alike; in others, they differed widely.
They were both tender in sentiment, sparkling in wit, and
glowing in fancy. Both appreciative by nature in all her
aspects. Both sportive and grave, by turns and both convivial
sometimes to a fault. But the errors of the one were life-
long, of the other brief. The one was often the leader of
forbidden paths - the other only a follower. The faults
of the one were serious - of the other menial. The first gave
a charm to vice and a pang to virtue, by the witchery of his
verse - the last never. At the precincts of the grave we drop
the comparison. During the funeral obsequies of the deceased,
his remains reposed on the spot where he received the ordinance of baptism in his infancy, and gave his hand to the Church
in his early boyhood. His last public address was on "Pa-
triotism", and the last scene of his life was a beautiful
illustration of it. He was among the first to volunteer in
the service of his State, after her second declaration of
independence. He was assigned to the defence of Fort Moultrie.
Here he renewed his covenant with his Maker, and now unitting
in himself the Christian, the scholar and the soldier, he discharged his duties to the admiration of everyone. Called
suddenly from his bed to his gun, upon a raw and chilly night,
he neglected the proper precaution for shielding his person
from the severities of the season. Exposed to them through
many hours, he contracted the disease which terminated his
existence. He lived to reach the paternal roof, leave his
parents the best consolation in their bereavement, and died
the first martyr to Southern independence. A. B. Longstreet

Issue of:
Thursday, July 27, 1865:
Married: On Tuesday morning the 11th inst., by the Rev. S. B.

Jones, Rev. Theodore Hunter, of Abbeville, and Miss Sue E.,
daughter of L. A. Osborne, Esq., of this village.

Issue of:
Thursday, August 3, 1865:
Obituary: Sergt. Wm. H. McClinton, of Co. "G" 2d S. C. Rifles,
was born Feby. 1st, 1844, and killed on the 20th April, 1865.
Seldom has it fallen to our lot to chronicle a death more
mournful or sorrowful. For more than three years he was a
soldier of Gen'l Lee's Army (...) of that great chieftain
(.....) on his splendid campaigns, enduring without complaint,
fatigue, privations and hardsips. He was severely wounded
while nobly doing his duty, on the bloody field of "Frazier's
Farm", but recovering he hastened to rejoin his comrades and
(.....) fortunes of his country, passing through unhurt, to
the close of the struggle ....which are without a parallel
in the annals of war. It was reserved for him to give up his
young life under circumstances peculiarly solomn and peculiarly interesting. After the surrender of Gen'l Lee's Army,
while returning to his distant home, with a heart buoyant with
hope at the prospect of an early re-union of friends and
kindred, he halted one evening at a farm house to find shelter
from an approaching storm and requested permission to take
refuge in a barn nearby. This modest request was denied him,
by the surly landlord, but an old delapidated shelter was
pointed out to him; hungry and exhausted, after many hard days
marching, he soon fell asleep, together with his companions.
There while lost in sleep forgetful of his toils and sufferage,
dreaming perhaps of his distant home and the loved ones there
a beam from the crazy structure was nailed down across his
breast by the fierce winds, and in a moment more his happy
spirit took its flight to the spirit land. He was a child of
the covenant, nursed in the lap of piety and indoctrinated
from his infancy in the principle of the christian religion,
and it is not surprising that his friends should have a comfortable hope that his end was peace. A tree is known by its
fruit. From early childhood, he was modest, prudent, discreet.
A mother's prayers followed him in all his wanderings and
perils, and although he never publicly made a profession of
his faith in Christ, yet the spirit of God evidently was often
with him. His chaplain had repeated conversations with him
upon the great interest of his sould, and he testified he
was ever sober and discreet and so far as he could judge, he
possessed a strong scriptural hope of salvation, and his
mind illuminated by the regenerating influence of the Holy
Spirit. And although this is a severe blow to the sorrow
stricken parents and friends, being the third son out of four,
who have fallen victims in this bloody war, and although it
would have been a great comfort could he have reached his
house and received the kind attention of friends, and to them
given his last dying testimony of his faith in Christ, yet it
is also comforting to cherish the fond hope, that he died the
death of the righteous and his last end was like His.
A Friend

Issue of:
Thursday, August 17, 1865:
Obituary: [From Columbia Guardian, Dec. 1864] Killed at
Fort Harrison, on the 30th of September last, Private George
Martin, company C, Palmetto Sharpshooters, aged about twenty

50

five years. The subject of this notice entered service in
April, 1861, as a member of the "Palmetto Riflemen of Anderson",
and faithfully performed the duties of a soldier in that
company until the fatal missil terminated his young and promising life. Through the arduous campaigns of Virginia, Maryland,
and East Tennessee had he passed with credit to himself; and,
by the unwavering consistency of his character, as a soldier
and gentleman, had endeared his name to the gallant associates
who best know him and appreicated his sterling worth and service. At the battle of Sharpsburg he received a severe wound,
and was conspicuous for his daring upon that as every other
field of conflict. His steady adherence to duty, upright conduct in every relation, and kind, generous nature, won him the
esteem of others and caused him to be spoken of frequently as
a model soldier. The most auspicious years of his life were
spent in the service, and his ardent nature and impulsive
disposition impelled him to a conscientious discharge of those
trying duties which are imposed upon the obscure but honored
and patriotic private in the ranks. However grateful poster-
ity may be for the liberty we shall bequeath for their indur-
rance, they can not bestow respect and honor upon the private
soldier, whether living or dead, commensurate with his in-
trinsic merits. In the bivouac, on the weary march, and
amidst the fury of fierce encounters with the enemy, the
humble private steadfastly pursues the line of duty, and by
his glorious deeds and unexampled courage, wins fame for the
more fortunate. Such a one was George Martin, and his name
deserves to be cherished amongst the bravest of the brave, and
the noblest of the noble. The deceased was a native of county
Monigham, Ireland, and came to this country some seven or eight
years ago. He was then quite a youth, but by his industry,
energy and genlemanly deportment, soon won friends who were
devoted and true. When the war commenced, he relinquished
amny cherished schemes and promptly enlisted for the defence
of his adopted home. For near four years had he fulfilled
the obligations thus selfimposed, then was called to rest from
his labors. During the last summer he had manifested a deep
interest in his soul's salvation; and we are led to believe,
from the evidence of his conduct, that he had experienced a
change of heart and found the way to life everlasting. His
mortal remains are interred beneath the soil of the Old
Dominion and his dust commingles with that noble army of
martyrs in freedom's cause who have found a resting place
there. May the green sod press lightly above him!
A Comrad Anderson Court House, S. C. December 1864

Issue of:
Thursday, September 21, 1865:
Married: At the Benson House, on Tuesday evening 12th instant,
by the Rev. J. Scott Murray, Mr. F. S. Rodgers of Charleston,
and Miss Lizzie Cochran, of Anderson.

Issue of:
Thursday, September 28, 1865:
Married: At the residence of the bride's father, on Thursday,
7th instant, by Rev. H. M. Barton, Dr. John N. Doyle and Miss
Lou M. Stribling, all of Pickens District.

Issue of:
Thursday, October 5, 1865:
Married: At the residence of the bride's father, in Anderson

District, on the 7th instant, by Rev. J. M. Gambrell, Mr. H. C. Poore, of this District, and Miss Elvena Amanda, second daughter of G. L. Wharton of Charleston.

Married: On Thursday evening the 21st instant, by the Rev. W. E. Walters, Capt. James M. Kidd, of Tennessee, and Miss Sallie C., daughter of W. W. Holland, Esq., of this District.

Obituary: Died, on the morning of the 21st inst., Ida Jane, aged 13 months and 5 days, infant daughter of Michael and Rachel Nicely.

Married: At the resident of the bride's father, on the 28th ult. by the Rev. Fletcher Smith, Mr. A. Evans Browne of Anderson District, and Miss Julia M. Miller of Pickens.

Issue of:
Thursday, October 19, 1865:
Married: On the 5th inst., by the Rev. Wm. Carlile, James A. Hall, Esq., and Miss Emma Carpenter, all of Anderson.

Issue of:
Thursday, October 26, 1865:
Married: On October 10th, by Rev. T. H. Edwards, Mr. Warren D. Marony and Miss Docia E. Watson, all of Anderson District.

Obituary: [From the Newberry Herald]: "The theme is old/Of 'dust to dust',/ but half its tale untold." Emma J. Goggans, daughter of Daniel and Emily Goggans, Newberry District, died at the residence of her father, on the 18th inst., of Congestive Fever, in the twenty third year of her age. When the King beheld the handwriting upon the wall, his terror, arose not from what he saw, but from what he could not see; for he was unable to discern the body to which the hand belonged. It is so in death. Our fears arise, not from what we know, but from what we do not know. To the Christian all things are revealed; the grave is diverted of its terrors and "Death is swallowed up in victory." Several years previous to her death the deceased connected herself with the Methodist Episcopal Church. She was ever assidious in promoting the welfare of others; constant in the discharge of both spiritual and temporal duties, and true to her God whom she professed and loved. In her last illness she was resigned and submissive. Fathering all her strength a few hours before the cool hand of death was laid upon her she sang "Rest for the weary", and to a friend who stood weeping by her side, she spoke words of comfort and said, "It is not hard to die." Of her approaching dissolution she seemed assured and met her destiny with Christian fortitude; for, amidst her sufferings and the struggle between life and death, a spirit presided that occupied her in all things to say "Thy will be done; ever so Father, for it seems good in thy sight." As a daughter, she was dutiful and loving; as a sister, confiding and affectionate; as a friend, wilable and constant. Possessed of rare intelligence and much amiability, she was the centre of many hopes and the pride of many friends. In a few weeks she would have gone to the hymenial altar, there to assume the duties and responsibilities, of life which she was so well qualified by nature and education. But man. like a pendulum, ever vibrates between a smile and a tear. It is as otherwise determined in the high courts of Heaven, and she was summoned from the uncertainties and frailties of life, to join in the marriage supper

of the Lamb. With the family so deeply afflicted many have shed
affection's tears, and in their bereavement have felt an honest
sympathy for, when the young and the gifted, the beautiful and
the good pass away, not so we gather on the heart as (shik-snik?)
the dews along the flower. A loving daughter, an affectionate
sister, a constant friend, she is gone; her body to its coffined
home, her spirit to mansions prepared where the weary are at
rest.

Obituary: Died, at the residence of Col. Hammond in Anderson,
S. C., Sept. 29, 1865, Ella Viola, infant daughter of W. Baylis
and L. A. Gaines, aged one year and nearly five months. Four
weeks of patient suffering with Pnuemonia, at last freed the
struggling spirit from the frail young body and good angels took
it home to unending blissful repose on the.....of our Father,
who has said, "Of such is the Kingdom of Heaven." While the
parents sadley miss their pet lamb from the fold, and the little
brother and sister, speak of her with fond regret and the household sigh to greet again their little "shepherd" with her winning
ways and sunny smiles, her baby prattle and wee tottering steps,
let them remember that she is far more blessed that their affection could tender her in this dark "vale of tears." The pain its
little body had already endured, and the trials and the cares
incident to a longer life in this poor world, should reconcile
the bereaved to the Divine decree which called her to rest ever-
more. Sad it was to see her bright Violet eyes closed, and the
pale lips of the little one speechless here forever; yet the
healing balm may drop into their wounded hearts, for those eyes
beholding glories, those lips chanting praises which only the
redeemed experience in mansions of eternal happiness.
Anderson, S. C., Oct. 18, 1865   E.

Issue of:
Thursday, November 2, 1865:
Married: On the 18th October, by the Rev. W. E. Walters, Mr. J.
D. Cook, of Pickens, and Miss Mary E. Maret, of Anderson.

Obituary: Died, at Pendleton, S.C., on Thursday night, October
9, 1865, Caroline, wife of William S. Hastie of Charleston, and
daughter of the late John Franklin, of New York, aged 54 years.

Issue of:
Thursday, November 9, 1865:
Married: In Abbeville, October 24th by Rev. C. McCartha, Mr. R.
W. Sassard, of Charleston, and Miss A. S. Fant, of Anderson.

Issue of:
Thursday, November 16, 1865:
Married: On the 2d November, by Rev. B. F. Mauldin, Capt.
Nathan McAlister and Miss Sallie V. Cooly, all of Anderson.

Married: On Tuesday evening, the 7th inst., by Rev. W. E.
Walters, Mr. Jasper N. Vandiver and Miss Emma T. Fant, all of
this District.

Married: On Thursday evening, 9th instant, by Rev. H. M. Barton,
Mr. W. T. Jordan, of Tennessee and Miss Nannie J. Maret, of Hart
County, Ga.

Issue of:
Thursday, November 30, 1865:

Married: At the residence of the bride's father, in this village on Tuesday evening, 21st instant, by Rev. J. Scott Murray, Mr. I. O. McDaniel of Atlanta, Ga. and Mrs. Lou C. Wilkes of Anderson

Issue of:
Thursday, December 7, 1865:
Married: On Thursday, November 30, 1865 by Rev. John L. Kennedy, Mr. Thomas W. Russell and Miss Alice M., third daughter of Dr. J. W. Earle, all of this District.

Married: On Thursday evening, Nov. 30, 1865, at the residence of John C. Whitner, Esq., Mr. Lawrence Orr Williams, of Anderson District, and Miss Elizabeth Garrifelia, daughter of Mr. D. G. Finley, of Spartanburg.

Obituary: Departed this life on the morning of the 15th November, Nettie S., consort of John L. Arnold and daughter of Wm. Banks of Forsythe, Georgia, in the 25th year of her age, after a painful and protracted sickness, which she bore with patience, sustained by a blessed hope in her Saviour. It seems but as yesterday that she, whose death we sorrowfully deplore, was among us in all the vigor of life, shedding light and joy around her, like some rare flower nourished by the hand of affection. She bloomed in all the loveliness of a devoted wife, mother and daughter; but oh! the void her early death has made in the loved one's hearts! No more will we behold her dear form in our midst, nor hear the cheeful voice, the ringing laugh, for all is hushed in death. She sleeps her last sleep in the quiet city of the dead. Scarcely had she bloomed in youth and beauty, ere she drooped and died. We bow in resignation to the Divine will.

Obituary: Death-We regret to record the demise of Thomas J. Eccles, Esq., which occured at Yorkville, S. C. on Sunday, Nov. 26th. He was a practical printer, and had long connected with the newspaper press of this State.

Issue of:
Thursday, December 14, 1865:
Married: At the residence of the bride's father, on Tuesday evening, Dec. 12th, by the Rev. W. E. Walters, Mr. N. A. McCully and Miss Carrie M., daughter of J. T. Fretwell, Esq.

Obituary: Death of Capt. Lee M. Pegg, Enrolling Officer of Green County, Georgia. Assinated by someone unknown on the night of 18th May, last, in the town of Greensboro, Georgia. [Lengthy article]

Obituary: In Memoriam - Departed this life, on the 12th November, Mrs. Hattie Earle, beloved wife of F. W. Earle, and daughter of Mrs. Wm. Hubbard. Having nobly fulfilled her mission on earth, she has passed away to that rest which "remaineth for the people of God." Early in life she united with the Presbyterian Church of Anderson, and dedicated herself to the service of her maker. She lived to his honor and glory. This was the crownist excellence of her life - a life alternating between the brightest sunshine and the deepest gloom. In all the endearing relations of wife, mother, daughter, sister, with her pure, ernest, self-sacrificing devotion, there was intimately blended a spirit so bright and joyous that while it considered one of the chief attractions of her character, and

54

at the same time served to secure for her the esteem and admiration of all who were brought within the sphere of her influence. Her friendships were steadfast and enduring unalloyed by envy or detraction.

Issue of:
Thursday, December 21, 1865:
Married: On the 16th November, by Rev. Wilson Ashley, Maj. L. W. Kay and Mrs. Hattie E. Stone, all of this District.

Issue of:
Thursday, December 28, 1865:
Married: On Sunday morning, December 24th, 1865 at the residence of the bride's father, in this village, by the Rev. W. H. Stratton, Mr. D. Sloan Maxwell, of Pendleton, and Miss Kate B., only daughter of B. F. Crayton, Esq.

Married: On Wednesday evening, December 20th, 1865, by the Rev. John Burdine, Mr. John Baylis Neal and Miss Sarah Caroline Pegg, all of this District.

Married: On Thursday evening, December 14th, 1865 by the Rev. John M. Carlisle, M. D. Hamilton Russell and Miss Fannie E. Smith, all of this District.

Married: On the 31st of October, by Rev. B. Hays, Col. Jesse McGee and Miss M. E. Chamblee, all of this District.

Married: On the 7th of December, by Rev. David Humphreys, Mr. J. M. Chamblee and Miss J. A. E. Williford, all of this District.

Issue of:
Thursday, January 18, 1866:
Married: On Thursday morning, January 11, 1866, by the Rev. W. H. King, Mr. J. Miles McGee and Miss M. J. Jones, all of Anderson District.

Married: On Wednesday evening, January 10, 1866, by Rev. W. P. Martin, Col. Warren D. Wilkes and Miss Isabella, daughter of Mr. Wm. Telford, all of this District.

Married: On Thursday evening, 11th instant, by Rev. W. B. Long, Mr. U. L. Gambrell and Miss Margaret Orr, all of this District.

Obituary: Died at Anderson C. H., Sunday, January 14, 1866, Keating L. Simons, in the 46th year of his age.

Issue of:
Thursday, January 25, 1866:
Married: At Pendleton, S. C., on the 17th inst., by the Rev. F. P. Mahaffy, W. Walker Russell and Miss Janie, youngest daughter of Jno. B. Sitton.

Issue of:
Thursday, February 1, 1866:
Married: At the residence of the bride's father, on Tuesday evening, Jan. 30th, 1866, by the Rev. J. Scott Murray, Mr. James A. Hoyt, Editor of the Anderson Intelligencer, and Miss Rebecca, daughter of Elijah Webb, Esq., all of this Village.

Married: On January 25, 1866, by Rev. Wm. F. Pearson, Mr. Jas.
J. Harkness and Mrs. Letitia Wallace, both of Anderson District.

Married: On the 18th January, at the residence of Martin Hall,
Mr. Wm. H. Long and Miss Agnes P. Nance, all of Anderson
District.

Married: On January 24th, at the residence of the bride's
father, Mr. Wm. G. Watson, of Anderson District and Miss Amanda
E. Allen, of Abbeville District.

Issue of:
Thursday, February 8, 1866:
Married: On Tuesday evening, February 1, 1866, by Rev. David
Simmons, Mr. Lee Linder and Miss M. Lou Webb, all of Hart County,
Ga.

Issue of:
Thursday, March 8, 1866:
Married: On the 28th of February, by Rev. W. E. Walters, at the
residence of the bride's father in Anderson District, Col.
Joseph N. Brown and Lizzie L. Bruce, only daughter of Thomas
Bruce.

Married: On the 18th February, by the Rev. H. M. Barton, James
H. Sullivan and Mrs. Mary Woodin, all of Pickens District.

Issue of:
Thursday, March 22, 1866:
Married: On Thursday evening, 15th instant, by Rev. W. E.
Walters, Mr. R. R. Beatty and Miss Anna E. Dean, youngest
daughter of Moses Dean, all of Anderson District.

Obituary: Died in Pickens District, on the 2d of January, 1866,
Sallie Lynch, daughter of J. W. and Susan Crawford, aged 3 years,
3 months, and 18 days. On New Year's morning she was quite
hoarse, from an apparently ordinary cold, but was playful until
later in the day, when she grew worse; still no danger was
apprehended until about dark, when the hoarseness assumed the
form of membranus croup. Before a physician could be obtained,
she was past recovery, her spirit winged its way to realms
above, just at dawn of day. Words cannot descirbe the anguish of the fond mother as she watched the little sufferer
through that long weary night - her husband far away, and no
friend to comfort - but surrounded by her weeping children, she
saw "Death" for the first time enter her household and lay his
icy hand upon the brightest, the purest, the best. Heartrend-
ing was the scence when the stricken father returned and found
his little Sallie, his darling, his pet, still, cold, dead.
The sweet voice, that rang in merry tones, bringing gladness
to his house and heart, hushed forever. The little arms that
were wont to twine in loving caress about his form, folded
humbyably upon her marble breast, and the warm pure heart that
loved him so dearly, beat no more in joyous rapture when his
well known footsteps fell upon the threshold. It is no wonder,
parents and children, you grieve to lay in dark tomb this
lovely, this beautiful, this bright jewel - lovely, aye, and
beautiful, even in death. She was a being not made for earth.
Often, while here, she seemed an angel of light - so pure was
she while guile, so far above her years was her understanding,

so kind, so gentle of nature, I marvel that we wished to keep her from the home where seraphs dwell. It may be, God has some mission for her glory, or has taken her from some great trials that would have crushed her gentle spirit, had she stayed. Let this soothe every regret, and feel that God has done it in loving kindness who oftentimes chasteneth those he loves. Is it not comforting to think of the blessings she now enjoys - safe from sin, free from pain, robed in spotless garments, praising the Lord and joining her supplications with the Lamb for mercy and acceptance to those on earth she loved? Oh, no, your sweet child, your little Sallie, with sky blue eyes, and soft golden hair, is not dead, but lives in Heaven, Weep not, but bow low at Jesus' feet, and you will be permitted to meet her in those green pastures, where flows the river of Eternal Life; there you may dwell an unbroken family, to be seperated no more forever.   Cold Springs, S. C.   One She Loved

Issue of:
Thursday, April 5, 1866:
Married: On the 3d inst., by the Rev. David Humphreys, at the residence of Mrs. Catherine D. Norris, Mr. John J. Hall and Miss Martha C. Keys, eldest daughter of Robert A. Keys, all of Anderson District.

Issue of:
Thursday, April 12, 1866:
Married: On Wednesday evening, March 28th, 1866, at the residence of the bride's father, by Rev. John H. [not legible], Mr. John L. Thornley, of Newberry, and Miss Eveline N., eldest daughter of O. H. Fant, Esq., of this village.

Issue of:
Thursday, April 26, 1866:
Married: On the 15th inst., by the Rev. W. H. King, Mr. Thomas Cobb, of Pickens, and Miss Matilda Elrod, of Anderson District.

Married: On the 22nd inst., by the Rev. W. H. King, Mr. W. P. Hewin, of Anderson, and Miss Nannie E. Prather, of Lowndesville, Abbeville Dist.

Married: On Thursday, 19th inst., at the residence of the bride's father, by the Rev. D. McNeil Turner, D. D., Rev. W. F. Pearson, of Abbeville, to Miss Eugenia Thompson, the only daughter of Maj. James Thompson, of Anderson District.

Issue of:
Thursday, May 3, 1866:
Obituary: Died at her residence in Anderson District, on the 5th of March 1866, Mrs. Mary K. Mattison, wife of Capt. James Mattison, deceased, and daughter of Charles Kizziah Stark, deceased, of Abbeville District. The deceased was gathered home at a good old age, having attained her 58th year. She was the child of pious parents, and at an early period of life, devoted herself to the service of her Redeemer, and united with the Baptist Church of Christ at Rocky River, of which she lived a consistent member for over thirty years until her master said "It is enough, come up higher." I suppose if anyone ever lived or died with a conscience void of offence towards God and then she was that one; humble and unassuming in all the relations of life. She was loved...most by those who knew her best and

whilst we mingle our sympathies with the deceased relations and children, we would say to them, mourn not as those who have no hope, "for if, we believe that Jesus died and rose again, even so them that sleep in Jesus, will God bring with him." May God by his spirit lead her children to choose that better part, which shall not be taken from them. Her sufferings were painful and protracted, but she murmured not, but bore all with patience and Christian fortitude. Her remains were deposited in the family graveyard on the 6th of March, in the presence of a large number of neighbors and mourning friends. We trust and believe she sleeps with Jesus.

Issue of:
Thursday, May 10, 1866:
Married: [Extract from Laurensville Herald] - In the Methodist Church in this village, by the Rev. J. R. Little, Mr. Julius W. Cay...?, Forman of this Office, and Miss Bell I. Anderson, all of this Village. (Laurens)

Issue of:
Thursday, May 17, 1866:
Married: On the banks of the Tugaloo River, on Sunday the 29th of April, by the Rev. Jesse Brown, Mr. Thomas M. Richardson and Miss Elvira E. Vandiver, all of this District.

Obituary: The Laurensville Herald announces with sincere regret, which is shared by all acquaintances, the death of Mrs. Jane C., wife of Dr. John W. Simpson, prominent citizen of that village.

Issue of:
Thursday, May 24, 1866:
Married: On Wednesday evening May 16, 1866, at the residence of the bride's Uncle Z. Hall, Esq., by the Rev. Wm. F. Pearson, Mr. Wm. A. McFall to Miss T. C. Swilling, both of Anderson District.

Issue of:
Thursday, May 31, 1866:
Obituary: In Memoriam - / Col. Herbert Hammond departed this life at his residence near Anderson, S. C., on the morning of the 20th May, 1866, after a painful and protracted illness. He was born in Elbert County, Georgia, March 17, 1797 - was married to Elizabeth Rich of Elbert, in 1824, and during the subsequent year, settled in Anderson District, S. C., where he spent the remainder of his life. In 1838 he was converted at Sandy Springs, under the ministry of Rev. James Stacy, and the following year was appointed class leader and steward of the Church, which offices he faithfully filled until death. He was elected Ordinary of Anderson District in November, 1847, and served as a public officer in that capacity near 20 years. His opinions in his civil and religious station were marked by superior sense and judgment, and a man can scarcely be found who possessed, in so eminent a degree, the confidence and respect of the entire community. This was shown by the large concourse of citizens that assembled in the Methodist Church to hear his funeral sermon, pronounced by Rev. S. H. Browne, and the closing all the stores during the sad occasion. It is often the case that sorrow for the dead is limited to the immediate kindred, but the death of a good man is a felt loss in every community. His living example, prayer and generous support of morality and religion are withdrawn, and in

proportion to his integrity as a man, and his piety as a
Christian, the community suffer. There are some men whose
practical life of piety is too valuable to the world to be
thrown away - too precious to be buried in the waters of
oblivion. Such a man was Herbert Hammond. When standing
around his grave, a leading member of another branch of the
Church, said, "We have put away a good man; there are no more
such as he, in any of our churches." Generous to fault, his
benevolence was proverbial and a strong believer in the Scriptural doctrine that liberality towards the Church is a Christian
virtue, his all was consecrated to the service of God, who
cared for him in life, and blessed his dying hours with the
consoling thought that wife, brother, and children were all
journeying with him to the Kingdom of Heaven. His seven surviving, around his cold form, hand in hand, vowed to try and
emulate his example and meet him in the home of the blest.
Devotion to God was a marked feature in the character of this
good man. The altar for family worship that he erected when
converted was never taken down, but morning and evening the
sacrifice of prayer and praise ascended to God. Possessed of
a catholic spirit, he loved the Church of his choice with a
devotion that grew with years; its claims to him were paramount;
and whether in prayer meeting, or the more public service of
the sanctuary, Providence permitting, his seat was never vacant.
His death was one of triumph-just such as we would expect from
the life of a good man. In his last moments he was unconscious
but often during his illness he spoke of his abiding trust in
God; and sometimes faith swelling into sacred joy, he would
speak of the preciousness of religion, and the prospect of
immortality, with a confidence and pathos that melted the
hearts of all who were privileged to hear. But he is gone-
gone we trust to the better and brighter world.
Soldier of Christ, well done!/Praise be they new employ;/And
while eternal ages roll,/Rest in thy Saviour's joy.   G.F.R.

Obituary: -Death of Major Bolling-
We regret to learn that Maj. Thad C. Bolling, of Greenville
District, died at his residence on Friday night last, after a
brief illness. He was a member of the recent State Convention
and was highly respected by his fellow citizens. His remains
were interred at Fork Shoals, in that District, on Monday in the
presence of a large assemblage of friends and acquaintances.

Issue of:
Thursday, June 7, 1866:
Fatal Accident: Preston Belcher, in wrestling with a younger
brother, a loaded pistol was discharged, and the contents were
lodged in his abdomen, from the effect of which he died Sunday
morning. His remains were interred in Baptist Churchyard.

Issue of:
Thursday, June 14, 1866:
Married: On the 31st ult., by Rev. W. E. Walters, Dr. O. R.
Horton, of Abbeville District, to Miss Fannie L. Charles of
Greenville District.

Married: On Wednesday evening, 6th inst., by the Rev. Henry
Tyler, Mr. W. K. Harris and Miss Eliza J. Browne, both of this
District.

Obituary: [see issue of June 7 also] Died, June 3, 1866 near Abbeville, So. Ca., Preston Belcher, in the nineteenth year of his age. He was a manly youth, an affectionate son and brother, and a warm hearted friend. He gave promise of becoming an honored and useful citizen. All who knew him loved him, and many there are to sympathise deeply with the bereaved household. He was spared through the closing scenes of the late war to die among those who were dear to him. He fell asleep in Jesus. It was given him to behold the Sinner's Friend, and by faith to stake the salvation of his immortal soul upon the Saviour's infinite love and mercy. None ever trusted him in vain. He is nto dead but asleep, and them that sleep in Jesus will God bring with Him. Weep not for him. Let his memory be cherished as of one who has only gone before us, and whom we shall see again; and let the Saviour be adored as the Redeemer of another of our loved ones.

Issue of:
Thursday, July 5, 1866:
Married: On the 26th ult, by Rev. J. B. Hillhouse, Mr. E. P. Moore and Miss M. A. Lewis, all of this District.

Issue of:
Thursday, July 19, 1866
Married: On Tuesday morning, 17th inst., by Rev. W. E. Walters, Col. Charles S. Mattison and Mrs. Mary J. Brown, all of this District.

Issue of:
Thursday, July 26, 1866:
Married: On Monday, July 19th, by Rev. J. B. Hillhouse, at the residence of Mrs. Mary Bellotte, the bride's grandmother, Mr. Samuel A. Bellotte and Miss Sallie E., daughter of Mr. Elias Tillinghast, deceased.

Issue of:
Thursday, August 2, 1866:
Married: At the residence of the bride's father, on the 25th of July, by the Rev. G. F. Round, Mr. A. H. Osborne and Miss M. E. McCully, all of this village.

Obituary: In Memoriam - Departed this life, Pendleton, S. C., July 26, 1866, Mrs. Floride Calhoun, relict of the late Hon. John C. Calhoun, in the 75th year of her age. She sleeps in Jesus, awaiting the trumpet's sound at the last great day, when those who, having finished their course in the confidence of a certain faith, and, in the comfort of a reasonable religious and holy hope, shall be received into everlasting habitations. By her removal, another link has been severed of the chain which united us with a free, happy and glorious Past. The wife of John C. Calhoun, Carolina's greatest statesman, and most honored son, it were better she should depart than longer live to witness the destruction which he so ably and earnestly endeavored to prevent. Few who have occupied a like elevated position. By her many noble traits of character, she had endeared herself to the community of which she had so long been an honored member; and heartfelt was the sympathy exhibited by her many friends during her painful and protracted sufferings; and now that she rests in peace, her memory will be cherished by them with peculiar respect and veneration.

Issue of:
Thursday, August 16, 1866:
Married: On Thursday evening, 9th inst., by Rev. F. G. Carpenter,
Mr. J. Baylis Smith and Miss Harriet, eldest daughter of Gen.
J. W. Guyton, all of this District.

Tribute of Respect: Williamston Lodge, No. 24, A. & F. M., Williamston, August 2, 1866. Extract from the Minutes: The announcement of the demise of Brother Van B. King will fall with sorrow
upon many a heart. He was called to his final account on 29th
July last. Brother King was a grandson of Rev. Robert King
and great grandson of Rev. Moses Holland.

Sudden Death: Mr. D. Alex Davis, for several years an employee
on the Anderson branch of the G. & C. R. R., died in this
place on Monday night last, after an illness of only a few
days. Mr. Davis was a warm-hearted, generous man and highly
esteemed by the community. His sorrowing family have our
deepest sympathies in this sad and unexpected bereavement.

Another Horrible Murder: On Monday last a soldier by the name
of Charles Kelley, belonging to the garrison stationed at this
place, was murdered in a most shocking manner, his throat
being cut by a razor and the body thrown in an old well. Suspicion at once rested upon several of his comrads and arrests
were immediately made. At the time of this writing (Wednesday
noon) the Coroner's examination is in progress and we forbear
stating further particulars until conclusion is reached by
the inquest.

Issue of:
Thursday, August 23, 1866:
The Murder of Kelley: [see above issue of August 16] The
Coroner's jury mentioned last week as investigating the murder
of a United States soldier by the name of Kelly, came to the
conclusion that "the said Charles Kelly came to his death
during the night of Monday the 13th inst., and at a point near
the mile post on the road leading from Anderson to Abbeville,
from the effects of a mortal wound inflicted by means of a
razor in the hands of one Thomas Berry, private Co. I, 8th
U. S. Infantry, of which wound the said Kelly did instantly
die." We learn that the accused Berry is in the custody of
the military authorities. He and the murdered man were intimate friends and the deed was evidently perpetrated to secure
money which he knew his friend possessed.

Issue of:
Thursday, September 20, 1866:
Married: On Tuesday evening, 4th inst., by Rev. A. C. Steppe,
Mr. John L. Arnold, of this village and Miss M. Ella Johnson
of Greenville District.

Issue of:
Thursday, September 27, 1866:
Obituary: Departed this life, Pendleton, S. C., on the 14th
inst., Mary Lorton, eldest daughter of Dr. and Mrs. Wm. B.
Cherry, in the 16th year of her age. Amiable and affectionate,
dutiful and lovely was our young friend and the general sorrow
consequent on her decease attests the high estimation in which
she was held. As mortals sorrow we must, when one so well
fitted to make home happy and to adorn society, is taken from

us; but we would not sorry [sic] as those who have no hope,
"For if we believe that Jesus died and rose again, even so
them also which sleep in Jesus will God bring with him."
"So blooms the human face devine,/ When youth its pride of
beauty shows;/ Fairer than Spring the colors shine,/ And
sweeter than the opening rose./ But, worn by slowly rolling
years,/ Or broke by sickness in a day,/ The fading glory dis-
appears,/ The short-lived beauties die away./ Yet these, new
rising from the tomb,/ With lustre brighter far shall shine,/
Revive with ever-during bloom./ Safe from disease and decline."

Issue of:
Thursday, October 11, 1866:
Obituary: Death of Rev. Dr. Francis Lister Hawks, Born New-
berry, N. C., June 10, 1798. [Front page - long article]

Issue of:
Thursday, October 25, 1866:
Married: At the residence of the bride's Uncle, on the 17th
inst., by the Rev. W. E. Walters, Mr. W. A. Fant and Miss
Kittie Jackson.

Married: On Wednesday evening, 10th inst., at the residence
of the bride's mother, by the Rev. S. (?) Gaillard, Mr. W. S.
Jenkins and Miss Sallie D., eldest daughter of Rev. T. L.
McBryde, deceased.

Issue of:
Thursday, November 1, 1866:
Obituary: Death of Old and Valued Citizens - We regret to
learn that our kind friend, Mr. D. T. Rainwater, a valuable
and useful citizen of this District, died at his residence
on Friday last. His upright conduct, stern integrity and
consistent course in life ranked him amongst the good and
faithful and we trust that an everlasting place has greeted
him beyond the shores of time.

     Mr. Stephen Leverette, one of the oldest and most honored
citizens, died recently at his home, ten miles south of this
place. For many years he was known as a successful and worthy
teacher and leaves behind him a name respected and revered
for all the noble qualities that adorn life.

Issue of:
Thursday, November 8, 1866:
Married: At the residence of Mr. Robert Smith, on Wednesday
evening, October 31st by the Rev. W. H. Stratton, Mr. Samuel
M. Crayton and Miss Sallie J. Nevitt, all of this District.

Married: On Wednesday October 31st, by Rev. W. H. McGee, Mr.
J. T. C. Jones and Miss Josephine McGee, eldest daughter of
Elias McGee, all of this District.

Obituary: -In Memoriam of Lelia Ligon- Only daughter of Mr.
Wm. J. Ligon of Pendleton, who departed this life October 29,
1866, aged two years and three months. Passed from the
shadows of earth, claimed by the angels ere her worldly pilgrimage had begun; she is tenderly gathered into the little
flock who roam amid flowers ever vernal through the glorious
valleys of the celestial hills. "Side by side they're sweetly
sleeping,/ Little lov'd ones early blest;/ Free from care and

pain and sorrow,/ Oh! rejoice! they are at rest."
A Friend

Issue of:
Thursday, November 22, 1866:
Married: On Tuesday, the 6th inst., at the residence of the
bride's father, by Rev. D. F. Maddon, Mr. James B. Burriss,
of Anderson and Miss Mattie A. Thompson, of Laurens.

Issue of:
Thursday, December 6, 1866:
Married: On the 29th ult., by Rev. W. F. Martin, at the
residence of the bride's father, Mr. Aris Cox, of this District and Miss Margaret C. Maupin of Greenville District.

Issue of:
Thursday, December 13, 1866:
Married: On the 5th inst., by Rev. Fletcher Smith, James D.
Warnock, of Anderson and Miss Hattie E., daughter of E. Hern-
don, Esq., of Pickens.

Married: On the 6th inst., by Rev. Fletcher Smith, Albert
Zimmerman and Miss Mary M., daughter of Capt. J. D. Kay, all
of Pickens District.

Married: On the 6th inst., at the residence of the bride's
father, by Rev. C. McKindry Smith, Mr. Theodore Smith and Miss
Esther Dice, youngest daughter of Rev. John Burdine, all of
this District.

Issue of:
Thursday, December 20, 1866:
Married: On Tuesday, Dec. 18th by Rev. Wilson Ashley, Mr.
J. M. Webb to Miss Lucinda Callaham, all of this District.

Issue of:
Thursday, January 3, 1847:
Distressing Casualty: One of the saddest deaths it has ever
been our duty to record, occurred in this village on Friday
21st ultimo. Mrs. Jane Owen, wife of ___?___? Owen and
daughter of Mrs. Eliza Robinson, while reposing before the
fire on the day previous, had her clothing ignited by a spark
and before assistance reached her, the flames had destroyed
nearly all her garments leaving the sufferer in a dying condition. Patiently enduring the Christian fortitude, the
agonizing tortures consequent upon this awful calamity, this
estimable lady expired on the afternoon of the 21st. The
funeral services were performed by Rev. W. H. Stratton at the
Episcopal Church, the following Sunday, amid a large concourse of relatives and sympathizing friends. In this afflictive dispensation of Divine Providence, the heartfelt condolence of the entire community is with the bereaved husband
and sorrowing little ones.

Obituary: Major Willis F. Jones - The old members of Fields
Division, A.N.V., will remember the gallant officer whose name
heads this article, and who was killed on the Darbytown Road
below Richmond in the fall of 1864. We learn from Kentucky
exchanges that the remains of Maj. Jones arrived in Lexington,
Ky. on the 14th ult., and were buried in the cemetery by his

wife the next day. His former chief, Gen. Fields, was present at the burial.

Issue of:
Thursday, February 7, 1867:
Married: At the residence of Mrs. J. V. Moore, on Wednesday the 30th of January by Rev. A. P. Cornish, Mr. E. Henry Shanklin and Miss Virginia, youngest daughter of the late Dr. William Robinson, all of Pendleton.

Obituary: Death of Col. B. F. Sloan, Sr. - We regret to learn of the death of Col. Benj. F. Sloan, which occurred at his residence in Pendleton on Saturday night last. The deceased was a prominent citizen of the District and for twenty years had charge of the Pendleton Factory. He was in the seventy second year of his age.

Issue of:
Thursday, February 14, 1867:
Married: On the morning of 16th January at the residence of the bride's mother, by Rev. David Humphreys, Col. J. W. Norris and Miss Susan Simpson, both of this District.

Issue of:
Wednesday, Feburary 21, 1867:
Married: On February 14th, by Rev. W. F. Pearson, Mr. A. M. Norris and Miss Ellen A. Mecklin, both of this District.

Issue of:
Wednesday, March 6, 1867:
Married: February 21st, at the residence of Mrs. M. H. Wither-spoon, Cabarrus County, N. C., by the Rev. John E. Pressly, Miss Maggie C. Woodside and Mr. D. J. Sherard of Anderson District, S. C.

Married: On the 28th ult., by Rev. W. P. Martin, at the residence of the bride's father, Mr. William Thompson and Minerva C. Cooley, all of this District.

Married: On the 28th ult., by Rev. J. B. Hillhouse, Mr. J. W. Lewis and Miss S. A. Millwee.

Issue of:
Wednesday, March 20, 1867:
Married: On Thursday, the 14th inst., at the residence of the officiating minister, by Rev. David Humphreys, Mr. Elbert F. S. Rowley, of Greenville, to Miss Anna Smith of Anderson District.

Married: On the 26th February, by the Rev. David Humphreys, Mr. Benjamin Maybin of Newberry, to Miss Ettie M. Sadler, of Hart County, Georgia.

Married: On the 23d February, by Rev. J. Scott Murray, Sear-gent John Smith of Chicago, Illinois, to Mrs. Martha J. Shanahan, of Anderson Village.

Obituary: Died, on 30th November, 1866 Robert A. Hutchinson, son of Capt. John and Eveline Hutchinson. He was deprived of an affectionate father at an early period; his father fell in that terrific battle near Jackson, Mississippi, where one

company had to confront one entire regiment of the enemy.
Not one was ever to waver. He fell nobly defending the honor
of his State, (S.C.) and the sunny South. He was the only son
of a noble sire. He had a kind stepfather, to whom he was
devotedly attached. Mr. Morrow treated him with all the kindness of a natural parent. Robert seemed to know no difference
between him and his own father. He was a lad of high promise,
for one of his tender years. His mother conversed with him
relative to his probable departure. He expressed a desire to
remain with his kind mother and papa, though he expressed no
fears to go to his Father in Heaven. He lingered with some
consuming diease that defied all medical skill for some weeks;
the careful nursing and watchfulness of parents and friends
failed to arrest the hand of the destroyer. Death often selects
one of brightest promise for its prey. It is a great trial
to a parent when, "in bitterness for a firstborn," to part with
one just at that period when they twine so strongly around a
parents heart; yet, when the Good Shepherd takes the lambs to
himself, the parent should ask for grace, and strength to say,
"Thy will be done." He has gone to the kind Saviour who said,
"Suffer little [children] to come unto me, and forbid them
not, for such is the kingdom of God." He was born 28th of
May, 1861. "What is your life, it is even a vapor that
appeareth for a little time and vanisheth away."

Issue of:
Thursday, March 27, 1867:
Married: On Monday afternoon, March 25th, by the Rev. Wallace
H. Stratton, Corporal Henry J. Ackley, Co. L., 8th U. S.
Infantry and Miss Adelia Parker of Anderson Village.

Obituary: -Death of Col. D. S. Taylor- We have to record this
morning the death of another old citizen of Pendleton. On
Friday last, Col. David S. Taylor departed this life in the
60th y ar of his age, after a brief illness, of apoplexy. His
summons was short, although premonitory symptoms of the
disease had been apparent for several years. Col. Taylor had
accummulated a large fortune before the war, and was regarded
one of our wealthiest citizens. He had recently accepted the
appointment of Assistant Assesor of Internal Revenue and was
at this place in the active discharge of his duties but a few
days previous to his death.

Issue of:
Wednesday, April 3, 1867:
Married: On March 26th, at the residence of the bride's
mother, by Rev. T. G. Herbert, Rev. Geo. F. Round and Miss
Julia A. Hammond, all of Anderson, S. C.

Issue of:
Wednesday, April 10, 1867:
Married: On the 10th March, by John Black, Esq., Mr. Caloway
Alexander and Miss Jane Wright, both of Anderson District.

Issue of:
Wednesday, April 24, 1867:
Married: On the 18th February last, by the Rev. Robert King,
Mr. Jno. S. Smith to Miss Sue L. Shirley, all of Anderson
District.

Issue of:
Wednesday, May 22, 1867:
Married: On the 14th inst., at the residence of the bride's
father, on Tugalo, by Rev. J. B. Hillhouse, Lieut. Wm. Steele
of Etowa, Georgia, and Miss N. R. Shelor.

Married: On the 11th inst., by Rev. J. J. Workman, Lieut.
P. A. McDavid and Miss Fannie M., daughter of Dr. J. M. Sullivan all of Greenville District.

Married: On the 9th inst., by the Rev. David Humphreys, Mr.
John McClinton and Miss M. Richey, at the house of her brother-
in-law, Mr. James Harkness.

Married: On the 16th inst., by the Rev. David Humphreys, at
the residence of the bride's father, Mr. James S. Beatty and
Miss Mary Williford, all of this District.

Obituary: Died, at her residence in this District, on the
first instant, Mrs. Mary Anderson Bellotte. She died in faith
and in the communion of the Church.

Issue of:
Wednesday, May 29, 1867:
Married: On the morning of the 16th inst., at the residence
of Z. Hall, Esq., by Rev. A. Rice, Mr. R. L. Pratt, of Abbeville District and Miss M. F. C. Swilling of Anderson District.

Married: By the Rev. A. Rice, on the evening of the 26th inst.,
at his residence, Mr. Mason Henderson, of Abbeville District,
and Miss Carrie Fisher of this District.

Issue of:
Wednesday, June 12, 1867:
Married: By Rev. [illegible] on the [?] June 1867, at the
bride's residence in Pendleton, [?] Virginia R. Hunter and Mr.
J. C. Stribling, [?]..Pickens District.

Issue of:
Wednesday, June 19, 1867:
Married: On Wednesday, June 12th, 1867, by Rev. W. H. Stratton,
at the residence of the bride's mother in this village, Mr.
Thomas W. White and Miss [....?] [....?]Brown, all of Anderson

Obituary: -Death of a United States Soldier- The garrison at
this place buried one of their comrades in the Presybterian
graveyard on Friday last. His name was Michael Scroghron,
private Co. I, 8th U. S. Infantry. We learn that he was a
married man from West Cambridge, Mass.

Issue of:
Wednesday, June 26, 1867:
Married: On Wednesday, June 10th, 1867 by Rev. W. H. Stratton
at the residence of the bride's mother, in this village, Mr.
William [illegible] and Miss Julia V. Robinson, both of this
village.

Obituary: -Death of Thomas B. Burriss- We are pained to
ammounce the death of Thomas B. Burriss, an estimable, warm-
hearted and generous citizen. He died at the residence of his

father, Rev. Jacob Burriss, three miles north of this place,
on Wednesday night last, in the 35th year of his age. In the
short career of our departed friend, there is much to admire.
Possessed of exalted virtues, true generosity and noble
principles, it is neither strange nor woderful that he was
highly appreciated by a large circle of friends and acquaintances. He was endowed by nature with rare intellectual gifts,
while a liberal education secured for him all the noblest
pleasures of the mind. Above all other qualities, however, his
wit was truly remarkable and to this we may add that the
exuberance of his spirits rendered him a most genial companion.
Such men seldom escape the temtations and allurements of society.
Our lamented friend had his frailities, alike human and
inevitable. Let those without sin alone reproach his memory.
We would rather cherish and imitate his virtues, for they
were numerous and draw the curtain of oblivion over his faults,
if they belonged to his manly nature. The decease entered the
service of his country in April, 1861, as a member of the
"Palmetto Riflemen", Co. B., 4th S. C. Vols. During that year
while in Virginia, the disease was developed that finally
terminated his earthly existence. In consequence of a protracted illness, he was discharged from the army and remained
at home until the latter part of 1863, when he again joined
his old comrades, then in East Tennessee. The command was
transferred to Virginia the following spring and through the
arduous campaigns of that year the deceased performed the
duties of a soldier with cheerfulness and alacrity. In October,
1864, he received a painful wound which caused him to be fur-
loughed several months. He returned to the army at the earliest
practicable moment and remained until the memorable day at
Appomattox. Since the war, Mr. Burriss has been preparing himself for the practice of Dentistry and a few months ago opened
an office with this intention. But alas! the vanity of human
hopes! His apparently robust health yielded rapidly to the
inroads of disease and in less than four weeks he was a
corpse. He was conscious of his critical condition and gave
evidence that he was prepared to meet the dread summons.
On Wednesday night, surrounded by aged parents, fond relatives
and sympathizing friends, the messenger appeared unto him and
his spirit returned to God who gave it. He was buried on
Thursday afternoon by the Masonic fraternity, among whom he
was held in high esteem. At the time of his death he was
Secretary of the Lodge and Chapter at this place.

Issue of:
Wednesday, June 26, 1867:
Fatal Duel: A duel was fought near Charlston, on Wednesday
last, between Mr. Edward Roe, formerly of Columbia and Mr.
Theodore G. Boag of Charleston, resulting in the death of the
first named party. The city papers contain the evidence
before the Coronor's jury relating to the actual occurrence
but no intimation as to the cause of difficulty. The surviving principal and the seconds of both parties have been
arrested and lodged in jail. The trial will probably take
place at the present term of the Court, now in session in
that city.

Obituary: The Selma [Ala.] Messenger chronicles the death,
in the Almshouse of Dallas County, on Saturday last, of Robert
McKnight in the 84th year of his age. Mr. McKnight was perhaps the oldest printer in the United States, having commenced

learning the "art preservative of all arts" in Georgetown, S. C. in 1798 and until within a few years was able to work at the case. He was an honest, industrious and good man and not withstanding the poverty in which he died, was much respected by all who knew him. He was the father of Maj. Geo. McKnight, better known as "Asa Hartz".

Issue of:
Wednesday, July 3, 1867:
Married: On Tuesday, 25th inst., at the residence of the bride's father, by the Rev. Wm. F. Pearson, Dr. James M. Sloan, formerly of Pendleton now of Pickens C. H., to Miss Sallie J. Linch of Abbeville, S. C.

Obituary: -Death of Wm. Van Wyck, Esq.- We regret to announce the death of William Van Wyck, Esq., at his residence in this village, on Sunday morning last. The deceased was a native of New York, we believe, but had been a resident of this District for a great many years. He was a member of the Episcopal Church and was highly esteemed by a large circle of friends and acquaintances. At the time of his death, Mr. Van Wyck held the office of Assessor of the Internal Revenue for his Revenue District and gave general satisfaction in the discharge of delicate and important duties. His health has been declining for some months and when the summons came, it was not unexpected. He was probably over sixty years of age.

Issue of:
Wednesday, July 17, 1867:
Married: At the residence of the bride's father, on Tuesday, July 2, 1867, by Rev. T. P. Gwyn, William Burriss, of Anderson District, S. C., to Miss Nannie L., youngest daughter of John Dickinson, of Calhoun County, Alabama.

Issue of:
Wednesday, July 24, 1867:
Obituary: -Death of John R. Horsey- We learn from the Charleston Mercury that John R. Horsey, Esq., for many years Clerk of the city council, died in that city on the 17th inst. He was taken suddenly ill in the forenoon and died about 11 o'clock that night. Mr. Horsey was formerly a resident of this place and was well known to the older citizens.

Obituary: -Death of Wm. N. White, Esq.- We learn from the Athens [Ga.] Watchman that Wm. N. White, Esq., of that place, died on the 14th inst. in the 48th year of his age. Mr. White was well known throughout the South as the proprietor of the Southern Cultivator. He was a native of New York but had been a citizen of Athens for some twenty years and was highly esteemed by a large circle of friends and acquaintances.

Issue of:
Wednesday, July 31, 1867:
Married: On the 13th inst., by Rev. W. D. Beverly, Mr. B. M. Clinkscales and Miss Jane E. Fant, all of this village.

Obituary: -Horrible Murder- We learn that on Tuesday of last week, Mr. Franklin A. Ragsdale, living in the eastern portion of this District, was found within three hundred yards of his own house, shot through the right wrist, with his left arm shattered at, above and below the elbow joint. He had been in

bad health for some time and was unable to give any account of
the occurrence and no satisfactory clue was obtained by the
Coronor's inquest. We have not heard how long Mr. R. survived
the injuries. He was quiet, inoffensive citizen and highly
esteemed. On Friday morning, a Negro was brought to jail on
suspicion of being implicated in this murder but there is no
definite evidence of such complicity, so far as we can ascertain.

Issue of:
Wednesday, August 14, 1867:
Obituary: Died at the residence of its great grandfather, Col.
D. K. Hamilton, on Tuesday morning, 6th inst., of whooping
cough, Martha Jane, infant daughter of David H. and Fannie
E. Russell, aged seven months and six days. Blessed, thrice
blessed, sweet little babe.   T. H. R.

Obituary: -Departed this life, at her residence in Townville,
July 12th, Miss Permelia Dickson, in the 66th year of her age,
Miss Dickson connected herself with the Presbyterian Church,
in 1852, but had been a possessor of that gift, which can only
be given through a crucified Saviour - religion, some thirty
years. To her, death, had no terror. "The narrow house and
pall and breathless darkness", and the funeral train, had no
terror for her. As she felt the pang of suffering cutting
asunder, one by one, the bonds that held her to earth, as she
felt the blushing current of life wearing away and the sharp-
ness of every keen emotion as they were shortening the moments
of the soul's connection and conflicts with the body and she
knew the silver cord would soon be loosened, she dreaded not
the awful grave, for the hope she had in her Saviour had broke
it's spell, i-s dread dominion. She looked upon death as a
friend, for she was well satisfied when the body returned to
dust, the spirit would return to the God who gave it. As a
Christian, she was consistent and zealous, always speaking a
kind, affectionate and encouraging word. Her love and kindness is indelibly stamped upon the minds of all those she
left behind, who knew her well. Her good deeds, kind words
and generous character, has left a shining monument in the
minds of the members of "Little Beaverdam" Church that will
never perish - encouraging them at all times by her cheerful
Christian example and precept. She leaves a large circle of
friends and relatives to mourn her loss, though they should
not mourn, as it is her eternal gain.   BEPPO

Issue of:
Wednesday, August 28, 1867:
Married: On 21st inst., by Rev. B. F. Mauldin, Mr. J. P.
Richardson of Pickens, to Miss Nancy K., youngest daughter of
Griffin Breazeale of Anderson District.

Issue of:
Wednesday, September 25, 1867:
Obituary: Died, at the residence of her son, Robert M. Anderson, at Chappell Depot, Newberry District, S. C., on the evening of the 14th September, 1867, Mrs. Susan Martin Anderson,
wife of Dr. George Thomas Anderson in the 57th year of her
age. "Blessed are the dead who died in the Lord."

Horrible Murder: John Henry McGill shot by a freedman, Elbert
Brownlee. [Lengthy, in detail article]

Issue of:
Wednesday, October 9, 1867:
Married: On the evening of the 3d inst., at the residence of
the bride's father, in Abbeville District, by Rev. A. Rice, Mr.
Robert M. Pratt and Miss Jane A. Bowen, all of Abbeville
District.

Married: On Thursday, 3d inst., at the residence of G. L.
McGee, by Rev. W. H. King, Mr. John B. Leverette and Lucy C.
McGee, all of Anderson District.

Issue of:
Wednesday, October 23, 1867:
Married: On Tuesday, evening, October 8th at the residence of
the bride's father by Rev. W. D. Beverly, Mr. John H. Clarke
and Miss Annie M., second daughter of Millford Burriss, Esq.,
all of this District.

Married: At the same time and place and by the Rev. Beverly,
Mr. Thomas M. Cater and Miss S. Elizabeth, third daughter of
Millford Burris, Esq., all of this District. May the happy
pairs live a thousand years and their honey-moon never end.

Married: On Wednesday evening, October 16th, at the Presbyterian Church in this village, by the Rev. W. H. Stratton, Mr.
Wm. F. Barr and Miss L. A. Hubbard, all of this village.

Married: At the residence of the bride's father, on Thursday
evening, October 17th, 1867, by Rev. W. H. Stratton, Mr. J.
Fleetwood Clinkscales and Miss Hattie, second daughter of Wm.
Archer, Esq., all of this District.

Issue of:
Wednesday, October 30, 1867:
Murder Charge: Alexander Bryce and nine negroes charged in
Pickens court with the murder of Miles M. N. Hunnicutt.

Issue of:
Wednesday, November 13, 1867:
Atrocious Murder: We are deeply pained to learn a former
citizen of this place, Mr. Edward N. Emerson, was brutally
murdered on Sunday night, 3rd inst., at Albany, Georgia. This
information is contained in private letters received by friends
here, and the murder is said to have occurred under the following circumstances: It appears that a bold robbery had been
committed in Albany on Saturday night and Sunday morning a
party of citizens, including the deceased, went in search of
the robber. Mr. Emerson, being ahead in the pursuit, came in
close contact with the supposed thief and fired at him several
times but without effect. The party returned to town and that
evening about 7 o'clock Mr. E. walked down to the hotel and
finding several men engaged in conversation respecting the
robbery and pursuit, joined in the conversation. The men were
sitting in chairs in front of the hotel and one of them named
Betts rose from his seat and ask him who he was, to which
Emerson replied, "My name is Emerson", and repeated it for
the third time. The man then asked, "Who are you and what
are you", to which E. replied, "I work for a living; I am a
hard working man." Betts said, "Clear the way men," and
immediately drew his pistol and fired twice, both balls entering the breast and Emerson fell dead, without speaking. The

murderer was formerly Colonel of the 14th Alabama Regiment,
lives in Atlanta, is a notorious gambler and has murdered six
men. He made his escape, but two of his friends and accom-
plices, who were endeavering to assist him in getting off, were
arrested by the citizens. The deceased had been in Albany but
a few months and had won many friends who now sincerely mourn
his ultimely death. The funeral services were performed the
next day by the Rev. Mr. Gaillard of Greenville, S. C. These
are particulars as obtained from private letters. Mr. Emerson
was well known in this community and leaves a large circle of
relatives and friends to lament his demise. He was a member of
the Palmetto Riflemen in the late war and was always a gallant
and true soldier. Poor Ned! May this sudden transition from
earthly scenes prove thy awakening to eternal bliss.

Obituary: -Death of Mr. Charles Haynie- We are grieved to
learn that our old friend, Mr. Charles Haynie, died at his
residence in this District, near Holland's Store, on Friday
last, of typhoid fever. He was truly one of the best citizens
of the District and highly esteemed by all who knew him. His
death will leave a void in his immediate neighborhood that
cannot easily be filled. Mr. Haynie's life had been marked
by an uprightness, honesty and integrity seldom equaled. Of
a warm, generous nature, he was frank and open in his friendships and ever won the affections of those around him. He was
a consistent member of the Presbyterian Church and prominently
active in his duties.

Issue of:
Wednesday, November 20, 1867:
Married: On the 12th inst., at the residence of Mrs. Robert
Catheart, in the city of Columbia, by Rev. W. E. Boggs, Mr. P.
K. McCully, of Anderson, S. C. and Miss Maggie J. Cathcart of
Columbia, S. C.

Issue of:
Wednesday, December 4, 1867:
Married: At the residence of the bride's father, in this vill-
age, on Thursday evening, November 28th, 1867, by Rev. J. S.
Murray, Mr. George W. Miller, of Abbeville and Miss Emmala T.,
eldest daughter of the Hon. J. P. Reed, of Anderson.

Married: On Wednesday evening, 27th ult., by Rev. Hugh McLees,
Mr. James A. Gray and Miss E. J. Sadler, both of Anderson
District.

Obituary: Died, October 3, 1867, Miss Laura Hatton, in the
28th year of her age. She was the youngest daughter of Mr.
William Hatton, late of this District. She was violently
attacked with Diptheria, her sufferings were very great and
the dease defied all medical treatment, but these extreme
sufferings were of short duration, as death terminated them
in less than a week. She confidently believed, at an early
period, she could not survive the attack. She was calm,
quiet, resigned, waiting the call of the Master. She was
early trained to industry and active business habits and
cheerfully aided her mother and sisters in attending to all
the domestic concerns of the family. She early "remembered
her Creator in the days of her youth". She was long a member
of a large Bible class at Good Hope Church. She diligently
studied the requirements of the Bible and endeavored to

regulate her conduct and conversation accordingly. She had
been for years a member of the Presbyterian Church at Good Hope.
She was a bright ornament to the church and her dying testimony was given in favor of the Christian religion and the consolations it gives in a dying hour. Hers was a quiet victory
over death, that severed all the tender ties that bound her
to an affectionate family, the church and the Sabbath School
and passed her into all the pleasures of the Celestial Paradise.
She was loved while living and lamented at her death. D. H.

Issue of:
Wednesday, December 11, 1867:
Married: At the residence of the bride's father, in this
District, on Thursday evening, December 5th, 1867, by Rev.
J. S. Murray, Dr. John Hopkins and Miss Sallie A., eldest
daughter of Mr. Thomas Harper, all of this District.

Issue of:
Wednesday, December 18, 1867:
Married: On Thursday, December 11th, by Rev. J. B. Hillhouse,
Mr. N. W. LaFoy and Miss Eugenia M. Erskine, all of this
District.

Issue of:
Wednesday, December 25, 1867:
Married: In the Baptist Church on Wednesday evening, December
18th, by Rev. Ellison Capers, Mr. William C. Davis of Charleston and Miss Eleanor C., third daughter of the Hon. J. P. Reed,
of this place.

Married: On Thursday, 19th inst., by the Rev. J. Scott Murray,
Mr. Jeptha Harper and Mrs. Violet Rainwater, all of this
District.

Married: By Rev. A. Rice, at his residence, on the afternoon
of the 17th inst., Mr. T. L. Clinkscales and Mrs. Mary C.
Wakefield, all of this District.

Married: On the 26th November, by Rev. D. Humphreys, Mr.
Lemuel Stribling to Miss Martha Brownlee, all of this District.

Issue of:
Wednesday, January 8, 1868:
Married: On the 26th inst., by Rev. W. L. Pressly, Mr. J. W.
Cook and Miss Emma C. Bryan, both of this District.

Issue of:
Wednesday, January 15, 1868:
Obituary: Died, of brain fever, on the 31st day of December,
1867, Kiturah Pauline, infant daughter of G. W. and E. S.
Maret, aged 10 months and 22 days. "Pauline has left this
world of trouble,/ And gone to shining realms above;/ Jesus
has called her to his arms,/ Around the throne of God in
Heaven,/ To join that heavenly, happy band,/ And be an angel
there forever."

Issue of:
Wednesday, January 22, 1868:
Married: On the 25th December, by Rev. Fletcher Smith, at the
residence of the bride's father, Mr. J. B. Carpenter of Anderson and Miss Fannie Mauldin, of Pickens.

Married: on the 14th inst., by J. C. Haynie, Esq., Joseph
Davis and Miss Eliza Shaw, both of Gwinnett County, Ga.

Married: On Wednesday, January 8, 1868, in Grace [Episcopal]
Church, by Rev. A. H. Cornish, James Munro, Esq., of this
place and Miss Lillie L., daughter of the late Thomas Roper,
formerly of Charleston.

Married: On the 16th of January, 1868, by Wm. Riley, Esq.,
Mr. William Bryson and Mrs. Elvira Major, all of Anderson
District.

Obituary: We regret to learn that Mr. Samuel Smith, an old
and respected citizen of this District, died at his residence
seven miles south of this place on Monday night last.

Issue of:
Wednesday, February 5, 1868:
Married: On the 24th of December, 1867, by Rev. J. B. Hill-
house, Mr. L. W. Gentry and Mrs. J. H. Poole, all of this
District.

Married: On the 29th of January, 1868, by Rev. J. B. Hillhouse, Mr. B. J. Poole and Miss R. J. Bailey, all of this
District.

Issue of:
Wednesday, February 12, 1868:
Married: On the 24th of December, 1867, at the residence of the
bride's father, by Rev. D. Humphreys, Mr. McDuffie Cothran, of
Abbeville and Miss Martha McClinton of Anderson.

Married: By the Rev. D. Humphreys, on the 6th February, 1868,
Mr. James Gilmer and Miss Martha Norris, daughter of Capt.
P. K. Norris, all of Anderson District.

Issue of:
Wednesday, February 26, 1868:
Married: On the 6th inst., by Rev. A. B. Stephens, Capt. D.
A. Switzer of Spartanburg, and Miss Kate A. Mahaffey, of
Laurens District.

Married: On February 20, 1868, at the residence of the bride's
father, by Rev. V. Young, Mr. W. C. Meredith of Orangeburg
and Miss Mattie Cummings of Anderson District.

Issue of:
Wednesday, March 4, 1868:
Married: In the Methodist Church on Thursday evening February
27th by the Rev. John W. Carlisle, Maj. W. W. Humphreys and Miss
Anna J. McCully, both of this village.

Married: On the evening of February 19th, by the Rev. C. C.
Pinckney, Col. Samuel B. Pickens to Miss Anna P., daughter of
Wm. P. Ingraham, Esq., all of South Carolina.

Obituary: Death of a Gallant Soldier - We are pained to record
the death of an old comrade in the Confederate service, Mr. Wm.
T. Cleveland of Pickens District, who died a few days ago of
disease resulting from severe wounds received in the discharge

of duty. Mr. C. was a graduate of the South Carolina College,
an accomplished gentleman and faithful soldier of the "lost
cause". He served as a private in the Palmetto Sharpshooters and was always reckoned among the most unselfish and
patriotic of that glorious Regiment. Peace to his ashes.

Article: - A Family Meeting - The family is an institution of
God, first formed in Paradise in the time of man's undepraved
innoccney[?] It is the germ of society and the source of
domestic enjoyments and when sanctified by the blessed influence
of the Gospel, it is the Church and to the State. On the 14th
inst., we were present at a "Family Meeting" at the residence
of Mr. Andrew McLees, a venerable citizen of this District, who
on that day attained to eighty years of age. His children
and some of his grandchildren and great grandchildren, with the
heads of several neighboring families, among whom was included
the aged Pastor of the family and his wife, met at the family
homestead and spent the day in pleasant social intercourse
and partook of a sumptuous dinner prepared for the occasion.
The ancestors of Mr. McLees immigrated to this country from
Antrim County, Ireland, in 1786. He was born in Newberry
District, S. C., on the 14th of February, 1788. He removed his
present location - then in Pendleton, now Anderson District -
in the year 1805. He was married to Miss B. Bennett in 1809.
They had twelve children - six sons and six daughters. The
eldest son has been a Ruling Elder in Roberts Church for more
than thirty years; the second son has been Pastor of Rock
Church, in Abbeville District, over twenty years; the third son
removed to Alabama where he died in 1844, leaving a small
family; the fourth son still resides with his parents, whom he
now watches over with almost that solicitude with which they
watched over him in his infantile days; the fifth son is now
the Stated supply of Hopewell Church, Pendleton; the sixth son
read medicine with Dr. Evins and soon after he commenced practice he was taken with typhoid fever and died in 1860. Of the
daughters, one died in infancy, three are married - Mrs. D.
Sadler, who lives in the lower part of this District; Mrs.
James Seawright and Mrs. J. W. Black, who live in Abbeville
District - all are heads of families. The two remaining daughters still reside with the aged parents and conspire with the
son to relieve their father and mother of every care and render
their declining days peaceful and happy. This aged couple
united with Roberts Church about 1814. They are the most
aged members in this church and perhaps, with one exception, are
the only persons living who were members of it when the present
aged Pastor took charge of it in 1821. Their children were all
dedicated to God by baptism in infancy and were brought up in
the nurture and admonition of the Lord. They all, excepting
the one who died in infancy, united with the church by a profession of faith in Christ. Mc McLees has been a worthy
citizen of this District for sixty three years. He and his
aged consort have been married fifty nine years. They were
industrious and economical and hence were in comfortable circumstances, although they owned no slaves. They brought up
their children to the same industrious habits, which proves a
peculiar benefit in these days of adversity and want. Mr.
McLees has ever led a quiet and orderly life. He never had any
quarrels with his neighbors nor any law-suits in Court. He says
that he has now the same stock of horses that he had when he
moved into the District and plants the same kind of corn that

he first planted, which, however, has been much improved by his care in selecting seed. Many persons in this and even in neighboring Districts, have sent to him for some of his choice corn for seed. Mr. McLees is now eighty and his wife seventy five years of age. Nine of their twelve children are still living. They have now twenty seven grandchildren; they lost four grandsons in the war and several others died in infancy. They have also several great grandchildren. The whole family would number about forty persons. Before the cheerful company who was present on this festive occasion dispersed, the Pastor read the 103 Ps., and sung the hymn, "O God of Bethel, by whose hand", etc, and offered up a special prayer for this assembled family and for all who were present. May the various branches of this family, as they enlarge and spread abroad, ever show the same habits of industry, the same honesty and uprightness of character and the same consistency of Christian deportment which have marked the lives of these aged paretns, now so near the end of their pilgrimage on earth and may they with their children and children's children, for successive generations, be all gathered into the "One Family" in Heaven, where seperations are unknown and where love and friendship shall reign to all eternity. It is a little remarkable that the sons-in-law are all members of the Presbyterian Church, two of them Ruling Elders, who adorn the office. Their daughters-in-law are also members of the Presbyterian Church. Some of their grandchildren have taken the vows of God upon them and one in a course of preparation for the Gospel ministry. Perhaps one cause, under God, of this singular success, is owing to the manner of training, especially by the mother. When she retired to some solitary place for making known her requests unto God, she took one of the children at a time with her and before kneeling down to pray, talked with it and endeavored to impress the young mind with the importance of an early conse-cration to God and to his service, the necessity of a change of heart, the precious promises to the young and while dwelling on the love of ye Saviour, she has seen the tears trickling down their cheeks and says she never asked of God to give them shining honors, great wealth or earthly distinctions, but grant them pardoning mercy and sanctifying grace. Many times has the Psstor felt cheered when in conversation with her about the state of the church, when it appeared more in a declining than a progressive state, to find one who, like the captive Jews who remembered Zion and was sorrowful for the moral desolation around. Soon these two aged servants of God, and Mrs. Martha Simpson, the other only surviving member of Roberts Church at that date and the Pastor, must soon, very soon, leave this church, with all its interests, to the care of One, "whose eyes can never slumber nor sleep", and surrender it unto the hands of another and a younger generation. But the church still lives. We would now commend this church, with its present members and their children to the watchful care of a covenant keeping God to the latest generation.

D. Humphreys

Issue of:
Wednesday, March 18, 1868:
Married: On the 23rd February last, by Rev. A. Acker, at the residence of the bride's father, Mr. J. W. Poor and Miss Corrie P. Cox, youngest daughter of Abner Cox, Sr.

Obituary: -Drowned - We regret to learn that Mr. E. J. McClure, of this District, committed suicide by drowning himself in Seneca River on last Saturday morning. He left his home about daybreak and proceeded directly to the river through his own plantation. His prolonged absence alarmed the family and search being instituted, his tracks were easily discovered and later in the day the body was found in the river. The deceased was a man of large family and maintained through life industrious habits. His mind had been affected for some days and there is no reason to doubt that he ended his life in a fit of insanity. He was about sixty years of age.

Issue of:
Wednesday, March 25, 1868:
Married: On Wednesday evening, the 18th inst., at the residence of the bride's father, by Rev. W. E. Walters, Capt. E. G. Roberts and Miss Ella, eldest daughter of William Perry, Esq., all of Anderson District, S. C.

Married: by the Rev. W. F. Pearson, Dec. 17,1867, at the residence of the bride's father, Mr. John L. Haynie and Miss R. P. Drake, both of Anderson District.

Married: By the Rev. W. F. Pearson, March 5, 1868, at the residence of the bride's father, Mr. Tucker W. Wood and Miss Mary C. McKee, both of Anderson District.

Married: On the 5th March at the residence of the bride's mother, by Rev. D. W. Humphreys, Dr. Wm. C. Holmes of Texas, and Miss E. A. Hamilton of Carroll County, Miss., formerly of Anderson District, S. C.

Issue of:
Wednesday, April 1, 1868:
Married: At the Benson House, on Thursday morning, March 26, by Rev. W. E. Walters, Mr. Edwin E. Keese and Miss Mollie E. Cochran, all of this village.

Obituary: Col. James F. Wyatt breathed his last on the 10th inst., at 10 o'clock and 45 minutes a.m. For nine weeks he had been painfully and unceasingly afflicted, during which time he had the constant attention of two practical physicians, as well as the unwearying viligance [sic] of a devoted family, joined with the unceasing attention of kind neighbors, but all in vain. He is gone. On Wednesday, 11th, his remains were carried into Pisgah Church where he held membership and at 3 o'clock p.m. a funeral sermon was delivered by Rev. T. R. Gary, from the text: "If a man die shall he live again", Job 14:14. The sermon was earnest and appropriate and listened to by a large congregation of weeping relatives, friends and neighbors and if sectarian prejudice exists, it seem to have been left behind on the occasion, for Baptists, Methodists and Presbyterians all seemed by their deportment to say - "we have lost a brother." The religious services were concluded by a few words of exhortation and kind cheer to the bereaved family, by Rev. J. M. Pickens and prayer by Rev. G. Carpenter and then the corpse was consigned to the grave in the burying ground near by, there to rest until the last, loud trump shall announce that time shall be no longer. Thus passed away one of Carolina's noblest sons, in his 67th year. He was born

May 1, 1801. Married early in life and commenced a career of usefulness which terminated only with his life. In politics he was an appreciative voter, in the military he delighted and early commenced a volunteer career, working up through the various grades of promotion until he honored the old 4th Regiment by being its Colonel. Afterwards, when he had become to[o] aged to endure the hardships of active field duty, he took the Colonelcy of the 42nd Regiment, while younger patriots went forth to battle for the sunny South. This position he held until our militia system became extinct. But the best remains to be told. He was not only a patriot and a gentleman, but a Christian, for "The tree shall be known by its fruit." The hungry went not from his door empty; the sick found him at their bedside; those in grief had his sympathy; they were at variance found in him a peace-maker. But the Judgement Day will open the book and there the fruit will be seen. He pondered well before he acted; for though strictly moral, he never joined the Christian church until 1860, when he united with the Baptist Church at Pisgah, where he was a zealous and attentive member and an officer in the church to the time of his decease. Fully conscious of his approaching dissolution, he set his house in order. Not only did he bear his affliction with Christian fortitude but looked forward to the future welfare of his bos[o]m companion and those over whom God had given him charge and having finished his course, he folded his hands over his heart and passed away without a struggle. A community feels sensibly the loss; but if our loss be his eternal gain, then let us dry up our tears and pray that we, too, may die the death of the Christian.   W.M.

Obituary: In Memoriam of Austin Williams, Dec'd. - Only a few brief months have passed since the Session and Church of Williamston were called upon to lament the loss of him whose name heads this brief notice. The deceased was born of reputable parents in the lower end of Greenville District, S. C., on the 21st of February, 1804. He died at his residence at Williamston, on the morning of September 9, 1867. Mr. John Williams, the father of the deceased, was a native of South Caroline and married Anna Wells, a native of this State also, where they settled down and raised a large family of children, of whom the subject of this notice was the eldest son. He remained with his parents until he was grown, when he went out West and was engaged for sometime in peddling dry goods through the States of Georgia and Alabama. He then returned home and soon after was united in marriage with Amry Anderson, of Greenville District, S. C., and settled near his father's residence where he resided until the year 1852, engaged in the vocation of farming, when he removed with his family to Williamston, Anderson District, S. C. and there spent the remainder of his days on earth. Not many years after his marriage, he was appointed Magistrate, the duties of which office he performed with credit and acceptance down to the time of his death. Being a sound reasoner and a good judge of law, his decisions in important and complicated law cases were invariable sustained by the higher courts whenever referred to them. In 1843, he became a member of the Presbyterian Church at Fairview, in Greenville District and with his family attended church regularly twice a month riding a distance of twenty two miles, there and back. His doors were always open to ministers of the gospel, of what ever name or order, many of whom have often

shared his hospitality and sheltered under his friendly roof
in going to and from their appointments. But a short time
after he united with the church, he was elected and ordained as
a Ruling Elder in the Fairview congregation. In 1852 he removed his membership to Broadway Church in Anderson District,
S. C. and was elected and ordained as Rider in the congregation. In 1852, the Presbyterian church at Williamston was
organized (in a great measure through his influence) of which
he became one of the leading members and he was again elected
and sat apart to the Eldership, in which capacity he continued
to act faithfully and with promptness to the time of his death.
The deceased was a business man, in every sense of the word,
of no ordinary talent and was very useful in his sphere. In
his death, the community and surrounding country have sustained
an irreparable loss, which is deeply felt and lamented by all
who knew him. He has left a disconsolate companion and four
children, one of them a widowed daughter with two promising
little boys, together with numerous relatives and friends to
mourn his departure, but they mourn not as those without hope,
having the blessed assurance "that all is well with him" and
they hope to meet him in that better world above. Whereas,
Almightly God, in His infinite wisdom, hath seen fit to call
from our midst our much beloved and esteemed brother, Austin
Williams, Esq.; Therefore- Resolved, That the Session and
Church of Williamston do deeply sympathize with the widow and
family in their bereavement. Resolved - That a page in our
session book be didicated to the memory of the deceased and
that the time of his birth and death be transcribed thereon.
Resolved- That the widow be presented with a copy of the above
preamble and resolutions. T. F. Anderson, S. C.

Issue of:
Wednesday, April 8, 1868:
Married: On the 31st of March, by the Rev. Baxter Hays, Mr.
D. S. Branyan, of Abbeville, and Miss Noriza Armstrong of
Anderson.

Issue of:
Wednesday, April 15, 1868:
Married: On the 22nd March by the Rev. G. W. Woodberry, Mr.
Thomas Jefferson John Scott Borum, of Williamsburg, S. C. to
Miss Rachel Sathina[?] Letson[?] of Marion District.

Issue of:
Wednesday, May 6, 1868:
Married: At the residence of the bride's father, on the 29th
April, by Rev. B. F. Mauldin, Mr. W. F. Smith of Georgia to
Miss S. Mary Williams of South Carolina. Thus are blended
two loving hearts. May their whole existence be one of joys
unmarred and prosperity untroubled. May no trivial sorrows
of earth ruffle the bright sea of life so confidently and so
happily embarked upon, "The foe is conquered now,/ Enraptured
joy enshrines your heart,/ And vistory's wreath is on your
brow."/ Take her and with her while away/ Earth's mortals
happiest hours;/ And may your pathway in this life,/ Be strewn
with beauteous flowers." Lucia

Issue of:
Wednesday, May 13, 1868:
Obituary: Died at Florence, S. C., on April 23rd, 1868, after
a painful illness of twelve days, Madora Ella McCall, relict of

J. Dewit McCall and daughter of J. P. and Mary E. Chase.

Issue of:
Wednesday, June 3, 1868:
Married: On Tuesday evening, the 19th inst., at the residence of the bride's father, by the Rev. A. H. Cornish, Mr. Vincent F. Martin, of Charleston, to Miss M. Lucia Harrison of this place.

Married: By the Rev. W. H. King, on the 21st of May, 1868, at the residence of the bride, Mr. Wm. B. Tate and Mrs. Martha E. Rice, all of this District

Issue of:
Wednesday, June 10, 1868:
Obituary: Death of Gen. Miller - Gen. Andrew Miller died at the residence of his son, Judge John C. Miller, in Henderson, Rusk County, Texas, at 20 minutes past 9 o'clock on 17th April, from general debility, arising from extreme old age, in his 89th year. Gen. Miller was born in Abbeville District, S. C., May 28, 1789, commencing life with the second year of the United States Government. He lived to see it subjected to many trials and revolutions; and leaves it in a very different condition from that which marked its early history. He public life commenced in 1819 (fifty four years ago) as Lieutenant in the army of the war of 1812. In 1816 he was elected to the Legislature from Pendleton, S. C. He served ten years in that body, distinguishing himself as a man of great energy and ready comprehension in legislative matters. Calhoun was then in his prime - he and Gen. Miller were friends and compeers. In 1820 Gen. Miller removed to Georgia - was elected to the State Senate in 1823 and remained a member of that body, with the exception of one year, till 1830. He wielded a large influence in the legislature. In 1827 he excepted the position of Major General in the Georgia Militia, which he held for many years. With the close of the Presidential campaign of 1840, he dated the close of his political course. During this campaign he filled the position of Elector, for the State at large, on the Houston ticket, with much honor to himself and to the Whig party. In the Spring of 1844 he removed to Texas, settled in Rusk County, directing his attention chiefly to agricultural pursuits. Though often solicited he would never run for office in Texas. Gen. Miller was a man of superior intellect and retained the vigor of his mind to the last. He was all his life a student - was a profound politician - an accurate historian - thoroughly versed in all agricultural subjects and one of the best Biblical scholars. He took great interest in the natural resources of the country. Gen. Miller, after his removal to Texas, gave much attention to domestic matters - to the making of his home pleasant and inviting. He planted and successfully grew the first apple orchard in Rusk county; demonstrating that this fruit could be successfully grown in this climate - thee prevailing opinion to the contrary notwith- standing. His orchard still remains in a flourishing condition - a monument to his enterprise and good taste. In the death of Gen. Miller, a great and good man has been removed. "Peace to his ashes."

Fatal Accident: The Abbeville Banner of last Wednesday gives the following account of a melancholy occurrence in that village. The young man was known in this community as an agent for sewing machines. Mr. R. J. Martin, a native of Greenville, as we are informed, who came to our town a few days ago as the agent of a sewing machine manufacturer, met with a fatal accident on Monday last. In the afternoon, about 4 o'clock, he called upon a citizen of this place, whose residence is accessible only by a long flight of stairs. Having transacted his business, he attempted to descend and being under the influence of liquor, he lost his balance and fell over the railing to the ground, a distance of about twenty feet, his head striking a stone, which produced congestion of the brain. Medical assistance was at once rendered and every effort made to alleviate his sufferings. He lingered in great pain until yesterday morning, about 2 o'clock, when he died.

Issue of:
Wednesday, June 24, 1868:
Married: On the 18th inst., by the Rev. J. I. Bonner, at the residence of the bride's father, Dr. H. T. Epting, of Williamston, S. C. and Mrs. Mary Jane Knox, daughter of William Hill, Esq., of Abbeville.

Married: On Wednesday evening, June 17th, at the Baptist Church by Rev. W. D. Beverly, Mr. William N. Clark and Miss Emma E. Beverly, eldest daughter of the officiating minister - all of Anderson C. H., S. C.

Obituary: Died, at Anderson, S. C., on the 28th of April, after a painful illness of ten days, E. Warren Webb, aged thirty one years. "Man cometh forth like a flower and is cut down, he fleweth also as a shadow and continueth not." Beloved, regretted and lamented.

Obituary: Mrs. Mary L. Black, wife of J. W. Black, Esq., of Abbeville District, S. C., departed this life on the morning of the 22nd of April, aged 42 years and 12 days. It is seldom our duty to record a more sad and melancholy event than the death of this good woman. She has been cut off in the prime of life, amidst scenes of great usefulness in the domestic circle, as well as in the church, leaving a husband and four little children, besides many relatives and friends, to mour her irreparable loss. She was, indeed a good woman, a good wife, a good mother and a sincere, devoted, consistent and humble Christian. She was the daughter of Mr. and Mrs. Andrew McLees, of this District, who taught her from early childhood the importance of entire consecration to God's service and at the age of 14 years she made a public profession of her faith and joined Roberts Church. At her marriage she removed her membership to Little Mountain Church in Abbeville and up to her death, the power of converting and sanctifying grace. She loved her church and the cause of Christ was ever near her heart. She was permitted to attend the meeting of the Presbytery at Greenwood, when the ordinances of God's house and the means of grace seemed to her more precious than usual - because her Saviour meant that to be her last time on earth to enjoy them. Immediately on her return home she took Pneumonia and for five or six days her suffering was very great; still she never murmured or complained; but calmly resigned herself to the will of God, she meekly said, "It is alright". When in reply to her own inquiries, her attending physician told she was near her end, she quietly said, "It does not disturb me, I have been looking forward to this time for years and I am

prepared to meet it." She expressed a desire to live on
account of her little children, but she committed them to God
and gave some special directions concerning them and after
giving a parting charge to her sorrowing family and friends to
meet her in Heaven - without a struggle or groan she died as
if she had been going to sleep! "Asleep in Jesus! blessed
sleep!/ From which none ever wakes to week!" For her to live
was Christ, but to die was gain.
Storeville, S. C.   June 16, 1868   W. F. P.

Issue of:
Wednesday, July 10, 1868:
Married: On the 16th June, by the Rev. E. H. Reid, Mr. L. T.
Mahaffy, of Reidville, Spartanburg District and Miss Sallie C.
Sullivan, of Laurens District.

Issue of:
Wednesday, July 15, 1868:
Obituary: Died, at Anderson, June 22nd, 1868, Mrs. Mary B.
Prevost, wife of Joseph Prevost, in the 57th year of her age.

Obituary: Died, at his residence in Tippah county, Mississippi,
June 1st, 1868, Col. James Simpson Liddell, in his seventy
eighth year. The deceased was born in Anderson, S. C. and emigrated to Mississippi in 1841, where he resided up to his death.
He leaves a widow, with children and grandchildren to mourn
his loss. Col. Liddell was a participant in the war of 1814.
He gave three sons to the service of his country in 1861 -
Samuel Baylis Alfred, fell at Gettysburg, Wm. Anderson at
Chicamauga and Charles Gaillard at Jonesborough, Georgia. His
health has been gradually failing him since their death. Peace
to his ashes.

Issue of:
Wednesday, August 12, 1868:
Married: On August 6, 1868, by Rev. Wm. Hodges, Mr. Allen
Rutledge of Tishimengo County, Mississippi and Miss Anna
Clinkscales of Anderson District, S. C.

Married: On August 6, 1868, by Rev. D. Humphreys, Mr. John
McMahan and Mrs. Bethia McAlister, all of Anderson District.

Issue of:
Wednesday, September 9, 1868:
Married: On the evening of the 1st inst., at the residence of
Mrs. Elizabeth Taylor, in Abbeville District, by Rev. A. Rice,
Mr. Phillip L. Hampton, of Stone Mountain, Ga., and Mrs. Joannah
S. Campbell, of Abbeville District, S. C.

Issue of:
Wednesday, September 16, 1868:
Obituary: Mrs. Harriet E. Boyd, wife of Rev. J. Marion Boyd,
of Newberry Circuit, died on congestion, September 4.

Obituary: Charles Hammond, Esq., formerly a well known merchant of Hamburg and one of the most honored and beloved
citizens of Edgefield District, departed this life on the
3rd inst., at his home.

Issue of:
Wednesday, September 23, 1868:
Married: On Thursday evening, September 10, 1868, at the

residence of the bride's father, by the Rev. W. B. Jones, Mr.
W. W. Farrow, Editor of the Abbeville Banner, to Miss M. A.
Parks, daughter of Dr. F. G. Parks of Greenwood, S. C.

Married: On the 12th inst., by Rev. Wilson Ashley, Mr. J.
Roddy Martin, of this District and Miss Lou McDavid, of Greenville District.

Obituary: Mrs. Sarah Hunter died at Orrville, in Anderson
District, on the 15th August, in the 92nd year of her age. She
was the daughter of Robert and Jane Gilky, born in Rutherford-
ton, N. C. and could remeber many incidents of the Revolutionary
War. The writer of this article has frequently heard her
describe a visit of the Tories to her father's house. She
married Thomas Hunter, in 1801, one of the first settlers
of Pendleton Village. At this place she resided till the death
of her husband. She possessed a remarkably vigorous constitution, a meek, quiet, amiable disposition. For many years of
her life she was nearly blind; but her sight improved for
several years before her death. She was the mother of two
children - a son and a daughter. Her son died at the age of
twenty four of consumption. Through her daughter, Mrs. Anderson
she leaves nine grandchildren and twenty eight great grandchildren. She professed religion in early life and united with
the Presbyterian Church. She continued a consistent member of
the church of her choice till death. She had no fears of death
but prayed that she might die saying, "That she was old, blind
and deaf and she wanted to go and be with Christ." Her body
lies at the old Stone Church, near Pendleton, waiting for the
coming of her Divine Lord and Master.

Obituary: The Pickens Courier is informed that George Green,
a citizen of that District, was shot recently, dying a short
time from the effects of the wound. No particulars.

Issue of:
Wednesday, September 30, 1868:
Obituary: Departed this life, Ella Amanda, fifth daughter of
Dr. James W. and Mrs. Amanda Earle. Born March 26, 1853 and
died August 31, 1868 in her fifteenth year. This pure flower
had scarcely unfolded its snowy petals ere it was bourne hence
to a bright home above. Dear Ella united herself a short time
before her decease to the Methodist Episcopal Church and died
in strong faith in the atoning merits of her Saviour's blood
and in prospect of a heavenly home. During her severe illness,
her meek spirit was not known to murmur and though the idol of
the family, she seemed resigned to the Will of her Heavenly
Father. Sorrowing ones, mourn not, for your lovely Ella. "She
is not dead but sleepth" - she is only gone before to beckon
you to mansions of eternal bliss. Look up! look up! Though
bitter I know the cup is to drain, your heavenly Father afflicts
you in love to draw your wandering thoughts to Him, where you
may be united in mansions of eternal bliss, where parting will
be no more.   C. L. G.

Obituary: "Death of an Old Citizen" - We are pained to record
the death of Capt. William Nevitt, an aged and highly respectable citizen of this District, which sad event occurred at
his residence near this village on Monday last, after an illness
of only a few days. He was a native of Maryland and emigrated

when quite young to Fairfield District in this State, where he
married and continued to reside for many years. He came to this
District some thirty years ago and has always been greatly
esteemed as a citizen of upright character and hones faithfulness to society. He was a Deacon of the Baptist Church at the
time of his death and for many years previous and had been a
member of that denomination for more than a half century. He
commanded a company in the war of 1812 and was stationed some-
where on the coast, we believe. After a long life of usefulness and honor, with a numerous line of descendants to mourn
his departure from this world, he has been gathered to his
fathers and is now enjoying the rest that remains for the
finally faithful. We are informed that this aged patriarch has
often expressed a desire, of late, to witness the country once
more at peace, and with this exception, was perfectly resigned
to death. His illness was of short duration and only three
days before being called to the realities of an eternal world,
he was engaged in the ordinary duties of life. He was nearly
eighty five years old and was regular in attendence upon divine
worship, up to the Sabbath before the illness which terminated
his career upon earth.

Obituary: H. H. Williams and E. W. Petit, both old citizens
and business men of Charleston, died last week.

Obituary: Mrs. Elizabeth Snider, a highly esteemed lady of
Orangeburg District, died on the 12th inst., at the extraordinary age of 104 years.

Obituary: A. D. Stainmaker, the mail rider between Tuscaloosa,
Alabama, was shot from his horse on the 10th inst., by negroes.
The mail bag was cut open and the letters destroyed. The un-
fortunate man, it is said, leaves a wife and two children.

Issue of:
Wednesday, October 7, 1868:
Married: On the morning of the 20th inst., at the residence of
the bride's father, by A. A. Porter, D.D., Mr. John P. Sitton,
of Anderson and Miss Myra M., daughter of A. F. Jackson, Jackson Hill, Spartanburg Dist., S. C.

Obituary: "Another Old Citizen Gone" - We are deeply pained to
receive the intelligence that our old friend, Abner Cox, Esq.,
died on Sunday last, at his residence near Belton. A correspondent informs us that for several weeks Mr. Cox had been
unwell but kept up attending to his farm; his ailment eventuated
in an attack of cholera morbus and on Thursday last, physicians
were summoned to attend him. He was not thought to be in a
critical condition, however, until the day before his death,
when it became manifest that the system, weakened by severe
exposure during the latter part of the summer, could not react
against this violent attack. On Sunday at midday, he passed
quietly and peacefully into the spirit land. He descended from
an ancestry who were among the first settlers in this section
and throughout life maintained a high character of honesty and
liberality. He leaves a wife and many children, besides a
numerous connection and a large circle of friends to mour his
death. He was a member of the Shady Grove Baptist Church where
he was buried on yesterday morning. He died in the 67th year
of his age.

Issue of:
Wednesday, October 21, 1868:
Married: On Wednesday evening, October 7, 1868, at St. Paul's
Church, Pendleton, by Rev. A. H. Cornish, Mr. B. C. Crawford,
of Pickens, S. C. to Miss Rebecca, eldest daughter of W. H. D.
Gaillard, Esq., of Pendleton, S. C.

Married: On the 6th of October, by Rev. W. F. Pearson, at the
residence of the bride's father, Mr. P. C. Hall to Miss Sally
Hall, both of Anderson District.

Issue of:
Wednesday, October 28, 1868:
Married: On the 25th inst., at the residence of the bride's
father, by W. S. Pickens, Esq., Mr. M. T. Fleming to Miss
Fannie, youngest daughter of N. S. Clardy, all of Anderson
District.

Married: October 27, 1868, at the residence of the bride's
father, near Lowndesville, by the Rev. W. F. Pearson, Dr. R. E.
Thompson, of Anderson and Miss Lou C. Groves of Abbeville.

Issue of:
Wednesday, November 4, 1868:
Obituary: Died at Anderson Court House, on the 24th of October
1868, Mrs. Catherine Benson, in the sixty eighth year of her
age. Thus has another of the Saviour's bidden ones departed
to be with him and like him. She went up through great suffering. Her chamber of disease was one of much pain but it was not
cheerless. The chastened spirit did not fret but calmly she
reposed all her interests and welfare of those dear to her
heart, into the hands of a covenant-keeping God. Her path was
that of the just, shining more and more unto the perfect day.
The gold grew brighter and more precious in the furnace. Her
faith was clear and scriptural. The roots of her piety were
down in deep waters. It was evident to all who knew her that
she shared largely in the benefits which believers receive in
this life - "assurance of God's love, peace of conscience, joy
in the Holy Ghost, increase of grace and perseverance therein
to the end." Nor is there a shadow of doubt that now "made
perfect in holiness she has passed immediately into glory."
The community has lost a useful member - her church will long
miss her prayers and efforts in its behalf, and her family.
As, who can describe the void now made in the household circle?
But all is well. The summons found her ready. She has gone to
be with Christ, where he is and to behold his glory. She died.
"But the sunshine of Heaven beamed bright on her waking,/ And
the song that she heard was the saraphim's song."

Issue of:
Wednesday, November 18, 1868:
Obituary: Died in Sumter, S. C., at the residence of S. P.
Gaillard, Esq., on the 6th of October, Mrs. Rebecca W. Gaillard,
wife of the late Peter Gaillard, Esq., in the 84th year of her
age.

Obituary: At the residence of her son-in-law, Dr. George W.
Foute, in Whitfield County, Georgia, on the evening of the 9th
of October last, very suddenly of apoplexy of the lungs, Mrs.
Lucinda Nash Broyles, widow of the late Cain Broyles, deceased,
in the 79th year of her age. The deceased was a devout

Christian, performed well her part in life and now rests from her labors.

Issue of:
Obituary: "Death of Gen. Waddy Thompson" - We learn from a dispatch received last night that Gen. Waddy Thompson, of Greenville, died on Sunday morning last in Tallahasse, Florida, aged seventy years. He represented the mountain District in Congress many years ago and was afterwards appointed Minister to Mexico. He was well known and greatly admired throughout this section and in the palmy days of his political career was noted as an effective popular speaker. For ten or fifteen years he has been altogether withdrawn from public life.

Issue of:
Wednesday, December 2, 1868:
Married: On the 19th November, at the residence of the bride's mother, near Fairview, by Rev. E. T. Buist, D.D., assisted by Rev. C. B. Stewart, Mr. John C. Bailey, Associate Editor of Greenville Enterprise, and Miss Maggie, youngest daughter of the late John M. Harrison, all of Greenville County.

Issue of:
Wednesday, December 9, 1868:
Married: On the 18th of November, by Rev. W. E. Walters, Mr. H. O. King and Miss L. C. Campbell, all of Anderson District.

Married: On December 6, 1868, by Rev. W. F. Pearson, Mr. George K. Shrimp and Miss T. M. Clinkscales, all of Anderson District.

Issue of:
Thursday, January 7, 1869:
Obituary: "Death of Rev. Basil Manly, Sr." - The Greenville Enterprise says: Dr. Basil Manly, Sr. was born in Chatham County, North Caroline, January 28, 1798. He was sent by his father to the South Caroline College in 1819 and graduated with the first honor in 1821. After leaving college he settled in Edgefield and preached in that district till 1826. He was then called to the pastorate of the First Baptist Church in Charleston. [Long details]

Issue of:
Thursday, January 14, 1869:
Married: On the 13th of December, 1868, by Rev. A. Rice, Mr. James Ibzan[?] Crowther, of Abbeville and Miss Elizabeth Jane Pruitt of Anderson.

Married: On December 24, 1868, by Rev. W. F. Pearson, Anthony F. Hanks, of Anderson and Miss Susan K. Little, of Abbeville.

Married: In Meridian, Mississippi, on Thursday the 3rd inst., at the bride's mother's, Mrs. Eliza McLaughlin, by Rev. W. E. Mabray, Mr. J. T. Kay, formerly of Anderson District, S. C. and Miss Marcella McLaughlin, of Meridian, Miss.

Married: On the 8th December, 1868, at the residence of the brides father, near Lowndesville, Abbeville District, S. C., by Rev. W. P. Mouzon, Mr. A. A. Dean, of Anderson District and Miss L. D., youngest daughter of Charles Allen, Esq.

Married: On Tuesday evening, December 22nd, 1868, at the residence of the bride's father, by Rev. W. H. Stratton, Mr. Robert L. Keys and Miss Anna C. Archer, eldest daughter of Wm. Archer, Esq., all of Anderson District.

Married: On the evening of the 31st ult., by Rev. J. L. Kennedy, at the residence of the bride's mother, Whitner Symmes, Esq., Editor Keowee Courier, to Miss Nettie, youngest daughter of Mrs. L. Alexander, of Pickens.

Married: On the 17th December, 1868, by Rev. George F. Round, Mr. Wm. H. Garrison to Miss Essie Reed, all of this District.

Issue of:
Thursday, January 28, 1869:
Married: On the 21st inst., by Rev. B. F. Mauldin, Mr. M. E. Telford to Miss Catherine T., eldest daughter of Rev. W. P. Martin, all of this district.

Issue of:
Thursday, February 11, 1869:
Married: At the residence of the bride's father, on the 24th of December, 1868, by Rev. Mr . Brown, Mr. Edward A. Russell, of Anderson County, to Miss Nannia A. Rosamond, of Greenville County.

Married: By B. F. Mauldin, on Thursday, 4th inst., at the residence of the bride's father, in this District, Capt. W. H. Austin to Miss Mattie, daughter of Matthew Breazeale, Esq., of this District.

Married: By B. F. Mauldin, in Williamston, on Friday, 5th inst., Mr. Samuel Davenport to Miss Lavania Summers, all of Williamston.

Married: By B. F. Mauldin, on Sunday 7th inst., Mr. H. T. McEllion to Miss Mary E., daughter of W. W. Holder, all of Williamston.

Issue of:
Thursday, February 18, 1869:
Married: On the morning of the 4th February, by Rev. David Humphreys, at the residence of the bride's father, Dr. R. F. Diver, of Greenville and Miss Fannie, youngest daughter of David Simpson, Esq., of Anderson.

Issue of:
Thursday, February 25, 1869:
Married: On Thursday, the 18th February 1869, by Rev. George F. Round, Mr. Berry T. Martin to Miss Mary Tallulah McPhail, the only daughter of Capt. Peter McFail, all of Anderson District.

Married: By the Rev. George F. Round, on Tuesday, 26th January Mr. ___ Duncan, of Georgia to Miss Rebecca Camenade, of Pendleton, S. C.

Married: On Thursday, the 18th February, 1869, by Rev. Thomas Crimes, Mr. R. F. White to Miss S. E. King, all of Anderson District.

Obituary: H. H. Knee, one of the original settlers of Walhalla, died last week.

Issue of:
Thursday, March 4, 1869:
Married: By Rev. B. F. Mauldin, at the residence of the bride's father, on Thursday evening, 25th inst., Mr. J. W. Sitton to Miss Tabitha J., daughter of Col. J. D. King, all of this District.

Married: On Thursday, February 4th, by the Rev. Mr. Grogan, at the residence of the bride's mother, Mr. Theodore Munro, of Anderson, S. C. and Miss Mary C. Baker, of Elbert, Georgia.

Married: On Sunday morning the 28th February, at 8 o'clock, at the residence of the bride's mother, by Rev. A. Rice, Mr. Robert Baylis Massey and Miss Cynthia Minerva Martin, all of this county.

Issue of:
Thursday, March 11, 1869:
Married: On Thursday evening, February 25, 1869, by Rev. L. W. Stephens, at the residence of the bride's mother, in Elberton, Georgia, Mr. S. N. Carpenter, Editor of the Elberton Gazette and Miss Maggie C. Stanford.

Issue of:
Thursday, March 18, 1869:
Married: On Sunday morning, the 7th inst., at 9 o'clock at the residence of the bride's mother, by Rev. A. Rice, Mr. William McGee and Miss Sallie Smith, all of this county.

Married: By the Rev. A. Rice, on the evening of the 10th inst., at the residence of the bride's father, Mr. Thomas Leak, of Stokes County, N. C. and Miss Anna L. Drake, eldest daughter of James Drake, Esq., of this county.

Married: On February 25th, 1869 at the residence of the bride's mother, near Charleston, Mississippi, Rev. David W. Humphreys and Miss Agnes Sherman.

Issue of:
Thursday, April 1, 1869:
Married: March 18, 1869, at the residence of Mrs. Lou Richey, by Rev. Wm. F. Pearson, Mr. John L. McLin of Anderson, to Miss F. Ann Richey, of Abbeville.

Issue of:
Thursday, April 8, 1869:
Obituary: Died, at his residence on March 4, 1869, Maj. James Gilmer. He and his wife had just returned from an evening visit to see an afflicted friend and complained of a sick brash [?] and passed away to the spirit land with but little pain, in half an hour. His parents were from the Emerald Isle, settled in Abbeville District, but removed at an early day to Pendleton and settled near Roberts Church. His father was one of the Elders of this church at its organization, or shortly thereafter. He himself was born in Abbeville District, March 22, 1794. Was elected to the Legislature of this State in 1840. Not ambitious for popularity, he never offered his

services again to the State. United with Robert's Church, Sept.
22, 1850; was ordained an Elder Oct. 1, 1854; appointed Clerk
of Session Jan. 20, 1855; resigned the office Aug. 2, 1859.
He was distinguished for truthfulness, moral honesty, great
accuracy and punctuality in the discharge of his duties as a
magistrate, surveyor and all other public duties. As a
Christian, uniform in his deportment-possessed the confidence
of the church, of the session and of the community at large.
The death of such a man is a loss to the family, the church
and the country.   D. H.

Issue of:
Thursday, April 29, 1869:
Married: On Thursday evening, April 22d, 1869, at the resi-
dence of the bride's father, by Rev. J. S. Murray, Dr. J. W.
Gurley and Miss Julia J., second daughter of O. H. P. Fant, Esq.
all of Anderson.

Obituary: Departed this life, on the 4th of February, 1869,
at her residence in this county, Mrs. Margaret Major, after a
severe illness of ten days, from a paralytic stroke. She was
the daughter of Kennon Breazeale, deceased, and was born in
Anderson County, November 14, 1793 and was married to James
Major, Esq., deceased, in her early maidenhood and became the
mother of a numerous offspring, many of whom are left behind
to mourn the loss of a good, kind and affectionate mother.
Many years ago, in the providential dealings of her Heavenly
Father, she was called upon to carry the remains of her beloved,
devoted and Christian husband, the happy partner of her best
and sunniest days, to their last resting place, beside which
hers now repose. And though the loss was great and the affliction severe, yet she bore it with pious and Christian submission
and became a widow indeed. She was mild, gentle and meek,
always adoring her widowhood, which ceased at her death, with
many Christian graces. She was naturally a woman of great
energy, perservance and activity. She studied carefully and
prayerfully the duties of wife and mother and always being
blessed with remarkably good health, she was enabled to discharge those duties which spread out before the wife and mother.
In September, 1831, she embraced the Christian faith and on the
24th day of the same month united with Neal's Creek Baptist
Church and was immersed into its fellowship by the Rev. Wm.
McGee and from that time till the day of her death she continued steadfast in the Apostle's doctrine, proved herself to
be faithful and ornamental member of the church. At all times
she gave strong and satisfactory evidence of a work of Divine
Grace upon her heart. We believe we can truly say, that
while she lived she lived unto the Lord, because she was the
Lord's through Jesus Christ her Saviour. Ready and willing
was she to make sacrifice for Him who loved her and gave His
beloved Son to redeem her. Observe the fact that just one
half of her long and eventful life was spent in the service of
her Heavenly Master and it is reasonable to hope that the talent
committed to her care has been returned with usury and that
her pure and Christ-like Spirit has been admitted into the
Paradise of Her God, living now in the bright fields of glory
beyond the skies. Weep not, therefore, ye berefit sons and
daughters. Imitate that example which was set by your departed
mother. Walk in that way in which her obedient feet walked.

Let her God be your God, her Saviour be your Saviour and then
her eternal home will be your eternal home.

Her Pastor

Issue of:
Thursday, May 6, 1869:
Married: On Sunday morning, April 25th, 1869, at the residence
of the bride's father, by Rev. A. Rice, Mr. Josiah Herford, of
Henry County, Virginia and Miss Anna R. Rice, eldest daughter of
A. E. Rice, of this County.

Married: On Sunday morning, May 2nd, 1869, at the residence of
the bride's father, by Rev. W. H. King, Mr. J. D. Welch, of
Tennessee and Miss Florence E., eldest daughter of B. A.
McAlister, of this county.

Issue of:
Thursday, May 13, 1869:
Married: On the 21st ult. at the residence of the bride's
father, in Greenville District, by Rev. B. F. Mauldin, Mr.
E. H. Archer to Miss Emma M., daughter of Israel Chenly.

Married: By Rev. W. P. Martin, on the 22nd ult., at the residence of the bride's father, Mr. Wm. L. Latimer, of Abbeville,
to Miss Emmaliza, youngest daughter of Mr. Joel Kay, of Anderson District.

Married: By Rev. W. P. Martin, on the 6th inst., at his
residence, Mr. A. P. Shirley, of Abbeville District to Miss
Laura K. Sotherland, of Anderson District.

Suicide: Margaret Pearce, of Charleston, committed suicide in
Philadelphia last Monday by taking oxalic acid. The cause is
said to be pecuniary difficulties.

Issue of:
Thursday, June 3, 1869:
Obituary: Died, of consumption, at the residence of his father,
in Williamston, S. C., on the 15th of November last, Dr. R. K.
King, for several years a resident and practicing physician of
the city of Columbia. This young and gifted gentleman graduated
with distinction at the Medical College in Charleston in 1866.
He was well known and highly respected by a large number of
persons here and secured many warm and attacked friends by his
amiable traits of character. During the late war he filled
the responsible station of druggist and assistant in the
Ladies Hospital, in the Eastern part of Columbia and by his
assiduity to the duties of the post and his attention to the
wants and his exertions in alleviating the sufferings of the
sick and wounded in that institution and by his universal
politness, he won the lasting regard of all the patients who
came under his care and secured the confidence and respect of
the ladies who had charge of the hospital. After the close of
war he established himself in the city of Columbia and devoted
himself to the practice of his profession with great devotion
and soon acquired a reputation for much skill and was rapidly
rising to well merited fame when the fatal disease, which
eventually ended his life, seized upon him and cut short his
future prospects. The writer of this imperfect tribute to his
memory knew him well and bears willing testimony to his noble-
ness of character and his great worth as a man and unites with

his family and friends generally in mourning his early death. He was without question a man of talent in his profession, liberal to fault, charitable and humane. Had he lived, he would have adorned the profession of his choice and reflected honor upon the character of a physician; for he was attacked to its practice and had just that order of mind and acuteness of perception and that peculiar benevolence of heart which are necessary for and which eventually lift its votaries to enviable distinction. He has gone to that "Home from whence no traveler returns", that unexplored country, unknown to mortals, except by the eye of faith in the promise of "Him who spake as never man spake", whose precepts and promises, if believed, secures an entrance into the rewards prepared for suffering humanity" "before the foundation of the world was laid!".
A Friend

Death: On Friday night last, near Salubrity, in Pickens County, a white man by the name of Willard was killed. The stable on the premises was discovered to be in flames, when the deceased and his father, with other persons, rushed out of the dwelling and a volley was fired into them with the result above stated. From all we can learn, the attack in this instance was expected and the combat between the parties was desperate, a number of shots being exchanged. As the matter will probably undergo official investigation, we will refrain from giving the particulars as related to us.

Issue of:
Thursday, June 10, 1869:
Married: On Wednesday, the 19th day of May, at the residence of the bride's father in this county, by Rev. J. Scott Murray, Mr. J. Haynes H. Earle and Miss Annie W. Earle.

Death: Mr. Timothy Norton, an old resident of Sumter, S. C., died in that place on last Tuesday.

Death: Mr. Lewis Watts, aged ninety two, died very suddenly on Sunday evening last, at his residence, three miles from Camden, in this State.

Death: A son of Mr. William Young, of Laurens District, was killed a few days since by accidentally falling into a well.

Death: Mr. F. A. Calhoun, of Abbeville, a nephew of the great statesman, died in that place on Sunday, 29th ult, after a short illness.

Issue of:
Thursday, June 17, 1869:
Married: On the 3rd of June, at Mount Ina, the residence of the bride's father, by Rev. A. H. Cornish, Mr. Robert Young, of the Keowee Courier and Miss Anna W., eldest daughter of Col. H. W. Kuhtmann, both of Oconee county.

Married: On the 10th of June, 1869, at the residence of the bride's father Mr. Stokes Stribling, near Richland Church, by Rev. D. Humphreys, Mr. Warren Shelor and Miss Rebecca Stribling.

Married: By the Rev. D. Humphreys, on June 13, 1869, Mr. Robert McGill and Mrs. Mary White, both of Anderson County.

Obituary: James J. Harkness, Esq., of Anderson, S. C., died of
chronic inflamation of the stomach and liver, at 12 o'clock on
the 24th of April, 1869, in the fiftieth year of his age. For
more than twelve months the heavy hand of disease spread through
the entire system, prostrating him so that for many months
previous to his death he was unable to attend or watch over his
private interests. He went down step by step to the grave,
giving him ample time to "set his house in order" and prepare
for his passage through the "dark valley and shadow of death".
He often spoke of his shortcomings as a Christian and Deacon
of Varrenes Church; yet he bore his afflictions without com-
plaints and calmly and unhesitatingly reposed his trust alone in
Jesus for salvation. He leaves five children by his first
marriage "without father or mother" and a wife and one child,
whose sad office now is to mourn over their sore bereavement
and irreparable loss. Truly, "Gods ways and thoughts are not
as ours", or he would not have smitten the head of the family
and left these little ones without a father's love; but blessed
thought, He doeth all things well and has promised "that everything shall work together for good" to them that love Him.
May this precious promise - "I will be a husband to the widow
and a father to the fatherless", be abundantly fulfilled in
the case of this afflicted family. "Judge not the Lord by
feeble sense,/ But, trust Him for His grace;/ Behind a frowning
Providence,/ He hides a smiling face."   W. F. P.

Issue of:
Thursday, July 8, 1869:
Deaths in This Village:
Mrs. Esther Benson, relict of Mr. E. B. Benson, formerly a
well known merchant of Pendleton, died at the residence of her
son-in-law, Dr. A. P. Cater, in this village, on Saturday
morning last, in the 75th year of her age. She leaves a
numerous line of descendents and a wide circle of friends to
mourn her loss.
Miss Carrie Horsey, second daughter of Mr. T. M. Horsey, recently of Charleston, but now a resident of New York, died suddenly
on Sunday morning last, of consumption, also at the residence
of Dr. Cater. She is cut off in the bloom of life and after
months of weary illness.

Suicide: The Greenville Mountaineer records the suicide of Mrs.
Joel Charles, in the vicinity of Grove Station, by cutting her
throat with a knife. Physical derangement is supposed to be
the cause of this sad termination of life.

Issue of:
Thursday, July 22, 1869:
Obituary: Died, of inflammation of the brain, July 16th, 1869,
Minnie Adelia Stacy, youngest child of R. W. and A. O. Todd,
aged two years and eleven months.

Issue of:
Thursday, August 5, 1869:
Obituary: "Death of Manson Jolly" - This news will be received
with regret by the many friends of this bold and daring Confederate soldier. We learn that a private letter has been
received, stating that Manson Jolly was drowned on the 8th
of July, near his home in Texas. He was building a residence
on the opposite side of the creek from where he lived and had

crossed over on horseback several times during the day. The
stream was greatly swollen and in attempting to cross for the
third or fourth time, he was carried with his horse down the
creek and in the struggle which ensued both were drowned. Mr.
Jolly had been married about one year and leaves a young wife,
the daughter of a former citizen of Anderson. The thrilling
exploits and adventures of Manson Jolly in this section of the
country, immediately after the war closed, are fresh in the
recollection of all. His name was a terror for a long time to
the garrison of United States soldiers, especially the volunteer white and colored regiments stationed at his place. When
the regular troops arrived, he removed to Texas, where he has
since been leading a quiet and peaceful life.

Issue of:
Thursday, August 12, 1869:
Married: On the 27th of July, 1869, at the residence of Mrs.
H. T. Browne, by Rev. David Simmons, Dr. J. B. Browne, of Town-
ville, S. C. and Miss Annie E. Simpson of Ripley, Miss.

Issue of:
Thursday, August 19, 1869:
Obituary: Died, on July 25th, 1869, in Dallas county, Texas,
Joseph Taylor, third son of Thomas A. and Mary A. Wideman,
aged nine years, seven months and seventeen days.

Issue of:
Thursday, September 2, 1869:
Married: On Thursday evening, August 26, 1869, by Rev. Wilson
Ashley, Mr. Ephraim B. Eaton and Miss Eliza Ann Hall, all of
this county.

Issue of:
Thursday, September 9, 1869:
Obituary: Departed this life at the residence of her husband,
in Anderson District, on the 24th of August, 1869, Mrs. Myra M.,
wife of John P. Sitton. The deceased had been a consistent
member of the North Pacolet Presbyterian Church in Spartanburg
District for a number of years. She leaves a husband and many
friends to mourn her loss.

Issue of:
Thursday, September 23, 1869:
Married: On Tuesday, September 14, 1869, by Rev. J. B. Adger
at Pendleton, S. C., Mr. John E. Breazeale and Miss Mollie J.,
youngest daughter of J. E. Belotte, Esq.

Married: On Tuesday, September 14, 1869, by Rev. J. B. Adger
at Pendleton, S. C., Mr. R. Marcus Burriss and Miss Carrie
E. Tillinghast, all of Anderson County.

Married: At the residence of the bride's mother, by Rev.
D. W. Humphreys, on the evening of the 16th inst., Mr. J. W.
Black, of Abbeville and Miss Eliza Hatton, of Anderson.

Married: At 4 o'clock on Thursday, the 9th inst., at his own
residence, by Rev. A. Rice, Mr. John Preston Cowan and Miss
Mary Jane Burton, all of this county.

Distressing Casualty: We have received a letter from our
esteemed friend, Maj. George Seaborn, giving the particulars

of a distressing and fatal accident which occurred at the
Pendleton Factory on Saturday last, resulting in the death
of Mrs. McDow, an estimable widow lady of that neighborhood.
The following embraces the particulars: "Mrs. McDow came to
the Factory to have some wool carded and from curiosity or
other motive, went in front of the machinery and putting her
hand and arm near the wool cylinder, the sleeve of her dress
was caught, pulling her into the machine and resulting in her
arm being broken and mangled in a most distressing manner.
The body was thrown over in the left of the machine from her
position when caught. The accident happened about two o'clock
p.m. The proprietor, Mr. Wm. Perry, had just left the Factory
and on being sent for, hastened in her assistance, removed her
to his residence and sent to Pendleton for physicians. Drs.
Pickens and Sloan responded promptly and found Mrs. McDow very
much exhausted, so much so that they declined to amputate the
limb until reaction should take place. They applied restora-
tives without effect - professional skill and the most devoted
of attention availed not and after four hours of great suffering, death closed the scene. Her son reached her bedside a
few minutes before she died."

Issue of:
Thursday, September 30, 1869:
Obituary: Departed this life September 14, 1869, at his
residence, in Anderson County, S. C., near Calhoun, Mr.
Daniel Mattison, in the sixty second year of his age. He died
of bilious cramp colic, surviving only about fifty six hours
after he was taken. He was born and raised within seven
miles of his late residence. By industry and economy, he had
accummulated an ample fortune but by the result of the war he
lost some thirty thousand dollars in property but still had
enough left for a good living. He was a good, quiet, unassuming citizen, a kind and obliging neighbor, a friend to the
poor, an affectionate and devoted husband. He joined the
Baptist Church of Christ at Broadmouth upon a profession of his
faith in the Lord Jesus Christ and was baptised into the fellowship of said church on the fourth Sunday in July 1842. Some
years afterwards he removed his membership to the Baptist
church at Shady Grove and lived a consistent member until his
Heavenly Father removed him by death to the church triumphant in
Heaven. He has left an affectionate and bereaved wife and
many relatives and friends to mourn his death but we trust
their loss is his infinite gain; therefore we sorrow not as
those who have no hope for if we believe that Jesus died and
rose again, even so them also which sleep in Jesus will God
bring with him. W. P. M.

Obituary: "Death of Rev. David Humphreys" - It is our mournful
duty this morning to record the death of Rev. David Humphreys,
which occurred at his residence in this county on Tuesday
night after an illness of a few weeks. This exemplary servent
of God, through a long and useful life, had the utmost confidence and respect of everyone with whom he came in contact.
No man in this section has been greater beloved in all relations of life and hundreds and thousands all over the land will
learn of his demise with sorrowing hearts. But he was faithful
in all things and has served the Lord with unabated zeal for
more than a half century. "Henceforth, there is laid up for
him a crown of righteousness." Mr. Humphreys was pastor of

Good Hope and Roberts Churches for nearly fifty years and during all that time, in season and out of season, his charges were never neglected on a single occasion. It was expected for him to preach his semi-centennial sermon at Good Hope Church on the second Sabbath in October. He died in the 76th year of his age. His remains will be interred at Robert's Church today, at 10 o'clock.

Obituary: "Uncle Bob Martin", of Milton, Georgia, died on the 27th of July last, aged 103 years. For 79 years preceding his death he was a Master Mason in good standing. He died in the full possession of his mental faculties.

Issue of:
Thursday, October 14, 1869:
Married: On Thursday evening, 7th inst., at the residence of the bride's father, in Laurens county, by Rev. B. F. Mauldin, Mr. Henry S. Shumate, of Anderson county and Miss J. [..?..] daughter of Mr. Joel Smith.

Obituary: "Death of Dr. William Henry Calhoun" - Our exchange ammounce the death of Dr. Wm. Henry Calhoun, in Lee county, near Tupelo, Mississippi, on the 24th ult. He died suddenly of disease of the heart, whilst visiting a sick patient. He was a native of Abbeville and emigrated to Mississippi in 1845, where he established a high reputation as a Physician and a successful planter. He married in Anderson many years ago, Miss Orr, a sister of Hon. James L. Orr. His wife and four children survive to mourn his loss. Dr. Calhoun was the youngest son of the late James Calhoun, of Abbeville and a nephew of Hon. John C. Calhoun. He was about fifty four years old.

Obituary: Mr. A. W. Shillito, an aged and respected citizen of Abbeville, died in that county, suddenly, on Wednesday last.

Issue of:
Thursday, November 4, 1869:
Married: In the village of Anderson, on Tuesday evening the 26th October, 1869, at the residence of the bride's father, by Rev. J. Scott Murray, Mr. James H. Thornwell, of Yorkville, S. C., son of the late Rev. James H. Thornwell, L.L.D. and Miss Florence L., youngest daughter of Mr. Elias Earle.

Married: In the village of Anderson, on Wednesday, the 27th of October, 1869, by Rev. J. Scott Murray, Mr. Lemuel G. Mauldin of Abbeville county, and Miss Mary J., daughter of the late Mr. H. B. Arnold.

Married: On the evening of the 13th October, 1869, at the residence of the bride's father, in Abbeville county, by Rev. A. Rice, Mr. Abner H. McGee and Miss Sallie M. Jones, all of Abbeville County.

Obituary: Mrs. Agnes Paschall, one of the last widow pensioners of the revolution, died in Georgia lately aged 94.

Obituary: Mr. Otis Mills, for many years a prominent citizen of Charleston and the original owner of the Mills House, died in that city on the 23rd ult., in the 75th year of his age.

Issue of:
Thursday, November 18, 1869:
Married: On Thursday, October 28th, by Rev. Wm. P. Tilden, at
Boston, Mass., Maj. E. W. Everson, of Anderson, S. C. and Miss
Hattie R. Fales, of Delham, Mass.

Married: By A. C. Stepp on Thursday, November 11, 1869, Mr.
Joel M. Acker and Miss Mary Harper, youngest daughter of William
Harper of Anderson county.

Issue of:
Thursday, November 25, 1869:
Married: On the 4th inst., by Rev. W. D. Beverly, Mr. N. O.
Farmer, of Greenville and Miss G. A. Earle, eldest daughter of
Rev. J. R. Earle, of Anderson county.

Married: On the 18th inst., by Rev. W. D. Beverly and Rev. A.
Rice, Rev. W. H. King of Anderson and Miss P. M. Pratt of
Abbeville county.

Obituary: "A Sad Accident" - We have a copy of the Daily Times
published at Jefferson, Texas, containing the particulars of
the death of Richard A. Taylor, eldest son of Isham. W. and
Caroline Taylor, formerly of this place. It seems that on the
first day of this month, in company with two other youths, young
Taylor was engaged in duck hunting, when a flock of ducks were
about coming over them and one of his companions turned to fire
and accidently shot Taylor in the left breast killing him
instantly. He was a quiet unobtrusive boy and was held in high
esteem among his associates. This heart rending occurrence is
deeply lamented by the citizens of Jefferson, who sympathize
alike with the bereaved parents and the unfortunate little
fellow in whose hands the gun was at the time of the fatal
accident. Richard was in the sixteenth year of his age and his
former playmates in this vicinity will receive the news of his
sudden death with unfeigned sorrow and regret.

Issue of:
Thursday, December 2, 1869:
Married: On Wednesday evening, November 24th, 1869, by Rev.
W. H. Stratton, Mr. J. Baylis Lewis and Miss Rebecca, daughter
of William Archer, Esq., all of Anderson.

Obituary: Died, on the 24th of October, last, Mr. George
Campbell, aged 97 years. He was a native of Newberry and when
about 19 years of age came to Anderson where he has resided
ever since. He joined the Presbyterian church about fifteen
years ago and has been a consistent member and on his death
bed professed a willingness to depart and be with Christ. He
left behind him many relatives and friends to mourn his loss.

Obituary: Dr. Wm. Michel, formerly of Charleston, died in
Greenville on Wednesday evening, 17th of November, after a
short illness, in the 76th year of his age. He was a skillful,
kind and attentive physician and greatly beloved by all who
knew him.

Issue of:
Thursday, December 9, 1869:
Married: On Thursday evening, December 2, 1869, by Rev. Samuel
A. Weber, Enoch B. Cater and Miss Lucy Osborne, daughter of

Wm. M. Osborne, Esq., all of Anderson.

Married: On the 2nd of December, by Rev. W. P. Martin, at the residence of the bride's mother, Mr. J. Franklin Gambrell to Miss Susan Austin, all of Abbeville.

Married: On the 25th of November, at 1 o'clock p.m., by Rev. W. F. Pearson, Mr. William J. Vandiver to Miss Nancy Lou, eldest daughter of Mrs. Keaton, all of Anderson county.

Married: By Rev. W. F. Pearson, at 6 o'clock p.m., on the 25th of November, at Centreville, Mr. James Prince to Miss Bell Robinson, both of Abbeville.

Issue of:
Thursday, December 16, 1869:
Married: On Monday evening, December 6, 1869, by Rev. W. P. Martin, at the residence of Mr. Wm. Holmes, in the town of Belton, Mr. Wm. S. Smith and Miss Sarah J. Maddox, all of Anderson.

Married: By the Rev. W. P. Martin, on the 9th December, 1869, at the residence of the bride's father, Mr. Sidney J. Burts and Miss Anna Eliza, youngest daughter of Stephen Latimer, Esq., all of Abbeville.

Issue of:
Thursday, December 30, 1869:
Married: On the 21st of December, 1869, by Rev. W. E. Walters, Dr. John A. Robinson and Miss M. Amanda Pratt, both of Abbeville.

Married: On Wednesday, 22nd of December, 1869, by Rev. D. L. Whitaker, Mr. Joseph L. Winter and Miss M. E. Hall, all of Anderson county.

Issue of:
Thursday, January 6, 1870:
Married: At the residence of the bride's father, on Tuesday 28th of December 1869, by Rev. J. W. Kelly, Mr. Wm. A. Diseker, of Columbia, and Miss Theodate M., second daughter of Col. J. P. Hoyt, of Laurensville, S. C.

Married: By Rev. George F. Round, Tuesday evening, December 28th, Mr. Dresden A. Smith, of Columbia, to Miss Gertrude Small, of Abbeville.

Obituary: "Death of Mr. Milford Burriss" - This sad event occurred at his residence in this town on the 25th of December last. Mr. Burriss had an attack of apoplexy and paralysis combined on Friday of the week previous to his death and never spoke afterwards. He lingered in this condition until Christmas day, when his spirit passed from earth. He was an upright and honest citizen and highly respected by all who knew him. He had been successfully engaged in planting for a number of years and recently moved to this place for the purpose of giving closer attention to his mercantile interests. He was a member of the Baptist church and gave evidence before his death that his faith was well founded.

Issue of:
Thursday, January 13, 1870:
Married: On Tuesday, 4th January inst., by Rev. W. D. Thomas,

Col. G. F. Townes, editor of the Greenville Enterprise and Miss
Mary I. Keith, daughter of the late Wm. L. Keith, Esq.,
formerly of Pickens, S. C.

Obituary: Departed this life, on the 25th day of December,
1869, at his residence in this town, Mr. Milford Burriss, in
the 55th year of his age. [see issue of January 6 above] - The
sadness produced by the death of this esteemed and useful
citizen will long be felt by many hearts. In no case, perhaps,
has death come more unexpectedly or more forcibly suggested to
our minds the solemn declaration of our Lord, "Therefore, be
ye also ready, for in such an hour as you think not the Son of
Man cometh." No man within the range of our knowledge seemed
to possess in a higher degree the elements of a physical
constitution which would encourage the hope of a long life than
did our departed friend. Suddenly, however, and to the aston-
ishment of all, were these hopes crushed by the fatal stroke
which told but too plainly that his days upon earth were
numbered, being deprived the power of speech, as well as in
part the use of his limbs. He remained speechless and helpless for a few days after the shock and then passed into the
spirit world. It is not, however, alone the suddeness with
which fills our hearts with saddness but also the loss which we
have sustained. Industry and perseverance in his chosen
pursuits were strikingly characteristic of him from early life.
To these he attributed, under God's blessing, the practical
knowledge and means which he had acquired and by which he could
be useful to those around him. But it in another and more
sacred relation that his loss is more keenly felt. As a husband he was devoted and kind; as a father affectionate, tender
and indulgent, ever ready to consult the interests and happiness
of those thus committed to him; as a friend, he was ardent and
confiding; but while our hearts are filled with sadness at the
loss which we have sustained in these respects, "we sorrow not
as those without hope." Several years ago he made profession
of religion and united with the Anderson Baptist Church.
Subsequently he removed his membership to a church in the
country, where it remained until about three years ago, when his
wife and two daughters joined the Anderson Church. He then
brought his membership again to the Church of which he was
first a member, where it remained until he was removed, as we
trust, to the church triumphant, where there is no more sickness, pain or death" and there is no night there and they need
no candle for the Lord God is the light of the City"; and there
is no more weeping for God shall wipe the tears from all
faces "and they shall hunger no more, neither thirst anymore".
"Asleep in Jesus, blessed sleep,/ From which none ever wakes to
weep;/ A calm and undisturbed repose,/ Unbroken by the last of
foes."   W. D. B.

Issue of:
Thursday, January 20, 1870:
Obituary: "Death of Another Old Citizen" - It is our melancholy duty to record the death of another useful and honorable
citizen of Anderson. Mr. Elias Earle died at his residence
in this place on Monday morning last, aged about 70 years. His
life was quiet and unobtrusive but he was widely known as a
pure and upright citizen and bore an exemplary character in
every relation towards his fellowman. He was an ardent and
earnest patriot and sacrificed much for the public good.
During the late war his benevolent character shone conspicuous

while his hospitable home was often the abode of weary and
suffering soldiers who will respect his memory and feelingly
revert to his kind attentions. Mr. Earle had never connected
himself with any religious denomination, but he was ever
foremost in all that pertained to the welfare and prosperity
of Zion and seemed to have an abiding interest in the preaching
of the Gospel. He has gone down to the grave full of years and
the honor of an upright course on earth and will be deeply
lamented by a wide circle of friends. The funeral services
were conducted by Rev. Messrs. Murray and Beverly at the Baptist
Church on Tuesday morning amid a large concourse of citizens
and his remains were carried to the family burial place, known
as Beaverdam, about eighteen miles northwest of Anderson, where
the last sad rites took place on yesterday morning.

Issue of:
Thursday, January 27, 1870:
Married: At Storeville, S. C., January 20th, 1870, by Rev.
W. F. Pearson, Mr. James A. Reid, of Abbeville and Miss M.
Marilla, eldest daughter of A. C. Jackson, of Anderson.

Issue of:
Thursday, February 3, 1870:
Married: On the 27th inst., at the residence of the bride's
father, by Rev. W. E. Walters, Mr. S. A. Skelton, and Miss Sue
Roof, all of Anderson District.

Married: At Symmes' Mills, near Pendleton, S. C., on the 27th
inst., by the Rev. Hugh McLees, Miss Marie Symmes, daughter of
the late Dr. F. W. Symmes, to Dr. J. H. Dean of Greenville.

Issue of:
Thursday, February 10, 1870:
Married: By Rev. W. P. Martin, January 30, 1870, at the
residence of the bride's father, Mr. Wm. N. Hammond, of Ander-
son Village and Miss Mary Hamilton, daughter of David Rogers of
Anderson County.

Obituary: Died, of Diphtheria, on the 10th of December, 1869,
Mrs. Laura Cox, wife of David Cox. The subject of this notice
was a daughter of Kenon Breazeale, deceased, who was well
known to many citizens of this county. Mrs. Cox was born
July 27th, 1807 and joined the Baptist Church at Friendship
in September, 1832. She subsequently removed her membership
to Shady Grove church, near Calhoun, where she remained a consistent member. She leaves a kind husband and five children
with many relatives and friends to mourn her loss.

Obituary: Mrs. Sallie Hammond, widow of Col. Le Roy Hammond,
both of them prominently known and honorably identified with
the history of old Edgefield, died recently, aged 87.

Issue of:
Thursday, February 24, 1870:
Married: On February 3, 1870, by Rev. W. P. Martin, Mr. William
Austin and Miss Julia Ann Ashley, all of Anderson county.

Married: On the 21st February, 1870, by Rev. J. I. Bonner, Mr.
W. Cowan Brock, of Honea Path and Miss Anna E. Seawright of
Donaldsville, S. C.

Thursday, March 3, 1870:
Married: February 15, 1870, at the residence of the bride's
father, by Rev. W. F. Pearson, Mr. A. C. Keys and Miss Tabitha
Hall, all of this county.

Issue of:
Thursday, March 10, 1870:
Married: On the morning of March 1, 1870, at the residence
of the bride's aunt, Mrs. Barmore, near Donaldsville, S. C.,
by Rev. Manning Brown, James W. Fowler of Abbeville and Miss
Ella V. Sharpe, of Mississippi.

Married: Near Columbia, S. C., on the 23rd of February, 1870
by Rev. Wm. E. Boggs, Mr. W. Cuttino Smith of Hillsboro, N.C.
and Miss Martha M., eldest daughter of Col. Hart Maxcy.

Married: On Tuesday, March 1st, by Rev. Wm. L. Pressley, Dr.
S. R. Haynie and Miss Lucy J. Norris, all of Anderson county.

Married: On the 3rd of March, at the residence of the bride's
father, by Rev. David Simmons, Mr. J. L. Hardin and Miss M. L.
Sears, all of this county.

Obituary: The Atlanta Intelligencer announces the death of
Mr. W. E. Archer, who was well known in this community. He died
in that city on the 28th of February after suffering twelve
days with a carbuncle. Mr. Archer was in the 54th year of his
age and was esteemed as a worthy and enterprising citizen of
Atlanta where he had been residing for a year or two past. He
has many relatives and friends in this vicinity who will mourn
his untimely death.

Issue of:
Thursday, March 17, 1870:
Married: On the evening of March 8, 1870 at the Methodist
Episcopal Church, Anderson, S. C., by Rev. A. B. Stephens, P. E.,
Mr. James B. Pegg of Anderson and Mrs. Mary Adeline Foran, dau-
ghter of John H. Sebreiner, Esq., of Charleston, S. C.

Obituary: Mr. W. K. Harris died in this village on Sunday
afternoon after a lingering illness of some months. He had
been a resident of Anderson for nearly five years and was
generally esteemed for his kind and benevolent disposition,
together with a faithful discharge of every duty in life. Mr.
Harris was a native of North Carolina though his youthful
days were spent in this vicinity. His family removed to Georgia
about twenty five years ago and afterward to Tennessee from
which latter State he came back to Anderson early in 1865. He
was in the 45th year of his age. The remains of Mr. Harris
were escorted from his residence by the Masonic fraternity and
the Sons of Temperance to the Methodist Church where the
funeral discourse was delivered by Rev. W. A. Hodges before a
large and attentive congregation. He was buried in the Presbyterian churchyard with Masonic honors.

Obituary: Mr. Jonathan T. Harrison departed this life at his
residence, three miles west of Anderson, on last Monday morning.
For more than five years Mr. Harrison has been a sufferer of
rheumatism and has nearly all that time been confined to the

to the house by this affliction. He bore his great sufferings
with an uncomplaining spirit and was at all times resigned
to the will of God. Mr. Harrison removed from Fairfield to this
place about seventeen years ago and has ever been held in high
esteem as a citizen. He served in the Confederate army for
several years and in the discharge of his duties as a soldier
contracted the disease which terminated his life. He was about
45 years of age. The funeral sermon over the remains of Mr.
Harrison was preached by Rev. W. D. Beverly in the Baptist
Church after which the Masons took charge of the body and with
appropriate honors deposited in the grave all that was mortal
of their deceased brother.

Issue of:
Thursday, April 7, 1870:
Sudden Death: The numerous friends and acquaintances of Mr.
John B. Smith will be pained to learn of his sudden death which
sad event occurred at his mother's residence four miles east
of this place on the 29th inst. Mr. Smith was a quiet, unobtrusive gentleman respected by all who knew him. He had been
in bad health for the last two years. He was buried with
Masonic honors in the Presbyterian churchyard on Thursday last.

Issue of:
Thursday, April 14, 1870:
Married: On Thursday evening April 7th, 1870, at the residence
of the bride's father, by Rev. W. E. Walters, Mr. George A.
Wagener, of Charleston, S. C. and Miss Eleanor E., eldest
daughter of J. Crawford Keys, Esq., of Anderson, S. C.

Issue of:
Thursday, May 5, 1870:
Obituary: Mr. Albert Hackett, an old and well known citizen,
died suddenly at his residence two miles north of this place on
Friday night last.

Obituary: Mr. William J. Hix, an energetic and useful citizen
of this county, died on Saturday last and was buried at the
Baptist church in this place on Sunday.

Obituary: The Walhalla Courier announces the death of Mr.
Elijah Alexander, Sr. one of the most highly respected citizens
of Pickens County, in the ninety eighth year of his age. The
deceased had lived to see his county achieve its independence
and through the mutations of time witness its demoralization,
degredation and loss of liberty.

Issue of:
Thursday, May 12, 1870:
Married: On May 5th, 1870 by Rev. J. B. Traywick, Capt.
Thomas L. Williams, of Greenville, Tennessee and Miss Mary M.
Simpson, daughter of Hon. R. F. Simpson of Anderson County,
South Carolina.

Obituary: Died, on the 28th of March, of typhoid fever, at his
residence near Water Valley, Mississippi, Mathew Thompson
Miller, in the 64th year of his age. The deceased was born
in Abbeville and spent the greater portion of his life in
Anderson District, S. C. He was beloved and respected by all
who knew him. He was a devoted and working Christian and a
member of the Methodist church. He was buried by the Masons
of which fraternity he was also a member.

Obituary: Died, on the 4th inst., Ellen Mazyck, youngest child of Robert W. and Jane W. Hume, aged one year and five months.

Issue of:
Thursday, May 19, 1870:
Married: On Thursday evening, May 12, 1870, by Rev. J. Kennedy, Mr. P. McD. Alexander of Oconee County and Miss Mary E. Hagood, eldest daughter of James E. Hagood, Esq., of Pickens C. H.

Married: On Tuesday, 10th of May, by Rev. W. E. Walters, Mr. John J. Hardy, of Lowndesville, S. C. and Miss Fannie M., daughter of Samuel Knox, Esq., of Franklin County, Ga.

Issue of:
Thursday, May 26, 1870:
Married: On the morning of the 22nd inst., at the residence of the bride's father, by Rev. A. Rice, Mr. Robert Hadden and Miss Emma Francis, second daughter of Mr. Roger Williams, all of Abbeville county.

Obituary: Died, at the residence of her husband in Belton on the 11th day of May 1870, Mary E. Stringer, wife of A. J. Stringer. She was born January 28, 1837 and was married November 3, 1857. From her youth she was the subject of serious religious impressions but professed no change of heart until during the summer of 1868. On the 30th of August, 1868, she united herself to the Belton Baptist Church and was baptized a few days afterwards with her husband and many others. From the time she identified herself with the Church she manifested the most untiring interest in everything in any way promotive of the interest of the Redeemer's Kingdom. Her place in the Church was never vacant when she was able to attend and she was ever ready to encourage others in the performance of Christian duty. Her intimate friends who were without hope in Christ found in her a quiet, faithful counsellor and realized that she felt a prayerful interest in their salvation. During her last illness, which was severe and lasted several weeks, eminently manifested that patience which comes from the exercise of a saving faith in the Lord Jesus Christ. Not a murmuring word escaped her lips and even when she knew that the disease could not be broken up, unmurmuringly she would take whatever her kind physician and friends thought best for her. During her illness she talked with her husband in reference to her hopes in Christ and spoke many words of consolation as to her future prospects. A few days before her death when asked by a friend if she enjoyed the presence of her Saviour in her afflictions she replied, "Yes, and in prayer I feel that I can draw nearer to God than ever before." When asked if she felt resigned to the will of God and could trust entirely in Him, she replied that "she could trust all in the hands of her Saviour and felt assured that He would never forsake her and that He would take care of those she loved in this world." When the last moment came she quietly fell asleep in Jesus, the immortal spirit passing from the conflicts of earth to the joys of the better world. She leaves a devoted husband and an affectionate boy, with many relatives and friends to mour her departure. Though the affliction is severe, yet it is best and though her death has made desolate the household of which she was the light, her friends should be encouraged with the hope "that they may meet her again in the heavenly land."

Obituary: The remains of Mr. John L. Humphreys did not reach this place until Saturday evening last. A large crowd of friends and acquaintances were assembled at the depot and the body was carried to Masonic Hall where it remained until next morning. The funeral services took place at Robert's Church on Sunday, Rev. W. E. Walters officiating. The untimely death of Mr. H. is truly lamented by our people, among whom he was reared and by whom he was warmly esteemed.

Issue of:
Thursday, June 9, 1870:
Married: On the 31st May, 1870, at the residence of Capt. F. W. R. Nance, by Rev. John M. Carlisle, Dr. T. A. Hudgens, of Honea Path, S. C. and Miss Ella Gaines of Anderson.

Married: At Tip Top, near Pendleton, June 1, 1870, by Rev. J. Scott Murray, Mr. R. E. Sloan and Miss S. M. Maxwell, second daughter of Mrs. C. L. Maxwell.

Obituary: "Death of Mr. Robert Brackenridge" - It is our duty this morning to announce the death of the oldest male inhabitant of Anderson county. Mr. Robert Brackenridge departed this life at his residence nine miles southeast of this place on Friday night last in the 91st year of his age. He was a native of County Antrim, Ireland and came to this country when quite a youth. Mr. Brackenridge was engaged in school teaching the greater portion of his long life, having entered upon that avocation in Abbeville about the year 1800. He taught consecutively from that time until within the past few months but for a number of years he followed the occupation only nominally. He was universally esteemed for his sterling worth and integrity and numbered among his friends, patrons and pupils nearly every prominent citizen of Anderson for the last half century. He was a member of the Masonic fraternity and probably the oldest Mason in this section of the State. He likewise belonged to the Presbyterian denomination and was a consistent member of that church. He possessed the genuine humor of his native country and we have heard several incidents in his life worth relating. It is said that on a certain occasion Mr. Brackenridge visited this place when Court was in session and looking around at the officers of the Court and members of the bar, remarked to a friend that he had whipped every one of them including Judge Earle who was presiding and Gen. Whitner then Solicitor of this circuit as well as the Clerk, Sheriff and all the lawyers. Of course the remark was repeated until it reached the ears of the Judge who shortly ordered an adjournment of the Court and every one began to gather around the old gentleman for he had then reached an advanced period in life. The scene which followed can better be imagined than described and it was one upon which this venerable citizen loved to dwell over afterwards. He survived the distinguished Judge many years and had lived to see many of those present go down to the grave. And now, at the close of a very long, useful and honorable career on earth, he has been fathered to his fathers and we trust that he reposes in eternal peace.

Issue of:
Death of Another Citizen: We are again called upon to record
the death of an esteemed, useful and honorable citizen of
Anderson. Mr. A. C. Jackson departed this life at his residence, in this county, on Thursday night last, after a long
and painful illness, aged about 50 years. He was stricken
down in the midst of an active life and is a serious loss to
his family and the community at large. Mr. Jackson was a native
of Spartanburg, we believe, and had resided in this county
for the past ten years. He was an Elder of the Presbyterian
church at Varennes and adorned the profession of a Christian.
He was a worthy member of the Masonic fraternity and was
buried with the honrs of that ancient institution on Sunday
morning at Varennes church. The funeral sermon was delivered
by Rev. W. F. Pearson in the presence of a large concourse of
sorrowing friends and neighbors.

Obituary: Mr. Richard Watts, an old and much esteemed citizen
of Laurens, died at his residence on the Saluda recently.

Issue of:
Thursday, July 7, 1870:
Obituary: Mr. John Barker, of Fairfield, died on the 26th
ult., aged 86 years. He was a soldier in the war of 1812.

Issue of:
Thursday, July 28, 1870:
Obituary: Died, January 4, 1870 at the residence of her husband near Townville, S. C., Mrs. Harriet N. Woolbright, wife of
Wm. S. Woolbright and daughter of the late James R. Fant. She
was about forty four years old. About fourteen years ago she
united herself to the Townville Baptist Church by a public
profession of her faith in Jesus Christ. She always manifested
the greatest interest in everything connected with the prosperity of her Church and when able she was a regular attendant
on the ministrations of the sanctuary. She was severly
afflicted for the last four years of her life, being often
entirely helpless. These sad afflictions she bore with that
resignation and christian fortitude which always adorned her
life. Her prayer was, "Not my will, O Lord, but thine be
done". She had a large circle of relatives and friends and
was universally beloved by all who knew her. For several days
before her death she exhorted all who visited her to lead a
godly life. Among the recollections of her last hours was the
very earnest prayers for the prosperity of her Church. When
the eve of life with her had truly come, she called her children
to her, one by one, gave them a mother's dying blessing and bid
them so to live as to meet her in heaven. At last she called
her husband to her and praying the blessing of God upon him and
and the children, bid him farewell for a little while, until
they should meet on the shores of the better land. When the
last moment came she was like the soldier who had fought the
good fight, ready to fall asleep in the arms of her Saviour.
"Asleep in Jesus, blessed sleep,/ From which none ever wake
to weep". She leaves a large circle of relatives and friends
to mourn her loss. Mourning friends, quell sorrowing tempest
of your souls and drive back the bitter tears for soon, by
the peace of God, you may greet her on the shores of a blessed
immortality.   A Friend

Issue of:
Thursday, August 4, 1870:
Married: At the residence of the bride's father in Hartwell,
Ga. on the 27th inst. by Rev. J. H. Grogan, Dr. Charlie Webb
and Miss Myra P. Benson, daughter of John B. Benson, Esq.

Issue of:
Thursday, September 1, 1870:
Obituary: Died at his residence near Pendleton Village, on
the morning of August 23rd, 1870, Capt. John Maxwell in the
79th year of his age.

Obituary: Mrs. Eliza C. Marshall, relict of Dr. S. Marshall,
formerly of Abbeville, died on the 11 th of August in the city
of Greenville, aged 72 years.

Obituary: Rev. John T. Pressley, D.D., an eminent divine of
the Associate Reformed church and formerly of Abbeville, died
at his home in Alleghany City, Penn. on the 13th of August,
aged 76 years.

Issue of:
Thursday, September 15, 1870:
Obituary: The Edgefield Advertiser records the death of Mrs.
Rebecca Griffin, relict of the late Col. Richard Griffin in the
84th year of her age.

Obituary: Also the death of Dr. W. M. Burt, who removed from
Edgefield to Louisiana some four years ago.

Issue of:
Thursday, October 20, 1870:
Married: At the residence of the bride's father in this
County, on Thursday evening, the 6th inst., by Rev. J. Scott
Murray, Dr. Thomas T. Earle, of Sumter County, to Miss Sallie
F., daughter of Mr. John B. Earle.

Obituary: "Death of an Aged Lady" - Mrs. Mary McMahon was
buried at Good Hope Church in this county on Saturday, Oct.
8th. She was a native of Ireland and was buried upon her
98th birthday. She had lived for many years in Anderson
county and was greatly esteemed among her neighbors. Up to
a few months since she was remarkably active for one of her
advanced age.

Issue of:
Thursday, November 3, 1870:
Married: On Tuesday morning, 25th of October, by Rev. O. T.
Porcher, W. A. Lee, Esq., Editor of the Abbeville Press and
Banner and Miss V. D. Cade, all of Abbeville District.

Married: On Thursday, October 20th, by the Rev. D. D. Byers,
Mr. W. Edward Sears and Miss Lucinda M. Hix, all of this County.

Issue of:
Thursday, November 10, 1870:
Married: At the residence of the bride's mother on the 27th
of October, by Rev. W. P. Jacobs, Mr. David H. Glenn, of Fair
Play and Miss Lucy H. Byrd of Laurens.

Obituary: Died, September 6, 1870, at the residence of his mother in Anderson county, W. H. Stephenson in the 27th year of his age. Mr. Stephenson was a brave soldier, a good citizen and an affectionate son. He has left a large circle of friends to mourn his loss.

Issue of:
Thursday, November 17, 1870:
Obituary: Died, in this county on the [?] of September, Maj. John M. Thompson, after a short illness, in the 58th year of his age. The deceased was a native of Anderson District, S. C. where he resided until 1843 when he moved to Lauderdale, thence to Carroll county, Mississippi, where he engaged in the business of planting. Here he reared a large family of children and surrounded himself with all the comforts of wealth and prosperity. But the rich lands of Arkansas which were then coming into favorably notice, attracted his attention in 1856 and he sold his plantation in Carroll county and moved to this county, in the Fall of that year, settling in Spring Creek Township. Unfortunately he selected extremely low lands which proved unhealthy, in consequence of which, sickness of his family and the trials incident to opening a plantation in the heart of an almost wilderness county, subjected him for the first few years to great hardships. His patient industry, however, finally overcame the numerous obstacles he had to encounter; but about the time he began to enjoy the fruits of his life-long labor, disaster made inroads upon his family fold and up to the period of his death he had buried his beloved wife and six out of eleven children. Two of his sons, Dr. James Thompson and Ben Thompson - both young men of fine education and promising talents, died in the Confederate service. These afflictive strokes of Providence sunk deep into his mind and saddened him to the day of his death. For the past few years, it may be said, affliction had marred his life; for there was not the brightness and the cheerfulness, the energy nor the enterprise which characterized his earlier days. In his walk through life, it can be emphatically said of Maj. Thompson, he was upright, generous and true. No husband or parent was ever more beloved; no neighbor was kinder; no citizen among us more esteemed for rectitude of conduct. For many years he was a member of the Presbyterian Church and died in the glorious belief and hope of a higher and better life in the realm of eternity. He was buried by the Mariana Chapter of Royal Arch Masons of which he was an exemplary companion. Five children, two grandchildren and a large circle of kindred in South Caroline and Alabama survive to mourn his loss. May they find consolation in the good life he lived and emilate the precious heritage of his good name. Helena, Arkansas Monitor

Issue of:
Thursday, December 15, 1870:
Married: On December 5, 1870, at the residence of Mr. Enoch Drake, by Rev. W. F. Pearson, Mr. James F. Rogers and Miss Fannie M. Robinson, both of Anderson County.

Married: On November 24, 1870, by Rev. W. F. Pearson, Mr. Isaac Robinson and Miss Polly Ann Strickland, both of Anderson County.

Issue of:
Thursday, December 22, 1870:
Married: On the evening of December 15, 1870 at the residence of the bride's father, in Abbeville county, by Rev. A. Rice, Mr. Samuel C. Riley and Miss Sallie H. Sharp, both of Abbeville County.

Married: On Sunday morning, December 11, 1870, by Rev. W. B. Singleton at the residence of the same, Mr. A. N. Mulligan, of Anderson County and Miss Mattie Ann Ellison of Pickens County.

Issue of:
Thursday, January 5, 1871:
Married: On Thursday evening, December 22, 1870, by Rev. J. T. Vernon, of Hart County, Ga., Mr. S. L. Bollman and Miss E. J. Dobbins, both of Anderson county.

Married: On Thursday, 22nd of December, 1870, by Rev. F. G. Carpenter, Mr. N. S. Maddox and Miss F. E. Bailey, all of Anderson county.

Married: On the 21st of December, 1870, by Rev. J. H. McMullen, Mr. Thos. J. Holland and Miss Sue E. Reeder, all of Hart Co., Georgia.

Married: On the 22nd of December, 1870, by Rev. Mr. Nicholson, Mr. John Brownlee, of Abbeville and Miss Cora C. Holland, of Anderson County.

Married: On the 22nd of December, 1870, by Rev. W. E. Welborn, Mr. Wm. M. Hall and Miss Mary E. Keown, all of Anderson county.

Obituary: The Laurensville Herald records the death of Col. John Hudgens, a prominent citizen and estimable gentleman. In his early days he served the people as Sheriff of the District and later in life represented Laurens in the Legislature. He was the father of Dr. Thos. A. Hudgens, of Honea Path.

Issue of:
Thursday, January 12, 1871:
Obituary: "Death of An Aged Lady" - Mrs. Elizabeth Emerson, widow of an old Revolutionary soldier, died at the residence of her son-in-law, Mr. John Carpenter, in this County, on the 29th of November last. She was born in Ireland on the 15th of August, 1770, and was consequently upwards of one hundred years old at the time of her death. Her parents removed to this country when was quite a child, and the last sixty years of her life were spent in Anderson County. During the past year we have recorded the deaths of three very aged residents of this county, and all of them were natives of Ireland.

Issue of:
Thursday, January 19, 1871:
Married: On Tuesday evening, December 27, 1870, by Rev. H. Nixon Hays, Mr. L. Orr Davis and Miss C. Malissa Grant, all of Oconee county.

Married: On Thursday evening, 29th of December, 1870, by Rev. J. R. Earle, Mr. Robert Dunlap and Miss Mary Fisher, all of Anderson County.

Married: On January 10, 1870 [should be 1871?] by Rev. A. P.
Nicholson, Dr. S. W. Clayton, of Pickens and Miss Lou F.,
youngest daughter of Rev. J. L. Kennedy of Pendleton, S. C.

Issue of:
Thursday, January 26, 1871:
Married: At the residence of the bride's uncle in Griffin, Ga.,
on the 12th inst., by Rev. B. F. Mauldin, Mr. J. L. Mauldin
of Charleston, and Miss Gena M. Evans, daughter of the late
J. E. B. Evans, of Griffin.

Issue of:
Thursday, February 2, 1871:
Married: On Sunday morning, January 15, 1871, at the residence
of the bride's mother in Williamston, by Rev. J. A. Wood, Mr.
John M. Gambrell, of Abbeville county, and Miss Cassie Clink-
scales, of Anderson county.

Married: On January 10, 1871, by Rev. W. P. Martin, at the
residence of R. D. Dean, Esq., the bride's stepfather, Mr.
A. J. Stringer and Miss Mary E. Rice, all of the Town of Belton,
Anderson county.

Married: By Rev. W. P. Martin, on January 5, 1871, at the
residence of the bride's father, Mr. James T. Greer and Miss
Francis E. Cummins, eldest daughter of Mr. William Cummins
[Cummings] all of Anderson county.

Married: By Rev. W. P. Martin, on November 27, 1870, at the
residence of the bride's mother, Mr. Warren S. Flemming, of
Anderson county, and Miss Mary F. Mattison, of Abbeville County.

Obituary: Mrs. Martha Gregg, consort of Mr. Hugh Gregg, was
born in Edgefield and died in Anderson County, S. C., January
6, 1871.   Our deceased sister had been a pilgrim on earth about
seventy years.   For something over twenty years she was a
member of the Baptist Church.   Meekly and unassumingly she
performed her duties, "looking unto Jesus", the "spring of her
joys, and life of her delights".   During her last sickness no
word of murmur escaped through her lips.   It is precious to
surviving friends to know that although disease made severe
inroads on her frail constitution, her faith in Christ enabled
her to meet them with calm resignation to His will.   It was the
privilege of the writer several times to visit her during her
protracted affliction.   Even to the last, when far out in
"deaths cold flood", she waved the signal of triumph and the
presence of Jesus.   May the God of all Grace, sanctify this
dispensation of His providence to the good of surviving husband, children and friends.   "Thy art gone to the grave, but
we will not deplore thee".   W. A. H.

Issue of:
Thursday, February 9, 1871:
Sudden Death: We regret to announce the sudden death of Mr.
John Baylis Earle, a well known citizen of this county, which
occurred on Friday last.   In crossing Seneca river, at Sloan's
Ferry, he was taken ill suddenly while in the flatboat and was
carried to his home, a few hundred yards distant, where he
breathed his last in about an hour.   Some mismanagement on the
part of the boat hands caused Mr. Earle to use great exertions

to remedy the defect, which brought on an attack of heart
disease to which he was subject, we understand. Mr. Earle
was in the 68th year of his age. He was buried on Sunday
at the Deep Creek place, where the funeral services were
conducted by Rev. J. S. Murray. The obsequies were largely
attended by relatives, friends and acquaintances.

Issue of:
Thursday, February 16, 1871:
Married: On Thursday, the 12th of January, by Rev. H. N. Hays,
Mr. Warren D. Moore, and Miss Eveline Baldwin, all of Oconee
county.

Married: By Rev. H. N. Hays, on Thursday, 26th of January, Mr.
William Campbell and Miss Mary Cox, all of Oconee county.

Married: By Rev. H. N. Hays, on Thursday, 2nd of February, Mr.
William Pitts, of Oconee county and Miss C. C. Patterson of
Anderson county.

Married: On the 9th inst., by Rev. S. Isbell, Mr. James A.
Weldon, of Hart county, Ga., and Miss Martha J. Elgin of
Anderson county.

Married: On the 4th inst., by Rev. S. Isbell, Mr. Franklin
Barton, son of Rev. H. N. Barton and Miss Nancy Isbell, all of
Oconee county.

Married: On the 22nd December, last, by Rev. S. Isbell, Mr.
Frederick Davis&Miss Eliza J. Maret, all of Oconee county.

Issue of:
Thursday, February 23, 1871:
A Terrible Tragedy: It is with much pain that we chronicle
the occurrence of an unfortunate tragedy in our community. On
yesterday morning, about 2 o'clock, Mr. James Hyde, a citizen
of this County, who lives but a few miles from the city, was
killed by Mr. W. G. Long, one of our citizens. The jury have
not yet completed their investigation of the affair; but we
are led to believe that the terrible deed was committed by
Long while he was laboring under a fit of mental hallucination;
to which he is known to have been subject. After shooting his
victim, he crushed his skull with blows dealth with the stock
of the gun. The unfortunate man lingered until last night, when
he died. Mr. Hyde was an old man, of peaceable habits and leaves
a family to lament his melancholy death.   Greenville Mountainee

Issue of:
Thursday, March 2, 1871:
Married: Near Oconee Station, on the 14th inst., by Rev.
Fletcher Smith, Mr. N. J. Brown, of Anderson, to Miss Margaret
E. Todd of Oconee.

Married: At the residence of the bride's father, on the evening of the 22nd inst., by Rev. W. H. King, Mr. D. J. Bohannon
and Miss N. E., eldest daughter of John H. Jones, all of
Anderson county.

Married: On the 21st inst., by the Rev. J. M. Moode, Mr. W. B.
Lowrance, of Columbia, S. C., to Miss Mamie, only daughter of
J. M. Cochran, Esq., of Cokesbury, S. C.

Married: On Thursday evening, February 23, 1871, by Rev. D. D. Byers, Mr. James Seaborn and Miss Anna Mason, all of Oconee County, S. C.

Married: On Sunday evening, February 10, 1871, at the residence of the bride's father, by Rev. A. Rice, Mr. Walker H. Higgins and Miss Annie Agnew, all of Abbeville county.

Issue of:
Thursday, March 9, 1871:
Obituary: Died, in Adnerson County, S. C., on the 19th of January 1871, Thomas McConnell, in the 84th year of his age. The subject of this notice was born in Newberry County, and in 1822 removed to what was then Pendleton District and settled in the neighborhood of Concord Church. Mr. McConnell was a man of more than ordinary intelligence, and the greater part of his active life was spent in teaching school in Newberry, Laurens and Anderson. He was an exemplary and active Christian and derived much comfort, when the infirmities of old age came upon him, from the reading and meditation of the Holy Scripture.

Issue of:
Thursday, March 23, 1871:
Married: On the 26th of February, 1871, by Rev. W. F. Martin, at the residence of Elihu Smith, Mr. John Davis and Widow Thana Griffin, all of Anderson county.

Issue of:
Thursday, April 13, 1871:
Married: On Wednesday evening, April 5th, at the residence of the bride's father, by Rev. D. E. Frierson, Capt. Thos. P. Benson, of Anderson, and Miss Mallie E. McGee, third daughter of G. W. McGee, Esq., of Belton.

Married: On Sunday morning April 2nd, by Rev. W. A. Hodges, Mr. Wiley S. Masters, and Miss Amanda Smith, all of Anderson County.

Death of An Honored Citizen: It is with sincere regret that we record the death of Col. D. L. Donnald, of Williamston, which occurred at his residence in that place on last Saturday morning, after an illness of less than 24 hours. The deceased was an honorable, upright citizen, greatly esteemed by a large circle of friends and acquaintances. He served with distinction as an officer of the Confederate army. Col. Donnald was a native of Abbeville District and removed to Williamston only a few years ago. His remains were buried on Tuesday last with Masonic honors.

Issue of:
Thursday, April 20, 1871:
Obituary: Mr. John Markley, of Greenville, died on the night of the 8th inst.

Obituary: David M. Glover, Esq., of Edgefield county, died on last Sunday, aged sicty-five.

Obituary: Mr. Jacob Rawl, the former deputy sheriff of Lexington county, died in Alabama a short time since.

Obituary: Miss Gussie Henry, daughter of Dr. Nathan Henry, formerly of Laurens, died at Due West on the 4th inst., of congestion.

Issue of:
Thursday, April 27, 1871:
Mrs. Atwood, an old and highly esteemed lady, died at Greenville on Sunday afternoon.

Henry Cannon and Taylor Palmer both colored, were hung at Union last Friday, for the murder of G. M. Stephens last December.

Mr. Berry Hawkins, a farmer living some eight miles above Greenville, and near Paris Mountain, committed suicide on Saturday morning, last, by shooting himself through the head with a pistol.

The Greenville Mountaineer states that the body of Mr. Porter B. Burnham was found lying on the ground in his mother's yard, on Sunday morning of last week, and although there were signs of life remaining, all efforts of resuscitation proved ineffectual.

The Greenville Mountaineer says that Mr. Campbell, a road carpenter on the Greenville and Columbia Railroad, was killed on Tuesday, 18th instant, in the vicinity of Williamston, by being run over by a dirt train.

Married: On Wednesday evening, April 19th, at the residence of Mr. M. J. Wilson, by Rev. J. S. Murray, Mr. R. F. McKinney and Miss Elizabeth Snow, both of this village.

Issue of:
Thursday, May 4, 1871:
Obituary: Col. David L. Donnald

Issue of:
Thursday, May 11, 1871:
Married: On the 2d instant, at Equality, Anderson County, S. C., at the residence of the bride's father, by Rev. J. L. Kennedy, Mr. Thomas W. Davis of Greenville, and Miss Carrie McCann, of the former place.

Issue of:
Thursday, May 18, 1871:
Married: On the evening of May 10th, 1871, by the Rev. A. Rice, at his residence, Mr. John R. Puckett, of Oconee County, to Miss Mary F. Browne, only daughter of J. M. Browne of Anderson County.

Issue of:
Thursday, May 25, 1871:
Married: At the residence of the bride's uncle, Major F. C. V. Borstel, on the 16th of November, 1870, by the Rev. W. E. Boggs, of Columbia, Mr. N. C. Joyner, of Richland County, and Miss Cassa B. Dorrill, of Anderson, S. C.

Married: At the residence of the bride's uncle, Major F. C. V. Borstel, on the 17th of May, 1871, by Rev. J. S. Murray, Mr. Samuel Cunningham and Miss Caro H. Dorrill, both of Anderson, S. C.

110

Married: In Townville on Saturday, the 13th of May, 1871, by
Rev. H. N. Hays, Mr. W. F. Jeans and Miss Mary S. Palmer, all
of Anderson County.

Married: On Sunday May 14th, 1871, by Rev. H. N. Hays, Mr.
James Barton and Miss Martha Simmons, all of Anderson County.

Death of a Worthy Citizen: We are pained to chronicle the death
of Dr. S. R. Haynie, an exemplary and worthy citizen of this
county, which sad event occured at his residence near Holland's
Store, on Friday morning last. Dr. Haynie was an energetic,
devoted member of the medical profession, and was highly
respected by the entire community. His remains were buried
with Masonic honors at Flat Rock Church, on Saturday afternoon,
in the presence of a large concourse of relatives, friends and
acquaintances.

Death of Capt. Wm. Steele: We learn with sincere regret that
this aged and honored citizen of Oconee county departed this
life on the 15th inst. Capt. Steele in early life belonged to
the United States Navy, but the greater portion of his lengthened existence on earth was spent in this section of the State
to which he was devotedly attached; and at various times in
his life, Capt. Steele served the people with fidelity and zeal
in the Legislature and in other positions of honorable trust.
He was a genial, pleasant gentleman, and warmly endeared to a
large circle of friends. He was upwards of eighty years of age.

Homicide in Winnsboro: Mr. John W. Clark, formerly of Pendleton, killed by W. D. Aiken.

Issue of:
Thursday, June 22, 1871:
Death of An Old Citizen: It is with sincere regret that we
record the death of Halbert Acker, Esq., which occured at his
residence near Calhoun on last Friday in the 73rd year of his
age. Mr. Acker was at work in a field some distance from his
residence, and not responding to the signal for dinner, the
family became alarmed, and went in quest for him, when he was
found lying dead in the field. It is supposed that he died
suddenly from heart diease. Mr. Acker was a worthy citizen
and most highly respected. He was one of the most prominent
citizens in this section of the county, and as a kind obliging
neighbor was loved by all.

Issue of:
Thursday, June 29, 1871: Married: On Thursday evening, June
22, 1871, at the residence of the bride's father, by Rev. D. E.
Frierson, Mr. H. B. Fant and Miss Eugenia Carlisle, all of
Anderson.

Obituary: Departed this life on the 26th of May, 1871, Mrs.
Fannie Leonora Horton, wife of Dr. O. R. Horton, and daughter
of Israel Charles. She was born the 31st of May, 1866. When
married, she removed to Abbeville County, near Cokesbury, where
her husband had been for sometime practicing medicine. In a
month or two after her marriage, she made a profession of
religion, and united herself to the Walnut Grove Baptist Church.
In the prosperity of the Church she felt the most abiding
interest, and in word and action did all she could for the
cause of Jesus. None who were associated with her ever for the
moment doubted the truth of her Christianity. "A tree is

known by its fruit", and such was the devotion and obedience of her life to the commands of God that all felt assured that her reward was in Heaven. Though naturally of a timid and withdrawing disposition, yet by her amiability, her sincerety, and her general loveliness of character, she soon gathered around her a large circle of friends who continued to admire and love her the more they knew of her. During last winter she removed with her husband to Belton, and united with the Baptist Church at that place. For some time previous to her death, she seemed impressed with the conviction that her departure was near at hand. She, therefore, often spoke of it, and always expressed her perfect resignation, if it was the Will of God to call her away. To those who survive her she has given every assurance "that her passing spirit gently fled, sustained by grace divine", to the Christian home in glory. During her last severe illness, not a murmuring word escaped her, and on the 26th day of May, 1871, she calmly fell asleep in Jesus—"that sleep from which none ever wake to weep." On the following day she was buried in the graveyard at the Baptist Church of Belton. The last solemn rites to the memory of the departed were performed in the middle of a large circle of afflicted relatives and friends. She leaves a kind husband and two sweet children with a large family circle to mourn her departure. Deep as in the grief this affliction brings, they are the subjects of that sweet admonition. "Weep not as those who have no hope; for if we believe Jesus died and rose again, even to them also which sleep in Jesus will God bring with him."
Pastor

Issue of:
Thursday, July 13, 1871:
Obituary: Died, on the 5th of June, at her residence in Anderson District, Mrs. Mary Campbell, widow of the late George Campbell, aged 84 years. She was born in Ireland, and was brought to this county in early childhood. She was for 17 years a member of the Presbyterian Church, and on her deathbed professed her willingness to depart and her expectation of returning into rest and being with Jesus. She left behind her many relations and friends to deplore their loss.

Issue of:
Thursday, August 10, 1871:
Married: At his residence, by Rev. A. Rice, on Monday morning, 31st of July, at eight o'clock, Mr. Benjamin Perry Gambrell, of Williamston, and Miss Mary Jane Bagwell, of Belton, S. C.

Married: On the 10th day of April, 1871, by Judge Spaulding, Dr. E. B. Moore, formerly of Anderson, S. C., and Mrs. Charlotte Minerva Dunlap, widow of Judge Dunlap, all of Callusa City, California.

Obituary: Mr. John C. Colwell, an aged and highly esteemed citizen of Spartanburg county, died at his residence on the 18th ult., in the 75th year of his age.

Obituary: Mr. A. G. Field, a highly respectable citizen of Pickens county, is dead. Mr. Field was a member of the Baptist Church, and highly respected by all who knew him.

Death of An Estimable Lady: It is our painful duty to announce the death of Mrs. Martha Cater, the wife of Dr. A. P. Cater, of this town, and third daughter of the late E. B. Benson, Esq., of Pendleton. Although in feeble health for some time, Mrs. Cater was not considered in a dangerous condition until two days before her death, which occured on Sunday night last, in the 52nd year of her age. Truly, a mother in Israel has fallen! Self-sacrificing in spirit, unselfishly devoted to the ties of domestic life, her home was the abode of tenderness, refinement and hospitality. Her benevolent disposition always found delight in deeds of charity, and her unobtrusive life was aseries of kind action and gentle ministrations to the wants of her fellow creatures. "Softly Death touched her, and she passed away - Out of this bright world that she had made more fair." The funeral obsequies took place at the Presbyterian Church on Tuesday morning, and were conducted by Rev. D. E. Frierson, assisted by Rev. J. S. Murray. A large and attentive congregation attended the deep sympathy of our community in this afflictive dispensation of Providence, and manifested the respect and esteem of all classes for the lamented deceased. A wide circle of friends, relatives and acquaintances will receive this sad intelligence with sorrowful hearts, but "they mourn not as those without hope", for she that was a blessing to them has only gone before, to join the ransomed throng beyond the skies.

Issue of:
Thursday, August 17, 1871:
Fatal Accident: A terrible accident occurred at Hunnicutt's Crossing, on the Blue Ridge Railroad last Thursday evening, resulting the death of Mr. John Calhoun Clemson, grandson of Hon. John C. Calhoun, and only son of Hon. Thos. G. Calhoun, of Pendleton. It appears, from the testimony taken at the inquest held by John C. Whitfield, Esq., Trial Justice and acting Coroner, that a lumber train belonging to the Greenville Railroad ran into the passenger train of the Blue Ridge Raod at the place designated, and that Mr. Clemson, in attempting to get into the second-class car, was thrown violently against the facing of the car door, and fatally injured in the region of the heart, one of his ribs penetrating that organ. [Lengthy article follows]

Issue of:
Thursday, August 24, 1871:
Married: On the 9th of July, by Rev. W. P. Martin, Mr. Baylis Kelly and Miss Elizabeth Kelly, all of Anderson County.

Sudden Death: We are grieved to record the sudden and unexpected death of Mr. T. F. Millwee, which occurred in Dallas county, Texas, on the 21st of July. He was engaged in work at a saw mill, and while assisting to take a log off a wagon, the log rolled upon him and crushed him instantly to death. Mr. Millwee was a native of Anderson, and had been on a visit to his mother and relatives the past spring, and only returned about three months since to his Western home. He was about 27 years of age. The unexpected news of his death is a crushing blow to an aged mother, with whom we deeply sympathize in this sad affliction.

Obituary: Death has again summoned from our midst an estimable wife and mother, who is affectionately lamented by all who knew her lovely character, and deeply mourned in that home

113

circle where she was the ornament and pride. Mrs. Martha Reeves, wife of Mr. John A. Reeves, departed this life on Saturday morning last, after a lingering illness of many months duration. She was the eldest child of Mr. Jesse R. Smith, of this village. As a consistent member of the Methodist Church, she gave in her life a bright example of Christianity, and in her last hours upon earth, left a most precious legacy of faith and reliance upon her Redeemer's promises. Her remains were buried at the Baptist graveyard on Sunday morning, attended by a numerous concourse of sorrowing relatives and friends.

Obituary: Rev. G. W. Boggs of Winnsboro, died at the residence of his brother, Thos. G. Boggs, in Pickens county, on the 14th inst., in the 76th year of his age. Mr. Boggs was a native of Pickens, and was on a visit to his brother for the purpose of recuperating his health. He has been a resident of Winnsboro for about 30 years.

Issue of:
Thursday, August 31, 1871:
Mrs. Clarissa Vance and Mrs. Louise Holland, of Laurens county, are dead.

Obituary: Mrs. Catherine Baker, aged over one hundred years, died at Marion on the 20th instant.

Obituary: Mr. Samuel W. Tucker, of Spartanburg county, died on the 19th inst., in the 70th year of his age. He was the father of Hon. Joseph W. Tucker, of Missouri.

Obituary: Rev. G. W. Boggs, whose death was chronicled in these columns last week, was a native of Anderson District, and for over seven years a zealous missionary in Hindostan, as we learn from the Fairfield Herald.

Obituary: The Edgefield Advertiser chronicles the death of Maj. John H. Hughs, a prominent and useful citizen. He died on the 18th inst., after a painful and protracted illness, aged about seventy years.

Issue of:
Thursday, September 14, 1871:
Obituary: (From the Dallas, Texas Herald) Accidentally killed, in Dallas county, July 28, 1871, Theodore Millwee, formerly of Anderson District, South Carolina. The subject of this sketch was born on the 31st day of May, 1844, and was consequently in his twenty eighth year when overtaken by the grim monster. He enlisted in the Confederate army in the spring of the year 1862, and served until the close of the war, as a soldier in the Army of Northern Virginia, under the immortal Lee, never being off duty for a single day from any cause. He was a member of Orr's Rifles, in Hill's Corps. No more feeling tribute can be paid to his memory than to say he was every inch a soldier in those days that tried men's souls. In the year * he became a member of the Masonic fraternity, in Williamston, S. C., and remained devotedly attached to the same and its teachings until his death. [*1865] He was buried by the Tannehill Lodge, 52, F. & A. M., with Masonic honors, in the beautiful cemetery belonging to said Lodge. He was the youngest son of Samuel Millwee, deceased, and Sophia Millwee, of Anderson District.   B.

Issue of:
Thursday, September 21, 1871:
Married: At the residence of the bride's father, Mr. Thomas
W. Martin, on the 6th of September by Rev. D. E. Frierson, Mr.
James M. Smith and Miss Palmyra Martin, all of Anderson County.

Married: On the 7th of September, 1871, at the residence of
the bride's mother, by Rev. S. A. Agnew, Mr. R. A. Simpson,
of Pendleton, S. C., and Miss Maggie J. Agnew, daughter of the
late Dr. E. Agnew, of Union County, Miss.

Married: On the 14th of September by Rev. H. N. Hays, Mr.
Sanford Whitfield, of Anderson County, and Miss Adaline Campbell
of Oconee County.

Obituary: Died, at his residence Mount Hope, on Santee River,
on the 24th of June, 1871, Mr. John A. Keels, a well known and
highly respected citizen of Williamsburg county, S. C. He had
for some years been in delicate health, but up to within a
few months of his death, was able to attend to his customary
duties. Of Mr. Keels, it may be said, that while he was unpretending in manner, he was firm and earnest in his convictions,
striving always to maintain right and justice. He served his
country in the Legislature, and in many ways his clear judgment
and conscientious nature enabled him to serve his fellow
citizens acceptably, and, at the same time with credit to
himself. A prominent lawyer, formerly of this county, but now
residing in a distant State, on hearing of his death wrote as
follows: "In all the relations of life, he fully merited the
confidence reposed in him by his friends. I have closely
observed his conduct as a Christian, and well might it have
been said of him, 'Mark the upright man, and behold the
perfect.' He served his master faithfully, and I feel well
assured that he has entered into the rest that 'remaineth for
the people of God!'" We need add no more to this testimony,
for kind words have no power to reach and soothe the dull ear
of death. He sleeps quietly now, and gradually sank to his
grave, watched and comforted, daily and hourly, by a wife whose
devotion was more than noble - almost more than human. With a
self sacrifice and love which forgot everything else, she
clung to him, and denied herself rest, or concern for her own
fast failing strength. After his death, she started with her
children for her old hom, near Pendleton. The task was too
great, and under a brother's roof, and in spite of his faithful
and loving treatment, Mrs. Martha P. Keels lay down to die.
On the 10th of August, 1871, her weary spirit took its flight
to that bright "land beyond the river", where we confidently
hope she has rejoined her husband and together they are waiting
for their loved ones. This is not the place to enter into any
extended sketch of her life, beautiful and Christian life as it
was, and we must confine ourselves to leading facts. Mrs. Keels
was the fifth daughter of the late Capt. John Maxwell. Her
youth was spent under every advantage, being surrounded by a
lovely family, and thrown into constant association with
refined society. No wonder, then, that when she left her happy
home as a bride, the fondest hopes and kindest wishes of a
wide circle of friends and relatives followed her. Some of
these have already "gone on before", many others have lived to
see her, widowed and almost broken-hearted, return to the
scene of her youth, as if only to evidence that she was still
beautiful and firm in faith, and then to die. Both she and

her husband were members of the Baptist Church, and as we
cease to speak of this scene of sorrow and death, we do so with
happy and reasonable hope that both have exchanged the troubles
and infirmities of this earthly life, for the fadless joys
which attend the spiritual life of "Christs own". Of Mrs.
Keels, a stranger has said: She was a lady of rare attractions;
intelligent, cultivated and refined, and of great personal
beauty and loveliness." Those who knew her best also best
know the truth of this remark. Four orphan children are left,
deprived of a father's quidence, and of a mother's care. Kind
hands have laid the mother down of her last rest amongst her
kindred, and kind hearts will remember and love her children
for her sake.

Deaths: We regret to chronicle the death of Gen. John W. Guyton
which occurred at his residence in this county on Saturday last,
after a brief illness. Gen. Guyton was a poplar and influential citizen, and served the people of Anderson most efficiently
as Sheriff for one term. He was Brigadier General of Cavalry
some years prior to the war, and always manifested great
interest in the volunteer organizations of this character. His
death will be lamented by a large circle of relatives, friends
and acquaintances.

Also, the sad intelligence has reached us that Mr. Preston L.
Dean, of Fair Play, is no more. He has been in failing health
for some months, and it was feared that he would never recover
from the prostrating illness. Mr. Dean was a native of Laurens
District, and had been a resident of this section about fifteen
years. He was a warm-hearted, generous friend and an exemplary
citizen. He was about 35 years of age.
**Issue of October 19, 1871 - see Page 251
Issue of:
Thursday, October 19, 1871:
Married: On Tuesday, October 2nd, 1871, at the residence of
the bride's father by Rev. J. L. Kennedy, Mr. John M. Glenn
and Miss Anna M. McCann, daughter of Maj. T. H. McCann, all of
Anderson County.

Issue of: Thursday, October 26, 1871:
Married: On Thursday afternoon, October 18, 1871, by Rev. C. L.
Gaillard, Mr. W. A. Williams and Miss Ruth, youngest daughter
of Abram Martin, Esq., all of Anderson County.

Married: On Sunday, October 15, 1871, by G. W. Hammond, Esq.,
Mr. John D. Hillhouse and Miss Mary E. Hix, both of Anderson
County.

Issue of:
Thursday, November 2, 1871:
Married: At the residence of the bride's mother, near Pendle-
ton, on Wednesday the 18th of October, by the Rev. J. S. Murray,
Mr. Thomas S. Crayton and Miss Nannie E. Sloan.

Death of Mr. William Hammond: The numerous friends and relatives of this estimable gentleman will be pained to learn of
his death, which occurred at Dalton, Ga., on the 19th of
October, in the 80th year of his age. Mr. Hammond was a native
of Anderson, and leaves a large circle of relatives in our
midst to mourn the loss of a good man and honorable upright
citizen. His nature was quiet and unpretending, and although
he was unusually intelligent and well informed upon all matters

of public moment, yet he never aspired to office position nor
was ambitious of this world's honors. The serenity of a calm
peaceful life comforted his declining years, and his faith and
trust was founded upon the Christian religion. Mr. Hammond
removed to Georgia many years ago, but returned to this neighborhood during the war. Here he was surrounded by children and
grandchildren and other relatives, but his strong attachment for
the beautiful section of country in the vicinity of Dalton
induced him to return four or five years ago to his former home.
For several months past, we have been apprised of his approaching dissolution, as he was a great sufferer from a lingering
disease. He is now gone from a world which he made brighter
and happier by an example of patience, diligence and uprightness.

Issue of:
Thursday, November 16, 1871:
Married: On November 1, 1871, by Rev. J. L. Kennedy, Mr. Miles
N. Sitton of Pendleton, S. C., and Miss Lillian A., daughter of
Mr. and Mrs. A. M. Holland of Anderson County.

Married: On November 2, 1871, by Rev. J. L. Kennedy, Major
Stiles P. Dendy of Walhalla, S. C., and Miss Alice E., daughter
of Mr. J. B. Sitton of Pendleton, S. C.

Married: On November 9, 1871, by Rev. W. A. Hodges, Mr. John J.
Dugan and Miss Martha E. Browne, all of Anderson County.

The Greenville Enterprise records the death of Mrs. W. K. Easley
which occurred in that place on the 1st inst. She was the
daughter of the late Thos. Sloan of Pendleton, and was a lady
of high character and eminent Christian virtues.

Death of Mr. Robert Pickens: Another old and highly respected
citizen of this County has passed from time to eternity. Mr.
Robert Pickens departed this life on Thursday, 2nd of November,
in the 77th year of his age. He retired at the customary hour
on Wednesday night in his usual health, but was aroused about
one o'clock by some disturbance in the house, and upon going
back to bed, remarked to his wife that he felt a little unwell.
Two or three hours later, Mrs. Pickens woke, and failing to
receive any response to her enquiries, she soon ascertained that
life was extinct. It is supposed that he died from heart disease
and that he never experienced any severe pain, but succumbed
to the grim monster as if dropping into gentle slumber. Mr.
Pickens had been a member of the Methodist Church from early
youth, and had always lived consistently with his professions.
He was born and reared upon the place where he died, and had
never lived elsewhere. His father's birthplace, and settled
by his grandfather, both of whom were named Robert Pickens, the
old homestead has never belonged to a person of any other name.
Mr. Pickens was twice married, and was the father of eighteen
children, seventeen of whom lived to be grown, and ten of them
are now living. He was an intelligent and upright citizen, and
greatly respected by all who knew him.

Issue of:
Thursday, November 23, 1871:
Married: In the Baptist Church, on Sunday evening, November
19, 1871, by Rev. J. Scott Murray, Mr. Wm. (?) Baker of
Charleston, and Miss Cora D. Wilhite, youngest daughter of
Dr. P. A. Wilhite, of Anderson.

Issue of:
Thursday, November 30, 1871:
Married: On Tuesday evening, November 28th, at the residence
of the bride's mother, by Rev. J. S. Murray, Mr. J. O. Jones and
Miss Pollie Millwee, all of Anderson County.

Issue of:
Thursday, December 7, 1871:
Married: On Thursday evening, November 30, 1871, at the resi-
dence of the bride's father, by Rev. W. A. Hodges, Mr. James
Wakefield, of Abbeville County, and Miss Elvira S. Clinkscales
of Anderson County.

Obituary: Died at Greenville C. H., on the 21st ult., Miss
Julia Werner, late of Pendleton, S. C., in the 29th year of her
age.

Issue of:
Thursday, December 14, 1871:
Married: On Wednesday, 22nd of November, 1871, by Rev. Robert
McLees, Mr. G. Marshall Jordan and Miss Nannie Creswell,
daughter of Mr. James Creswell, all of Greenwood, S. C.

Suicide of Col. John D. Ashmore: A telegram from Memphis announces the fact that Col. John D. Ashmore blew out his brains at
Sardis, Miss., one day last week. We have no further particulars
at this writing, than the bare announcement. Col. Ashmore was
formerly a resident of this place, and at one time a most
popular citizen. He was a native of Greenville and in early
life removed to Sumter, where he married and engaged in farming
pursuits. . . etc., etc.

Issue of:
Thursday, December 21, 1871:
Married: On December 13, 1871, by Rev. J. Scott Murray, Mr.
E. L. Clark and Miss Bettie N. Crosby, second daughter of
David Crosby, Esq., all of Anderson.

Issue of:
Thursday, January 4, 1872:
Married: On Wednesday, December 20th, 1871, at the residence
of the Bride's father, near Anderson, by the Rev. Edward R.
Miles, Mr. E. A. Bell and Miss Mary Alice Prevost, all of this
State.

Married: On Tuesday, 19th of December, 1871, at the residence
of the bride's father near Pendleton, by the Rev. J. L. Kennedy,
Mr. J. J. Miles, of Charleston, and Miss Anna D., daughter of
Col. T. J. Pickens.

Married: On Wednesday evening, 20th December, 1871, by the
Rev. J. K. Mendenhall, Mr. Wm. S. Brown, of Anderson, and Miss
Maggie S. Longshore, of Newberry.

Married: On the 26th of December, 1871, in the Presbyterian
Church, Orangeburg, S. C., by the Rev. Edward Palmer, the
bride's grandfather, Rev. John T. McBryde and Miss Frances S.
Hutson, youngest daughter of Wm. F. Hutson, Esq.

Issue of:
Thursday, January 11, 1872:
Obituary: Died, at Pendleton, S. C., on the 7th inst., Mrs.

Elizabeth Sharpe, in the 81st year of her age.

Married: On Sunday morning, December 17, 1871, by Rev. H. N. Hays, Mr. Asbury Cox and Miss Ritta Grant, all of Oconee.

Married: On Thursday evening, December 28, 1871, by Rev. H. N. Hays, Mr. Wyatt Mattison, of Anderson County, and Miss Elizabeth E. Hopkins, of Oconee County, S. C.

Married: On Wednesday evening, January 3, 1872, by Rev. H. N. Hays, Mr. Richard W. Anderson and Miss Gustus Wilson, all of Oconee County, S. C.

Married: On January 4, 1872, by Rev. J. Scott Murray, Mr. G. D. Williams, and Miss Amanda Thomas, all of Anderson.

Issue of:
Thursday, January 18, 1872:
Obituary: Rev. John C. Galloway, of Oconee County, died suddenly on the 4th Inst., aged 77 years.

Obituary: Mrs. Rice, a highly esteemed and estimable lady, for many years a teacher in the Greenville Female College, has recently deceased. Latterly, she had been residing in Abbeville County.

Issue of:
Thursday, January 25, 1872:
Married: At the residence of the bride's brother on Wednesday, 10th of January, 1872, by Rev. Sidi H. Browne, Mr. Thos. P. Hoyt, of the "Keowee Courier", Walhalla, and Miss Mattie P. Ready, only daughter of the late Dr. J. C. Ready, of Edgefield, S. C.

Married: On Thursday morning, January 4th, 1872, at the residence of the bride's brother, Honea Path, S. C., by Rev. A. C. Stepp, Mr. J. J. Ward of Darlington, and Miss Lou M. McCullough of Greenville.

Issue of:
Thursday, February 1, 1872:
Married: On the 10th of December, 1871, by J. F. Clardy, Esq., Mr. John C. Spearman and Miss Ann Martin, all of Anderson Co.

Married: By Rev. W. P. Martin, December 17, 1871, at the residence of the bride's mother, Mr. David T. Cox and Miss Harriet Amanda Josephine Kirby, all of Anderson County.

Obituary: We regret to learn the demise of Col. Samuel Donnald, which occurred at his residence in Donaldsville on last Friday night, from a stroke of paralysis. Col. Donnald was a worthy citizen of Abbeville and was known to many of our readers.

Homicide in Walhalla: We are informed that a bloody rencontre took place in Walhalla last Saturday night, in a liquor saloon on Main Street, between John Petty and John Dale, resulting in the latter being shot in three or four places, from the effects of which he died on Monday afternoon. Both were drinking characters and a difficulty arose between them several days before, terminating finally as above stated. Petty was arrested and lodged in jail.

Issue of:
Thursday, February 8, 1872:
Married: At Mr. Stephen McKee's in Abbeville County, by
Rev. A. Rice, on the evening of the 1st instant, Mr. William
B. Miller, of the State of New York and Miss Josephine Rosanna
Stark, of Abbeville County.

Issue of:
Thursday, February 15, 1872:
Married: At the residence of the bride's brother, on January
25, 1872, Col. W. G. Burt and Miss Mary F. Belcher, both of
Bossier Parish, Louisiana, formerly of South Carolina.

Issue of:
Thursday, February 22, 1872:
Death of Maj. Wm. H. Whitner: It is with sincere regret that
we announce the death of Maj. Wm. Henry Whitner, a native of
our town and fourth son of the late Judge Whitner. We have
not heard the particulars of his death which occurred at his
residence in Madison, Florida, on last Friday evening, as we
learn from the telegraphic dispatch to his family. Maj.
Whitner was a warm friend and genial companion and during the
late war served with distinction in the Confederate army. He
was for a time upon the staff of Gen. Roger A. Pryor and
afterward served a considerable period with Gen. M. Jenkins,
during that lamented officer's most brilliant services. After
the death of Gen. Jenkins at the Wilderness, Maj. Whitner was
transferred to the division of Gen. Bushrod Johnson and continued with that distinguished officer until the war closed.
Maj. Whitner enjoyed the confidence and esteem of all with
shom he was associated and was frequently commended for his
bravery and gallant conduct. When the war ended, he sought
a home in the land of flowers and has devoted his talent and
energies to the practice of law, for which he was peculiarly
qualified by nature and education. Maj. Whitner was twice
married. He was probably about thirty three years of age.

Issue of:
Thursday, February 29, 1872:
Obituary: Died, at the residence of Dr. G. H. Symmes, (near
Symme's Mills, in Pickens County) of Cynanche Trachealis,
John Hamilton, infant son and only child of Dr. and Mrs.
John H. Dean, of Greenville, aged nine months. Dear little
Hamilton. He was the pet of all who knew him. His spright-
liness, his dear, beaming little countenance, full of intelligence and affection, so endeared him to us, that twas hard to
resign him, who was the light and joy of his parents, to the
cold clay; but God called him and we bow in humble submission
to the mysterious dispensation of His providence, knowing that
He who so heavily afflicts will give sustaining grace to those
who trust in Him. "Our darling! thou has left us/ We thy loss
do deeply feel/ But 'tis God who has bereft us/ He can all
our sorrow heal."

Issue of:
Thursday, March 7, 1872:
Obituary: Died, at Anderson C. H., on the 22nd of February,
Mr. John H. Schreiner, aged 78 years. He was a native of
Hamburg, Germany and for thirty five years was a merchant in
the city of Charleston.

Obituary: Died, at Columbia, S. C., Mr. John Brinsdon, of Powderham, Devonshire, England and for many years a resident of Havana, in the island of Cuba.

Obityary: Died, at Madison, Florida, on Friday, 16th of February, of pneumonia, after a brief illness, William Henry Whitner, a son of the late Judge J. N. Whitner, in the 36th year of his age.

Issue of:
Thursday, March 14, 1872:
Married: On Wednesday evening, at the residence of Alex. Oliver, Esq., by Rev. Edward R. Miles, Col. J. Townes Robinson, of Abbeville and Miss Eugenia A. Miller, of Lowndesville.

Issue of:
Thursday, March 21, 1872:
Obituary: On the 24th February, 1872, our community suffered an irreparable loss, in consequence of which it is now draped in mourning. That day Mrs. Nancy Wyatt, widow of the late Col. J. F. Wyatt, in the 68th year of her age, ceased to contend with the ills incident to mortality and fell sweetly asleep. She was a most estimable lady and one of our best and most devoted members of the Baptist Church, to which she attached herself in early life and from that time her whole life was an exemplification of religion. Her piety was neither superficial nor spasmodic, but deep and consistant as the ceaseless flow of majestic waters. Her place in the church was occupied and her charity was only limited by her means. She was found often at the bedside of the sick and in alms giving her hand was outstretched while at home those who shared her hospitality were convinced that it was dealt by no stinted hand. As a wife and mother her example was such as deserves to live in the memory of her surviving children, who have reason to thank God for such a mother and that she was spared until their maturity. Oh! what priceless legacy is the memory of a praying mother - her influence does not end with death. Bereft friends, cheer up; we shall not miss her long. Thank heaven, the grave is not the goal of human hope. While we feel sure that our departed mother is safely housed in that world of unalloyed bliss, yet a little while, if faithful, and our bark, too, will be safely stranded upon the immortal beach of that heavenly world. With the light of the Gospel penetrating the tomb, we "sorrow not as others who have no hope."   P.   Newell, S. C.

Obituary: Death of An Aged Citizen: It is with sincere regret that we announce the death of Capt. Wm. Saunders, one of our oldest and most esteemed citizens. He died at the residence of his son-in-law, Capt. P. K. Norris, and was buried on last Sabbath, at Bethesda Church. Capt. Saunders was a patriotic and honorable citizen and served his country in the war of 1812 as a Captain of volunteers. He was born near Charleston, we believe, and had been living in Anderson for nearly forty-five years. As a peaceful, quiet and exemplary man, he was most highly esteemed by all who knew him. We are informed that he was in the 87th year of his age.

Obituary: We regret to learn, also, that Andrew Todd, Esq., died at his residence in this County on last Monday morning. Mr. Todd had been a sufferer from dropsy for the past year

and his death was not unexpected. He was sicty eight years
of age and had been a Magistrate in his neighborhood for the
last thirty-seven years.

Issue of:
Thursday, March 28, 1872:
Obituary: Died, near Kosse, Limestone county, Texas, on the
27th November, 1871, Mr. H. Cater Todd, in the 33rd year of
his age. On the 19th of November he fell from a tree, which
injured him internally so severely as to cause his death in
eight days after, although the tenderest nursing and most
skillful medical aid was given him. He was born and raised
in Anderson County, S. C. and scarcely one year ago, amid the
deep regrets of many friends, he left there with his wife and
babe to join his kindred who had preceeded him to Texas. Well
pleased with his new home, he had made many new friends and
his prospects seemed fair for a long life of usefulness and
domestic happiness, when suddenly he was stricken down by an
untoward accident and taken from the dear ones who loved him
so well. But, oh! the sweet consolation to his mourning
friends to know he was prepared for the Master's coming, tho'
he came in an unexpected hour. He appeared entirely resigned
to his Creator's will; the day before his death he was perfectly happy and the last coherent words he uttered were
praises to his Redeemer for his glorious feelings. For many
years he had been a member of the Presbyterian Church, in which
his sober life and earnest piety soon called him to the
position of an Elder, which office he filled to the entire
satisfaction of the church. Every position in life he was
called to fill he filled it well. He was a dutiful son,
an affectionate brother, a devoted husband, a tender father,
a faithful friend, a kind neighbor, a brace soldier and a
consistent Mason, who faithfully squared his life by the royal
precepts of the fraternity. All who knew him will testify to
his honorable upright life and strict integrity; but such
was his modesty that only those who knew him best, knew the
brightest of his intellect and the keener sensibilities of
his heart. Such was the purity of his character that from his
youth up he was never know to speak falsely or profanely, or
commit any act that would sully the bright record of his life.
Oh, how hard to be resigned to the loss of such as he, but
"God doeth all things well." He is now supremely happy in
Heaven and those who loved him so tenderly here will strive
faithfully to meet him there. May God guard and protect his
young desolate wife and little babe and comfort his aged
father, his brother and sister and many friends who with me
mour his irrepable loss.   A Friend

Obituary: Mr. Wiley Hill, a much respected citizen of Laurens,
died on the 18th instant.

Obituary: Mrs. Nancy Harrison, widow of the late Dr. James
Harrison, of Greenville, died suddenly in that city from an
attack of paralysis, on the 13th inst.

Obituary: The Greenville Enterprise announces the death of
Wm. Bates, Esq., long identified with the manufactoring
interests in that County and the founder of Batesville Factory.
He was seventy five or eighty years of age.

Obituary: Death of Dr. E. E. Whitner: We are deeply pained
to record the death of Dr. Elias E. Whitner, which occurred in
Greenville last Thursday, after a brief illness. Dr. Whitner
lately removed to Greenville for the purpose of practicing
medicine and was scarcely established in his new home when the
fell Destroyer came. The sad intelligence of his death was
almost the first tidings received by many of his friends in
this community, where he was born and reared. He resided in
Florida for several years, returning to this State about
eighteen months ago, we believe. He graduated in medicine
since the war. Dr. Whitner was a warm friend and genial
gentleman and was greatly endeared to the friends of his earlier
life in Anderson. His remains were brought to this place on
Friday, and interred in the Presbyterian churchyard on Saturday
morning. He was in the 33rd year of his age. It is only a
few weeks since an older brother died in Florida and the grief
stricken family receive the warmest sympathies of our entire
community in this deep affliction.

Obituary: The Abbeville papers record the death of Dr. Isaac
Branch, a prominent citizen of that town, who was well known
throughout the State. He was a native of Vermont, but had been
a resident of Abbeville for more than fifty years. He was a
zealous and devoted member of the Presbyterian Church and was
an active energetic worker in the Master's vineyard. Of late
years Dr. Branch was engaged in the insurance business and
especially as superintendent of agencies in this State for the
Piedmont and Arlington Life Insurance Company. Dr. Branch was
in the 72nd year of his age.

Issue of:
Thursday, April 4, 1872:
Married: On March 24, 1872, by Rev. B. F. Mauldin, Mr. E. T.
Gambrell and Miss Dorsie E. Wardlaw, youngest daughter of the
late H. H. Wardlaw.

Married: On the 14th of March, by Rev. S. Isbell, Mr. Z. L.
Burress and Miss Clara Lou, second daughter of William Riley,
Esq., all of Anderson County.

Obituary: Fell asleep in Jesus, March 28, 1872, at Anderson
C. H., S. C., Julia Motte daughter of Margaret A. and the late
Edward Morris, of Charleston, S. C.

Issue of:
Thursday, April 11, 1872:
Obituary: The Greenville Enterprise records the death of Mr.
Wm. Berry, of that County, who was said to be about 108 years
of age.

Issue of:
Thursday, April 18, 1872:
Obituary: Died, at her residence in Anderson County, S. C., on
the 16th of February, 1872, Miss Nancy R. Campbell, who was
born April 30th, 1829. For nearly twenty years of her life she
was a member of the Presbyterian Church and for more than
twenty-five years she was an invalid. She bore her suffering
with patience and died professing fath in Christ, submission to
the devine will and a hope of the eternal rest which remaineth
for the people of God.

Obituary: Capt. Wm. Sanders sweetly feel "asleep", in Anderson
county, March 15th, 1872. The light of his 85th birthday fell
upon his lifeless remains, awaiting their burial. And although
the immortal part was gone, the precious assurance was felt
that it was spending that day in a more congenial clime than
that on earth. He was first a member of the Episcopal Church,
in Charleston, but, after his removal to the up-country, he
united with the Methodist E. Church, South, in which he died.
In 1811, he was married to Miss Martha Ditmer, by whose side he
fought life's battle and then laid down his armor. For over
sixty years they toiled together and then ceased to labor
almost at the same time. He was greatly respected in the
community in which he lived. As the sunset of life approached,
he seemed to feel a deeper interest in the cause of the
Redeemer, the neighborhood and country at large. More than a
year before death, it was evident that disease was making fearful inroads on the body, During all this time no murmuring
word escaped his lips calmly, patiently, he awaited the issue.
For days and weeks before his death, perfectly conscious of
his approaching dissolution, faith towered above "the general
wreck" and clung to the promises of Jesus. Sometime before
growing speechless, while the icy arms of death were around him,
he said, "All is well." Then passed away our departed brother.
And though surviving wife, children and friends entertain the
sweet assurance that he rests with Jesus, yet it is natural
that sadness should reign in every heart and throughout the
house. But, oh! who would have believed that the sadness of
that household would, in so short a time, have increased
almost to desolation? Yet in a few short days his remains were
followed to the grave by those of his wife, sister Martha
Sanders, who was born in Charleston, about the year 1795 and
died March 29, 1872. With her husband she united with the
Methodist E. Church, South, and remained a consistent member
to the close of life. In all the relations of life, she seemed
to "Adorn the doctrine of Christ." Amid the cares, labors and
responsibilities of wife, mother, sister and friend, the clear
light of her religion beamed. It especially pleased her to
minister to others. Around the bed of sickness and suffering
she lingered like an angel of mercy. When care heavily rested
on her husband's brow, she delighted to remove it if possible.
Standing up with him through prosperity and adversity, she
shared in his sorrows and his joys. Often has the writer
enjoyed their society at the House of God and in their own home,
for they loved to have their Ministers with them. Having watched
with unwearied attention around her husband's bedside for a long
while and being ripe in years, her system yielded to the ravages
of pneumonia. On the morning of the 29th of March, ere the
natural sun had risen the great "Sun of Righteousness" was
shining on her redeemed spirit. She gave directions as to her
coffin and to a number of other things just as if going on
some pleasant journey in the community. She felt her own
pulse some half hour before death and said, "I'm going", and
afterward added "suffering much but I'll have joy to-night."
She was sensible to the last. How touching was her request -
"Write to my children and tell them to meet me in Heaven."
God grant that that request may be complied with! Brother and
Sister Sanders ended their earthly pilgrimage at the residence
of their son-in-law, Capt. P. K. Norris. Their remains
sweetly sleep in the graveyard at Bethesda Church waiting to
"have part in the first resurrection." Let us low and respect

Christ's aged servants while they live, for, "like the few
fleecy clouds that linger in life's evening skies, they are
painted with hues prophetic of Heaven."   W. A. H.

Issue of:
Thursday, April 25, 1872:
Obituary: Andrew Pickens Calhoun died recently at the resi-
dence of his maternal grandfather, Gen. Duff Green, near Dalton,
Ga. He was a grandson of John C. Calhoun.

Issue of:
Thursday, May 2, 1872:
Obituary: Departed this life, in a blessed hope of a glorious
resurrection, Mrs. Mary Randal Dawson, beloved wife of Rev.
Thomas Dawson, in the 70th year of her age. She was baptized
by Rev. James Welch, at Burlington, N. J. and joined the Church
at that place when 12 years old; was united with her husband
Aug. 10, 1822, at the Valley Town's Mission Station, Cherokee
Nation and has ever been a devoted Christian, wife and mother,
and now rests forever on the breast of her adoreable Redeemer
and Saviour.

Issue of:
Thursday, May 9, 1872:
Accidental Drowning: It is our sad duty to chronicle the
death of George Moore, eldest son of the late Col. John V. [U]
Moore, by accidental drowning in the mill pond at Pendleton
Factory on Sunday morning last. It appears that, in company
with other boys, George went in bathing and after remaining
sometime in the water, he was attacked with a sudden cramp.
Before assistance could re rendered, the lifeless form sunk
to rise no more. George was a bright, promising and intelligent youth and his death will be sincerely regretted by the
numerous friends of his family. He was in the 15th year of
his age, and was employed in a mercantile establishment at
Pendleton.

Issue of:
Thursday, May 30, 1872:
Married: At the residence of the bride's father, on Wednesday
evening, May 22nd, 1872, by Rev. J. S. Murray, Mr. B. Frank
Mauldin, of Columbia, and Miss Mamie E. Reed, daughter of Hon.
J. P. Reed, of Anderson, S. C.

Issue of:
Thursday, June 6, 1872:
Sad Case of Drowning: We have to record one of the most
melancholy cases of accidental drowning ever known in this
section, which occurred on Thursday last at Johnson's mill,
on Brushy Creek, in the upper portion of this County. It
appears that four little boys, returning from school on the
day specified, went into bathing and were seen by Mr.
Johnson in the water. An hour afterwards, a colored man
passing that way noticed clothing on the banks of the millpond and not seeing any person in the vicinity, reported the
fact to Mr. Johnson. The water was immediately drawn from
the pond, and the worst fears were realized, as the bodies were
found intheir watery grave. Three of the boys had their
arms clasped around each other and the remaining one was
close by. Two of the boys were sons of Mr. Joel Ellison,

aged respectively ten and twelve years. The other two were cousins, the sons of Sidney and Thomas Couch and aged about nine years. The supposition is made that one of them got beyond his depth in the water and that the others went to his assistance, with the fatal result above stated. But this is mere conjecture, as nothing certainly is known as to the cause of this most fearful accident.

Remarkable Longevity: We are informed that Mr. Henry Jolly and his wife died within an hour of each other on last Sunday night, at their residence six miles north of Anderson. Mr. Jolly was nearly ninety years of age, while Mrs. Jolly was about eighty seven and they had been married for seventy years! This aged couple, after a pilmigrimage together for near three-quarters of a century, ended life's fitful fever within the same hour. Both were confined during their last illness for about four months. "In death they are not divided."

Issue of:
Thursday, June 13, 1872:
Fatal Accident: A terrible accident occurred at the Anderson Depot on last Saturday afternoon, resulting in the death of Mr. Sanders Smith, a well known school teacher of this County. It seems that Mr. Smith was desirous of taking the train for Belton at 2½ o'clock and went to the Depot for that purpose. He was considerably intoxicated and went near the edge of the platform. The cars were being shifted at the time and the freight cars were run out on the track next to the platform with the intention of leaving the hindmost car. When this was "cut off" from the train, one of the hands called out "all right" as is customary and it is supposed that Mr. Smith concluded that this signal meant to get aboard, which he attempted just as the train moved rather briskly, when the car striking him, he was thrown down next to the platform, in which position he was turned around several times with a space of less than six inches. crushing him most horribly and breaking his left arm and right thigh. Although the alarm was instantly given the train could not be stopped until the entire length of the car was passed, with the unfortunate man being crushed within the narrow space. His mangled body was taken into the reception room of the Depot, where he breathed his last in a short time. A telegram was sent to his friends in Belton and the up-train brought several of his relatives, who took charge of the body and carried it to Shady Grove for interment.

Issue of:
Thursday, June 27, 1872:
Death of a Prominent Citizen: We have to record the untimely death of Mr. David M. Watson, which occurred at his residence in this County on Sunday night last, in the 44th year of his age. Mr. Watson was a prominent and useful citizen, an active and zealous member of the Baptist Church at New Prospect and an intelligent, successful farmer. He was identified with the mercantile interests of this town, as a member of the well known firm of Watson & Bros. His remains were interred at the family burying ground near the residence of his father-in-law, Rev. Jacob Burriss, on Monday afternoon, amid a large concourse of sorrowing friends and relatives. As atoken of respect to his memory, the stores and business houses of this town were closed from 2 P.M. on Monday until Tuesday morning.

Issue of:
Thursday, July 11, 1872:
Married: July 4, 1872, in the morning, at the residence of
the bride's father, by Rev. W. E. Walters, Mr. John J. Price,
of Anderson County and Miss S. A. E. Burditt, only daughter
of Mr. George F. Burditt, of Abbeville County.

Issue of:
Thursday, July 18, 1872:
Death of Gen. W. K. Easley: A telegraphic dispatch received by
the Columbia Carolinian from James A. Hoyt, Esq., dated
Atlanta, July 11, conveyed the sad intelligence of the death
of Gen. W. K. Easley, of Greenville, who was on a visit to that
city on business connected with the Air Line Railroad. From a
private communication from the editor of the Intelligencer,
who was in Atlanta at the time, we learn that Gen. Easley had
only reached Atlanta the day before his death. After breakfast
on the morning of his arrival, he went on a trip up the Air
Line Railroad, rode on the engine, was absent all day, ate
nothing during his absence and his physician expressed the
opinion that this was the exciting cause of his illness. He
was taken violently ill on the next morning with congestion
of the entire abdominal viscers, from which he died at 3
o'clock p.m. He had the best medical attention from the
beginning, and was kindly attended by some of his old friends
from South Carolina, among them Gen. A. C. Garlington and Col.
C. D. Farrow. In the death of Gen. Easley, the State has lost
one of her most gifted sons.

Issue of:
Thursday, August 8, 1872:
Married: On the evening of August 1, at the residence of the
bride's father, by the Rev. W. A. Hodges, Mr. John A. Reeves
and Miss Fannie M., daughter of J. B. and M. J. Clark, all of
this place.

Issue of:
Thursday, August 15, 1872:
Married: At the residence of the bride's father, on Tuesday,
6th inst., by Rev. Daniel Paine, Mr. James W. Eskew, of
Anderson, S. C. and Miss Mollie F. Wheeler, of Franklin County,
Ga.

Married: At the residence of the bride's mother, on Wednesday
evening, 31st of July, by Rev. W. E. Walters, Mr. John A.
Reese and Miss Sue Carpenter, all of Anderson County.

Fatal Accident to a Young Carolinian: The Augusta train
yesterday brought to the city the remains of a young man
named Theo Farmer, a native of Williamston, S. C., who was
killed on the Western and Atlantic Railroad, on Saturday last,
at a point near Chattanooga. He was employed as a train hand
and was standing on the top of the car when he was knocked
off while passing through a bridge and instantly killed. His
body was forwarded by the Company to his home at Williamston,
where his father, Elijah Farmer, resides, and is accompanied
by Mr. Hamilton, a Carolinian also, residing in Atlanta, who
was one of the few acquaintances of the deceased youth. He
was a young man, only nineteen years of age.
                              Carolinian - 13th inst.

                              127

Obituary: We learn that Mr. Samuel Reid, an estimable citizen
of Oconee County, died last Saturday, aged 70 years. He was
buried at Walhalla on Sunday.

Obituary: We are informed that Mr. Andrew Shearer, of the
Rock Mills neighborhood, died last Sunday night after a brief
illness in the 83rd year of his age. His remains were buried
at Providence Church on Tuesday morning.

Issue of:
Thursday, September 5, 1872:
Obituary: Died, August 19, 1872, at her residence near Pendle-
ton, Mrs. Elizabeth H. Maxwell, wife of the late Capt. John
Maxwell, in the 73rd year of her age.

Issue of:
Thursday, September 19, 1872:
Obituary: Died at Williamston, on Tuesday morning, 20th
of August, our promising young man, Willie Pickel, son of
J. E. Pickel, aged 20 years. He was kind and gentle in his
associations and much beloved by all who knew him.

Issue of:
Thursday, October 3, 1872:
Obituary: Died, on the 26th of September, of congestive fever
Mrs. Martha M. Orr, wife of Capt. James Orr, of Slabtown,
Anderson County, S. C. in the 34th year of her age.

Issue of:
Thursday, October 31, 1872:
Obituary: Died in Anderson County, S. C., on 16th of October,
1872, Sylvestor Bleckley, son of Mr. James A. and Mrs. C.
Bowie, age 2 years, 4 months and 2 days. May the parents
prepare to meet their loved infant in the Great Day, knowing
that of [..?...] in the Kingdom of God.

Obituary: Died, at his home sixteen miles northwest of
Anderson, C. H., S. C., on Friday, the [...] day of October,
1872, Thomas F. Rankin, in the 65th year of his age. After
a severe illness of thyphoid fever, of twenty-two days duration,
his released spirit winged its flight - humbly trust - to that
upper and happier rest where sufferings are unknown. Father,
may we meet thee again in a far better home when life with its
doubts and journeys is done and the rich and the poor of the
earth are one, Resting with God.

Issue of:
Thursday, November 7, 1872:
Obituary: Death of Wm. O. Alexander: Mr. Alexander left his
home near Craytonville in this County, in the fall of 1870, for
Falls County, Texas; but not satisfied with that part, he
removed last fall one hundred miles west, into the upper
Cross Timbers, in Johnson County. Returning to Falls County in
January last on business, he encountered a "Norther" in crossing
the prairie and his feet were so frozen that he was unable to
walk. The shock to his system and the sufferings he endured
superinduced dropsy, which his physicians combatted with varied
success until August 23, 1872, when he died at a Sulphur
Spring, in Hood County, in the 57th year of his age.

Married: At the residence of the bride's father, October 30, 1872, by Rev. H. Tyler, Mr. D. Sloan White and Miss Virginia C. Cox, only daughter of Maj. D. L. Cox, both of Anderson County.

Married: At the residence of the bride's father, on October 29, 1872, by Rev. W. E. Walters, Mr. Robert L. Clinkscales, of Anderson County and Miss Ella Kay, daughter of Mr. J. B. Kay, of Abbeville County.

Married: At the residence of the bride's father, on 23rd of October, by Rev. W. B. Jones, Mr. Lindsay Pratt, of Due West and Miss Emma Holloway, daughter of Mr. G. W. Holloway, of Ninety-Six, S. C.

Married: At the residence of the bride's mother, in the town of Anderson, on Wednesday evening, 23rd of October, by Rev. W. E. Walters, Mr. John P. Sullivan and Miss Lizzie Vandiver, only daughter of Mrs. Mary E. Vandiver, all of Anderson.

Married: On the 17th of October, at the residence of the bride's grandfather, Capt. M. Hall, by Rev. Wm. L. Pressley, Mr. R. P. Clinkscales, of Anderson, and Miss M. Corrie Hall, of Due West.

Married: On Sunday, 3rd of November, by Rev. Ezekiel Long, Capt. James Orr and Miss Georgianna Ricks, all of Anderson County.

Issue of:
Thursday, November 14, 1872:
Married: On Thursday, 31st day of October at Anderson Court House, by Rev. J. Scott Murray, Mr. M. M. Seawright, and Miss Augusta Pruitt, both of Donaldsville, Abbeville County, S. C.

Obituary: Died, in Anderson County, S. C., Nov. 5th, 1872, Mrs. Mary Claudia Reed, second daughter of S. J. and N. L. Emerson and consort of Mr. C. C. Reed, in her 21st year. She leaves a kind husband, fond parents and many friends to mourn their loss. Of her virtues we need hardly speak. These were daily exhibited in the various relations of life. As a wife, devoted; a daughter, cheerful and obedient; a sister, "mild and lovely" and as a neighbor and friend, kind and sympathetic. For several years a member of the Baptist Church, she adorned the doctrine of Christ by a godly walk and conversation. Read and loved to read her Bible and was regular in her secret devotions. Her interest in the Sabbath School is expressed in the following tribute of respect:
Resolved, By the Sabbath School at Ebenezer, that in the death of Mrs. M. C. Reed, this School has lost one of its most useful and zealous members. Kind and efficient as a teacher, she was beloved by her class and obtained the respect and esteem of the entire school. She loved the Sunday School cause. While as a school we bow with humble submission to this Providence, we feel assured that our loss is her eternal gain.   C. V. Barnes, Sec. pro tem
                    J. W. Brothers, Sup't.

Issue of:
Thursday, November 21, 1872:
Married: On the 24th of October, by Rev. W. E. Walters, Mr.

W. A. Breazeale and Miss Alice Wakefield, all of Anderson
County.

Married: On the 12th November, by Rev. W. E. Walters, Mr.
Joel T. Rice and Miss Sadie A. McGee, both of Belton.

Married: On the 6th of November, by Rev. A. P. Nicholson,
Mr. Thomas A. Sherrard, of Anderson and Miss Virginia C.
Baskin, of Abbeville.

Married: At the residence of the bride's father, by Rev.
W. A. Hodges, on the 29th October, Mr. B. A. McConnell and
Miss M. C. McConnell, all of Anderson County.

Married: On Tuesday evening, October 15th, at the residence
of the bride's father in Columbia, S. C., by the Rev. W.
Cuttino Smith, Prof. Jas. F. Latimer, of Davidson College,
N. C., and Miss Sue H. Maxcey, of Columbia, S. C.

Obituary: We are pained to record the death of Mr. B. C.
Snipes, which occurred in this town on last Monday morning,
after an illness of two or three weeks. Mr. Snipes was a young
man of excellant character and fine intelligence and enjoyed
the respect and confidence of the entire community.

Obituary: Death of Dr. Thomas A. Evins: This announcement
will not come unexpected to the majority of our readers, who
have been aware of the long and serious illness of this
eminent physician and well known citizen. For many months,
Dr. Evins has suffered from disease of the kidneys and the
fatal termination of this dread malady was expected by all of
his friends, scattered far and near. The icy hand of the grim
monster ended the sufferings of our friend and neighbor on
last Friday night, at ten o'clock. Dr. Evins was a native of
Spartanburg and while yet a youth, he came to this place and
studied medicine with his uncle, Dr. Alexander Evins and when
he had graduated at the schools of medicine, he began the
practice in this town. For more than twenty-five years, Dr.
Evins has occupied a close and sacred intimacy with the families
of this community and has faithfully served a large practice
by unremitting skill and devotion to his profession. He was
a hightoned, honorable man, upright in his dealings with all
and thoroughly imbued with a refined taste and correct principles. His extraordinary success as a physician gave him the
unbounded confidence of the multitude, while his professional
attainments were recognized and admired throughout the State.
At the breaking out of the war, he was appointed Surgeon to
Orr's Rifles and served in that capacity until he rose to the
position of Brigade Surgeon and afterwards was honored with
the appointment of Medical Director of the Division in which he
served. Returning from the army, Dr. Evins resumed the
practice of medicine in this town, although strongly solicited
by friends elsewhere to occupy a more lucretive field, but his
strong attachment to Anderson urged him to remain. He was
married in the fall of 1866 to Miss E. E. Holcombe of Pickens
and settled permanently in our midst. Early in the present
year, he was attacked by the first symptoms of the disease
which terminated his existence on earth and from day to
day grew worse, until he was forced to abandon the active
duties of his profession. Three or four months ago, he was

confined to his room and mortal cannot estimate the physical
pain endured for that length of time. Kind and loving friends
gathered around his bed-side and endeavored to administer
comfort in his affliction, but earthly help was in vain. Yet
the consolations of religion were to him a priceless jewel
and he was calmly resigned to the will of his Creator, feeling
prepared for the mighty change from time, to eternity and relying upon the merits and atonement of Christ for salvation in
a better world. He was an Elder in the Presbyterian Church,
with which he had been connected for several years. He was in
the 47th year of his age and leaves a wife and three children
to lament the loss of a noble husband and affectionate father.
His remains were carried to Greenville on Saturday afternoon
and from thence to the family burying ground at Nazareth Church
in Spartanburg County, where his parents and grandparents are
buried.

Murder: R. M. Hughs, a white man, was brutally murdered by
a drunken man, not knowing what he was doing, in Pickens
County, on the 8th instant. There was no political or personal
quarrel. Hughs was shot dead in his wagon by the murderer
after the latter had snapped his revolver at the negro on the
road and his victim had chided him for being careless. The
murderer's name is Julius Durham.

Issue of:
Thursday, November 28, 1872:
Married: At the residence of the bride's parents, by Rev. E.
R. Miles, of Abbeville, Mr. S. H. Prevost and Miss Pallie V.
McCully, both of Anderson.

Married: On the evening of the 19th inst., at the residence
of the bride's father, by Rev. A. Rice, Mr. B. F. Gassaway and
Miss Esther Pruiet, daugher of E. D. Pruiet, all of Anderson
County.

Married: On the evening of the 21st inst., by Rev. A. Rice, at
his own residence, Dr. Lucius Montgomery, of Florida and Miss
Lou J. Hall, of Anderson County, granddaughter of the officiating clergyman.

Married: On the evening of November 20th, at the residence
of the bride's mother, by Rev. I. Goss, Mr. A. E. Scudday and
Miss Lela McGee, daughter of Mrs. Sarah McGee, both of Anderson County.

Married: On Thursday evening, November 21st, at the residence
of the bride's father, by Rev. R. L. Harper, Mr. B. A. Davis
of Abbeville County and Miss Cynthia Scudday, daughter of Dr.
H. H. and S. Scudday of Anderson Village.

Obituary: Robert Hayne Perry, the youngest son of Hon. B. F.
Perry, died on the 18th inst. at Aiken, whither he had gone in
search of health. He was a young man of fine reputation and
intelligent promise and was just verging upon manhood. His
remains were carried to Greenville for interment.

Issue of:
Thursday, December 5, 1872:
Married: On the 21st of November, at the residence of the

bride's father, Mr. John R. Holcombe, of the <u>Pickens Sentinel</u> and Miss Fannie E. Williams, all of Pickens County, S. C.

Married: On the 20th of November, by Rev. Wm. Williams, D.D., Mr. Robert G. Williams, of Newberry and Miss Lidie S. McKay, only daughter of Robert McKay, Esq., of Greenville.

Death of a Veteran: We are pained to record the death of Mr. William Mattison, an aged and respected citizen, which occurred at his residence near Honea Path on last Sunday morning, Dec. 1st., in the 86th year of his age. Mr. Mattison was a soldier in the war of 1812 and was an upright and useful member of society. He joined the Baptist Church last summer.

Issue of:
Thursday, December 12, 1872:
Married: On the evening of the 21st ult., at the residence of the bride's father, by Rev. Mike McGee, Mr. C. E. O. Mitchell and Miss Fannie Geer, all of Anderson County.

Married: At the residence of the bride's father, on the evening of the 4th inst., by Rev. Mike McGee, Mr. James E. Anderson and Miss Mollie Earle, daughter of Rev. J. R. Earle, all of Anderson County.

Deaths:
Our town has again been saddened by the visits of the insatiate archer, whose shafts are aimed alike at the old and young. On last Wednesday morning, the community was shocked by the sudden death of Mrs. John H. Clarke, who was in the bloom of life and had been married only a few years. She had been an invalid for months but death came suddenly and bereft husband and children of an affectionate wife and fond mother.

On Thursday morning, the family of Hon. James L. Orr was plunged into grief by the death of Amelia, the youngest daughter, who was in the 13th year of her age. She was a bright, intelligent child - the pet of the household.

Issue of:
Thursday, January 9, 1873:
Married: On the 2nd of January 1873, by Rev. R. M. King, Mr. W. L. Green and Miss Savannah E. Williams, all of Anderson County.

Married: On the 18th of December, 1872, by Rev. Manning Brown, Mr. John T. Watkins and Miss Mattie E. Scudday, both of Anderson.

Married: On the 26th of December, 1872, by Rev. D. L. Whittaker, Mr. J. P. McDonald, of Oconee and Miss Julia A. Winter, of Anderson.

Married: On the 26th December, 1872, by G. W. Maret, Esq., at the residence of the bride's mother, Mr   Robert Smith, of North Carolina and Miss Mary Palmer, of Anderson County.

Married: On the 27th December, 1872, by G. W. Maret, Esq., at his own residence, Mr. John Partener and Miss Susan Lewis, all of Anderson County.

Obituary: Death of J. Overton Lewis: It is with sad regret
that we learn of the death of Col. James Overton Lewis, one of
the oldest and most highly esteemed citizens of Oconee County.
He died suddenly on the 31st of December, from an apoplectic
stroke. Mr. Lewis was a native of Virginia, we believe, but
had spent the greater portion of his lengthened life in the
upper section of South Carolina. He was an intelligent,
active and upright citizen and prominent for his advocacy of
all that concerned the material progress and development of
this section.

Issue of:
Thursday, January 16, 1873:
Married: On Tuesday evening, 14th inst., at the residence of
the bride's father, by Rev. J. R. Earle, Mr. Thomas H. Burriss
and Miss Bella Breazeale, daughter of Kenon Breazeale, Esq., all
of Anderson County.

Married: On the 30th of October, 1872, by Rev. W. [?] Martin,
Mr. Jasper N. Pool and Miss Nancy E. Cox, all of Anderson
County.

Married: By the Rev. W. Martin, on the 18th of December,
1872, Mr. Augustus W. Poor and Miss Margaret Jane Holland, all
of Anderson County.

Married: By the Rev. W. Martin, on the 23rd of December 1872,
Mr. Joseph Johnson Vaughn and Miss Margaret Clement, all of
Anderson County.

Issue of:
Thursday, January 23, 1873:
Married: At the residence of the bride's father, on the evening
of January 15, 1873, by Rev. T. H. Pope, Dr. West A. Williams,
formerly of Anderson County, and Miss Georgia Camilla, fifth
daughter of Dr. F. G. and M. E. Parks, all of Greenwood,
Abbeville County.
Two trusting hearts are thus united/ With the golden bands of
love;/ May all their steps by faith be guided,/ And their
journey end in heaven above.

Issue of:
Thursday, February 6, 1873:
Married: January 30, 1873, by Rev. [?] P. Martin, at the
residence of the bride's father, Mr. John H. Breazeale and Miss
Sarah Ann Cooley, second daughter of Wm. M. Cooley, all of
Anderson County.

Married: On Thursday evening, January 30th, by Rev. Wilson
Ashley, Mr. E. R. Kay, of Anderson County and Miss Jane
Walker, of Abbeville County.

Married: On Thursday evening, January 30th, by Rev. W. A.
Hodges, Mr. E. W. Stewart and Miss Sallie P. McAlister, all of
Anderson County.

Issue of:
Thursday, February 27, 1873:
Obituary: From the Eutaw [Alabama] Whit and Observer - Mr.
J. W. Coates, son of the late Dr. James Coates, of South

Carolina, and nephew of the Drs. Sanders, of Clinton and Pleasant Ridge, died suddenly - living only about 48 hours after being attacked - at the residence of Mrs. Strait, near Clinton, on the 8th inst. The deceased was an exemplary young man, industrious and energetic and although he had been in the county but a short time, his friends were numerous, as was evidenced by the large concourse that attended the funeral obsequies. We learn he leaves a mother and four sisters and although deprived of their tender care, he received the motherly attention of Mrs. Strait, together with lady relatives and many friends, who watched his dying moments with those tender emotions only known to woman's heart. We tender his bereaved mother and sisters our condolence in this severest of all afflictions.

Issue of:
Thursday, March 6, 1873:
Obituary: We regret to learn of the death of Mr. William Knox, of Franklin Co., Georgia, who was well known to many of our citizens as an intelligent and upright gentleman. He died suddenly on Tuesday, 25th ult., of heart diease. He leaves a wife and seven children to mourn this irreparable loss.

Issue of:
Thursday, March 13, 1873:
Obituary: Died, on the 4th of February, at her residence, on Little River, Miss Anna Robinson, in the 81st year of her age. She was a native of Abbeville and a consistent member of the Methodist Church.

Issue of:
Thursday, March 20, 1873:
Married: On the 13th inst., at the residence of the bride's mother, by Rev. A. H. Cornish, Mr. John E. Lebby, of Wadmalaw Island, to Miss Lucy Virginia, youngest daughter of the late J. Overton Lewis, of Perryville Oconee County, S. C.

Issue of:
Thursday, March 27, 1873:
Married: On Thursday evening, March 20, 1873, at the residence of the bride's father, by Rev. D. E. Frierson, Dr. M. E. Parker and Miss M. Rebecca Humphreys, eldest daughter of S. C. Humphreys, Esq., all of Anderson County.

Married: At the residence of the bride's mother, near Honea Path, on Sunday, March 9, 1873, Mr. Joel Kay and Miss Mollie Bigby.

Married: By Rev. W. P. Martin, at his residence, Feb. 18, 1873, Mr. Jonathan Vaughn and Mrs. Minerva Stone, all of Anderson County, S. C.

Obituary: Mr. William Bailey, an esteemed citizen, died at his residence three miles northeast of town, on Monday night last, in the 75th year of his age, after an illness of only five days. He was a member of the Presbyterian Church at Midway, where his remains were interred on Tuesday afternoon.

Mrs. Mary Rankin and Mr. Baylis Watkins, of the Slabtown

neighborhood, died recently. Both were octogenarians, we believe,and were universally respected wherever known.

Obituary: Death of Col. D. K. Hamilton - This brief announcement will bring sadness to the numerous friends of this venerable and esteemed citizen, who has stood like a beacon of the past to rising generations and was greatly admired for his sterling, noble qualities. Col. David K. Hamilton was a native of Anderson, born and reared in the vicinity of Slabtown and resided there during the entire time of his lengthened existence upon earth. He has been in feeble health for several years and during that period was attacked with erysipelas three or four times, but medical skill overcame the disease, until about a week before his death, when the fatal attack came on, which baffled the powers of physicians as the patient old man knew that death was drawing nigh. He lingered until Tuesday, 18th inst., in the full possession of his mental faculties and calmly resigned to the will of his Father, when death ended his sufferings and his spirit passed away peacefully into the realm of bliss. Col. Hamilton was a member of the Presbyterian Church, with which he had been connected for upwards of sixty years and the greater portion of that time occupied the position of an Elder, in which he faithfully served the cause of his Master. He was eighty years old on the 22nd of February last and lived an honorable and useful life, leaving many descendants to rise up and bless his memory.

Obituary: Death of John Hugh Marshall, Esq. - We are pained to record the death of our valued friend, John H. Marshall, Esq., which sad event took place at his residence in Greenville on Tuesday night, 18th inst. He was stricken with paralysis, eight days before his death - the diease attacking the lower portion of his body, beginning at the abdomen and rendering that portion of his person entirely useless and dead. In this condition he lingered, until the paralysis gradually and certainly extended to the heart and upper portion of his body, after which his recovery was considered impossible and his death speedily expected. Mr. Marshall was a native of Abbeville and was a brother of Mrs. James L. Orr, of our town. Prior to the war, he resided in this place for several years, engaged in the practice of law, in partnership with Judge Orr and during his sojourn in our town, he made many warm friends by his kind, affable disposition and courteous manners. When the war ended, he engaged in planting near Abbeville, for several years and two or three years ago he removed to Greenville, where he had recently purchased a large place in the immediate suburbs of the city. Life seemed to open anew before him, but in the midst of busy energies and hopeful anticipations, the summons came suddenly for his entrance upon the realities of eternity. We knew him well and intimately for many years and admired his genial qualities and upright character. Possessing a fine education, he was likewise inbued with a cultivated literary taste, which was continually improved and enlarged by extensive reading. We deeply sympathise with the relatives of our departed friend in this sore affliction.

Issue of:
Thursday, April 3, 1873:
Married: On the 27th of March, 1873, by Rev. E. F. Hyde, Mr. B. F. Gantt and Miss Alice McCrary, all of Anderson County.

Obituary: Died, at his residence near Slabtown, in Anderson
County, S. C., of Erysipelas, on the 18th ult., Col. David
K. Hamilton, in the 81st year of his age. For more than a
half century he had been connected with the Carmel Presbyterian
Church, as a member and Ruling Elder and exemplified in his
death, as in his life, the happiness and conscious serenity of
a constent Christian character. He lived to bury the wife of
his bosom and four out of five of his children, leaving only
one to drop the tear of filial affection over his remains.
"Let me die the death of the righteous; and let my last end
be like his."

Obituary: Death of Mr. Hampton Stone - The numerous friends of
Mr. Hampton Stone will be grieved to learn that he is no more.
He died on the 11th of March last, at his home in Jasper
County, Texas, after a long and painful illness, of diease of
the heart. Mr. Stone was a native of Greenville District, but
was a resident of Anderson for many years and was widely known
among our people. In the fall of 1866, he removed with his
family to Texas and settled in Jasper County. Two or three
years ago, Mr. Stone returned on a visit to this section and
was then in the enjoyment of excellent health, bidding fair to
attain a green old age. He was a member of the Baptist Church
and filled the office of Deacon at the time of his death. As
a citizen, friend and neighbor, he was greatly esteemed for
sterling qualities of head and heart and the news of his death
will shed a gloom among a large circle of friends. Mr. Stone
was in the 64th year of his age.

Issue of:
Thursday, April 24, 1873:
Obituary: Died, on Sunday the 6th instant, of diease of the
lungs, Clara, infant daughter of E. A. and N. A. Russell, aged
15 months. "Of such is the kingdom of Heaven."

Obituary: On the 23rd of March, 1873, at Hutchins, Dallas
County, Texas, of menigitis [sic] Robert Keys Norris.

Issue of:
Thursday, May 15, 1873:
Married: On the evening of May 8, 1873, by Rev. A. Acker, Mr.
Joel M. Harper and Miss Mary Jane, eldest daughter of Wm.
Riley, Esq., all of Anderson County.

Issue of:
Thursday, May 22, 1873:
Married: On Sunday morning, May 18th, 1873, by Rev. W. P.
Martin, at the residence of the bride's mother, Mr. Marshall
B. Gaines and Miss Loutetia Emaline, eldest daughter of Mrs.
E. Caroline Mattison, all of Calhoun, Anderson County, S. C.

Married: By Rev. W. P. Martin, on May 22, 1873, at the resi-
dence of the bride's father, in Greenville County, Mr. George
W. Clement, of Anderson County, and Miss Cyntha, daughter of
Rev. K. Vaughn.

Issue of:
Thursday, June 5, 1873:
Married: On Wednesday evening, 21st of May, 1873, at the
residence of the bride's mother, by Rev. J. H. McMullen, Mr.
E. Berry Benson and Miss Alice E. Adams, all of Hartwell, Ga.

Issue of:
Thursday, June 26, 1873:
Obituary: "Gone Home" - Mrs. Emily Palestine Wright, the beloved
wife of James A. Wright, of Abbeville, died June 11th, 1873,
aged 31 years, 3 months and 13 days. Her maiden name was
Robinson. She gave her heart to her Saviour in 1861, uniting
with the Methodist Episcopal Church South, at the Old Turner's
Chapel, near Honea Path, where we buried her "natural body"
in hope of a glorious resurrection. Married to the playmate
and lover of her childhood, in 1865, she soon revealed the
character of a true wife. As a mother, she was tender and
judicious. As mistress of the household, her rule was marked
by energy, gentleness and love. Her person was attractive,
her manners winning, her mind practical, her affections warm,
her self control remarkable, her piety a principle. During the
last year of her life she suffered much and gradually lost
strength and her beauty, like a fading flower, was consumed.
Not her beauty! Real human beauty cannot perish. Disease
cannot touch it. Death cannot harm, but only sends it to
Heaven. It blooms in the night. It flourishes most when its
roots are covered with the mold of its decaying leaves. It is
psiritual loveliness. The trials of this life develops it.
Its features are meekness, goodness, faith, charity, patience,
truth. This was our sister's imperishable beauty. She has
gone with it to "the bos'm of her Father and her God." She
clung to life long. The wifely love was strong - the mother
heart was strong - but the love of Christ at last was strongest
and she calmly counseled and blessed her husband, prayed for
her children, sent messages to her friends and with childlike
trust and unruffled serenity waited for the Master. It was
touching to hear her singing the night before her death,
"Rock of Ages cleft for me, let me hide myself in Thee." Her
calmness, her thoughfulness, her lovingness and sweetness, her
submission to God and faith in the Redeemer were beautiful
indeed. Love drove her chariot-wheels. Death was conquered.
    W. T. C.

Issue of:
Thursday, July 3, 1873:
Obituary: Died, at his residence in Senatobia, Mississippi,
on the 15th of June, 1873, Henry L. P. McGee, a native of
Anderson District, S. C., in the 35th year of his age. Grim
monster, death has taken from our midst a generous, kind-
hearted friend, a pure and upright citizen and fond and
devoted husband and father, and many are the hearts sorrowed
by the demise of him who had so much good and noble qualities
to endear him to the people. By his death the community has
sustained irreparable loss - society a useful member and
relatives an affectionate and loving kinsman. To all we
tender deepest sympathy and especially would we invoke the
comiseration of "Him who tempers the wind to the shorn lamb"
upon the grief stricken widow and the helpless orphans. May
they be consoled with the belief, yea knowledge, that while
he is dead to them in this world, his sould has winged its
flight to brighter realms where, with arch-angels, he awaits
their coming.   Senatobia [Miss.] Times

Issue of:
Thursday, July 10, 1873:
Obituary: Died at the residence of her father in Williamston,
S. C., on Sunday evening, June 29th, 1873, Miss Sallie Hamilton

Mauldin, daughter of Rev. B. F. and Mrs. A. T. Mauldin.

Obituary: Death of Dr. J. J. Wardlaw - We learn with sincere
regret that Dr. J. J. Wardlaw, formerly of Abbeville, died
at his residence in Walhalla on Wednesday evening, 2nd inst.
He had one of his thighs broken two or three weeks since and
his system never rallied from the terrible shock occasioned by
this accident. Dr. Wardlaw was a native of Abbeville and a
brother of the late Judge Wardlaw. He was a kind-hearted
intelligent and upright man and at one time represented Abbeville in the lower branch of the Legislature. He removed to
Walhalla three or four years ago.

Issue of:
Thursday, July 17, 1873:
Obituary: We are informed that Dr. John G. Gantt, of Honea
Path, died on Monday last and was buried on Tuesday. He was
stricken with paralysis some time ago, which we suppose even-
tuated in his death. Dr. Gantt has been post master at Honea
Path for a number of years.

Obituary: Died, of that fell-destroyer - Consumption - at the
home of her mother-in-law in this village, July 1, 1873, Mrs.
Jaqulene T. Fant, wife of Preston C. Fant. The deceased was
born in Gwynette County, Georgia, Sept. 24, 1850. Her parents
Thomas and Caroline Todd, were born and reared in this State,
moved to Georgia, where she, their only daughter was born.
Her mother died when she was only four years old. Her uncle,
James Todd, brought her and younger brother to his home in this
State, where he and wife reared and taught them until they
were grown "in the way they should go." They were the instru-
ments used by our blessed Saviour, verifying his promist, "I
will be a father to the fatherless." In 1865, she joined the
Methodist Episcopal Church in this place. Thus in early life,
while young, she gave her heart to God. She adorned the Church
of her choice and the doctrine of God, lived the life of a
Christian in deeds and died as she had lived, in the hope of
a bright and glorious future beyond the grave. Fully conscious
of her near approach to death, yet with calmness that only
faith in Jesus Christ could inspire, she called her husband
and the family, bid them farewell, gave a shout of triumph,
clapped her hands and exclaimed, "I am ready and willing;
Lord Jesus receive me to thyself" and breathed her last without
a struggle. Good thus to live, but glorious, thrice glorious
thus to die! with the full assurance of that peace which
surpasseth all understanding, reserved alone for the people of
God. She leaves a doting husband, one little boy, four years
old, brothers, relatives and many friends to mourn their loss;
but those mourn not as those who have no hope - their loss is
her gain. May God grant that the words of one so young in her
last moments pressing the duty of personal piety upon her
relatives and friends produce in their hearts "fruits meet
for repentance". Visions of glory and happiness in heaven
were continually before her mind and by faith she saw and
heard things which her language was impotent to describe.
Was it not for better for her to go and enjoy heavenly delights,
of which God was then giving her a foretaste, than to remain
in the body contending with the powers of sin. May the grief-
stricken husband be comforted by God's sustaining grace and
be enabled in the spirit of meekness to say, "Lord not my will,

but Thine be done." May He who has smitten given to them
the consolations of His spirit. [Two verses of poetry follow]

Obituary: Died, in the town of Williamston, on the 18th ult.,
Mrs. Ruth Odell, aged 71 years. The deceased was a native of
Laurens County and has left several children and grandchildren
to mour her departure. Her last days were spent in the family
of her son-in-law, Dr. W. A. McCorkle, where she died.

Obituary: Dr. Matthew Thomson, died at Northport, Alabama,
on the 11th of June in the 79th year of his age. He was a
native of Anderson District and removed to Alabama in 1856.
Many of our old citizens will remember the deceased, who had
an extensive acquaintance and connection among our people. He
was a brother of Maj. James Thomson, who resides in the lower
portion of this County.

Obituary: The funeral services of Mrs. Wm. A. McFall took
place in the Presbyterian Church on Monday last, in the presence of a large congregation of friends and acquaintances.
Appropriate remarks were made by Revs. D. E. Frierson and
A. Rice, after which the remains of the deceased were buried
in the adjoining graveyard. Mrs. McFall died on Sunday morning
at High Shoals, the residence of her husband. Her character
was exceedingly lovely and her life a faithful testimony of
the religion she professed. [Note: Her give name - Tabitha]

Obituary: Dr. H. C. Cooley died at his residence near Brown's
Ferry, on the Savannah River, on Tuesday evening last, of
congestive fever, after a short illness. He was a native of
Greenville District, graduated in medicine at the schools in
Philadelphia and Paris and settled in practice at this place
in the Spring of 1857. He retired from the practice of medicine at the close of the war and has been engaged in planting
since that time. Dr. Cooley served in the capacity of Surgeon
to the Fourth Regiment S. C. Vols. during the first year of
the war.

Issue of:
Thursday, July 24, 1873:
The Greenville Mountaineer and Enterprise records the death of
Maj. George Addison, formerly of Edgefield, who has been
residing in Greenville for several years. He has been suffering
from dyspepsia for a long time and for the last several weeks
all hope of restoration to health was gone. Maj. Addison was
a genial, kind-hearted man and greatly esteemed by a wide
circle of friends and acquaintances throughout the State.

Issue of:
Thursday, July 31, 1873:
Obituary: Died, at the residence of his daughter, Mrs. Jane
Hall, on the 12th of July, A. D. Gray, Esq., in the 78th
year of his age. The deceased was a native of Abbeville, a
soldier in the war of 1812 and a member of the Baptist Church
for upwards of forty years. He was thrown from his buggy on
Sunday previous to his death and it was from the effect of
injuries received that he died. He was an upright, honorable
citizen and greatly esteemed by his neighbors. He leaves one
son and two daughters to mournthe loss of a devoted parent.

Killed by Lightening: We are informed that a young man was killed by lightening near Walhalla, on last Saturday afternoon, during the storm which prevailed in that section. He was a son of Thomas Massey, about sixteen years of age and grandson of Mr. Silas Massey, of this County. The lightening struck him on the top of his head and ranged down the back, tearing his clothes to pieces. The body was brought by train on Monday morning to Sandy Springs, where the funeral services took place.

In Memoriam: [Excerpts from a long write-up] Col. J. Perkins Hoyt departed this life at the residence of Mr. John L. Gilkerson, near Tumbling Shoals, in Laurens County, on Wednesday morning, 23rd July, in the 68th year of his age. He was a native of New Hampshire and removed in early life to Virginia, where he married and settled. Twenty-five or thirty years ago he removed farther South and for a few years made his home in Georgia, but subsequently removed to Laurens C. H., of which place he was a citizen until April last, when he came to Anderson and expected to spend the remainder of his life at the residence of his eldest son.

Issue of:
Thursday, August 7, 1873:
Married: On Wednesday evening, July 30th, at the residence of the bride's father, by Rev. Lewis M. Ayer, Mr. Joseph R. Fant and Miss Sallie A. Sharpe, eldest daughter of Mr. E. Sharpe, all of Anderson.

Obituary: [Excerpts from death of Homer L. McGowan, Esq.] Of Laurens, died at Caesar's Head on Monday 28th of July in the 37th year of his age. He married Miss Farrow of Laurens.

Issue of:
Obituary: Mrs. Hannah Taylor, relict of the late Col. David S. Taylor, departed this life on Monday morning last, at her residence in this town, after an illness of only five days. She was the mother of a large family, who are suddenly called upon to sustain an irreparable loss and who will tenderly cherish the memory of their best and dearest friend on earth. Mrs. Taylor was in the 67th year of her age. Her remains were carried to Pendleton and buried by the side of her husband in the Episcopal graveyard.

Obituary: Dr. W. H. Pegg, an excellant physician and highly respected citizen of Atlanta, Ga., fell dead in the streets of that city on Sunday, 10th inst., from apoplexy. Dr. Pegg was a native of Anderson County and has a large number of relatives and friends here. He was in the 59th year of his age.

Issue of:
Thursday, August 28, 1873:
Obituary: [Excerpts from long article] Death of Elijah Webb. Died Monday morning, 25th of August, inst. Born on Seneca River, in Anderson County, on the 13th of January 1806. Moved to Anderson from Pendleton, where he worked for Messrs. Benson, in 1827. In 1828 he married Caroline, daughter of Col. Dudley Hammond. He was the husband of three wives and three sets of children. His first, Caroline, died in 1841, leaving a son and a daughter. The daughter became the wife of Gen. Samuel M.

Wilkes, who was killed at the battle of Manassas. She remarried
to I. O. McDaniel, Esq., of Allatoona, Ga. In 1843, Mr. Webb
married his second wife, Rebecca Scott, daughter of Charles
Gaillard, of Charleston. The fruit of this marriage was an
only daughter, who became the wife of James A. Hoyt, editor of
the Anderson Intelligencer. The second wife, Rebecca, died in
January, 1848 and during the year following he married Rosa H.,
daughter of Wm. Waller, Esq., of Charleston. The fruit of this
marriage was a daughter and two sons.

Sickness and Deaths: There is much sickness in the neighborhood southwest of this place, in the vicinity of Pendleton,
about Five Forks and in other portions of the County. Whole
families are prostrated with Chills and Fever and in several
instances with ravages of this disease have proved fatal. We
have heard with regret of the death of Mr. Edmund McCrery, a
respected and useful citizen of this County, living near
Pendleton and also of his son who was living with him. They
died within an hour or two of each other and were interred in
one grave. Mr. McCrery leaves a family smitten with the
disease which terminated his life. Mrs. Hillhouse, the widow
of Mr. Porter Hillhouse, deceased, Miss Josephine Hix and a
little son of Mr. Todd and several colored persons have died
within the last few days.

Issue of:
Thursday, September 4, 1873:
Obituary: "Death of a Young Lady" - Among the deaths recently
occurring near this town, it is our sad duty to record that of
Miss Arabella E. Lewis, which occurred at the residence of her
uncle, Mr. J. Crawford Keys, on Sunday night, 31st of August.
She was the youngest daughter of Robert B. and Juliet A. Lewis,
both deceased, formerly of Dahlonega, Ga. Her life was chiefly
spent in her uncle's family, after the death of her parents.
Lovely, gentle and kind in diposition, warmly attached to
relatives and friends, she will be sadly missed in the circle
of her acquaintances. The funeral services were conducted by
Rev. D. E. Frierson, who made touching allusion to her christian
experience in her last illness and the body was consigned to the
grave in the Presbyterian churchyard, amid a large concourse of
sorrowing relatives, friends and acquaintances.

Issue of:
Thursday, September 11, 1873:
Obituary: We regret to announce the death of Maj. George W.
Rankin, which occurred at his residence near Slabtown on Sat-
urday last, after a brief illness, of intermittent fever. Maj.
Rankin was a prominent and influential citizen in his neighbor-
hood.

Obituary: Mr. James H. Land, of Rock Mills, died on Friday
night and was buried with Masonic honors at the Baptist graveyard, in this town on Sunday morning. He was a member of
Furman Lodge, No. 170.

Issue of:
Thursday, September 25, 1873:
Married: By G. W. Hammond, Esq., on September 23rd, 1873 at
Sandy Springs, Mr. John Elmore and Miss Nancy Lee, both of
Anderson County.

Issue of:
Thursday, October 2, 1873:
Married: On September 25th, 1872 (should this be 73?), by
Rev. W. P. Martin, at his own residence, Mr. James R. Nelson
and Miss Sallie Josephine Smith, all of Anderson County.

Married: By Rev. W. P. Martin, on September 28th, 1873, at
the residence of the bride's mother, Mr. Joseph J. Copeland
and Miss Josephine A. Poor, eldest daughter of Mrs. Neighra
Poor, all of Anderson County.

Obituary: The Walhalla Courier records the death of Mr.
Charles Thompson, a worthy and highly esteemed citizen of
Pickens County, which occurred at his residence, five miles
above Pendleton, on the morning of the 17th ult., aged 74
years.   He was the father of Col. R. A. Thompson of Walhalla.

Issue of:
Thursday, October 9, 1873:
Married: On the 25th of September, at the residence of the
bride's mother, by Rev. John M. Carlisle, Mr. C. E. Stubbs and
Miss Alice Hoyt, all of Sumter, S. C.

Married: On the 30th of September, at the residence of the
bride's father, by Rev. W. P. Martin, Mr. John T. Chapman of
Greenville County and Miss Mary Jane Smith, eldest daughter of
Mr. Joel Smith, of Anderson County, S. C.

Obituary: Capt. Duff Green Calhoun, formerly of Pendleton,
died in Texas on the 25th of August, in the 35th year of his
age.   He was the eldest son of Col. A. P. Calhoun, deceased.
He leaves a wife and one child.

Issue of:
Thursday, October 16, 1873:
Obituary: Death of an Aged Citizen - We regret to announce the
death of Mr. John Stephenson, an upright and respected citizen
of this county, which occurred at his residence on Tuesday
last, after a long illness.   He was upwards of seventy years of
age and has always been greatly esteemed for his integrity and
faithfulness in the discharge of every duty as a good citizen.
His remains were buried at Mountain Creek church on Monday last.

Obituary: Mrs. Louisa M. Cunningham, relict of Capt. Robert
Cunningham and mother of Col. John and Miss Ann Pamela
Cunningham, died at her residence in Laurens County on the 6th
inst.

Issue of:
Thursday, October 23, 1873:
Married: On the 15th inst., at the residence of the bride's
father, by Rev. J. H. McMullan, Mr. Willie W. Burriss and
Miss L. America Snipes, all of Anderson County.

Issue of:
Thursday, October 30, 1873:
Obituary: Departed this life on the 7th day of August, 1873,
at his reisdence on Wilson's Creek, Anderson County, S. C.,
Mr. Martin Hall, in his 76th year.   He was one among the oldest
men in the community, in which he lived, and was generally
beloved and respected by all who knew him.   He was ever kind

and curteous to all with whom he was brought in contact and was
ever ready to speak a word of comfort and encouragement. The
bed-side of the afflicted and suffering among those in his
community were never neglected or forgotten by him, but such
places found him a constant visitor, ever ready to extend his
sympathy and aid. The high esteem in which he was held was
abundantly attested by the large number of relatives and friends
who visited him constantly during his brief but distressing
illness. As a husband, he was tender and affectionate; as a
friend, he was frank and sincere; as a neighbor, he was kind
and obliging and as a citizen, he was pure and honest. Although
not a member of the Church at the time of his death, yet
he was a constant and regular attendant on the services of the
sanctuary and always evinced the most ardent interest in all
that pertained to the interest of the Redeemer's Kingdom.
During his last illness, he gave unmistakable evidences of the
surety of his hope in Christ and that he would be admitted into
the home of the blessed. Feeling that he was ready at the
bidding of his Master to enter upon his rest in heaven, just as
the sun lowered in the horizon, casting the last golden tints
upon all around, the spirit passed from its earthly house to
the Mansions above, where doubtless it now rests in that
glorious land. His remains were interred at the graveyard at
First Creek Church, to rest until summoned from the tomb to
the judgment of God. He left an affectionate wife to mourn
an irreparable loss and many relations and friends, whose
hearts are deeply grieved over the departure of one so dear to
them and one, the memory of whom will ever live fresh in their
hearts.   A Friend

Obituary: Mrs. Fannie King, who was the daughter of Rev.
Moses Holland and the wife of the Rev. Robert King, was born
April 15, 1794; was married in early life; consecrated herself
to the service of Christ while yet young and when her husband
was called to the work of the Gospel Ministry and set apart
by the Church at Neal's Creek to that sacred office, her's was
a privilege of teaching him to read the Word of Divine Truth,
which he has so faithfully since declared to others, making
many wise unto salvation. She was indeed a devoted wife to
the husband of her choice and by reason of her superior
attainments, and constant study of God's word, she became not
only his literary teacher but his theological instructer,
comprehensive commentator and home concordance. She became and
was at the time of her death, the mother of twelve children,
four sons and eight daughters, all of whom she had instructed
in the ways of the Lord and by word and example, constrained
them to "remember their Creator in the days of their youth."
She lived to see them all consistent and useful members of the
Baptist Church and two of her sons ministers in the same. When
her work on earth and in the Militant Kingdom of our Lord was
completed, she heard the blessed invitation from the King of
Kings, "Come up higher, and she quietly and peacefully fell
asleep in Jesus, the 15th of July, 1873, aged 70 years and 3
months. Hers was a triumphant death; no dread, no sting was
felt. May our last end be like hers!   M. M.

Obituary: Mr. George W. Reid, a veteran of the war of 1812 and
also the Indian war of 1836, died in Walker County, Ga. on
the 13th inst. Mr. Reid was between eighty-five and ninety
years of age at the time of his death. He was raised in
Anderson District, S. C. but had been a citizen of Georgia for
thirty years.

Thursday, November 6, 1873
Married: On the 29th of October, 1873, at the residence of the bride's father, Mr. Wm. B. Todd of Anderson and Miss Janie F., youngest daughter of Mr. B. B. Harris, of Oconee.

Married: On Thursday evening, October 23, 1873, by Rev. Baxter Hays, Mr. A. J. Howell and Miss Lettie A. Elgin, all of Anderson County.

Married: On the 28th of October, by Rev. James L. Martin, Hon. T. C. Gower, of Greenville and Miss Sallie A. Martin, of Abbeville.

Married: On the 16th of October, 1873 at the residence of the bride's mother, by Rev. W. H. King, Capt. G. W. Belcher and Miss Mary J. Morgan, all of Anderson County.

Married: On the evening of the 6th inst., at the residence of the bride's father by Rev. L. M. Ayer, Mr. John H. Clarke and Miss Ramah, eldest daughter of David Crosby, all of Anderson County.

Married: On the 23rd of October, at the residence of the bride's father, by Larkin Newton, Esq., Mr. J. T. Boggs and Miss Mary Ann, third daughter of Capt. James Welborn, all of Anderson County.

Obituary: Died, of typhoid fever, in Anderson County, S. C., on the 18th of October, 1873, Miles E., son of Thos. R. and Mary C. Gerard, in the sixth year of his age. The deceased lived but a few days, consequently his sufferings were severe but in all his agony he retained the full powers of consciousness and told his friends that he was going to die. Thus, he has passed to the arms of Him who has said, "Suffer little children to come unto me and forbid them not" - another addition to that happy myriad of little ones who bask in the sunlight of a glorious immortality, to be and reign with Jesus forever. Z. A. Foster.

Obituary: Death of Mr. W. C. Davis, in Charleston yesterday morning at 10:45 o'clock. He was a native of Abbeville County and 32 years of age.

Thursday, November 13, 1873:
Obituary: Rev. C. H. Spears of Oconee County, died at his residence on the 22nd inst. His death was preceded, only a few weeks, by the death of his son and wife.

Married: At the Methodist Church, in Greenville, S. C., on Wednesday evening, Nov. 12th, by Rev. E. J. Meynardie, D.D., Mr. James L. Orr, Jr., of Anderson and Miss E. B. Hammett, second daughter of Col. H. P. Hammett, of Greenville.

Married: On Thursday evening, 6th of November, by Rev. J. L. Vass, Mr. William M. Hagood, of Pickens and Miss Katie Cleveland of Spartanburg.

Married: On the morning of the 18th inst., at the residence of the bride's father, by Rev. Mr. McMillan, Mr. William S. Elrod and Miss Anna M. Bolt, all of Anderson County.

Obituary: We are informed that Mr. David A. Geer, formerly of Anderson County, died at his residence in Rusk County, Texas on the 6th of October, of malarial fever, after a brief illness of only thirty-six hours. Mr. Geer removed to Texas nearly two years ago and had the misfortune to lose his wife in December last. His children are left orphans in a strange land.

Obituary: Death of James Birnie, Esq., in Greenville on Wednesday, 12th instant, aged 32. He was a native of Charleston and had lived in Greenville for 10 years.

Issue of:
Thursday, November 27, 1873:
Married: In the Baptist Church, on Tuesday evening, November 25th, 1873, by Rev. L. M. Ayer, Mr. Luther P. Smith and Miss A. I. Ayer, daughter of the officiating clergyman, all of Anderson.

Married: On November 20, 1873, by Rev. W. A. Hodges, Mr. E. B. Hall and Miss Mary E. Webb, all of Anderson County.

Obituary: Mrs. Gena Evans Mauldin departed this life in Atlanta, Georgia, on the 18th of June 1873, in the twenty second year of her age, in the full assurance of a blessed immortality. Mrs. Mauldin was the daughter of Mrs. Sarah E. and the late Dr. Jno. E. B. Evans, of Columbia, S. C. When a little child the deceased was very bright, cheerful and affectionate and showed evidence of piety at a very early age. In the summer of 1863, she professed conversion, joined the Baptist Church in Columbia and was baptised by her beloved pastor, Rev. J. M. C. Breaker. From that time until her death she was a zealous member and by Divine strength was enabled to sustain a happy, cheerful, Christian character. She was commended to others by a most engaging cheerfulness and a disposition highly social, which enabled her at once to enter into cummunion with friends and strangers. On the 12th of January 1871 she became the wife of Joab L. Mauldin, who has experienced life's keenest anguish in her untimely death. She exhibited the untiring and affectionate anxiety of a Christian mother for little Guy, her only child. As a wife she was watchful and affectionate and faithfully discharged the duties of that sacred relation. The happiness of her companion perpetually occupied her thoughts. None but he who was the dearest object of her love could know its depth, the strength and the purity. This sweet flower was doomed soon to fade. The seeds of fatal consumption were lurking in her frame and in the fall of 1871 began to make themselves known. In August of the following year she had a severe attack of fever and sank into a fatal decline. She suffered long and often intensely, but in all her conflicts with her sufferings the Good Shephard afforded her the support of His Grace. She conversed with much composure about her approaching dissolution. On the day before her death, though she was too weak to express but a few brief thoughts, her mind was in a state of perfect peace. Calmly she left us for the arms of her precious Saviour. She sleeps beside her father in Madison, Georgia. Her tuneful lips are silent forever and her dear hands are folded 'neath the clay.

But she herself is not there; her delighted spirit joins its voice to the melodies of angels and lingers among the flowers of an eternal May. Brief at longest will be our seperation. Ere long she will beckon to us from that shining shore. May each one, husband, child, mother, sister and friends meet her there and receive her heavenly welcome.

Issue of:
Thursday, December 11, 1873:
Married: At the residence of Capt. P. K. Norris, the bride's father on the 4th inst., by Rev. John S. Young, Mr. L. H. Seel and Mrs. L. J. Haynie, all of Anderson County.

Married: At the residence of the bride's father, on the 7th inst., by Rev. W. A. Hodges, Mr. W. M. Harden and Miss Anzie E. Stuart, all of Anderson County.

Married: At the residence of the bride's grandfather, Mr. John Davis, of Abbeville, on the 2nd inst., by the Rev. W. T. Capers, Mr. James H. Bewley of Anderson C. H. and Miss Jennie McCord of Abbeville.

Obituary: We are pained to announce the death of Mrs. Eleanor Stringer, wife of Mr. A. J. Stringer of Belton, which took place on Monday last. She was an estimable lady and leaves many friends to lament her loss.

Issue of:
Thursday, December 18, 1873:
Married: In this town, on the 1st inst., by Rev. J. Scott Murray, Mr. T. A. Williams, of North Carolina and Miss S. E. Roberts, daughter of Mr. C. E. Roberts, of Anderson.

Married: On November 20th, 1873, by Rev. W. P. Martin, at the residence of the bride's father, Mr. Francis Ibsan Bell and Miss Emma Rintha Victoria Branyan daughter of Robert Branyan, all of Anderson County.

Married: On the 3rd inst., by Rev. R. F. Bradley, at the residence of Mr. John Stevenson, Mr. John D. McDonald, of Hart County, Ga. and Miss M. Julia Stevenson of Anderson County, S. C.

Obituary: Mary Eleanor Stringer, (wife of A. J. Stringer, of Belton, S. C.) was born Dec. 31st, 1846 and died from Puerperal Fever, Dec. 6th, 1873, aged 26 years, 11 months and 5 days. She was born of the Spirit and consecrated herself to the service of Christ in early life; united with the Baptist Church and remained a useful and devoted member until translated to the Church Triumphant in Heaven. She was amiable and lovely in all her deportment; as a Christian, meek, humble and relying, carrying about in her body the image of our Lord Jesus Christ; as a mother, patient, tender and forbearing; as a wife, devotedly attached to the husband of her choice, striving at all times to make her home a quiet, happy retreat into which her beloved companion and friends could continually resort and find sympathy in trials, a cheerful greeting when the outside world scoff or taunt. So gentle and loving, so Christ like, was she, that unkind words, unthoughted expressions, murmuring at the treatment of friends, or the dealings of her Heavenly Father, seldom, if ever, escaped her lips. She leaves mother, brothers, husband, two darling children, (one just budded forth) a host of kindred and friends to mourn over her early departure. But they should not murmur, nor mourn excessively, as she is now delivered from the evils of this present world; her spirit is resting in the realms of the blest and her corruptible body, which now rests in the quiet churchyard, will soon come forth glorified to meet the spirit in the air. And those who now mourn will also have passed away or be changed and if found clothed with the righteousness of Christ, will meet her where parting will be no more. Let this glorious thought revive the courage and drooping spirits of grief-stricken ones, and let them strive more earnestly to obtain that world and the resurrection from the dead, that they with her may enter into that rest which remains for the people of God.   M. M.

Obituary: Died, at Anderson, S. C., of rheumatic fever, on the morning of the 5th inst., in the fifth year of her age, little Sarah Church Whitner, daughter of B. F. and Anna Church Whitner. (One verse of poetry follows)

Issue of:
Thursday, December 25, 1873:
Tribute of respect to Mary Susannah Floyd, deceased, wife of John S. Floyd.

Married: On Tuesday evening, December 16th, at the residence of the bride's mother, near Townville, S. C., by Rev. Mr. Crymes, Mr. William N. Alexander and Miss Maria L. Ledbetter, only daughter of Mrs. E. E. Ledbetter, both of Anderson.

Married: At Orrville, S. C., on the 17th of December, 1873, by Rev. R. H. Reid, assisted by Rev. J. D. Burkhead, Mr. James L. Anderson of Talladega, Ala., and Miss Augusta V. Anderson youngest daughter of Mrs. Mary D. Anderson

Married: On Wednesday evening, December 17th, at the Baptist Church in this town, by Rev. L. M. Ayer, Mr. J. A. Brock and Miss Theodosia D. Copeland, all of Anderson.

Married: On Tuesday evening, December 23, 1873, at the resi-dence of the bride's father, by Rev. J. S. Murray, Mr. E. T. Cashine and Miss A. O. Fant, daughter of O. H. P. Fant, Esq., all of Anderson.

Married: In Marion Street Church, Columbia, S. C., Tuesday November 25th, 1873, by Rev. Sidi H. Browne, Mr. H. Bascom Browne and Miss Mollie M. Moody.

Married: On Wednesday, December 17th, at the residence of the officiating minister, by Rev. John Leavell, Mr. Albert A. Jeffers and Miss Fannie M. Moore, all of Anderson County.

Issue of:
Thursday, January 8, 1874:
Homicide: At Calhoun, on 27th of December, Mr. Robert Holliday, Sr., killed by his nephew, John Henry Vermillion, age 17.

Issue of:
Thursday, January 15, 1874:
Married: On January 11th, 1874, by Rev. Robert King, at the

residence of the bride's father, Mr. Hugh M. Knox and Miss Lucy M. Griffin, all of Anderson County.

Married: On Tuesday, 6th of January, 1874, at the residence of Maj. W. B. White, by Rev. H. N. Hays, Capt. Elisha King, of Oconee County and Miss Margaret McClure, of Anderson County.

Married: On Thursday, 8th of January, 1874, by Rev. H. N. Hays, Mr. Robert Moore and Miss Amanda Tannery, both of Oconee.

Married: On the 2nd of December, 1873, at the residence of W. B. Dorn, Esq., by Rev. G. M. Boyd, Mr. Benj. F. Hutchins, of Anderson County and Miss Mary Jeanette Dearing of Edgefield County, S. C.

Married: On December 17th, at the residence of Gen. Arthur of Lexington, by Rev. A. J. Canthen, Rev. G. T. Harmon, of the S. C. Conference and Miss Maggie Seibles.

Married: On Thursday morning, December 25, 1873, by Rev. F. G. Carpenter, Maj. J. M. Hamlin and Miss Hester J. Rogers, all of Anderson.

Married: On the 23rd of December, 1873, at the residence of the bride's father, Thomas L. Reid, by Rev. J. B. Adger, D.D., Mr. Samuel McCrary and Miss M. Montie Reid, all of Anderson County.

The homicide reported in our last issue occurred in Greenville and not in Anderson County as stated. Mr. Holliday lived at the Cooley place and it was there the difficulty took place which ended in his death.

Issue of:
Thursday, January 22, 1874:
Information Wanted: The heirs and descendents of Isaac West, deceased, can hear something to their advantage by communicating with McDowell & McClintock, Carmi, Illinois. These gentlemen wish to know something of the relatives of Mary West, (daughter of the said Isaac West,) who was married in Anderson County nearly 45 years ago to Henry Bugg. Shortly after the marriage they moved to Kentucky, from thence to Indiana and afterwards to White County, Ill., where both of them died a few years ago, leaving no heirs in that country. Any person acquainted with the history of Isaac West's family will confer a favor by writing to the law firm above named, or giving the requisite information to Capt. John W. Daniels, Clerk of Court, at this place.

Issue of:
Thursday, January 29, 1874:
Married: By Rev. A. Rice, at the residence of the bride's father, Jan. 15, 1874, Rev. Edwin Clarence Rice, of Dallas, Texas and Miss Lucy Agnes Pinson of Ninety-Six, Abbeville County, S. C., youngest daughter of T. J. and Gilly Pinson.

Married: On January 8, 1874, at 4 p.m., by Rev. Edwin C. Rice, Mr. Rob't F. Spearman and Mrs. T. N. Boazman, all of Laurens County.

Married: At the residence of the bride's father, on Thursday

evening, Jan. 22nd, by Rev. D. E. Frierson, Dr. D. B. Darby, of
Columbia and Miss Ida Harrison, daughter of Gen. J. W. Harrison
of Anderson.

Married: On Thursday evening, January 8, 1874, at the residence
of the bride's father, by Rev. J. S. Murray, L. L. Gaillard and
Miss Kate Hammond, youngest daughter of Mr. B. F. Hammond, all
of Anderson.

Married: On Thursday evening, 15th inst., by Rev. J. R. Earle,
at the residence of Wm. McCown, Mr. David A. Skelton and Miss
Jeanette McCown, all of Anderson County.

Married: By Rev. J. R. Earle, on Sunday morning, December 6th,
at the residence of the bride's father, Mr. [?] Moore and Miss
Martha L. Sanders of Anderson County.

Obituary: "Death of a Worthy Citizen" - We are pained to record
the death of Mr. James L. Simpson, an estimable and worthy
citizen, which occurred at his residence in this County on
Tuesday night, 20th inst., after a brief illness, from billious
pleurisy, in the 51st year of his age. Mr. Simpson was an
intelligent and cultivated gentleman and only the Friday before
his death was in attendance upon the meeting of Rock Mills
Grange, where he read an essay upon an interesting topic. He
leaves a family of seven children.

Issue of:
Thursday, February 5, 1874:
Married: In the city of Charleston, on the 27th of January,
by the Right Rev. Bishop Lynch, Capt. F. W. Dawson, Editor of
the Charleston News and Courier and Miss Sarah Morgan, youngest
daughter of the late Judge Morgan, of New Orleans, La.

Obituary: "Death of An Aged Citizen" - we are pained to record
the death of an estimable and aged citizen, Mr. Thomas O. Hill,
which occurred at his residence in the Dark Corner on Sunday
afternoon in the 82nd year of his age. He was thrown from a
horse on Saturday morning and it was from the effect of
injuries received that death ensued. Mr. Hill was unusually
vigorous and energetic for one of his advanced age and was
personally supertending some business pertaining to the farm
when he met with the accident which eventuated in his death.
He has been a member of the Methodist Church for upwards of
fifty years and was always faithful in his private devotions
and in attendance upon public worship. He was the father of our
townsman, Col. R. S. Hill, who is the only surviving child of
the deceased. The remains of Mr. Hill were buried at Robert's
Church on Tuesday.

Issue of:
Thursday, February 12, 1874:
Married: On Feb. 3, 1874, at the residence of the bride's
father, Col. F. E. Harrison, Mr. E. Preston Earle and Miss
Antoinnette Harrison, all of Anderson County.

Married: On the 15th of January, 1874, by Rev. F. G. Carpenter,
Mr. Benjamin D. Martin and Miss Mattie Smith, all of Anderson
County.

Issue of:
Thursday, February 19, 1874:
Married: On the 5th February, 1874, at the residence of the
bride's father, Col. R. E. Hill, by Rev. W. W. Mood, Mr. James
M. Moore, of North Carolina and Miss Janie Hill, of Anderson
County.

Issue of:
Thursday, February 26, 1874:
Married: On the 19th of February, 1874, by Rev. F. G. Carpenter,
Mr. D. M. Stott, Jr. and Miss Mary F. Williams, all of Anderson
County.

Married: On the 29th of January last, by Rev. W. E. Walters,
Mr. H. O. King of Anderson County and Miss Lou L. Miller of
Abbeville County.

Issue of:
Thursday, March 5, 1874:
Married: On the 14th of February, 1874 by Rev. Baxter Hays,
Mr. Thomas F. Drake and Miss Flora Snipes, daughter of Matthew
Snipes, Esq., all of Anderson County.

Issue of:
Thursday, March 12, 1874:
Married: On the 26th of Feburary, by Rev. A. J. Cauthen, Dr.
O. R. Horton, of Belton and Miss Ella Latimer, daughter of
Mr. James M. Latimer, of Lowndesville.

Obituary: Died in Bloomfield, Ky., February 17th, 1874, Thomas
Hall, Jr., eldest son of Rev. Thomas Hall, aged 19 years and
17 days. This noble youth was born in Charleston, S. C., but
he sleeps his last sleep in the distant West, far from the
graves of his kindred. On his last birthday he was taken
with a slight chill, the precurator of typhoid fever, which on
the seventeenth day, terminated his earthly life. Amiable,
truthful and dutiful, as a boy he was maturing into a vigorous
manhood, in which the gifts of nature, blended with those of
piety, gave promist of great satisfaction to his friends and
usefulness to the world. Last November, he was baptised by
his father and during his brief Christian profession, the
genuineness and depth of his piety were clearly shown. His
end was calm and trimphant. He yearned to "go home" and "be
with Christ". Brother Hall will receive the sincere sympathy
of his many friends in this State - especially those of them
who have looked upon the face of a dead son and know the anguish
of such a loss. J. L. R.

Issue of:
Thursday, March 19, 1874:
Married: On March 4th, 1874, by Rev. A. J. Cauthen, at the
residence of the bride's father, Mr. James Bruce, Dr. J. B.
Moseley and Miss Anna Bruce, all of Abbeville.

Issue of:
Thursday, March 26, 1874:
Married: On Thursday evening, 5th of March, 1874, by Rev.
D. D. Byers, Mr. John M. Freeman and Miss Laura E. Graham,
daughter of Mr. A. J. Graham, all of Anderson County.

Married: On the 17th of February, by Rev. A. J. Cauthen, Mr.
Thomas Mauldin of Abbeville and Miss Amelia Craft of Anderson
County.

Married: On March 19th, 1874, at the residence of the bride's
mother, by Rev. D. J. McMillan, Rev. J. C. C. Newton, formerly
of Anderson County and Miss Lettie E. Lay, of Pickens County.

Issue of:
Thursday, April 9, 1874:
Married: March 26th, 1874, by Rev. W. P. Martin, at his own
residence, Mr. Charles Sullivan, of Illinois and Miss Susan
C. Harris, of Anderson County, S. C.

Married: By Rev. W. P. Martin, on March 28th, 1874, at his
own residence, Mr. John N. Sutherland and Miss Fannie Willingham, daughter of A. P. Willingham, all of Belton, S. C.

Obituary: "Death of An Estimable Citizen" - The grave has just
closed over the mortal remains of Mr. Joseph W. Carpenter, an
estimable and honorable young man, whose days of anguish and
suffering were ended at the residence of his mother-in-law,
Mr. Martha Webb, in this town, on Monday evening last. Mr.
Carpenter has been suffering from pulmonary disease for several
years and for the space of many months has lingered between
life and death, where the brittle thread of existence seemed
almost severed. His case excited the sympathies of the entire
community, while his patient resignation and cheerful acquies-
cence, mingled with a trusting, unshaken faith in the Saviour
of mankind, was the highest admiration from every one who came
into his sick chamber. When in the enjoyment of good health,
Mr. Carpenter was an active, energetic and useful citizen,
maintaining a high character for strick integrity and upright
dealing in business. His kind and courteous bearing rendered
him poplar [sic] among his acquaintances and there seemed a
bright and promising future for him, when disease began to
undermine a system naturally frail and delicate. Mr. Carpenter
was buried at the Baptist Church in this town on Tuesday afternoon. The religious services were conducted by Rev. L. M. Ayer
and Rev. W. W. Mood, whose truthful and touching references to
the sad event were most impressive upon the large audience
assembled in respect to the deceased. The remains were finally
interred with the imposing ceremonies of the Masonic fraternity,
of which the deceased was a faithful and honored member for a
number of years.

Issue of:
Thursday, April 16, 1874:
Married: On the 26th of February last, by the Rev. Jacob
Burriss, Mr. S. Lawrence Eskew and Miss Nannie S. Reid, third
daughter of Thomas L. Reid, Esq. all of Anderson County.

Issue of:
Thursday, April 30, 1874:
Married: April 26, 1874, by Rev. W. P. Martin, at the residence
of Mrs. Ann Mattison, the bride's aunt, in Calhoun, Anderson
County, Mr. Robert J. Mattison and Miss Martha Sandassie,
eldest daughter of Mr. John R. Sutherland, of Pickens County.

Obituary: It is with a feeling of sadness that we record the

death of an estimable lady, Mrs. F. E. Harrison, wife of Col.
F. E. Harrison, which took place at her residence, Andersonville,
onThursday last, 23rd inst. Her illness was of short duration,
she surviving only about two days from the time she was first
taken ill. The deceased lady was a daughter of Hon. Thos. C.
Perrin, of Abbeville and was highly respected and much beloved
by all who knew her. She leaves behind to mourn her loss a
kind husband and loving children. Our sympathies are with the
bereaved family.

Obituary: Mrs. Isabella Kay, of Honea Path, died at her residence on the 15th inst., after a painful illness of two weeks
duration. She was about eighty five years old and was for many
years a shining light in the Baptist Church.

Issue of:
Thursday, May 7, 1874:
Sudden Deaths:
We have to record the sudden death of Mr. Griffin Breazeale,
a highly respected citizen of this county, who departed this
life at his residence near Belton on Wednesday morning of last
week. He was stricken with paralysis the night before and
survived only about eight or nine hours. Mr. Breazeale had reached
the venerable age of eighty one years and has been quite feeble
for months before his death. He was a good, substantial citizen
and was justly esteemed by a large circle of relatives and
friends.

The painful news reached here on Tuesday that Mrs. William Fant,
of Five Mile, in Pickens County, died suddenly on Monday evening, of heart disease. She was the mother of Messrs. George W.
and James L. Fant, of this town and was in the 70th year of her
age.

Mrs. Caroline Wilson, wife of Mr. John Wilson, of Oconee County,
died at her residence on Thursday last, after an illness of only
a few hours. She was the daughter of the late Wm. Webb, of this
County and leaves many friends and relatives to sympathize with
her immediate family in this sad affliction. Truly, in the
midst of life we are in death.

Issue of:
Thursday, May 14, 1874:
Deaths:
It is with regret that we chronicle the sudden death of Mrs.
M. F. Freeman, which sad event occurred at her residence a
few miles below Craytonville on Thursday evening last. Mrs.
Freeman was unwell for sometime, but not seriously and on
Thursday after retiring for the night, she got up to procure
some water and instantly dropped dead.

Also, Mrs. John M. Smith died on Monday the 4th inst., at her
residence near Deep Creek, after an illness of only a few
days. Both were estimable ladies and their loss will be deeply
felt both by their families and friends.

Mr. Charles H. Whitworth, a worthy citizen of Oconee County,
died on the 23rd ultimo, in the 35th year of his age.

Issue of:
Thursday, May 21, 1874:
Deaths:
Millie Belle, 2 year old daughter of Dr. J. W. Gurley, died on
14th inst., from teething. She was buried in the Baptist
graveyard.

Mrs. Margaret Gasaway, an estimable lady living in the lower
portion of the County, died at her residence on Friday last
after a lingering and painful illness. The deceased was
advanced in years being at the time of her death 83 years old.
She was the mother of Mrs. Dawson in town.

Mr. William Long, an old and highly respected citizen of our
County, died at his residence, South of this place, on Saturday morning last, from an attack of bilious cramp colic. The
deceased was ill but a short while before he died; the attack
being violent. He was in his 75th year at the time of his
death and had always been a true citizen.

Issue of:
Thursday, May 28, 1874:
Married: In the Presbyterian Church on Wednesday evening,
May 20th, 1874, by Rev. D. E. Frierson, Mr. John W. Todd and
Miss Mattie E. Frierson, daughter of the officiating clergyman,
all of Anderson, S. C.

Married: On May 20th, 1874, by Rev. W. P. Martin, at his own
residence, Mr. John L. Norrell, of Abbeville C. H. and Miss
Dora Kuhlmann of Greenwood, S. C.

Obituary: "Death of John D. M. Dobbins" - The solemn truth that
"in the midst of life we are in death", is seldom so forcibly
illustrated as in the demise of this estimable citizen. On
Saturday morning, the second of May, he came from his residence
in the suburbs to his place of business in town, apparently in
his usual health, and particularly impressed, as it would
seem, with a sense of the duty resting on him as a good citizen.
On the Monday following, which would be Saleday, certain
official transactions were to be had, involving the pecuniary
interests of a number of his old friends, as to which he was in
possession of information acquired years before when Sheriff,
that was unknown to others. At 11 a.m. he called on the writer,
avowedly to communicate the information he possessed in relation to these matters, which he did with great particularity,
stating that if present on Monday he would make the facts
known himself, but if not, justice demanded that they should be
communicated. This solicitude for his friends being in
character with the fidelity of his whole life, attracted special
attention at the time, but recalling the circumstances, it
might be conjectured that he had some premonition of his
impending fate. After the lapse of perhaps half an hour, he
returned to his store, where, in a very few minutes, whilst
sitting conversing in his usual cheerful manner, his tongue
suddenly refused to give utterance, friends and physicians
near by were called in and it was ascertained that he had been
stricken with paralysis. All the aid that kindness and medical
skill could render was promptly administered, but to no avail.
Without the power of speech, he gave evidence of consciousness
and the recognition of friends for perhaps an hour, when
growing gradually worse, he lingered, manifesting neither

mental nor physical suffering, until the setting of the sun, when his spirit departed to "that bourne whence no traveler returns". Mr. Dobbins was, perhaps, as well known and highly respected by the people of Anderson County as any man who had lived in it and his loss will be felt and mourned in all circles of society; more especially will he be held in fond remembrance by that numerous class - the poor and the needy who have been the recipients of his gushing kindness. [Followed by one verse of poetry] Mr. Dobbins was born and raised in Anderson, and his whole life was devoted to the service of her people - not so much in official position, as in the discharge of the duties of those trusts that invariably seek the public spirited and patriotic citizen, in whom all confide and whose nature will not permit him to refuse a kindness. True, in addition to numerous minor offices which he held at different times, he was from 1858 to 1862 Sheriff of his county, and in these positions, as in the private trusts confided to him, invariably discharged his duties with an earnestness and fidelity that met the undivided "well done" of all the people. Mr. Dobbins passed his fifty sixth birthday on the 26th of March last, and although somewhat feeble for a year past as compared with his former vigor, his friends had reason to hope that several years of usefulness remained to him; but he is gone, at the places that knew him "shall know him no more forever". Four children had proceeded him to the grave - three sleep gently by his side in Robert's Churchyard, one rests on a Virginia battlefield and a wife, four children, brothers and sisters, with numerous relatives and friends survive him to mourn his loss. But they do not mourn without hope. He had been a number of years a consistent and worthy member of Hopewell Baptist Church and his walk and conversation was such that they feel their loss is "his eternal gain". A kind husband and father, a more devoted friends, or better citizen, wife, children, friends or county have seldom been called to mourn.

Issue of:
Thursday, June 4, 1874:
Married: At the residence of the bride's father, On Tuesday, May 26th, at 2 o'clock p.m., by Rev. M. McGee, Mr. William C. Jackson, of Amelia County, Va. and Miss P. Victoria McGee, daughter of G. W. McGee, Esq., of Belton, S. C.

Married: At the residence of the bride's father, on Thursday, 21st of May by Rev. L. H. Shuck, Mr. Curran H. Sloan of New York and Miss Kate Tupper second daughter of Simeon Hyde, Esq., of Charleston.

Married: On Thursday evening, May 7th, 1874, at the residence of the bride's father, by Rev. J. G. Law, Mr. John W. Shelor and Miss Jane, daughter of M. Stokes Stribling, Esq., all of Oconee County.

Married: On Tuesday evening, June 2nd, by Rev. P. F. Stevens, Mr. R. Edmund Belcher and Miss Lucie C. Taylor, daughter of the late Col. D. S. Taylor, all of Anderson.

Issue of:
Thursday, June 25, 1874:
Obituary: Died, on the 17th inst., Louisa Ellen Kay, only child of Lawrence and Nancy B. Kay, aged 13 months and two weeks.

Obituary: Mr. John McGregor, an old and highly esteemed
citizen of this County, died at his residence five miles southwest of town, on Tuesday evening, last, from Bright's disease
of the kidneys. He was born and raised in Anderson County
and was sixty five years old at the time of his death. An
honest man, an upright citizen, he was beloved and respected
by all who knew him. During his long and painful illness, he
bore his sufferings with fortitude and Christian resignation.
He leaves behind to mourn his loss an affectionate family and
a host of kind friends. Our sympathies are with the bereaved.

Issue of:
Thursday, July 9, 1874:
Obituary: Died, on the 24th June, Anna Camilla Smith, daughter
of Wm. P. Smith, aged 27 years. She was painfully ill more
than three months. She cast her lot with believers ten years
ago - died a member of Big Creek Baptist Church on the 25th,
Rev. W. L. Ballard preached her funeral; then we laid her in
Big Creek Cemetery. The first Sunday Rev. R. W. Burts, her
pastor, closed the memorial services with the song - "Sister,
thou wast mild and lovely,/ Gentle as the Summer breeze;/
Pleasant as the air of evening/ When it floats among the
trees." - Then closing with prayer for the family.
Williamston   July 6, 1874   A. W. C.

Obituary: Elijah Holden, of Oconee, is dead. He had many
friends in Orr's Rifles.

Issue of:
Thursday, July 30, 1874:
Suicide: We are pained to learn that Mr. Joshua Smith, an old
and highly valuable citizen of this County, committed suicide
on Monday, the 20th inst. at his residence near Slabtown. It
appears that Mr. Smith was in good health and spirits, his only
affliction being a slight attack of rheumatisim. About noon
he went out of the house and nothing was apprehended until
supper-time, when his sister went out on the piazza to call him
to supper and upon his not answering the summons, she went to
the carriage-house near by and found him suspended by the
neck with the reins of a bridle and not quite dead. Mr. Smith
was an able and efficient school teacher for a number of years
in the neighborhood of Slabtown and was at the time of his
death about fifty-five years old.

Murder: Miss Mary C. Tucker murdered by Henry Ziegler on 28
July 1874 by shooting her in the head with a pistol.

Issue of:
Thursday, August 6, 1874:
Obituary: "Death of a Prominent Citizen" - It is with sadness
that we record the death of Dr. C. L. Gaillard, an old, estimable and prominent citizen of this County, which occurred at
his residence about 10 miles north of this place, on the night
of the 29th July last, after a long and painful illness,
occasioned by dropsy. The deceased was born in St. James Santee,
formerly one of the low-country parishes, but now included in
Charleston County and came to the up-country at an early age
and settled in what was then known as Pendleton District, but
which is now Anderson County. He was twice elected to the
Legislature, once when he was quite a youngman from Pendleton
District and during the war from Anderson District. He was a

155

local Methodist Preacher for a number of years and was most zealous in his endeavors and teachings. During the last few years of his life he devoted himself to his earlier profession of Medicine and did much good as a Physician. He was earnest in whatever he undertook and did his utmost to do right. By his death the County loses a most valuable citizen, the community a true friend and his bereaved family a kind and indulgent parent and protector. At the time of his death he was in his 66th year. Beloved and respected by all who knew him, his memory will long be cherished. His remains were brought to this place on Thursday evening last and interred in the Presbyterian Cemetery. Our sympathies are with the bereaved family in their present sad affliction.

Additional Particulars of the Murder: It seems evident from the testimony of the witness at the inquest held upon the body of Miss Mary C. Tucker, that the killing was premeditated. Peter Carroll, one of the witnesses, testified that Henry Ziegler, in conversation with him sometime before the murder took place, said that if he did not get Miss Tucker she would never do anybody else any good. Further testimony went on to show that Ziegler came to town with Elbridge Tucker (a brother of Miss Mary Tucker) on the 28th July and returned home about 9 o'clock p.m. and while on the way home from town said that Miss Mary was angry with him. After going into the house, Ziegler took up Elbridge Tucker's pistol and examined it, saying that it was alright. Tucker told Ziegler to be careful with the pistol as it was loaded and sometime afterwards Miss Mary remarked to him that it was not right for a young man to carry a pistol. At the time she said this young Tucker had gone to bed, but a young man named Brooks Gailey was present with Miss Mary. Soon after she made the remark about carrying weapons, Zeigler presented the pistol and shot her through the forehead, the ball entering the brain. She fell over and said, "Henry what made you do that", and he made no reply. He then procured water and a towel and washed the blood from her face twice. Brooks Gailey ask Zeigler to assist him in removing her to another place and he refused. Young Tucker who was in bed at the time, (10 o'clock p.m.) upon hearing the report of the pistol, got up and came to the assistance of his sister. He examined the pistol and found one of the chambers empty, one ball having been fired out. He then went out after assistance and during his absence Zeigler left the premises running. Before assistance arrived, Miss Tucker had breathed her last. An inquest was held upon her body on the following morning, the 29th July, Trial Justice John Bryant acting Coroner. The verdict of the jury was, that "Miss Mary C. Tucker came to her death at 10 o'clock, on the night of 28th July, in her father's home, from a pistol ball entering the forehead and brain, the pistol being in the hands of one Henry Zeigler." Parties soon started in pursuit of Zeigler, and succeeded in capturing him the following day at Ruckersville, Ga. The parties who captured him were Messrs. Wiles, John H. Morgan and Andrew Craft. They brought him to this place the next day and lodged him in jail. Zeigler states that the shooting was accidental, that he examined the pistol before presenting it at Miss Tucker and could not perceive any loads in it.

Issue of:
Thursday, August 13, 1874:
Mrs. Annie Bailey, an aged lady of this County, died at her
residence on Friday last after a long and painful illness.
The deceased was in the 78th year of her age.

Issue of:
Thursday, August 20, 1874:
Married: By Rev. W. T. Martin, August 13th, 1874, in the
Baptist Church, at Friendship, Anderson County, Mr. G. Griffin
Cason and Miss Mary Ann Davenport, daughter of Mr. Francis
Davenport, all of Greenville County.

Married: On August 5th, by the Rev. Wm. Haynes, D. D., Mr.
Richard Pinson and Miss Alice C., eldest daughter of Thos. A.
Wideman, all of Dallas Co., Texas.

Obituary: We are pained to record the death of Mrs. Ezekiel
George, an old and highly respected lady of our town, which
sad event occurred about 11 o'clock, Sunday night last. Mrs.
George has been suffering for a long time from the effects of
cancer, which finally terminated her existence. She bore her
long and painful illness with Christian fortitude and resignation. She was at the time of her death in the 58th year
of her age. Our sympathies are with her bereaved family and
friends, who will long have cause to mourn her loss. She was
interred in the Presbyterian Cemetery at 5 o'clock on Monday
evening last.

Issue of:
Thursday, August 27, 1874:
Married: On the 20th August, by Rev. Wm. W. Mood, Mr. David
White and Miss Malissa N. McMillan. All of Anderson C. H.

Married: On the 13th of August, by Rev. W. P. Martin, in the
Baptist Church, at Friendship, Anderson County, Mr. G. Griffin
Cason and Miss Mary Ann Davenport, daughter of Mr. Frances
Davenport. All of Anderson County.

Issue of:
Thursday, September 3, 1874:
Obituary: Died in Cobb County, Ga., on the 22nd of August,
1874, of consumption, Martha W. Leverett, youngest child of
John and Ursula Laverett, aged 21 years and 13 days.

Married: On Tuesday evening, 18th of August, in the Presbyterian Church, at Williamston, by Rev. B. F. Mauldin, Mr. R. E.
Hill, of Abbeville and Miss Mamie T. Hamilton of Williamston.

Obituary: Mr. Joseph Keese, well known in this community as
the father of our worthy townsman, Mr. E. E. Keese, died at
his home, Fair Play, Oconee County, on Wednesday morning last,
from liver complaint. Mr. Keese had been suffering for about
three months from the disease but was prostated only one day
before his death. He was in the 64th year of his age.

Obituary: Mrs. Ellen Hamilton, an aged lady and sister of
Mrs. L. A. Osborne, died at the residence of the latter on
Saturday morning last. She resided in town upwards of thirty
years and was at the time of her death about 70 years old. Her
remains were interred in the Presbyterian Cemetery on Sunday.

Issue of:
Thursday, September 24, 1874:
Married: On Thursday, September 17th, by Rev. D. D. Byars,
Mr. Andrew J. Graham and Miss Mary Ann Heller, all of Anderson
County.

Issue of:
Thursday, October 1, 1874:
Married: On Tuesday evening, 25th of September, by Rev. J. L.
Kennedy, Mr. Nathaniel Elrod and Miss Mary Lou Simpson, all of
Anderson County.

Obituary: We are pained to record the death of Miss Mattie
Vandiver, which sad event occurred at the residence of her
mother, near Neal's Creek Church, on Thursday evening last,
from consumption. During a long and painful illness of more
than a year, the deceased bore her sufferings with christian
fortitude and resignation. She was a kind and loving daughter,
an affectionate sister and a warm, generous friend. Amiable
in character and gentle in manners, she was beloved and respected by all who knew her. Our sympathies are with the bereaved
family and friends who are left to mourn her loss. Her
remains were interred in the Neal's Creek cemetery on Friday
evening last.

Obituary: Preston Fant, infant son of our worthy townsman,
Mr. W. A. Fant, died at his residence on Wednesday, September
23rd, from whooping cough. He was a promising child and his
loss is deeply felt by his parents.

Issue of:
Thursday, October 8, 1874:
Married: On Thursday, October 1st, by Rev. D. E. Frierson,
Mr. E. A. Smith, of Charleston and Miss Mary E. Lewis of
Anderson.

Married: On 4th October, 1874, by Rev. W. P. Martin, at his
own residence, Mr. Ambrose T. Fleming and Miss Carrie C.
Kilgore, all of Anderson County.

Issue of:
Thursday, October 15, 1874:
Married: On the 8th inst., at the residence of the bride's
father, by Rev. Cuttino Smith, Dr. G. W. Earle and Miss Jeanette
daughter of Mr. Matthew Breazeale, all of Anderson County.

Issue of:
Thursday, October 22n, 1874:
Married: October 18, 1874, by Rev. W. P. Martin, in the
Baptist Church at Friendship, Mr. Allen M. Smith and Miss Mary
E. Smith, all of Anderson County.

Issue of:
Thursday, October 29, 1874:
Married: On Thursday evening, 22nd October, by Rev. H. Tyler,
Mr. A. W. Palmer and Miss Mary E. Palmer, all of Anderson
County.

Married: In Atlanta, Ga., on Thursday, 22nd October, by Rev.
David Willis, D.D., of that city, Dr. John W. Simpson and Mrs.
John D. Williams, both of Laurens, S. C.

Married: On the evening of the 27th inst., at the residence
of Col. J. C. Haynie, the bride's father, by the Rev. M.
McGee, Mr. J. Albert Langston and Miss Mary J. Haynie, all of
Anderson County.

Obituary: Died in Anderson County, S. C., Oct. 17th, 1874,
David Curtous, infant son of Mr. Wm. J. and Mrs. Mary C.
Gentry, aged two months and three weeks, "Suffer little children
and forbid them not, to come unto me, for such is the Kingdom
of Heaven." W. M. K.

Obituary: We are pained to record the death of Mrs. A. S.
Sadler, which sad event occurred at the residence of her husband,
near Sherrard's Store, on Tuesday, the 20th ult., from fever of
a malignant type. She was an estimable lady, beloved and
respected by all who knew her and her loss will be deeply
felt by a kind husband and four loving children, one of whom is
an infant and by the many relatives and friends whom she leaves
behind. Our sympathies are with the bereaved ones.

Issue of:
Thursday, November 5, 1874:
Married: On 27th of October, at the residence of the bride's
father, by Rev. J. L. Kennedy, Mr. J. P. Smith and Miss Corrie,
only daughter of Mr. F. M. Glenn, all of Slabtown, Anderson
County.

Married: On Sunday morning, 1st November, at the residence of
the bride's father, by Rev. F. G. Carpenter, Dr. R. G. Sloan
of Columbia, S. C. and Miss Sallie C. Carpenter of Anderson
County, eldest daughter of the officiating minister.

Married: On the 13th of October, at the residence of the
bride's father, by Rev. Edwin G. Weed, Mr. T. Douglas Sloan of
Pendleton and Miss Fannie M. Dye, daughter of James M. Dye, of
Augusta, Ga.

Married: On Wednesday evening, October 28th, by Rev. W. W.
Mood, Mr. W. C. Scott and Miss Ida Scott, all of Anderson.

Homicide: Wm. Martin shoots Stephen Chastain, Jr.

Death: Mr. Wm. Moorhead died suddenly.

Death: Died, B. Rush Campbell, Esq., a native of Laurens.
Buried Magnolia Cemetery near Charleston.

Issue of:
Thursday, November 12, 1874:
Married: On Thursday, November 5th, at the residence of the
bride's father, in Pickens County, by Rev. L. M. Ayer, Mr.
John R. Williams of Anderson and Miss Sallie A. Lenhardt of
Pickens.

Married: On November 5th, by Rev. W. P. Martin, at the residence of the bride's mother, Mr. Grief Tate of Anderson County
and Miss Margaret Murff of Laurens County.

Obituary: Died, on Thursday morning last, at his residence
near Sandy Springs, after a long illness occasioned by
consumption, Mr. John McLain, in the 40th year of his age.

The deceased was a highly respected citizen. His remains were interred with all the honors of the Grange Order in the Cemetery at Sandy Springs on Friday last.

Issue of:
Thursday, December 3, 1874:
Married: At Varennes, Nov. 26, 1874, by Rev. W. F. Pearson, assisted by Rev. D. E. Frierson, Mr. John W. Thompson and Miss Mattie L., eldest daughter of Col. J. W. Norris, all of Anderson County.

Married: On Thursday evening, Nov. 19th, at the residence of the bride's father, Capt. J. W. Major, by Rev. D. D. Byars, Mr. Willie L. Blackman and Miss Bettie A. Major, all of Anderson County.

Obituary: Miss Nancy Erskine died at the residence of her father, Mr. Thomas Erskine, near Broadway, on Friday last, after a long and painful illness.

Issue of:
Thursday, December 10, 1874:
Married: In Williamston, S. C., Thursday, December 3, 1874, by Rev. S. A. Weber, Miss Mollie Prince, daughter of W. L. Prince, Esq., of Williamston and Mr. L. H. Fouche, of Ninety Six, S. C.

Married: In Pendleton, S. C., on Thursday, 24th November, at the residence of Maj. George Seaborn, by Rev. A. H. Cornish, Mr. Robert G. Gaillard of Savannah, Ga., and Miss Mary A. Gilreath of Pendleton.

Death: James Trotter was killed by Dyer McJunkin on Sunday night last in Pickens. McJunkin cut Trotter's throat from ear to ear. Whiskey was the cause of the dispute which led to the bloody deed.

Obituary: Death of Mr. J. Milton Brown, at Townville, on Sunday morning last. He was a brother of Col. J. N. Brown and Mr. W. S. Brown, of Anderson.

Issue of:
Thursday, December 17, 1874:
Married: On Wednesday evening, Dec. 16, 1874, at the residence of the bride's father, Hon. Wm. Perry, by Rev. W. C. Smith, Mr. Joseph T. Keys and Miss Mary V. Perry, all of Anderson County.

Married: On Thursday evening, Dec. 2nd, at the residence of the bride's father, by Rev. J. R. Earle, Mr. T. Richardson of Hart County, Ga. and Miss Fannie L. Burriss of Anderson County.

Married: By Rev. J. R. Earle, on Tuesday evening, Dec. 8th, at the bride's residence, Mr. Timmons of Wilkes County, Ga. and Mrs. M. E. Holland of Anderson County.

Married: On Thursday evening, December 10th, by Rev. W. P. Martin, at the residence of the bride's father, Mr. Oliver M. Hanna and Miss Sarah Cordelia Elrod, eldest daughter of Adam Elrod, all of Anderson County.

Married: On Tuesday morning, 8th inst., at St. Luke's Church, Newberry, by Rev. Ellison Capers, Mr. Merver Brown of St. Louis, Mo. and Miss Mary Arthur of Greenville, S. C.

Married: On November 25th, by Rev. Mr. McMillan, Mr. R. M. Jenkins and Miss A. A. Gaillard, all of Anderson County.

Obituary: Death of Mrs. Mary Hammond, consort of Mr. B. F. Hammond, at her son-in-law's Mr. S. Bleckley, on Monday evening last, in her 62nd year. Buried in the Baptist Cemetery.

Issue of:
Thursday, December 24, 1874:
Married: On Tuesday, December 15th, by Rev. R. F. Bradley, Mr. William Hamilton and Miss Sallie Clinkscales, all of Anderson County.

Married: On Thursday, December 17th, by Rev. J. S. Young, Mr. Robert S. Sherard and Miss Sue Davis, all of Anderson County.

Married: On Thursday, December 17th, at the residence of the bride's father, by Rev. W. A. Hodges, Mr. Samuel Murphy and Miss Anna Osborne, all of Anderson County.

Married: On Thursday, 17th December, 1874, by Rev. W. P. Martin, at the residence of the bride's mother, Mr. Thomas A. Pearkins of Pickens County and Miss Mary Jane, eldest daughter of Mrs. McDowell, of Anderson.

Married: On Thursday evening, December 17th, by Rev. L. M. Ayer, Mr. A. L. Welch and Mrs. H. J. Stone, all of Anderson County.
** Issue of Thursday, January 7, 1875 additions - see Page 251
Issue of:
Thursday, January 7, 1875:
Married: On Tuesday, Dec. 22nd, 1874, at the residence of the bride's father, Banister Allen, Esq., by Rev. L. M. Ayer, Mr. J. Belton Watson of Anderson County and Miss Lizzie H. Allen of Abbeville County.
Issue of: January 21, 1875:
Married: On Thursday morning, January 14th, at the residence of the bride's father, by Rev. J. E. Earle, assisted by Rev. Jacob Burriss, Dr. D. S. Watson and Miss Corrie A. Watson, eldest daughter of John B. Watson, Esq., all of Anderson.
** Issue of Thursday, January 14, 1875 - see Page 251
Issue of: Thursday, January 21, 1875 - see Page 251 & 252
Thursday, January 28, 1875:
Married: Jan. 21, 1875, at the residence of Mrs. Mary Dean, by Rev. H. M. Barton, Mr. Asbury Wiggins and Miss M. L. Gibson, all of Fair Play.

Issue of:
Thursday, February 4, 1875:
Married: Jan. 28, 1875, by Rev. W. P. Martin, at the residence of the bride's brother, Mr. Andrew S. Drake, of Abbeville County and Miss Fannie E. Wardlaw of Anderson County.

Married: On Thursday evening the 14th of January, by Rev. H. N. Hays, Mr. John J. Martin of Anderson and Miss Lucy Cleveland of Oconee County.

Married: In this town, on Thursday evening, the 2nd inst., by
Rev. J. S. Murray, Mr. Charles O. Spencer of Ashland, Mississippi
and Miss Mamie Arnold of Lowndesville, Abbeville County and
formerly of Anderson.

Obituary: Death of a Noble Patriot - The Pickens Sentinel
brings the announcement of the death of that sterling old
patriot and honest citizen, Gen. F. N. Garvin, which occurred
at his residence in Pickens County on Friday night, 22nd ult.,
in the 73rd year of his age. Gen. Garvin was one of the
prominent men of better days and represented Pickens District
in the Senate and House of Representatives before the war and
likewise served as Sheriff for one term. He was generous,
hightones and honorable in every relation of life and was
unswerving in devotion to principal, always true as steel in
whatever he thought was right. South Carolina has lost a
devoted and faithful citizen whose place is not easily supplied.

Issue of:
Thursday, February 11, 1875:
Obituary: Death of Judge John T. Green - Judge John T. Green
departed this life at his residence in Sumter on Wednesday
afternoon, January 27th, remaining conscious to the last and
with the power of speech unpaired. The following sketch of
his career is copied from the Charleston News and Courier:
Judge John T. Green, of Sumter, was the son of Rev. Henry D.
Green of Mechanicsville, S. C. and was born at Mechanicsville
on October 18, 1827. At an early age he entered the South
Carolina Collect where he remained for three years. He subsequently entered the law office of Mr. F. J. Moses, Sr., the
present chief justice of the state and after a thorough course
of study was submitted to the bar in 1849 when he had just
passed his twenty first year. In 1852 Judge Green was elected
to the State Legislature on the Co-operation ticket and being
re-elected served for six successive years. Being again put
forward in 1858, he declined to be a candidate and continued to
practice his profession in Sumter until 1864 when he was again
elected a member of the Legislature. There having been some
irregularity in the preceeding election, a new one was held in
1865 and Judge Green was once more nominated and elected. In
the following year, 1866, Judge Green ran against the Hon.
John N. Frierson for State Senate from Sumter County and was
beaten by sixty six votes. During the war and for some years
afterward, Judge Green was in delicate health as he took no
part in the struggle he was regarded as a Union man. In 1866
he was appointed President of the Provost Court in Sumter and
held that post until civil authority was restored. When the
reconstruction government was organized he was unanimously
elected by the General Assembly Judge of the Third Judicial
Circuit, was re-elected upon the expiration of his term of
office and was still incumbent of that office at the time of
his death. Judge Green was a Republican in good standing and
his learnin, imparitality and square dealing on the bench
and in private life won for him the respect and confidence of
all classes and parties. For the past three years Judge
Green has been in bad health, his malady, consumption, assuming
a more dangerous aspect within the past three months and
finally causing his death.

Dreadful Calamity: The following letter copied from the
Greenville News of Tuesday last contains an account of dreadful

calamity which occurred in this county on Saturday last. The
News says:
It appears that on yesterday morning (Saturday) the 6th,
Aaron Holland a respectable and substantial farmer living some
two miles from Grove Station on the Anderson side of Saluda,
left his home together with his wife to attend a church meeting
at Grove Station, the only person left at home being his daughter Amanda, a maiden lady some thirty years of age - those
three comprising the family. While at church, at 11 o'clock, he
received information that his house was burned and upon hurry-
ing home learned to his horror that his daughter was burned
to death, together with the dwelling, kitchen smoke house and
other out-buildings and nearly all their contents. A sewing
machine, some chairs, bacon, etc. were saved, some neighbors
having reached there in time, being attracted by the smoke.
The family had mostly used the kitchen in the day time during
cold weather in which there were a stove and fire place and it
is supposed that the daughter may have accidently caught fire
to her clothing in the kitchen and from thence fled to her own
room in the house, a few steps distant and was there burned
to death, thus setting a fire to the room, as at that place
the fire was first seen from a distance and there her remains,
consisting of the heart entire, a few bones and a portion of
one arm, were found, all of which were carefully gathered for
burial. It is perhaps possible she may have been taken with a
fit, to which she was sometimes liable. thereby setting her
clothing on fire. The sad calamity has sent a thrill of horror
throughout the neighborhood.

Issue of:
Thursday, February 18, 1875:
Married: (From the Honolulu Commercial Advertiser) In this
city, at St. Andrews Temporary Cathedral, on Monday, December
21, 1874, by the Right Rev. Bishop of Honolulu, assisted by
Rev. J. Mackintosh, Mr. Frederick Harrison Hayselden, formerly
of Brighton, England, to Miss Talula Lucy, only daughter of
Mr. Walter Murray Gibson, of Lanai and formerly of Pendleton,
S. C.

Issue of:
Thursday, February 25, 1875:
Married: February 18, 1875, by Rev. W. F. Martin, at the
residence of the bride's mother, Mr. John J. Cooly and Miss
Missouri E. Breazeale, all of Anderson County.

Tribute - of respect to Martin H. Smith, who died 31st January
1875, by the Flat Rock Grange No. 295.

Issue of:
Thursday, March 4, 1875:
Married: At Vallambrosa, near Pendleton, on Wednesday, 24th
of February, at the residence of the bride's father, by Rev.
A. H. Cornish, Mr. Wm. Wragg Simons of Charleston and Miss
Carrie T. Miller, daughter of Dr. H. C. Miller of Pendleton.

Obituary: Dear little Lizzie, infant daughter of Dr. George
R. and Hattie C. Dean, died on Wednesday evening, February 3,
1875, aged 10 months, 2 weeks and 2 days. "Our dove-eyed
darling, our sweet little dear,/ Has left us to mourn, but the
angels to cheer;/ She has been called by the "God-one" to

missions above/ Where sorrow is unknown, but all is love./
Our church was too pure for a world like this,/ Her home is in
heaven, an abode of bliss,/ Of the one who said, "Let them
come unto me"/ Where she will rest in the bos'm through
eternity./ Though the blow seems hard-seems in cruelty sent,/
The father knows best, and in love it is meant;/ And of such
is His Kingdom, does he not say?/ To us says come - and we
should obey."   D. C. A.

Obituary: Mr. John Simmons died at his residence in Laurensville on the 20th inst., in the 73rd year of his age. He was
widely known to the traveling public as a genial and accommodating landlord for the last forty years.

Issue of:
Thursday, March 11, 1875:
Melancholy Accident: We learn from Dr. W. T. Holland, who was
attending a professional call in the neighborhood of Knox's
Bridge over Tugalo River, in Oconee County, that on Thursday
last two little boys, aged respectively seven and five, the
sons of John C. Neville, were playing on the bank of the river
and fell in. One of them cried out and was heard by a colored
woman, who ran some distance and informed a colored boy of the
occurrence, when he ran immediately to the river, plunged in,
and succeeded in bringing them to the bank. One of the little
boys was found to be quite dead, while the other, who had
fallen in last, was resuscitated by Dr. Holland and others who
came up soon after they were brought out of the water. This
was a sad affair and should warn all parents to keep their
children away from water courses, especially when they are
unaccompanied.

Issue of:
Thursday, March 18, 1875:
Obituary: Died, in Charleston, on the 8th inst., Bertha,
infant daughter of George A. and Eleanor M. Wagener, aged
two weeks. "Of such is the Kingdom of Heaven." L. D. K.

Married: On the 24th ult., at the residence of the bride's
mother, by Rev. J. R. Earle and H. J. Goss, Mr. G. W. Richardson of Athens, Ga. to Miss Fannie Magee, of Anderson County.

Married: On March 10, 1875, by Rev. W. P. Martin, at his own
residence, Mr. E. Wallis Ragsdale and Miss Texannah Chapman,
all of Anderson County.

Issue of:
Thursday, March 25, 1875:
Obituary: Death of Capt. James M. McFall - It becomes our sad
and painful duty to announce the death of Capt. James M. McFall,
a prominent and influential citizen of Pickens County, which
occurred on Saturday morning last, 20th of March, in the 32nd
year of his age. The deceased was a native of Anderson County
and a son of the late Col. John McFall. He lived in our midst
until a few years ago when he removed to Pickens C. H. and
entered upon a prosperous career as a merchant, building up a
substantial and lucrative business within a very short time.
His quiet, engaging manners, strict integrity and faithful
adherence to business principles won for him an enduring
popularity among the people with whom his fortunes were

identified and it is simple truth to aver that no man of his
years was so thoroughly appreciated or more strongly beloved by
the honest people of Pickens County, nor whose loss could be
more keenly felt in that community. Capt. McFall was a gallant
and faithful soldier in the Confederate army. He was our
friend and comrade-in-arms during the protracted struggle and
we can testify to his unwavering fidelity as an officer and
soldier throughout the entire war. He entered the service as
a private in the ranks of the "Palmetto Riflemen", which was
raised chiefly in this town and at the First Battle of Manassas
he was captured by the enemy and for months endured the rigors
of prison life in the Old Capitol Prison at Washington City.
He was exchanged the following spring and returned at once to
duty. Later in the war he was appointed Sergeant Major of the
Palmetto Sharpshooters, when we were serving as Adjutant of
that command and subsequently he received the appointment of
Adjutant from the War Department, which gave him the rank of
Captain. In that capacity he continued to serve with fidelity
and honor until the close of the war when he returned to the
peaceful pursuits of the private citizen. No man was more
greatly endeared to the entire command. Officers and men will
unanimously concur in expressing the highest admiration for his
undoubted courage and unflinching adherence to duty. Soon
after the war Capt. McFall was married to Miss Mildred Robinson,
of this town and for several years he was engaged in mercantile
employment here. His popularity in the army was maintained
at home and none will mention his name save with the utmost
respect and kindly feeling. He joined the Presbyterian
Church and always lived a consistent and unblemished life,
being recognized as an earnest and zealous worker in the vineyard of his Master. Indeed, it was a peculiar and beautiful
trait of his character that he was ever mindful of the religious training of the rising generation, for whose welfare and
happiness he was constantly laboring. The hand of friendship
would fain trace other incidents and characteristics of this
noble and generous man, whose loss is so universally deplored
and whose memory and good deeds will be cherished in after
years by all who knew him. Just and true in every relation
of life; liberal hearted, philanthropic in his nature; with
undaunted bravery and manly self-reliance, none excelled him
in all that makes up thenoblest speciman of humanity. The
remains of Capt. McFall were brought to this place on Monday
morning under the escort of a large delegation of the Masonic
fraternity who were met at the depot by another delegation from
Hiram Lodge No. 68, of which the deceased was formerly a member.
The body was carried to the Masonic Hall and remained there
until eleven o'clock a.m., at which hour the funeral services
took place. The procession of Masons was unusually large and
the congregation at the Baptist Church was imposing in numbers,
embracing all classes of our citizens. The stores and
business houses were closed as a mark of respect to the occasion.
The funeral sermon was delivered by Rev. J. S. Murray, in which
the life and character of the deceased was feelingly portrayed
and the most useful lessons to the living were included in an
earnest and eloquent manner. The discourse created a profound impression among the listeners, whose enrapt attention
showed the effect of the speakers solemn entreaties to emulate
the example of the deceased, in making preparation for the
inevitable change from time to eternity. After the religious
services were concluded the remains were committed to the charge

of the Masonic fraternity and with the usual ceremonies of the
order were deposited in the adjoining churchyard. The service
was conducted by M:.W:. James A. Hoyt, Grand Master of Masons
in South Carolina, who was requested to officiate on behalf
of the several Lodges represented.

Issue of:
Thursday, April 1, 1875:
Married: On the 4th of March, by Rev. Samuel Weber, Mr. E. K.
Hardin of Chester and Miss Ida Clinkscales of Williamston.

Married: At the residence of the bride's father, on Thursday
25th of March, by the Rev. W. A. Hodges, Mr. M. B. Jackson
and Miss Euphemia Bolt, daughter of Mr. Wm. Bolt. All of
this County.

Sad Death: It is our painful duty to announce the death of
Mrs. Theodosia D. Brock, the beloved wife of Mr. J. A. Brock,
which occurred on Tuesday evening after a long and painful
illness. The coming of the Destroyer's footsteps is at all
times sorrowful and distressing to relatives and friends but
when death strikes down innocent and young, we realize more
keenly the anguish of sorrowing hearts, whose only consolation
is that he lets the panting spirit free from earth's tribula-
tions and there springs up bright creations to defy his
power, while his dark paths become a way of light to Heaven.
With the bloom of youth upon her cheek and the brightest
prospects of the world before her, none can fail to sympathize
in this painful bereavement. She was gentle and loving in
character, modest and unassuming in demeanor, faithful and
devoted in her profession as a Christian. How short and
fleeting the time since the bridal wreath was worn! The pale
flowers of the tomb take its place so soon and the tears of
surviving kindred and friends fall upon the newly made grave.
May His infinite mercy and love attend the bereaved husband
and the little innocent boy so unconscious of his loss - a
mother's love and watchful tenderness.

Accident: We are sorry to learn that little Baylis, son of
our worthy townsman, Mr. John H. Clarke, met with severe injury
on Friday last. It seems that Mrs. Clarke went to the residence of her father (Mr. David Crosby) on that day, bringing
little Baylis with her and while playing in the yard he was
attacked and bitten through the upper lip by a fierce bulldog.
The wound inflicted was severe and painful but at last accounts
the little fellow was doing well.

Obituary: Mr. James Nesbit, Sr. of Spartanburg, died recently
at Rome, Ga. where he was on a business tour. He was over
seventy years of age, a man of considerable means and highly
respected by the people of Spartanburg.

Issue of:
Thursday, April 8, 1875:
Married: At the residence of Mr. John Dobbins, on Sunday
morning last, by Rev. J. S. Murray, Mr. J. Jesse Dobbins and
Miss Florence Skelton, daughter of the late Thomas Skelton,
all of this County.

Death: Rev. Wm. Banks, of York County, died in Georgia on the
17th ultimo.

Obituary: Mr. David Dickson died at his home in Oxford, Ga., on the 15th inst., after a protracted illness of several weeks. He was a gentleman well and widely known for his many virtues as well as for being the originator of the delebrated "Dickson Cotton" so universally used in the cotton States.

Obituary: Gen. Thomas F. Anderson, a prominent citizen of Banks County, Ga. died a few days ago in the 98th year of his age. He took an active part in the war of 1812, a member of the Georgia Legislature at various times and always a leading man in his section. He was brave and generous to a fault and retained his faculties in a most wonderful degree.

Issue of:
Thursday, April 15, 1875:
Obituary: The Greenville News announces the death of Dr. James M. Sullivan, a prominent and influential citizen of that county, which occurred at his residence on Friday night last. Dr. Sullivan was known to many of our readers. He had been in bad health for some months and had recently suffered from a severe nervous attack but his friends were not seriously concerned about his condition. Late on Friday afternoon he was stricken with paralysis which caused his death in a few hours. In the death of Dr. Sullivan, says the News, the community will suffer a great loss as he was one of the most progressive and public spirited citizens of Greenville. He was skillful and success- ful as a physician and was engaged in an active and extensive practice for thirty years. Hones, upright, liberal and chari- table, he was a fine type of the Southern Gentleman.

Issue of:
Thursday, April 22, 1875:
Married: April 11th, at the residence of the bride's father, Mr. Cyrus Stephens, by Rev. B. S. Gaines, Mr. C. W. Young and Miss Kate Stephens, all of Pendleton.

Obituary: Died, April 13, 1875, Mrs. E. P. Clardy, wife of N. S. Clardy, in the 66th year of her age. She was an affec- tionate wife and mother. She was born May 28, 1809, in the State of North Carolina and moved to South Carolina, Anderson County, at an early age and was married to N. S. Clardy January 11, 1831. She united with the Baptist Church at Big Creek at an early age and adorned the profession of her faith through life. She leaves a disconsolate and blind husband, eight children and twenty seven grandchildren to mourn her departure. But their loss is her gain.

Obituary: We regret to learn of the death of Mr. John Carpenter an aged and highly respected citizen of this County, which sad event occurred at his residence about six miles southeast of this place on Wednesday night last after an illness of only three hours, occasioned by disease of the heart. The deceased had been suffering for upwards of a year from the same cause, but nothing serious was apprehended until the attack came on which terminated in his death. He was seventy one years old and during his long life was ever the constant Christian, kind parent, faithful friend and upright citizen. His remains were interred in the cemetery at Neal's Creek Church on Friday morning last. Mr. Carpenter was born near Calhoun in Anderson County on the 20th of February 1805. When he was two years old and his father, (Burrell Carpenter) moved to the place where he died and he had lived on this place for sixty eight years. He is the last one of a large family. His father emigrated from Wake County, North Carolina in the fall of 1796. Mr. Carpenter joined the Methodist Church in 1828 and he was married to Elizabeth Emerson (daughter of Samuel Emerson) in the year 1825. We are indebted for these particulars to a near relative of the deceased.

Hanging: Elijah Adkins and Scipio Bryan, both colored, were hung at Beaufort on Friday last. Adkins was the murderer of Thomas Behn, who kept a county store near Bluffton and was killed in June last. Bryan killed another negro in December, shooting him in daylight from ambush in order to obtain ten or twelve dollars, the proceeds of some cotton sold that morning. Both murderers made full confessions and professed penitence. The execution was witnessed by five thousand colored people.

Issue of:
Thursday, April 29, 1875:
Married: April 22, 1875, by Rev. E. F. Hyde, Mr. T. W. Whitfield and Miss Ida E., daughter of Mr. R. T. Tucker, all of Anderson County.

Married: On Sunday morning, April 25th, at the residence of the bride's mother, by James McLeskey, Esq., Mr. Isham Elrod and Miss Sarah Jane Bolt, all of Anderson County.

Issue of:
Thursday, May 6, 1875:
Obituary: Miss Ann Pamelia Cunningham of Laurens County, departed this life at her residence on Saturday last. She was the daughter of Mr. Robert Cunningham and was the originator of the movement to purchase Mt. Vernon. Her contributions on the subject to the public press aroused much attention and were mainly instrumental in the organization of the Ladies' Mount Vernon Association which subsequently made the purchase and consecreated the home of George Washington. Miss Cunningham was highly gifted as a writer and her patriotic effusions were models of chastediction and earnest zeal to the cause.

Issue of:
Thursday, May 13, 1875:
Married: On April 8, 1875, by Rev. D. E. Frierson, at the residence of the bride's father, Mr. M. R. Casey of Donaldsville and Miss Mattie C. Wright, daughter of Mr. T. B. Wright of Anderson.

Married: At the residence of the bride's mother on Sunday evening last, by Rev. Wm. Carlisle, Mr. Frank M. Norris and Miss Susan Acker, all of this County.

Issue of:
Thursday, May 27, 1875:
Obituary: Death of Rev. A. H. Cornish - We are pained to record the death of Rev. A. H. Cornish, of Pendleton, which occurred at Newberry on Monday last after an intense suffering for two weeks. Mr. Cornish was a delegate to the Episcopal

Convention which met in Charleston on the 13th inst. and was
taken sick upon the cars when on his way down which compelled
him to forego the fatigue of travel and remain over at Newberry
where he received the kindest attention and the best medical
skill. His sufferings were acute and exceedingly painful until
death came to his relief. Mr. Cornish was greatly esteemed
by all who knew him for gentleness of manner, dignity of character and scrupulous fidelity in the discharge of responsible
duties. He resided at Pendleton for upwards of twenty five
years in charge of the Episcopal Church and a portion of that
time he gave his valuable services to the congregation at
Anderson where he was equally beloved for many noble qualities.
His remains were taken to Pendleton on Tuesday evening and
the funeral obsequies took place yesterday afternoon.

Issue of:
Thursday, June 3, 1875:
Married: On Thursday evening, May 20th, in the Methodist
Church, Newberry, by the Rev. Manning Brown, Mr. J. Clark
Wardlaw of Walhalla and Miss Bettie Moorman, daughter of the
late Col. Rob't Moorman of Newberry.

Married: On Sunday morning, May 25th, by James McLesky, Esq.,
Mr. John T. Fowler and Miss Sarah J. R. Morgan.

Obituary: Died, on Tuesday morning, May 25, 1875, of Paralysis,
Mrs. Elvira Browne, wife of Dr. Jasper Browne, in the forty
third year of her age. For five days previous to her death
she was deprived of reason and speech, consequently unable to
state her prospects beyond the grave; yet, the life she
lived was such as to establish beyond a reasonable doubt that
she was fully prepared to meet her God without condemnation.
Always patient, submissive and cheerful under all circumstances,
never murmuring in sickness of health but always exhibiting
that patient resignation to the will of God as becomes a
true Christian. Although she was unostentatious in the Christian
religion which she professed, yet it was manifested constantly
in all her acts of life. She has left an example behind worthy
to be followed by her husband and children and all that desire
to live and die a true Christian.   J.

Issue of:
Thursday, June 17, 1875:
Married: By Rev. W. H. Flemming, D. D., at the Methodist
Church in Yorkville, S. C., June 10th, 1875, Rev. J. Walter
Dickson of the South Carolina Conference to Miss Annie M.
Schorb of Yorkville.

Married: On June 13, 1875, at the residence of the bride's
father by Rev. J. M. Lander, Mr. James T. Kay and Miss Emma
A. Keys all of Anderson County.

Obituary: Death of Gen. Duff Green - The venerable and distinguished journalist, Gen. Duff Green, departed this life on
Thursday last in the 85th year of his age at his home near
Dalton, Ga. He was a remarkable man in many respects and once
achieved a natural reputation as an editor and bold, vigorous
writer. He was a native of Kentucky and early in life assumed
a prominent position in political circles. During the admin-
istration of President Jackson he established a newspaper in
Washington City called the United States Telegraph which

attained great celebrity from the able and independent position upon public measures and its warm devotion to the interests of Andrew Jackson. Subsequently, Gen. Green attached himself to the nullification party and became identified with the views and utterances of Mr. Calhoun. He was a kind, amiable and sociable gentleman, pure in character and steadfast in principle. His later years were spent in quiet, unobtrusive life in Dalton, Ga. where he was surrounded by numerous friends and relatives. His daughter married the late Andrew P. Calhoun of Pendleton whose family were part of his household since the war.

Obituary: We regret to learn the sudden death of Maj. John Wells Simpson, an estimable and upright citizen of Laurens, which occurred on the 3rd inst., of heart disease. He was about sixty years old.

Obituary: Eugene Harvey Williams, son of Rev. Wm. Williams, D.D., of Greenville, died at his father's residence on the 9th inst. after a protracted illness, aged 15 years. He was an unusually intelligent and promising youth.

Issue of:
Thursday, June 24, 1875:
Married: On the 17th of June 1875 at the residence of the bride's father, by Rev. E. Z. Brown, Mr. C. M. Hall and Miss Mattie J. Williams all of Anderson County.

Issue of:
Thursday, July 1, 1875:
Married: On Thursday evening, June 17, 1875, near Maysfield, Milam County, Texas, by Rev. J. Nabours, Mr. Thomas Herbert Williams formerly of Pickens District S. C. and Miss Emma Massengale of Milan County, Texas.

Obituary: Death of An Estimable Lady - We are pained to record the death of Mrs. Ellen C. Poe, of Pendleton, which occurred at her residence on Friday last, 25th of June, of paralysis, produced by softening of the brain, after a lingering and painful illness. Mrs. Poe was the daughter of Col. Joseph Taylor and was born at the then residence of her father on Seneca River, about six miles from Pendleton, on the 14th of January, 1811. She was the relict of the late Wm. Poe of Montgomery, Ala. and the mother of a large and interesting family. Her character was sterling and attractive and she was greatly endeared to a large circle of relatives and friends with whom we deeply sympathize in this sore bereavement. The funeral services were conducted at the Presbyterian Church in Pendleton on Saturday afternoon, by Rev. W. C. Smith and the remains of Mrs. Poe were buried in the Baptist Churchyard.

Obituary: Mrs. Nancy Massey, the consort of Mr. Silas Massey, departed this life on Tuesday 22nd of June, aged 85 years. She was a consistent member of the church for many years and leaves a wide circle of relatives and friends to mourn the loss of an aged and respected mother in Israel. Her remains were buried at Mountain Creek Church on Wednesday morning.

Obituary: We regret to chronicle the death of Mr. Wilson Drennan, which took place at his residence three miles north

of this place on Sunday morning last in the 78th year of his
age. Mr. Drennan was a quiet and respected citizen and an
elder in the Presbyterian Church. His funeral took place at
Concord on Sunday afternoon and the services were conducted
by Rev. D. E. Frierson who delivered an earnest and eloquent
discourse in the presence of a large congregation.

Issue of:
Thursday, July 15, 1875:
Obituary: Rev. Thomas H. Pope of Greenwood died on Thursday
night last after a brief illness. Mr. Pope was a pure and
upright gentleman much beloved where ever known and the Baptist
denomination sustains a heavy loss in his early and unexpected
death.

Issue of:
Thursday, July 29, 1875:
Married: At the residence of the bride's mother, Mrs. R. J.
Moorhead, on the 18th of July, 1875 by Rev. D. J. Huggins, Mr.
L. J. Burriss of Anderson County, S. C. and Mrs. M. E. Blanton
of Forsyth County, Georgia.

Married: At the residence of the bride's father by Rev. Jacob
Burriss on Tuesday July 6th inst., Mr. W. B. Hall to Miss Mary
L., daughter of Mr. M. B. Hembree, all of Anderson County.

Married: On the 25th of instant, by Rev. J. S. Murray, Mr.
J. H. Cobb of Texas to Mrs. Martha Dawson of Anderson, S. C.

Obituary: Departed this life July 13, 1875, M. S. Kate Baker,
daughter of A. T. and Arenie E. Baker, aged ten months and
eighteen days. Our little Kate is gone. She was too pure for
this world.

Obituary: We are pained to record the death of Mr. Hugh McGukin
which occurred at his residence near Holland's Store on Friday
last, 23rd inst., in the 69th year of his age. He was a native
of Ireland and emigrated to this State in 1825. He lived in
Abbeville County until 1851 when he removed to this County.
The deceased was a member of the Presbyterian Church for the
last twenty years and was highly esteemed as an upright citizen.

Issue of:
Thursday, August 5, 1875:
Married: On Sunday the first of August by the Rev. Mr. Bowman,
at the residence of Mr. J. C. Smith in Anderson County, Mr.
A. M. Smith of Indiana to Mrs. M. E. Martin of Anderson County.

Tribute of Respect: Jesse F. Campbell, of Williamston Lodge
No. 24 A. F. M., died at Williamston on 23rd June 1875.

Issue of:
Thursday, August 12, 1875:
Obituary: An obituary notice in the A. R. Presbyterian records
the death of Mr. Samuel Stewart in Union County, Mississippi
on the 6th of July last in the 75th year of his age. Mr.
Stewart was a native of Anderson County and some thirty years
ago removed from this State.

Issue of:
Thursday, August 19, 1875:
Obituary: We regret to announce the death of Mr. A. N. Alexander
an excellent and intelligent young gentleman living near Pendleton Factory. His death occurred suddenly on last Saturday,
though he had been in declining health for a long time.

Issue of:
Thursday, September 9, 1875:
Married: In Grace Church, Anderson, on Thursday morning,
Sept. 2nd, 1875, by Rev. Ellison Capers, Mr. Samuel M. Orr
and Miss Pet Allen, both of Anderson.

Married: At the residence of the officiating minister on the
1st of September by Rev. W. P. Martin, Mr. Augustus Poore of
Anderson County and Miss Nancy Caroline Bagwell of Greenville
County.

Obituary: Died, on Monday the 6th of September, William Riley,
aged 20 months, son of Zerah and Carra Lou Burress, after an
illness of two weeks. He is gone where there is no pain or
sorrow.   R. B.

Issue of:
Thursday, September 16, 1875:
Married: On the 9th of September inst., at the residence of
the bride's father, Mr. Haines Mullikin, by Rev. A. Acker,
Mr. Joseph M. Cox of Anderson County to Miss Flora D. Mullikin
of Greenville County.

Issue of:
Thursday, September 23, 1875:
Married: On the 15th inst. at the residence of the bride's
father by the Rev. J. H. Gilmore, Mr. J. Reese Fant of Anderson
S. C. and Miss Julia A. Naramore of Rochester, N. Y.

Married: On the 16th inst., by Rev. Wilson Ashley at his
residence, Mr. Jesse Kay and Miss Joe Williams, all of Anderson
County. This was the five hundredth couple married by this
clergyman, according to an account kept by himself.

Obituary: We regret to announce the death of Mr. John Dalrymple
an aged citizen of our County, which occurred at his residence
some miles northeast of this place on last Thursday afternoon.

Issue of:
Thursday, September 30, 1875:
Married: At the residence of the bride's father in Anderson
County on the evening of Sept. 16th, 1875, by Rev. Hugh McLees,
Mr. John M. Guyton and Miss Emma, daughter of Maj. T. H. Russell.

Sudden Death: Mrs. Clemson, the last surviving child of the
Hon. John C. Calhoun and wife of Hon. Thomas G. Clemson, died
at five o'clock p.m. on Wednesday the 22nd inst. near Pendleton at Fort Hill, the former residence of her own family.
She was the last link of a distinguished family of the past
generation from which Carolina's favorite son figured so
extensively in the councils of the Union and of this, his
native State. Her decease will be regretted not only by her
own circle of relatives and friends but also by the people

of Carolina who have so often attested their appreciation of and love for the many virtues and acquirements of her father.

Issue of:
Thursday, October 7, 1875:
Married: On Thursday evening September 30, 1875 at the residence of the bride's father by Rev. W. E. Walters, Miss N. Eugenia Drake of Anderson County, S. C. and Mr. Calvin N. Kay of Smith County, Texas.

Issue of:
Thursday, October 21, 1875:
Married: In the Anderson Baptist Church on Thursday morning October 14th, 1875, by Rev. J. S. Murray, Mr. Thomas R. Ayer of Barnwell and Miss Kitty B. Burress of Anderson.

Married: On Tuesday evening Oct. 19, 1875 at the residence of the bride's father by Rev. J. S. Murray, Mr. Jeff D. Maxwell and Miss Alice V. Borstel, all of Anderson.

Married: On the 12th inst. by Rev. Asa Avery, Mr. W. T. Carter and Miss Lina C. Heller, all of Anderson County.

Married: On the 13th inst. by Rev. Asa Avery, Mr. J. F. Graham and Miss Telula F. Bruce, all of Anderson County.

Married: On the 14th inst. by Rev. Asa Avery, Mr. Andy Hembree and Miss Susan Simmons, all of Anderson County.

Married: On the 13th inst. by Rev. E. F. Hyde, Mr. J. B. Hix and Miss Jenetta A. Graham, all of Anderson County.

Married: On Tuesday, 12th inst. by James McLesky, Esq., Mr. John Brown and Mrs. Elizabeth Davis, eldest daughter of Capt. Robert McJunkin, all of Anderson.

Married: By J. L. Bryan, Trial Justice, October 9th, Mr. William Moore and Miss Julia McGee.

Married: By J. L. Bryan, Trial Justice, October 14th, Mr. J. D. McCullough and Miss Lucy A. Simpson, all of Anderson County.

Married: At the residence of the bride's father on the evening of October 14th by the Rev. E. Z. Long, Mr. F. M. Davis and Miss Louisa, daughter of Mr. J. L. Byrum, all of Anderson County.

Issue of:
Thursday, October 28, 1875:
Married: On Thursday evening October 21st, 1875 by Rev. R. W. Burts, Mr. John H. Harrison of Greenville and Miss Nannie Latimer of Abbeville.

Married: On the 13th inst., by Rev. J. Z. Stockman, Mr. F. A. Lewis of Seneca City, S. C. and Miss Mattie M. Erwin of Brevard, N. C.

Issue of:
Thursday, November 4, 1875:
Married: By Rev. Mike McGee at his own residence on Thursday,

October 28, Mr. E. Harleston Poore and Miss Flora H. Mitchell, daughter of W. N. Mitchell, Esq., all of Belton, S. C.

Married: By Rev. Mike McGee at his own residence on Sunday night October 24th, Mr. J. N. Duncan and Miss Martha A. Davis, all of Anderson County.

Married: On Sunday night October 31 by Rev. John Campbell, Mr. James H. Ellison and Miss Mary Jane Lolis, all of Anderson County.

Obituary: We regret to learn that Rev. J. M. Landress died at his residence near Williamston on Wednesday morning. He had been very low with consumption for several weeks past. He was known to many in this County who will hear with sorrow of his death.

Obituary: Mr. J. Newton Cox died in Greenville on Friday last from the effects of a wound received in a difficulty over there during the first part of the week. His remains were interred in Shady Grove burying ground on last Sunday. He leaves a wife and five little children who are left desolate by his death.

Obituary: Miss Martha Neal, a young lady of our County who was beloved by all who knew here, died at the residence of her father, Mr. A. M. Neal, on Thursday last. Her death was unexpected and sudden, though she had been in feeble health for some time since. Her remains were committed to rest in the Hopewell burying ground some six miles northeast of this place.

Obituary: Charley Bewley, youngest son of Mrs. C. D. Bewley, of our Town, died of typhoid fever on last Friday morning at six o'clock after an illness of seven weeks. Charlie was an interesting and bright boy whose death leaves a void in the affections of his family. His remains were borne to their resting place in the Baptist Church yard by six young boys and followed by the Baptist Sabbath School of which he was a member. The funeral services were solemn and impressive.

Obituary: Death of Mrs. McGukin - We regret to announce the death of Mrs. McGukin, wife of our Sheriff, Mr. William McGukin which occurred on last Sabbeth morning after an illness of only a few days. Her remains were interred on Monday last in Mountain Creek Churchyard, where other members of her family are buried.

Issue of:
Thursday, November 11, 1875:
Married: On the 29th of September 1875 by Rev. R. W. Barbour, J. F. J. Caldwell, Esq., of Newberry and Miss Rebecca C., daughter of F. A. Connor, Esq., of Cokesbury, S. C.

Married: On the 19th of October by Rev. R. W. Barbour at the residence of the bride's father, John S. Fair, Esq., of Newberry and Miss Hannie, third daughter of Col. B. Z. Herndon of Cokesbury.

Issue of:
Thursday, November 18, 1875:
Married: On the 16th of November 1875, by Rev. Jacob Burriss,

Mr. John McPhail and Miss Maggie Richardson, all of this County.

Married: On Thursday the 4th inst. by Rev. H. Tyler, Mr. S. M. Milford and Miss F. Maria T. Palmer, eldest daughter of Thomas B. Palmer, all of Anderson County.

Married: In Pickens County, S. C., November 4, 1875 by Rev. Hugh McLees, Mr. W. W. Ford and Miss M. A. Rogers.

Obituary: We are pained to record the death of Mrs. Catherine D. Norris, relict of the late John E. Norris, Esq., which occurred at the residence of her son-in-law, Dr. J. L. Crumley, on Sunday morning last in the 87th year of her age. She had been an invalid for two years and for the last six months suffered greatly. Her remains were buried at the Presbyterian Church on Monday last in the presence of many relatives and friends.

Issue of:
Thursday, November 25, 1875:
Married: In Columbia on the 6th inst. by Rev. P. J. Shand, Mr. Ernest M. Taylor of Greenville and Miss Mary D. Bacot, second daughter of the late Col. R. H. Bacot, formerly of Charleston, S. C.

Married: On Thursday evening November 16th by Rev. W. L. Pressley, assisted by Rev. J. I. Bonner, Mr. Clarence Dunn of Donaldsville and Miss Maggie J. Nance, daughter of Capt. F. W. Nance of Due West.

Issue of:
Thursday, December 2, 1875:
Married: At the residence of Mr. Curran D. Sloan in the city of Greenville on Tuesday afternoon 23rd of November 1875 by Rev. J. C. Hiden, Rev. Ker Boyce Tupper, pastor of the Baptist Church in Charlottesville, Va. and Miss Cilla Sloan, youngest daughter of the late John B. Sloan, Esq., of Anderson.

Married: At the residence of the bride's father near Greenville, S. C. on Wednesday evening November 24th, Capt. J. Walter Gray and Miss N. E. Vance, daughter of Maj. J. K. Vance.

Obituary: We regret to announce the death of Mrs. Polly White, wife of the late Bartholomew White of this County which event occurred on Friday last. Mrs. White was one of the oldest ladies in our County, having been born in 1790. Her remains were interred in Hopewell burying ground on Saturday afternoon.

Issue of:
Thursday, December 9, 1875:
Married: On Sunday morning December 5th, 1875 at the residence of the officiating magistrate in Hart County, Ga. by Joseph Glover, Esq., Mr. M. C. Masters of Anderson County and Miss Sallie Moorhead, daughter of John Moorhead, Esq. of Hart Co., Ga.

Married: On Thursday morning 2nd inst., in Memphis, Tenn. by Rev. Dr. White, Dr. J. Wistar Vance of Greenville, S. C. and Miss Susa S. Vance of Memphis.

Married: On the 5th December in Adnerson County by Rev. John J. Campbell, Mr. John D. Garrett and Miss Cornelia C. Garrett.

Married: On Tuesday the 7th inst. by Rev. J. S. Murray, Mr. W. A. D. Finley and Miss Mary E. Bailey, all of this County.

Issue of:
Thursday, December 16, 1875:
Married: On the 8th inst. at the residence of Mr. L. N. Clinkscales, the bride's father, by Rev. C. V. Barnes, Mr. Samuel Jackson and Miss Cena A. Clinkscales, all of Anderson County.

Married: On Sunday, December 12th, 1875, at the residence of the officiating clergyman, by Rev. W. A. Hodges, Mr. S. P. Wilson and Miss Kate Shields, all of Anderson.

Married: On the 9th inst. by Rev. W. P. Martin at the residence of the bride's father, Mr. Enoch Breazeale Keys and Miss Ella Louise Kay, second daughter of Mr. Silas Kay.

Married: On the 30th ult. at the residence of the bride's father, by Rev. N. K. Melton, Col. M. C. Dickson of Anderson County and Miss Addie A. Gilkerson of Laurens County, S. C.

Married: On Tuesday the 14th inst. at the residence of the bride's father by Rev. J. S. Murray, Mr. John F. Wilson of Hartsville, Darlington County and Miss Fannie E., only daughter of Rev. J. S. Murray of Anderson, S. C.

Issue of:
Thursday, December 23, 1875:
Married: On Wednesday the 16th last by Rev. F. G. Carpenter, at the residence of the bride's mother, Mr. Wm. J. Guyton and Miss Julia A. Kay, all of Anderson, S. C.

Married: At the residence of the bride's mother, December 7, 1875, by the Rev. Broaddus, Mr. W. C. Latimer of Abbeville and Miss Susie J. Mobley of Edgefield, S. C.

Married: On Sunday evening the 12th inst. at his own residence by Rev. A. Rice, Mr. Noah W. Alewine and Miss Narcissa Davis, all of this County.

Married: On Thursday afternoon the 15th inst. of the residence of Mrs. Catherine Ranson, by the Rev. A. Rice, Mr. J. M. Stacks and Miss L. Eunice Ranson, all of this County.

Death: Mr. Lawrence Clinkscales, son of Mr. Frank Clinkscales formerly of this County, but more recently residing near Lowndesville in Abbeville County, was thrown from his horse on last Sunday and received injuries by the fall from which he died in a few hours.

Issue of:
Thursday, December 30, 1875:
Married: On Thursday evening, December 23, 1875 at the residence of the bride's mother by the Rev. R. A. Reed, Mr. Elbridge Tucker and Miss Tilman T. Bozeman, all of Anderson Co.

Married: On the 9th of December, 1875, at the residence of the bride's father, by Rev. Fletcher Smith, Dr. Wm. F. Wright and Miss Mary C., daughter of Dr. B. S. James, all of West Union, S. C.

Married: At the residence of the bride's grandmother, Mrs. Eliza Robinson, on the 23rd of December, 1875, by the Rev. D. E. Frierson, Mr. Samuel T. Craig and Miss Mamie Partlow, all of Anderson.

Married: At the Anderson Baptist Church on the 22nd of December, 1875 by Rev. J. S. Murray, Mr. William S. Ligon and Miss Cora S. Reed, daughter of Hon. J. P. Reed.

Married: On the 12th of December, 1875 by J. L. Bryant, Esq., at his residence, Mr. John Spearman and Miss Scyntha Dunlap, all of Anderson County.

Married: By J. L. Bryant, Esq., on the 21st inst., at the residence of Mr. Lent Hall, Mr. G. M. Leapard of Greenville and Miss Susan M. Adams of Anderson.

Issue of:
Thursday, January 6, 1876:
Married: On December 15th, 1875 at the residence of the bride's father, by the Rev. G. M. Rodgers, Mr. W. Holbert Pickens and Miss L. Josephine Wiginton, all of Anderson County.

Married: On December 16th, 1875 by Rev. G. M. Rogers, Mr. John Spearman and Miss Sallie Martin, all of Anderson County.

Married: At the residence of the bride's father on the 2nd inst. by the Rev. L. W. Tribble, Mr. R. B. Kay and Miss F. E. Wright, youngest daughter of R. N. Wright, Esq., all of Anderson County.

Married: By James McLesky, Trial Justice, on Sunday morning, December 26th, 1875 at the residence of the bride's father, Mr. R. P. Wilson of Greenville County and Miss Lucinda Abercrombie of Anderson County.

Married: By Rev. G. H. Cartledge on Thursday, December 23rd, 1875 at the residence of the bride's father, Mr. John L. Telford and Miss Mollie Elizabeth, daughter of Mr. Burton Rucker, all of Banks County, Ga.

Married: On Tuesday the 4th inst. at the bride's residence by Rev. J. S. Murray, Mr. John Dickinson of Calhoun County, Alabama and Miss Rosanna Scott of Anderson County, S. C.

Married: On December 28th, 1875 at the residence of the bride's father, by Rev. J. A. Porter, Mr. Henry G. Reed of Anderson and Miss Mamie E. Calcutt of Spartanburg.

Obituary: Mr. Preston C. Fant died at his residence in Anderson on Saturday last after a long and painful illness. Mr. Fant was a quiet citizen who had the friendship and respect of his neighbors. He bore his sufferings with great resignation and died as calmly as if death were only going to sleep. Mr. Fant was about 30 years of age and leaves a little orphan

son of about six years. His funeral services were conducted
in the Baptist Church on last Sabbath afternoon by Rev. J. S.
Murray and were attended by a large number of our citizens
who were present to pay this last mark of respect to the
departed.

Issue of:
Thursday, January 13, 1876:
Obituary: Died, on Sunday evening 9th of January, at his residence in the town of Anderson, Mr. Joseph Prevost, in the 70th
year of his age.

Death: On Saturday afternoon Mr. Calhoun Clinkscales met with
an unfortunate accident by which he lost his life. While
driving in his buggy on his way home from Belton, he lost his
hat and in an effort to catch it, fell out of the buggy in
such a way as to pull his horse back so as to step on his
stomach, thereby inflicting a wound from which he died at
about 10 o'clock on Saturday night at the residence of his
father, Mr. Reuben Clinkscales.

Issue of:
Thursday, January 20, 1876:
Married: At Cedar Grove, January 11th, 1876 by Rev. Elias Z.
Brown, Mr. James Stone and Miss Susan Crumpton, all of Anderson
County.

Married: At the residence of the bride's father, J. L. Fowler,
Esq., on the evening of Thursday January 13th, 1876 by Rev.
L. K. Glasgow, Mr. M. Scurry Mays and Miss Lizzie Fowler.

Married: At the residence of the bride's brother, J. R.
Holcombe, Esq., on Thursday the 6th inst. by Rev. Fletcher
Smith of Walhalla, Mr. R. A. Child of Pickens C. H. and Miss
Essie Holcombe, daughter of the Hon. W. E. Holcombe of Liberty
Station.

Issue of:
Thursday, January 27, 1876:
Obituary: We regret to announce the death of Mrs. Warren D.
Wilkes which occurred at the residence of her husband near
Belton after a short illness on last Saturday morning. The
funeral services were conducted on last Sabbath by Rev. W. P.
Martin and were attended by a large concourse of people who
were present to pay the last tribute of earth to the departed
one. Her remains were interred in the family burying ground
near Calhoun.

Obituary: We regret to announce the death of Mrs. Floride
B. Darracott which occurred at the residence of her daughter,
Mrs. L. O. Hammond near Belton, on last Saturday night. Mrs.
Darracott was one of the oldest ladies in our County, being in
the eighty first year of her age. Her remains were interred
in the Presbyterian churchyard on Tuesday last, the funeral
exercises having been performed by Rev. W. W. Mood in the
Methodist Church, of which the deceased was a member.

Issue of:
Thursday, February 3, 1876:
Obituary: Died, at the residence of her son-in-law, J. G.
Cartee, on the 8th of January, 1876, Mrs. Mary Barkley, in the

178

77th year of her age. She was a member of the Baptist Church for forty years and was greatly beloved by a large circle of friends.

Married: December 30th, 1875 by Rev. E. F. Hyde, at his residence, Mr. A. P. Graham and Miss E. E. Palmer, daughter of Mr. W. D. Palmer, all of Anderson County.

Married: On Sunday 16th inst. at the residence of the bride's father, by Rev. Robert King, Mr. B. S. Davis and Miss Sarah Willingham, all of Anderson Co.

Married: On Thursday the 20th inst. by Rev. W. A. Hodges at the residence of Mr. Ira C. Williams, Mr. Erasmus F. Reed and Miss Nannie McDavid, all of Anderson County.

Married: On Sunday 9th of January by G. W. Maret, Esq., Mr. Hiram King and Miss Sallie Odel, all of Anderson County.

Married: On the 13th of January 1876 by Rev. Wm. T. Norman, Mr. L. M. Cunningham and Miss Louannah C. Shiflet, daughter of Mr. John and E. E. Shiflet, all of Hart Co., Ga.

Married: On January 17th by Rev. Jacob Burriss, Mr. Wm. Frost of Pickens Co. and Miss Emma Jolley of Anderson County.

Married: On January 16th, 1876 by Rev. M. McGee at the residence of the bride's father, Mr. George A. Bowen and Miss Fannie S. Williamson, only daughter of Matthew Williamson, Esq., of Anderson County.

Obituary: We are pained to record the death of Dr. Jasper Browne which occurred at his residence near Storeville on Friday last in the 52nd year of his age. Dr. Browne was a useful and patriotic citizen and belonged to one of our most respectable families. He had been in bad health for the last year or two and knew that his days were few in the land of the living but expressed himself as prepared for the change. His wife preceded him to the grave about eight months ago and he leaves a family of eight children to mourn the loss of affectionate and devoted parents. His funeral was preached at Ebenezer Church by his brother, Rev. Sidi H. Browne, of Columbia, on Sunday last in the presence of a large congregation.

Obituary: S. L. W. Elrod died at his residence in Piercetown on Wednesday 26th ult. after a long illness. He was buried at Snow Hill church on Friday by the Masonic fraternity.

Obituary: Mr. John Miller died at his residence near Pendleton in the early part of last week in the 82nd year of his age. He was a son of the original John Miller, who established the Pendleton Messenger and who was said to have been connected with the printing of the celebrated Junius Letters.

Obituary: Mrs. Burns, an excellent and highly esteemed lady of Anderson County, died recently of apoplexy at the residence of her sister, Mrs. Abbott, near Walhalla.

Thursday, February 10, 1876:
Mr. David Morris, one of the oldest citizens of Anderson County, died at his residence near Centreville Mills on Monday night in the 88th year of his age.

Obituary: On last Monday afternoon at about four o'clock, Mr. John D. King fell from his mule while on his way home from Anderson and broke his neck, so that he died instantly. This occurrence took place on the old Gambrell's bridge road, some nine or ten miles from town. Trial Justice Wilkes held an inquest of the body on Tuesday and the jury rendered a verdict of "Died from the effects of a fall from his horse". The deceased leaves a wife and several children to mourn an unfortunate death.

Issue of:
Thursday, February 17, 1876:
Married: On Thursday February 3d, 1876, by Rev. R. A. Reid, Mr. T. J. Williford and Miss Mary Jane Todd, all of Anderson County, S. C.

Married: On Thursday February 10th, 1876 by Rev. W. P. Martin at the residence of the bride's father, Mr. S. N. Poore, and Miss Matilda Ann Smith, daughter of W. P. Smith, all of Anderson County, S. C.

Obituary: We regret to announce the death of Mrs. Sarah Smith which occurred recently at her residence near Pendleton. She was the widow of John G. Smith who died in the late war and leaves an only surviving daughter.

Obituary: Death of Mrs. Nancy Burriss - We regret to announce the death of Mrs. Nancy Burriss which occurred at the residence of her husband, Rev. Jacob Burriss, some three miles north of this place on [..?..] morning last at two o'clock after a long and painful illness. Mrs. Burriss was born in this County in 1803 and in 1820 became a member of the Baptist Church at Mountain Creek and remained a consistent and [..?..] member of this faith up to the time of her death. She was married in 1822 [?] and has thus lived in married life with her husband for fifty four years. For many years past she has been connected with the Salem Baptist Church of which her husband has been an influential and zealous member. The funeral exercises were conducted at the residence of Rev. Jacob Burriss on last Sabbath morning at 12 o'clock by Rev. J. R. Earle and her remains were deposited in the family burying ground to rest with her kindred who have gone before her. Mrs. Burriss was an excellant lady and leaves behind her memories which will long be cherished by a large circle of relatives and friends.

Issue of:
Thursday, February 24, 1876:
Married: On Thursday February 17th, 1876 at Mr. E. D. Pruitts by Rev. C. V. Barnes, Mr. Jocob Yilkowsky and Miss Francis Wenjinowska, both lately of Germany, now of Anderson County, S. C.

Married: On Tuesday the 22nd inst. at the residence of the bride's father, Maj. A. R. Broyles, in this town, by Rev. J. Scott Murray, Oliver Hewitt, Esq., of Barnwell County, S.C. and Miss Clara Broyles.

Obituary: Miss Mary Geer, daughter of Mr. Thos. Geer, died at
the residence of her father some six miles east of this place
on last Sunday morning from an attack of pneumonia.

Obituary: A man by the name of H. C. McGrady was taken sick
with congestion of the brain at the residence of Mr. G. F.
Burton in the lower part of this County on the 9th inst. and
died on the 12th. He was buried in Union Church Yard on the
following day.

Obituary: Mr. Asa Bolt, an aged citizen of this County, died
at his residence nine miles west of this place on last Sunday
from an attack of fever. Mr. Bolt was near eighty years of
age and up to the time of his late sickness was very active
and strong for a man of his years.

Obituary: Mrs. Jane Richey, wife of Mr. Reuben Richey, late
of this County, died in Bowie County, Texas on the 11th of
January last of apoplexy. Mrs. Richey was a Miss Stevenson
and has many relatives and friends in this County who will
regret to learn of her death.

Obituary: We regre to announce the death of little Gertrude,
infant daughter of Dr. and Mrs. James T. McFall, which occurred
at their residence in Anderson on last Thursday morning from
an attack of Pneumonia. She was just one year old and her
remains were placed in the Baptist church yard on Friday
last to sleep beside her relatives who rest there.

Issue of:
Thursday, March 2, 1876:
Married: At the residence of Thos. J. Adams, Esq., in Edge-
field on Wednesday 16th of Feburary 1876, by Rev. Luther
Broadus, Col. John Peter Phillips of Ninety Six and Miss Kara
Adams of Edgefield.

Obituary: A daughter of Mr. John Carwile died on Friday last
at the residence of the late A. O. Norris, deceased, at the
age of eleven years, from an attack of pneumonia.

Obituary: William Massey, a son of Mr. Duff Massey, died on
last Tuesday night of membranous croup. He was about fifteen
years of age and had been subject to attacks of croup for some
time past.

Obituary: It is with sadness that we record the death of Wm.
C. Lee, Esq., of Walhalla, which occurred on Sunday, 20th inst.,
after a long illness in the 68th year of his age. Mr. Lee
was a native of Charleston and at an early age settled in the
up-country, residing the greater part of his life in Anderson
and Oconee Counties. He married Miss Kiturah H., the youngest
daughter of Maj. David Humphreys. He lived for a number of
years at Sloan's Ferry on the Seneca River and was greatly
esteemed by his neighbors. Mr. Lee was an upright, honorable
citizen and sustained a good name in every relation of life.
His remains were carried to Bachelor's Retreat for interment,
where he has some children buried. He was the father of our
esteemed friend, Mr. Wm. Lee, a prominent merchant in Honea Path.

Obituary: Death of Mr. James Steele - (From the Cherokee
Georgian, February 23, 1876) After a protracted illness, which

he bore with great patience and resignation, Mr. James Steele departed this life on the 19th instant in the 74th year of his age. He was born in Pendleton District, S. C. and removed to Cherokee County in 1861. Here he resided until his death. Mr. Steele was a man of strong practical sense, a great reader, a close observer of passing events, a good judge of men, modest and retiring in his disposition, honest and sincere in his intercourse with his fellow men, sociable and hospitable at home, strongly attached to his personal friends and devoted to the welfare of his family. He was twice married and leaves by his first wife four sons and two daughters and one son by his last wife who survives him. He lived to see his children all settled in life, in easy and comfortable circumstances and useful members of society.

Issue of:
Thursday, March 9, 1876:
Married: February 27th, 1876 by Rev. P. Martin, at the residence of the bride's mother, Mr. B. P. Trammell and Miss Mary A. Coker, all of Anderson County.

Obituary: Died, on Tuesday night the 29th of February, 1876 after a brief but painful illness with Croup. William A. Massey, son of S. McDuffie Massie and Annie H. Massey, aged 13 years, 4 months and 5 days. He was the only remaining son and his death creates a sad void in the family circle where he was so much beloved for his many amiable traits of character. His short but very trying illness, was borne with great courage and resignation. He trusted in his Saviour to carry him safely over the dark river and land him on the shores of a blessed immortality. Let this thought, then console his bereaved parents - "That he is not lost, but gone before!" "Yet again we hope to meet thee,/ When the day of life is fled;/ Then in Heaven with joy to greet thee,/ Where no farewell tear is shed." Special thanks are due to Mr. O. Geisberg and other neighbors for the kind consideration tendered to the deceased in his last illness.   X.

Death: A young man named Lesley, living on the farm of Dr. W. T. Field in Pickens County, while cutting timber in the woods was unfortunately caught under a falling tree and instantly killed. His head was horribly smashed.

Issue of:
Thursday, March 16, 1876:
Married: At the residence of the bride's father, in this County, on Thursday the 9th inst., by the Rev. J. S. Murray, Mr. L. Reid Watson and Miss Sarah E. Moseley, all of this County.

Obituary: Mrs. Leckart, wife of Stanislaus Leckart, a recent Polish immigrant, died suddenly on the premises of E. J. Earle, Esq. of this County on last Friday morning leaving two small children - the younger only a few months old. The situation of Mr. Leckart, a stranger in a strange land, unable to speak English and with two small children on his hands, appeals strongly to the sympathies of the charitable.

Issue of:
Thursday, March 23, 1876:
Married: Wednesday evening, March 15th, 1876, by the

Rev. H. T. Gregory, J. B. Prevost of Charleston and Miss Mary
Orr of Anderson.

Married: On Tuesday 21st inst. by the Rev. M. McGee, at the
residence of J. Bryson Armstrong, Esq., Mr. Silas McDuffie
Hall and Miss Minerva Alice Armstrong. All of Anderson County.

Obituary: Mr. J. Ward Motte, a former citizen of Laurens, who
has lived in Newberry for several years, died in the latter
place on the 14th inst. in the 61st year of his age after a long
and painful illness.

Obituary: Dr. David C. Means of Fairfield died suddenly last
week. He was returning home from his brother's residence when
he either fell from his horse and was killed by the fall or he
died from an apopletic fit.

Sudden Death: On Friday last, 17th inst., Mr. William Bell from
the neighborhood of First Creek Church, was enroute to Belton
with his wagon in company with his son and other persons. Before
the party reached Belton they got out of the wagon to walk and
refresh themselves and stopped at the blacksmith shop of
Dr. W. C. Brown to warm, where Mr. Bell lit his pipe and was
quite lively, talking and laughing with those around him.
Shortly after leaving the shop, when they had passed Mr.
Joel T. Rice's residence in the town of Belton, Mr. Bell fell
down lifeless in the road, while in the act of speaking. He
expired without a struggle and it is thought his death occurred
from heart disease as he had been subject to symptoms which
lead to this conclusion.

Obituary: Mr. Stephen Chastain died at his home some eight
or nine miles west of this place on last Friday night of the
dropsy of the heart.

Obituary: We regret to announce the death of Rev. K. Vaughn
which occurred on the 7th inst. at his residence on Saluda
River in Greenville County, near Cooley's Bridge place. He
had been in declining health for some time but was not complaining more than usual for only a few days and his death was
unexpected by his own family. Mr. Vaughn was an ordained
minister of the Baptist denomination, a member of the Shady
Grove church and consequently belonged to the Saluda Association. He was more than sixty years of age and had reared a
large family of children all of whom have reached maturity.

Issue of:
Thursday, March 30, 1876:
Obituary: Died, in this County on the 15th March, 1876, Mrs.
Emily E., consort of Samuel R. Bryson, in the 27th year of her
age. Mrs. Bryson joined the Baptist Church in early life and
although for a number of years greatly afflicted, she lived a
devotedly Christian life and so triumphed in death, that her
last words were, "I am going to that sweet home." She leaves
behind her a devoted husband and three children to mourn their
loss and yet consoled with the hope that they shall all meet
again in the home above.

Issue of:
Thursday, April 6, 1876:
Married: By Rev. W. P. Martin, April 2nd, 1876 at the resi-
dence of the bride's father, Mr. John C. Rhoads and Miss Mary

Griffin, daughter of Elijah Griffin, all of Anderson County, S. C.

Obituary: Departed this life Thursday, March 23rd, 1876, Mrs. Frances C. Dean, wife of Major J. Dean, in the 42nd year of her age. The deceased was born in Anderson County, South Carolina the 3rd of May, 1833, united with the Baptist Church at Anderson C. H. about the year 1850 and was married on the 23rd of September 1852 and lived in Anderson County until the Fall of 1859 when she removed with her husband to Dallas County, Texas where they remained until the ensuing year when they removed to Smith County where they have ever since lived. It is useless to attempt to comment on the many virtues of the deceased in the space commonly allowed to an obituary notice and we must be content with stating that in her death the Church has lost one of it's brightest ornaments, the community in which she lived a cherished friend and benefactor, her children a kind and indulgent mother and her husband a dutiful and affectionate wife. She was ever a consistent Christian, practicing daily the religion she professed and during her long and severe affliction she never murmured at her condition but was perfectly resigned to the will of her Heavenly Father. None knew her but to love her and it is believed she died without an enemy. She was noted for her sweetness of temper and kindness of heart. Her ears were ever open to the cries of the needy. She has left a large circle of relatives and friends, both in South Carolina and Texas, to mourn her loss but it is a great consolation for them to know that she had "set her house in order" and was perfectly willing to die. The disease which terminated her life had been preying upon her for more than two years yet she bore it with all Christian fortitude and meekness even appearing cheerful in her affliction. What a consoling thought to her family and friends to know that her sufferings are over.   A. W. R.

Obituary: Gen. G. W. Hodges, died at his residence at Hodges' Depot on Friday night March 24th after a short illness. He was one of the oldest men in Abbeville County and one of the few remaining links connecting this with the past century. He was born in Abbeville County about the year 1792 and lived near the place of his birth for almost his entire lifetime. He was one of a family of twenty one children.

Issue of:
Thursday, April 13, 1876:
Obituary: Death of Miss Parker - Our readers will regret to learn that Miss Emma Parker, whose unfortunate accident we announced last week, died on last Saturday morning at about 10 o'clock from the effect of her injuries. Her father, mother and two sisters had been her constant attendants for several days previous to her death and rendered every kind- ness and attention which it was possible for professional skill or tender love to administer for the alleviation of her usffering, which, though intense, she bore with marked patience and christian resignation until death ended them. The manner in which she caught fire is a mystery and must ever remain so, as she herself was unable to give any account of it.

Another Melancholy Accident: We learn that a most distressing and fatal accident occurred in the Dark Corner on Thursday last, which almost beggars disciption for its sadness and

horror. It appears that a son of Mr. James Simpson, a lad
of nine or ten years of age, went to the well for the purpose
of drawing water. The well was not securely covered and when
the little fellow drew up the bucket and attempted to catch
hold of it, he missed his footing and fell head long into the
well, which is about forty five feet in depth. His mother
heard the noise and made the discovery that her son had fallen
into the well. Upon going to his assistance she ascertained
that he was alive and attempted to draw him up by the rope
but when he got near the mouth of the well her hold upon the
windlass was slackened and for the second time he fell again
to the bottom. By this time the father came to the relief
of the mother and concluded not to trust to the windlass but
to draw the little fellow up by the rope itself in his own
hands and when he had succeeded in bringing the brave boy
nearly to the suface the grip of the child upon the rope was
relaxed and he fell back for the third time. Of course, life
was extinct when his body was recovered. This is one of the
most distressing and melancholy occurrences we have ever known
and we deeply sumpathize with the unfortunate parents who
were compelled to witness the harrowing scene.

Obituary: Mrs. Mary Reid, the relict of the late George Reid
of Aberdeen, Scotland died suddenly in London on the 6th of
March at the extreme age of 88 years. The deceased had many
friends in Charleston and in Columbia, Yorkville and other
places in the state.

Obituary: Departed this life in Anderson County, S. C. March
16th, 1876, Mrs. Elizabeth Hall, wife of Martin Hall, deceased.
Mrs. Hall was born in Union County, S. C. March 5th, 1800 and
was married to Martin Hall of Anderson County in the year 1825,
into which county she immediately removed and lived until the
day of her death. Mrs. Hall was a wife indeed. As such, she
may have been equalled but not surpassed. She always prided
herself in the happiness of her husband; always found her
happiness in his; his joys were hers, though they came to him
often through sacrifices which she willingly made. She lived
nearly fifty years in true and devoted love and sympathy with
her husband. And although she never was a mother in reality,
yet she filled the capacity of a mother, (and Mr. Hall that
of a father) for a number of years to the commendation of all;
giving that advice, that training and religious instruction
to the orphans that were in the providence of God placed in
her hands for maternal care, as would necessarily lead the
mind to that Redeemer whom she in early life had embraced,
loved and served. Truly, she was a faithful and affectionate
mother to the motherless. As a church member she can very
appropriately be numbered among the first class of Baptist
women. She was always found in her seat at the Cross Roads
Baptist Church only when prevented by Providence. She loved
and delighted in the Kingdom of her Lord, "the house of His
abode." What a great blessing it might be to all Baptist
churches and their churches and pastors as she was. But
she is gone, no more to help the church, no more to assist
the pator. She has doubtless gone to receive her great reward
for she was eminently a Christian woman ready and willing to
engage in every good work.   Her Former Pastor

Issue of:
Thursday, April 20, 1876:
Obituary: Information has been received of the death of Mrs.
Mary Prince, of Ripley, Miss., which occurred at the residence
of her son-in-law, Capt. A. C. Rucker, on Friday March 31st in
the 76th year of her age. The deceased was the widow of Mr.
Richard Prince, one of the early settlers of Anderson who
removed to Mississippi about thirty years ago.

Obituary: Mrs. Amanda Bowen, the wife of Mr. T. J. Bowen,
living near the Abbeville line, was fatally wounded by an
accidental pistol shot on Saturday morning, 9th inst. She was
attempting to get her bonnet from a nail in the wall, upon
which a pistol was also hanging. In reaching for the bonnet,
the pistol fell to the floor and in picking up the pistol, she
let it fall again, when the pistol was discharged and the ball
entered the body of Mrs. Bowen. She survived until Tuesday
afternoon, when death released her from agony. The deceased
was formerly Miss Amanda Armstrong, daughter of Wm. Armstrong
and was a most estimable woman. She leaves a husband and
four children.

Issue of:
Thursday, April 27, 1876:
Married: At the residence of the bride's father, April 12th,
by the Rev. R. N. Wells, Mr. Alex. McBee Jr. of Greenville,
S. C. to Miss Annie B., daughter of W. J. Crosswell of Sumter.

Married: By Rev. W. P. Martin, April 16th, 1876 at his own
residence, Mr. George M. Braswell and Miss Nancy Caroline Poore,
daughter of Baylis Poore. All of Anderson County, S. C.

Obituary: We regret to announce the death of Mrs. Rebecca
Clinkscales, wife of the late Maj. Abner Clinkscales, which
occurred at her residence in this County on Saturday last
from erysipelas of the neck. Mrs. Clinkscales was about sixty
five years of age at the time of her death. Her remains were
interred in the burying ground at Cross Roads Church on Sunday
last.

Obituary: We regret to record the death of Mrs. M. R. Casey
which oqcurred at the residence of her husband at Due West
on Monday morning last. Mrs. Casey was a daughter of Mr.
T. B. Wright of this place and her remains were brought to
Anderson and placed to rest in the Presbyterian Cemetery on
last Tuesday.

Obituary: It is our painful duty to announce the death of
Mr. William M. Leavell which occurred at his residence near
Belton on last Saturday night from inflammation of the liver
of which he had been suffering for a long time. He had been
for the last two terms a member of the Board of County
Commissioners of Anderson County and was esteemed for his
integrity and upright character. The funeral services were
conducted in the Baptist Church at Belton on last Monday morning after which his remains were interred by the Sons of
Temperance, of which he was a member. The burial service of
this order was very solemn and beautiful.

Issue of:
Thursday, May 4, 1876:
Obituary: Mrs. Margaret Attoway, wife of the Rev. John Atto-
way of the South Carolina Methodist Conference, died in
Williamston on Monday the 24th of April last.

Obituary: Death of Mrs. Borstel - The reaper death has again
invaded the sacred precincts of a happy home and taken its
chief ornament away. On last Friday, after an illness of
several weeks, Mrs. Cassandra H. Borstel departed this life
in the 47th year of her age. Mrs. Borstel came to this town
in 1849 from Charleston, where her parents resided and entered
as a student in the Johnston Female Seminary and in 1850 was
married to Maj. F. C. V. Borstel, since which time, with the
exception of one or two years during the war, she resided in
Anderson. Mrs. Borstel was intimately connected with the
educational interests of the town for more than twenty years.
She was one of the teachers in Johnston Female University and
occupied important positions in the literary and musical de-
partments of that institution when its prosperity was second
to no similiar institution in the State. For the last two
or three years she has been in charge of the musical department of the Carolina Collegiate Institute and has aided
materially in enhancing its reputation. Her dignity, sound
judgement and acquirements always gave her great influence
with the faculty of instruction, and commanded the highest
respect of the students. Many of the latter, in different
parts of the State, will hear of the death of their beloved
instructress with the deepest regret and while they will
fondly cherish her memory they will commingle their sympathy
with the bereaved ones. Mrs. Borstel was a consistent and
devoted member of the Baptist Church for a number of years.
Although her health was frail, there was no enterprise which
had for its end the promotion of education or the advancement
of the interests of the church which did not enlist her heart
and command her energies. Her life was a useful one. Unselfish by nature, she lived to do good unto others and hence the
universal esteem in which she was held by the whole community.
The very large attendance of her funeral attests the appreciation of her worth by all classes of our people. In the
death of Mrs. Borstel the church has lost an exemplary member
and the community one whose place it will be difficult to fill.
In all the relations of life she was most useful and valuable
and while the loss to the community is great, none can estimate
the void in the hearts of the loved ones of her household. All
we can do is to sympathize with them most deeply in their sore
bereavement. The funeral services were conducted at the
Baptist Church on Saturday afternoon by Rev. J. S. Murray in
the presence of a numerous congregation whose tearful eyes
bespoke the estimation with which they regarded the deceased.

Issue of:
Thursday, May 11, 1876:
Married: On Tuesday the 9th instant in Pendleton at the resi-
dence of the bride's mother by Rev. J. S. Murray, Mr. E. B.
Murray and Miss Eva Sloan.

Visitor: Mr. Wm. L. Massey of Winston County, Mississippi,
who has been a regular subscriber to the Intelligencer for a

number of years, paid us a visit on a visit on Monday last.
He is a son of Mr. Silas Massey, of this County and removed to
Mississippi over thirty years ago.

Obituary: We regret to announce the death of Mrs. Polly
Bannister which occurred at the residence of her husband, Mr.
James Bannister, of this County, on the 30th of April last
from an attack of billious fever. She was sixty three years of
age and had been a member of the Baptist Church for years.
A husband and several children together with many friends are
left to mourn her death.

Issue of:
Thursday, May 18, 1876:
Obituary: Death of Dr. Alexander Evins - We are pained to
announce the sad intelligence that Dr. Alexander Evins departed
this life on Sunday night last at the residence of Col. John H.
Evins in Spartanburg. His disease was consumption and for
many years Dr. Evins has been in delicate health suffering from
a bronchial affection. He has declined rapidly for the last
several weeks and when we visited him only one week ago we felt
that his days were few in the land of the living. On Sunday
evening, as we learn from the Spartanburg Spartan, Dr. Evins
was sitting up with the family and received his friends with
his usual cheerfulness. He retired shortly after nine o'clock
going upstairs with great difficulty, supported by his nephew.
In less than an hour he was a corpse. Thus passed away one who
was greatly beloved and honored in our community and whose
memory will be cherished in numerous households. Dr. Evins
was born on the 17th day of March, 1802 in Spartanburg County.
He studied medicine and graduated at Lexington, Ky. which was
then one of the first schools in the country. There were no
railroads in those days and the young student rode to college
on horseback. He practiced his profession for a short time at
Fairview in Spartanburg County and then removed to Pendleton
District where he made hosts of friends and for a long time
enjoyed a most lucrative practice from which he retired many
years ago. He was genial and popular in his manners and soon
won the confidence and support of the people. He represented
Old Pendleton in the State Senate and when the District was
divided, Dr. Evins was elected Commissioner in Equity for
Anderson County. He was afterwards sent again to the State
Senate and until within a few years was always most active
and useful in every relation of life. He was a delegate to
the Knoxville Convention in 1836 which discussed and planned
the grand scheme for a railroad connection with the great
West and his interest in the promotion of similar schemes
was unabated to the end of life. Dr. Evins was one of the
earliest settlers of our town and until a few years ago resided
in our midst. He was warmly esteemed for his gentle, dignified
manners, firm and decided views of men and things and strong
espousal of whatever measures for the public good he deemed
right. In every circle of society he was regarded with great
respect and to his intimate friends and acquaintances there
was always frankness and candid bearing which could not fail
to elevate him as a true man and unshaken friend. He left our
place several years ago after the death of his nephew, Dr.
Thomas A. Evins and has since resided in Spartanburg. This
hurried sketch is necessarily imperfect as to the life and
character of the deceased, whose position and influence for
so many years entitled him to rank as an honored landmark

of Anderson where his memory will be revered and his virtues
tenderly cherished.

Issue of:
Thursday, May 25, 1876:
Obituary: We regret to learn of the death of Mr. W. O. Sharpe
of Alabama who was formerly a citizen of Pendleton and a
brother of our esteemed townsman, Dr. M. L. Sharpe.

Obituary: Mr. William Vandiver, Sr., of Franklin County, Ga.,
died on the 8th inst. in the 86th year of his age. He was a
native of Anderson, we believe and has many relatives and
friends in our midst.

Obituary: The late Dr. Alexander Evins was buried at Nazareth
Church in Spartanburg County where his remains were deposited
in the old family burying ground among their kindred dust of
several generations. The funeral services took place on Monday,
15th inst. Dr. Evins made a public profession of faith in the
Presbyterian Church of Spartanburg two years ago and frequently
expressed his readiness for the change from this world to the
realization of hopes in a better land.

Obituary: Death of Mr. W. H. Cater - We are pained to record
the death of Mr. William H. Cater, lately a resident of
Charleston, which occurred at the residence of his brother,
Mr. E. B. Cater, on Thursday afternoon 18th inst. in the 35th
year of his age. Mr. Cater had been confined to his room for
nearly three months and was a great sufferer for the most part
of the time. He was a native of Anderson and the eldest son
of the late Dr. A. P. Cater. He was twice discharged from the
army of the Confederate States on account of feeble health
and after his last discharge engaged in the drug business in
this town which continued for several years after the war. Of
late he was represented the drug house of Dowie & Moise, of
Charleston and was traveling for that firm when he was attacked
by his last illness. His kind and accommodating disposition
gained for him many friends who will deplore his untimely
death. He was a member of the Presbyterian Church for seven
or eight years and gave strong evidence of exceptance and
salvation through the Saviour. Mr. Cater leaves a wife and
five children with numerous relatives and friends to mourn the
loss sustained by this afflictive dispensation of Providence.
His remains were buried in the Presbyterian Cemetery on Friday
afternoon.

Issue of:
Thursday, June 1, 1876:
Married: At the residence of the bride's father on Tuesday
morning 30th of May by Rev. D. E. Frierson, Mr. David S. Taylor
and Miss Bessie W. Rucker, all of Anderson.

Married: On Sunday 28th ultimo by Notary Public Dr. W. K.
Sharpe at the residence of Solomon Perry, Esq., Mr. Norris E.
Edwards and Miss Lena Pickens. All of Townville, S. C.

Issue of:
Thursday, June 8, 1876:
Obituary: Died, in Anderson June 3, 1876, Rose Ella, daughter
of John J. and R. A. Smith, aged 1 month and 6 days.

Issue of:
Thursday, June 15, 1876:
Married: At the residence of the bride's father Thursday
evening May 18th by Rev. Mr. Ashley, Mr. S. J. Brown and Miss
Mary Shirley, all of Anderson County.

Obituary: We are pained to chronicle the death of Viola and
Lora, twin children of Mr. and Mrs. W. F. Barr of this town,
aged six months. One died on Tuesday afternoon and the other
on Wednesday morning from cholera infintum.

Death: W. S. Brown, Esq., Trial Justice and acting coroner,
held an inquest on Friday last upon the body of John Smith
who was drowned the day previous in the mill race at Anderson's
Mills, eight miles northwest of this place. We learn that the
deceased was enfeebled and emaciated and it is thought he was
attempting to drink water from the race when he was seized
with vertigo and was drowned in consequence as he was found
with his face in the water which was not more than a foot deep.
He was a stranger almost in the community and it is believed
that he came from Rabun County, Ga. where he has a wife and
children living. The verdict of the jury was accidental
drowning, in accordance with the facts above stated. The
deceased was about forty three years of age.

Obituary: John Watson Esq., of Greenville, died on Friday
last in the 89th year of his age. He was Ordinary of Greenville District for more than twenty five years.

Suicide: Mrs. Caroline S. Smith, wife of Capt. F. R. Smith of
the United States Navy, committed suicide in Beaufort by
shooting herself through the body. Domestic infelicity was
the cause of the suicide.

Issue of:
Thursday, June 22, 1876:
Obituary: Departed this life on June 8, 1876 at his residence
in Anderson County, Texas of bilious fever, Mr. Alexander H.
Waddill. Mr. Waddill was born August 1, 1810 in South Carolina.
He moved from there to Texas in the Fall of 1855. By his death
we lose an honest and upright citizen. He leaves a devoted
wife, three loving children and a large circle of friends to
mourn his loss - though we should not mourn as for those for
whom we have no hope.

Obituary: Mr. James McGrady, the oldest Mason in North
America, residing about ten miles east of Winnsboro, departed
this life on the 10th instant. Mr. McGrady was born in Ireland
on the 18th of February 1788 and was at the time of his death
over eighty eight years of age. He left his native county for
America in October 1816 and had been a resident of this county
ever since he landed. He was made a Mason in Crumlin Lodge
No. 180 of Ireland in the year 1814 and served as Worshipful
Master for two years and at the time of his death was a member
of Winsboro [sic] Chapter No. 2, R. A. M.

Obituary: We regret to announce the death of Mrs. James Wilcox
which sad event occurred at the home of her husband about one
and a half miles south of this place on yesterday morning. She
has for many years been a consistent and devoted member of the

Methodist Church and in her death the Church sustains a
sad loss. We understand she died from the effects of an
apopletic stroke. She leaves a husband and large family of
children to mourn her loss.

Issue of:
Thursday, June 29, 1876:
Homicide: On the night of the twenty second instant, Mr.
Allen S. Barksdale went to the house of Mrs. Mary A. Gray, one
of his tenants and a difficulty ensued which terminated in the
death of Barksdale from a cut in the head by an axe. Trial
Justice J. L. Bryant held an inquest over the body and a ver-
dict that the deceased was killed by an axe in the hands of
Mrs. Mary A. Gray in self defense was rendered. Upon this,
Mrs. Gray was committed to jail and on Saturday last was
brought before Trial Justice John E. Breazeale and G. W.
Hammond, upon Habeas Corpus. Gen. J. W. Harrison represented
the State and Maj. John B. Moore appeared for the prisoner.
Mrs. Gray's affidavit setforth, that on the night in question
Mr. Barksdale came to her house with a drawn knife and threatened to cut her throat, because she had taken a warrant for
him before J. L. Bryant, Esq., that he then rushed on her; she
gave back to the corner of her room; he followed and cut her;
she got an axe and struck him twice; he cut her again; she
tried to escape; he kicked her so that she fell and he fell
two [sic]; she got a hoe and struck him twice; he cut her about
the face and neck and swore he would kill her; she then got the
axe and struck him a lick which killed him; as soon as he fell
she sent for neighbors. No one was present except her little
children. Doctors Scudday and Wilhite submitted affidavits
that the cuts upon Mrs. Gray were from a knife or some sharp
instrument. Mrs. Gray was bailed on her own reconizance in
the sum of five hundred dollars, to appear for trial at the
next term of Court of this County.

Obituary: We regret to announce the death of little Eugene,
son of Mr. W. H. Cater, whose death we announced but a short
time since. The little boy was with his mother at Atlanta and
died of cholera infantum on the 22nd inst. His remains were
interred beside his father's grave in the Presbyterian cemetery
at this place.

Obituary: Mr. Martin S. Kay, who was for very many years a
respected citizen of this County, fell dead on the 20th inst.
in one of his fields near Carnesville, Georgia, whither he had
removed a few years ago. He was an old gentleman whose death
will be regretted by the many friends he left in Anderson County
the place of his nativity, Squire McKay [?] was widely known
through the upper portion of the State as a reliable and careful surveyor. He was also in the service of the Blue Ridge
Railroad as an engineer in the location and construction of
a portion of the road.

Issue of:
Thursday, July 6, 1876:
The many friends and relatives of Mr. John M. Jolly, who was
formerly of this County, will be glad to learn that he has
recently been elected Sheriff of Falls County, Texas. His
success in the home of his adoption is no doubt fully merited
for he was a worthy and energetic citizen while a resident
of Anderson County.

Funeral: The remains of Mr. R. P. Welch, the young man killed by the engine explosion at Townville on last Monday, were interred in the Presbyterian Church yard on yesterday morning. Solemn funeral rites were conducted by Rev. D. E. Frierson. Mr. Welch leaves quite a number of relatives and friends who mourn his sad untimely death.

Issue of:
Thursday, July 13, 1876:
Married: On the 6th inst. by Rev. S. A. Weber, Mr. H. Dobson Reese and Miss Ella Bradley, all of Williamston.

Obituary: We regret to announce the death of Dr. John H. Dean, a prominent citizen of Greenville which occurred on the 3d inst. after a long and painful illness. He was stricken with paralysis about six months ago. Dr. Dean had a lucrative and extensive practice in medicine and was always greatly esteemed by the citizens of Greenville. He married a daughter of the late Dr. F. W. Symmes, of Pendleton.

Death: Richard Branyon, son of Thomas Branyon, of Abbeville County, (near the Anderson line) left home on Thursday last. The family became alarmed at his protracted absence and search was commenced on Saturday for him. On Sunday his hat was found and at a late hour on Monday evening his body was discovered near the same place. A jury of inquest was summoned but we have no report of its deliberations.

Issue of:
Thursday, July 20, 1876:
Obituary: We regret to announce the death of a little son of Mr. John H. Hembree, which occurred on the 12th inst. after a brief illness. The funeral services were performed by Rev. D. L. Whitaker and the remains interred on the 13th inst.

Obituary: We are pained to record the death of Mr. W. L. Cornog, an esteemed citizen of Hart County, Ga., which occurred on the 26th ult. in the 34th year of his age. He was a warm hearted, genial gentleman and greatly respected wherever he was known. He was an active, influential citizen of our neighboring State and was much endeared to numerous friends and acquaintances in South Carolina.

Tribute of respect to Rev. Thomas R. Gary who was born in Laurens County, S. C. on 19 September 1818 and died in Pickens County, S. C. at 5 o'clock a.m. 1 May 1876. Buried at Enon Church near Easley, S. C.

Issue of:
Thursday, July 27, 1876:
Obituary: The neighborhood of Centreville mourns the loss of a popular and worthy man, Mr. William C. Hale, who died on the 19th inst. after a brief illness in the 25th year of his age. The deceased was held in great esteem by his neighbors and the large attendance at his funeral attested this fact. He was buried at Asbury Chapel on Thursday last, the religious service being conducted by Rev. D. L. Whitaker after which the beautiful and impressive funeral rites of the Sons of Temperance and Patrons of Husbandry were conducted by the officers of New Prospect Division and Deep Creek Grange to which the deceased belonged.

Thursday, August 3, 1876:
Married: On Wednesday evening 26th of July at St. Paul's
Church, Pendleton, by Rev. W. H. Gregory, Mr. Joseph J. Sitton
and Miss Susie H., third daughter of W. H. D. Gaillard, all
of Pendleton, S. C.

Obituary: Death of W. N. Alexander - The reaper has again
visited our community and removed from us a useful citizen,
a kind husband, a devoted father, an affectionate friend
and a promising young man. Mr. William N. Alexander had for
some time since been suffering from an attack of chronic
diarrhea but had not been considered dangerously ill until on
last Thursday the approach of the reaper was foreseen and on
Friday afternoon at about half past 3 o'clock his spirit
passed from earth. During his illness he was watched over and
cared for with the greatest anxiety both by the skill of medical
attendents and by the tender solicitude of a wife but nothing
could be done to arrest the conqueror. Mr. Alexander had
excellent business attainments and from the position of a
clerkship a few years he became the junior member of the
firm of N. K. Sullivan & Co., one of the best business houses
in Anderson. He was originally from Oconee County, but has
been a citizen of this place for the last eight years. In 1873
he was united in Marriage to Miss Maria, daughter of the late
Col. Daniel Ledbetter, of Pickens County and by his death
leaves a devoted wife and interesting daughter to sustain the
sad bereavement of his early demise. He had not reached his
twenty seventh year when he removed from the dear and sacred
relations he had assumed but three years ago. His death is
regretted by all who knew him for his was a nature which made
no enemies. On Sunday afternoon the stores of the town were
closed in respect to the departed merchant and many persons
gathered at the Baptist Church yard to render the last tribute to the remains of a friend who had been called hence in
the pride of his early manhood.

Obituary: Mr. Newton Bryson, of Centreville Township, lost a
little daughter two years of age on last Saturday from an
attack of dysentery. The little child had been delicate for
some time previous to the attack of sickness which terminated
her life. We sympathize with the parents in their bereavement.

Obituary: We regret to announce the death of Miss Mary E.
Dobbins, daughter of Mrs. Mary Dobbins of the Fork Township
which sad event occurred on Tuesday morning 25th ult. after
a protracted illness. Miss Dobbins was much beloved by her
acquaintances and her death is much lamented by many relatives and friends. Her remains were deposited to rest in
Robert's Church Yard on Wednesday last by the Fork Grange of
which she was an esteemed member.

Issue of:
Thursday, August 10, 1876:
Obituary: Mrs. Nancy Abercrombie, wife of Mr. Calvin Abercrombie, died on Wednesday the 2nd of August after a long
and painful illness. She was about sixty years of age.

Obituary: We are pained to record the death of Mrs. Callie
Townsend, the beloved wife of J. F. Townsend of Cokesbury,
which occurred at the residence of Mr. Samuel J. Emerson of this

County, on the 7th inst. She was a daughter of the late Col. Abner H. McGhee of Abbeville County and was greatly beloved by a large circle of relatives and friends.

Obituary: Death of Rev. W. R. Hemphill - The Associate Reform Presbyterian Church has lost one of its most honored and able divines in the death of Rev. W. R. Hemphill, D.D., which occurred at his residence in Due West on Friday, July 28th in the seventy first year of his age. Dr. Hemphill was a man of extraordinary energy and fine attainments. He was an incessant contributor to the religious and secular press. His labors have done much to build up his town and the interests of his denomination. He was for many years a professor in Erskine College and had for the last few years devoted his energies to raising an endowment of one hundred thousand dollars for this College. Dr. Hemphill was the father of Messrs. Hemphill of the Abbeville Medium and we extend our sincere sympathies to them in this serious loss and sore bereavement.

Obituary: Death of Mrs. H. H. Scudday - We regret to announce the death of this excellent lady which occurred at the residence of her husband of this town on Wednesday 2nd instant about 3 o'clock. Mrs. Scudday had suffered a long and painful illness and was calm and resigned in the hour of her death which freed her spirit from its suffering and gave her rest. She was a daughter of the late Maj. Hugh Gregg, a respected citizen of the Dark Corner township of this County and had been a resident of this town for several years past. Her death leaves a void in the home circle which will long be mourned by her husband and children. It makes a blank in the circle of her friends which will be long lamented. Solemn and impressive funeral services were conducted in the Presbyterian Church on last Thursday afternoon and her remains were interred in the adjoining cemetery.

Issue of:
Thursday, August 24, 1876:
Married: On the 8th inst. by Rev. F. R. McClanahan, Rev. D. W. Hiatt of Colleton, S. C. and Miss Ella E. Martin of Anderson.

Obituary: We regret to announce the death of Mrs. C. C. Pegg, wife of Capt. S. M. Pegg, which occurred at his place on last Saturday morning after a protracted and painful illness. Mrs. Pegg was the proprietress of the "Ladies Store" in Anderson and leaves many friends and acquaintances in our midst. who will regret her death. On Sunday morning her remains were placed to rest after impressive funeral services in the Presbyterian Churchyard in this place.

Issue of:
Thursday, August 31, 1876:
Obituary: Mrs. Nancy E. Cornog, daughter of W. W. Holland, Anderson County, S. C. and relict of W. Levis Cornog of Hart County, Ga., was born January 9, 1844 and died August 1, 1876. Sister Cornog had been a great sufferer for several years much of her time confined to her room and during this year her health had been very poor up to the latter part of May when her husband was stricken down with paralysis. Though so very feeble herself she left her bed and gave him her undivided and constant attention until the 28th June when he was relieved of his sufferings

194

and went to his eternal rest. Being overwhelmed with grief
and heart-broken, she was prostrate again and was taken the
next day after her husband was buried from her residence in
Hart County, Ga. to her father's in South Carolina where she
continued to sink until the 1st August when in great peace and
full faith she bid adieu to her two children, (a son and daughter), father and sister, father and mother-in-law and
numerous weeping friends, she joined her husband in "that
beautiful land" where the weary are at rest. She had been for
several years a member of the M. E. Church and from the time
of her connection with the church she manifested in every
department of life a meek, quiet and christian spirit, loved
the church and the people of God with an ardent love and
never more happy than when the Ministers of Christ and Christian people were being entertained on the (to her) all absorb-
ing subject of salvation. She, with her husband, was giving
special attention to the religious training of their children,
the fruits which are seen in the moulding of their character
as they are quiet and lamblike in all their bearing. This
lovely mother and Christian has ceased from her labors and is
at rest, while her works follow her. May the blessings of the
Redeemer, whom she loved, rest on the fatherless and motherless
children. May they know the God of their father and serve him
with perfect hearts and finally meet their loved parents in
that glorious world where their troubles will be over.
    Her Pastor

Obituary: Little Ernest, nearly four months old, son of Mr.
G. M. and Mrs. Annie Harper, died near Anderson, S. C.
August 18, 1876. "Yes, Ernest has left a vacant place/ To
the sorrowing ones beneath;/ But Oh! in heaven, with radiant
face,/ He wears an angel's wreath."   F & N

Obituary: Funeral of Gen. Wagener: The mortal remains of
Gen. John A. Wagener were deposited in their last resting place
in the Lutheran Cemetery at Walhalla on last Tuesday morning.
A very large concourse of people, composed of all classes
and orders of Walhalla and vicinity, attended his remains in
procession from Biemann's Hotel to the Lutheran Church where his
funeral services were conducted by Rev. J. F. Probst in the
German language followed by Dr. J. P. Smeltzer in a discourse
in English, after which his remains were taken charge of by
Blue Ridge Lodge No. 92, A.F.M. and buried with the usual
ceremonies of the order, which were solemn and impressive.

Issue of:
Thursday, September 7, 1876:
Obituary: We regret to announce the death of Mr. Luke Hamilton,
an aged citizen who resided near Storeville in this County,
which occurred on the 5th inst., from dropsy. He was seventy
six years of age. On Wednesday last his remains were deposited
to rest in Varennes churchyard.

Obituary: We regret to announce the death of Mrs. Martha,
wife of W. L. Dobbins, which occurred at the residence of her
husband in this County on Wednesday morning at 2 o'clock after
a protracted and painful illness of four or five months
duration. Her remains are to be interred by the Double
Springs Grange on this morning in the Robert's Church graveyard
at 11 o'clock.

Issue of:
Thursday, September 14, 1876:
Death of A Centenarrian: We regret to announce the death of
Mr. Silas Massey, an aged and well known citizen of this
County, which occurred at his residence on last Monday night,
a little after 10 o'clock. Mr. Massey had been paralyzed
for several years back and it was known that his end was
approaching several days before his death. Mr. Massey had been
a member of Robert's Presbyterian Church for more than twenty
years and died a member of that faith. According to his
record he was born on the sixth day of March, 1776 and was
consequently a little more than one hundred years old. He saw
the birth of the American Union and lived to see its centennial
anniversary, attaining an old age which is reached by very few
of the human family of this day. He leaves a number of children
who, in common with his friends, mourn the departure of the
aged one. His remains were interred in Mountain Creek Church
yard on Wednesday morning.

Obituary: We regret to announce the death of Mrs. Benjamin
Hapholdt, which occurred at her residence in Pendleton on
last Friday. She leaves a family of several children to mourn
the death of a mother.

Obituary: We regret to announce the death of the little child
of Mr. S. P. Tate, whose injuries from being kicked by a horse
we noticed some time since. Death came on last Monday evening
and called the little one from the sufferings of this life.

Obituary: We regret to announce the death of Mr. David F. Hale,
which occurred on last Sabbath afternoon from typhoid fever.
Mr. Hale was an excellent young man in the eighteenth year of
his age. He was a son of Mr. Wm. Hale, who has, by this sad
bereavement, been called upon to bear the loss of two sons
within the last two months. His remains were placed to rest
in the Asbury church yard on Monday afternoon.

Issue of:
Thursday, September 21, 1876:
Obituary: We regret to announce the death of Mrs. Nancy
Braswell, which occurred at her residence near Honea Path on
Friday last. She was eighty six years old and died within
a few days of her elder brother, the late Mr. Silas Massey.
She had been a member of the Baptist Church for fifty one years
and had raised sixteen children. Hermany relatives and friends
mourn her death.

Issue of:
Thursday, September 28, 1876:
Married: In Anderson, S. C. September 20th, 1876, by Rev.
D. E. Frierson, Wm. H. Overman, of Salisbury, N. C. to Miss
Flora Calhoun, eldest daughter of the late Col. Elliott M.
Keith.

Married: On Sunday afternoon, September 26th by Rev. J. R.
Earle, Mr. Daniel Kay and Miss Sarah Jane Hembree, daughter
of M. B. Hembree, all of Anderson County.

Married: At the residence of the bride's father, September
19th, 1876, by Rev. W. W. Mood, Mr. Abe Clark and Miss Mattie
F. Wilcox, all of Anderson.

Married: On the 14th of September by Rev. J. S. Murray, at
the residence of the bride's father, near Townville, Mr. William
L. Bolt and Miss Mary A. Woolbright, all of Anderson County.

Issue of:
Thursday, October 5, 1876:
Obituary: We learn that Wm. M. Gambrell, who resided near
Honea Path, in this County, died on the 19th of September and
was buried by the Patrons of Husbandry on the 21st ult.

Obituary: The Abbeville Press and Banner announces the death
of Mr. Banister Allen one of the oldest citizens of Abbeville
County, which occurred at his residence near Lowndesville on
Sunday night, 24th of September, after an illness of only a
few days. Mr. Allen was about eighty five years of age and
lived all his life within a mile of the spot where he was born.
He was remarkable for great business qualifications and possessed in a large degree all the elements necessary to financial
success, which he achieved in an eminent degree. His honesty
and fair dealing were known to all. Mr. Allen leaves a number
of relatives and friends in Anderson County who will sincerely
mourn his demise.

Married: On the 28th of September, in Seneca City, at the
residence of the bride's brother-in-law, Col. J. W. Livingston
by Rev. W. Cuttino Smith, Mr. Gideon Lee, of Carmel, N. Y.
to Miss Ella Lorton of Pendleton, S. C.

Obituary: Mrs. Nancy Braswell was born in Anderson County,
S. C., about 86 years ago, according to one account and 95
years ago by another and died on the 15th day of September,
1876 after a long and painful illness. She lived, died and
was buried on the place where she was born. She was the mother
of 17 children, 16 of whom she raised and became head of
families. Only one of the children was privileged to be
present at her burial. Her brother, Silas Massey, died a
few days ago at the advanced age of 100 years. She lived a
quiet, useful life, 39 years of which were spent in widowhood.
She early connected herself with the Baptist Church, held an
uninterrupted membership therein and fell sweetly asleep in
Jesus. Peace to her memory.

Tribute of Respect: James R. Dougherty died in Bristol,
Tenn. on the 14th instant.

Issue of:
Thursday, October 12, 1876:
Obituary: We regret to learn the death of Mrs. Jesse P. McGee
which occurred yesterday morning after a long illness. She
was a most estimable woman and greatly endeared to a large
circle of friends. Her remains will be buried at First Creek
Church today.

Obituary: Mr. Jacob Martin, one of the oldest citizens of
Anderson County, died on the 6th inst. at his residence near
Piercetown. He was in the 87th year of his age.

Obituary: Mr. Paris.Hawkins, another old citizen living on
Rocky River, departed this life yesterday morning after a
short illness. He was probably 70 years of age.

Issue of:
Thursday, October 19, 1876:
Obituary: Mr. D. J. Hix died at his residence west of Anderson
on last Sunday from a cancer with which he had been afflicted
for a long time previous. He was near sixty five years of age.
His death will be lamented by his many neighbors and friends.

Married: At the residence of the bride's father, Sept. 19,
1876 by Rev. J. L. Kennedy, Mr. J. Perry Glenn and Miss
Hettie A. Smith, all of Slabtown, Anderson County.

Married: On the 28th September, by Rev. J. R. Earle, Mr.
L. C. Chamblee and Miss Miriam McGregor all of Anderson.

Married: On the 13th of September, at the residence of J. M.
Lewis Esq. by Rev. Wm. B. Pressley, Mr. W. H. Reid, formerly
of Charleston, S. C. and Miss Mollie V. Emmons of Iredell Co.,
N. C.

Married: On the 12th October, 1876 in the Presbyterian Church,
Pendleton, S. C. by the Rev. W. Cuttino Smith, Mr. John Hackett
of Atlanta, Ga. to Miss Ida Robinson of Pendleton, S. C.

Issue of:
Thursday, October 26, 1876:
Obituary: Died, with croup, near Anderson C. H., October 13,
1876, little Lula Amis, eldest child of D. J. and N. E.
Bohanon, aged four years, ten months and thirteen days. "Dear
little pet thou art gone,/ Those bright eyes no more we see,/
I know thou has a better home,/ Than if you were with me."
        Parent

Issue of:
Thursday, November 2, 1876:
Married: At the residence of the bride's mother, October 25th,
1876 by Rev. W. L. Pressley, Mr. H. H. Acker of Anderson County
and Miss Joicey Moore of Abbeville County.

Married: By Rev. W. P. Martin, October 26th, 1876 at his own
residence, Capt. Willis Allen and Miss Fannie Moore, second
daughter of Mr. Grant A. and Mrs. Letty Moore, all of Anderson
County.

Issue of:
Thursday, November 16, 1876:
Obituary: Mrs. Margaret Massey, wife of Mr. John Massey, died
suddenly on the 5th inst. at her residence near Honea Path.
She was an old lady, having attained the age of seventy years.

Obituary: Mrs. Elizabeth Armstrong, an aged lady, died on the
9th inst. at the residence of her husband near Honea Path,
S. C. She was seventy one years old at the time of her death
and leaves a husband with many friends to lament her departure.

Obituary: We regret to announce the death of Mrs. Nancy Webb,
which occurred at the residence of her husband, Mr. James
Webb, on Wednesday morning at 6 o'clock from pneumonia. Her
remains will be interred at Sandy Springs burial ground today.
She leaves many relatives and friends who mourn her death.

Obituary: Dr. A. Walker, an old and highly respectable citizen of the Dark Corner Township of this County, died at his residence of last Friday afternoon at the advanced age of sixty six years. He was in usual health until Thursday afternoon, when he received a severe paralytic stroke, which terminated his life on the following day. His death is mourned by many relatives and friends.

Sudden Death: Once again the hand of death has removed from our midst a devoted wife and fond mother, who was an exemplary and useful member of society. The summons came suddenly in the morning of womanhood on last Monday afternoon to Mrs. Jemima Roof, wife of Mr. Walter Roof, of Charleston, who was stricken down by apoplexy at the residence of her father, Mr. J. B. Clark, in this town. She only survived about three hours and died without an utterance after the attack, which came upon her in health with no premonition of its approach. She was a faithful and pious member of the Baptist Church at this place and her remains were placed to rest in the Baptist Church yard after beautiful and solemn funeral services by Revs. J. S. Murray and L. M. Ayer. The deceased leaves a little daughter not yet a year old, with a husband and many relatives who, together with a large circle of friends, grieve for her untimely death.

Issue of:
Thursday, November 23, 1876:
Married: On Thursday the 16th inst. at the residence of the bride's mother in this town, by Rev. J. S. Murray, Mr. William W. Keys and Miss Vashti Burriss, all of Anderson.

Married: On Thursday the 16th inst. at the residence of the bride's father, in Williamston, by Rev. B. F. Mauldin, Mr. Thomas Archer and Miss Ruth Acker, all of this County.

Obituary: Departed this life on October 12, 1876, Mrs. Lucinda E. McGee, wife of Jesse P. McGee and daughter of Col. James Emerson. She was born January 28, 1827, was baptized and received into the fellowship of First Creek Baptist Church in 1846 and was married to Jesse P. McGee February 10, 1848. She ever adorned the profession she made of religion in an orderly and practical life of godliness. It was not difficult for even strangers to soon known from her conversation that she was extremely attached to her church. She early in life exhibited those traits of character which in all after years marked and distinguished her life for active and constant usefulness in the cause of her Redeemer. She was not less favorably known in the social circle among the people of her community. It was not only an assured fact that all met a hearty welcome at the threshold of her door, but were made recipients of all that heart could wish when once admitted her happy home. She was ever in the van in every good word and work and many who have passed through scenes of affliction and over whom dark and lowering clouds of sorrow have gathered, will bless her memory and respect her grave as the resting place of a true and sincere friend. During her last long and painful affliction she was never known to murmur and constantly expressed the most explicit confidence in and reliance on Christ - her friend - ever feeling and seeming to realize in its fullness, the precious truth that in His providence over her He would do that only which would be for her good and His

glory. Her only anxiety seemed, as it is with every Christian,
for the loved ones left behind. Many earnest prayers fell
from her dying lips for the husband and children whom she loved
as her own life. When the last moment came, without one
doubt or fear, she quietly breathed life's last moment away
and fell gently asleep in the arms of a blessed Saviour. It
is sad to know that we shall see her in life no more. Her
place in the church and family are vacant forever in time, but
we may meet her where no adieus are spoken and no farewell
tears are shed.   W. E. W.

Issue of:
Thursday, November 30, 1876:
Married: At the residence of S. M. Geer, Esq. on Thursday
23rd inst. at 2 o'clock p.m. by Rev. M. McGee, Mr. D. D. Gentry
and Miss Martha J. Holland, all of this County.

Married: On Thursday the 23rd of November at the residence
of the bride's mother, by the Rev. David Hiat, Mr. P. W. Leach
of Easley Station to Miss Victoria Campbell of Williamston.

Married: By Rev. W. P. Martin, November 26, 1876 at the resi-
dence of the bride's father, Col. Warren D. Wilkes and Miss
Miriam C. Harper, youngest daughter of Mr. John H. and Cloe
Harper, all of Anderson County.

Death of Rev. George Smith: We give below a notice of the death
of the gentleman whose name heads this article, which we copy
from the Rushville Jacksonian, of Indiana. In addition to the
facts stated in the obituary notice, we may mention as matters
of interest to our people that Mr. Smith married Miss Elizabeth
Brown in 1817, a daughter of Mr. John Brown, who at that time
lived upon the hill at Prevost's Mill. Previous to his removal
to Indiana he found a chapel for the worship of God in this
County, which is situated some seven miles southwest of Anderson and bears the name Smith Chapel, in honor of its founder,
whose death we now announce. He left three brothers in this
country, one of whom, Mr. Benjamin Smith, resided in Abbeville
County and the other two, Messrs. Samuel and Robert Smith,
resided in this County. Rev. George Smith left a large circle
of relatives and connections, besides very many friends in this
country, who will regret his death, although he has lived
beyond the allotted years of man. The Jacksonian says: The
subject of this sketch was born in Abbeville District, in the
State of South Carolina, May 13, 1794 and was married in the
same State, July 15, 1816. He was one of the early settlers
of Rush County, having moved to this State and county in the
year 1832, settling in Union township where he resided until
the year 1854: when he removed to Fayette county, where he
resided until the 25th day of October, 1876, at which time
he was called from labor to rest at the ripe old age of 82
years, 5 months and 2 days. He was a local preacher of the
Methodist church for 48 years prior to his death, always
taking a deep interest in all affairs of the church, especially
in her missions and charities, all of which received substantial aid and support from his purse. His life was
unostentatious but his memory will long be cherished by all
his old neighbors and more especially by the members of the
church to which he belonged. He was buried in the church yard
at Wiley Chapel, October 26th, 1876. Funeral services conducted by the Rev. Jesse Miller, of Glenwood. The deceased

leaves a widow 80 years of age with whom he had lived happily
for over 60 years. Ebenezer Smith of Union township was his
youngest brother. His widowed wife, his brother and family,
and his large circle of friends, though they feel sad at
parting with their long lived friend and companion, "mourn not
as those without hope", believing that in crossing of the
Jordan of death he was translated from this imperfect to that
all perfect celestial world beyond the skies.

Issue of:
Thursday, December 7, 1876:
Married: August 25, 1876 by J. L. Bryan Esq., Mr. S. M.
Latham and Miss Martha Driver, all of Anderson County.

Married: By J. L. Bryan Esq., November 9, 1876, Mr. A. A. S.
Galbreath and Miss Alice Stevenson, all of Anderson County.

Married: By J. L. Bryan Esq., December 3, 1876, Mr. W. D.
Chapman of Hart County, Ga. and Miss Mary M. Wardlaw of Anderson.

Death of Maj. F. C. V. Borstel: It is with sad feelings that
we record the death of Maj. Frederick Charles von Borstel, who
died at his residence in this town on Wednesday morning, the
6th instant, after an illness of several weeks. Maj. Borstel
was born on the 6th day of February, A.D. 1819, in Pommern,
Prussia, in Europe. While quite young, he went to London, where
he spent several years. From thence he sailed for New York
and after spending several years there and in New Jersey and
Georgia, in the spring of 1848 he came to Anderson and settled
permanently. In 1850 he married Miss Cassandra Hewitt of
Charleston, whom he survived only eight months. Maj. Borstel
was an honest, upright and useful citizen and possessed in
an eminent degree the confidence and respect of all who knew
him. His character was decided and in every enterprise upon
which he entered, he displayed an energy which is seldom
surpassed. He was a consistent, energetic and working member
of the Baptist Church for more than twenty years and in all
the relations of life he exemplified the religion of his
Saviour. He was for several years the Superintendent of the
Baptist Sabbeth School. In this work his whole heart was
enlisted and in it he never tired. As a meber and Deacon of
the Church, liberal in his contributions and devoted to its
best interest, he set an example worthy of the imitation of
all. The Church, the Sabbeth School and the community will
miss him and the bereaved ones have the sympathy of the community
in their affliction.

Issue of:
Thursday, December 14, 1876:
Married: At the residence of the bride's father on November
16th by Rev. L. W. Tribble, Mr. J. N. Shirley of Anderson
and Miss E. Tribble of Abbeville.

Married: On Sunday morning December 3rd at the residence of
the bride's father, by Rev. L. W. Tribble, Mr. T. Q. Cox
and Miss M. A. Grubbs, all of Anderson.

Obituary: Departed this life on Dec. 5, 1876, Reuben Cartee,
aged 85 years, whose remains were placed in the cemetery at
Big Creek, of which Church he was a consistent member. He
died as he had lived - a firm believer in the saving mercy of
a risen Saviour.

Issue of:
Thursday, December 21, 1876:
Married: By Rev. W. P. Martin, December 14th, 1876 at the
residence of W. C. Martin, near Hodges, Mr. James W. Gray and
Miss Grace G. Weatherall, daughter of William Weatherall,
deceased, all of Abbeville County, S. C.

Death of an Aged Citizen: The reaper of Death has been in our
midst again. All classes and conditions of society are subject
to the inevitable and irresistable power of the grim monster
and the community has realized of late the truth that "the
young may die and the old must die and the wisest knoweth
not how soon". It is our painful duty this morning to announce
the death of Daniel Brown, Esq. which occurred at his residence in this town on Friday night, 15th inst., in the 78th
year of his age. Mr. Brown was born in Abbeville County
within one mile of Donnaldsville on the 27th of October, 1799.
When he was about seventeen years old his father moved to
Pendleton County and settled on Broadway Creek, near the place
now known as Prevost's Mill. Mr. Brown was first married to
Miss Rhoda Acker when he was in the 21st year of his age.
By this marriage he had eleven children and eight of them
lived to be grown, surviving their mother. He was married the
second time on the 7th of May, 1840 to Mrs. Eleanor Nardin, by
whom he had two children. He commenced life by farming and
merchandizing in 1822, one mile below Varennes, on the
General's road and afterwards removed to a place known as
Tucker's mill on Wilson's Creek, where he remained two years.
Upon the division of Pendleton District into Anderson and
Pickens, Mr. Brown purchased and improved one of the original
lots in the town of Anderson and moved here on the 5th of
November, 1827 where he engaged in the mercantile business
and has been a citizen of the town ever since. He was the
oldest resident of Anderson at the time of his death and one
of its ancient landmarks. (long eulogy follows)

Issue of:
Thursday, January 4, 1877:
Married: By Rev. J. L. Kennedy on November 16th at the
residence of the bride's father, Mr. Tilman Cartee and Miss
Sallie, eldest daughter of Mr. Sam Poore.

Married: By Rev. J. L. Kennedy on the 26th November, at the
residence of the officiating minister, Mr. Thomas Garrett and
Miss Emma Garrett.

Married: By Rev. J. L. Kennedy at his residence in Williamston,
December 14th, Mr. Warren Cartee and Miss Sarah Cartee.

Married: By Rev. J. L. Kennedy, on December 20th at the
residence of the bride's father in Williamston, Mr. John A.
Reese and Miss Anna, daughter of Mr. A. J. Bradley.

Married: At the residence of the bride's father, W. W. Knight
Esq., on December 20th, by Rev. Hugh McLees, Mr. W. E.
Bellotte and Miss C. E. Knight.

Obituary: We regret to announce the death of Mrs. Martin, wife
of Col. John Martin, of this County, which occurred on last
Sunday night. Mrs. Martin was an excellant lady and lived to

a ripe old age and leaves a family with many friends to lament her death.

Obituary: Capt. William J. Broome, an old and respected citizen of Anderson County, died at his residence near Belton on last Monday and was buried on Wednesday by the Masonic Fraternity of which he was an acting and influential member. He was an upright and useful citizen, whose death will be regretted by the community in which he lived.

Issue of:
Thursday, January 11, 1877:
Married: In Anderson, S. C. January 4, 1877 by the Rev. David E. Frierson, Mr. William A. Chapman of Williamston and Miss Virginia E., second daughter of the late Col. Elliott M. Keith.

Married: On the 21st of December, 1876 at the residence of the bride's father, by Rev. R. D. Perry, assisted by Rev. J. Lowery Wilson, Mr. George B. Moseley of Greenville and Miss Annie B. Lowery, daughter of Maj. J. G. Lowery of Chester, S. C.

Married: On January 4th, by Rev. E. F. Hyde, Mr. J. L. Sears, and Miss S. M. Stribling, all of Anderson County.

Married: By J. L. Bryan Esq., December 21, Mr. J. A. Adams and Miss Alikina Adams.

Married: By J. L. Bryan Esq., December 24, Mr. W. G. Hall and Miss Julia Todd.

Married: By J. L. Bryan Esq., January 1, Mr. John Stewart and Miss Mattie Brown.

Married: On Thursday evening, December 14, by Rev. H. N. Hays, Mr. Benjamin Whitten and Miss Ann McCrary.

Married: On Thursday evening, December 21, by Rev. H. N. Hays, Mr. Wm. L. Harbin and Miss Susan A. Phillips.

Married: On Wednesday evening, 27th of December, by Rev. H. N. Hays, Mr. Eli Fletcher and Miss Amanda Sheriff.

Married: At the residence of the officiating clergyman, Rev. A. Rice at 11 o'clock on the 7th inst., Mr. William L. McClellan and Miss Emma Clamp.

Death: W. O. Hamilton accidentally killed when he dropped his shot pouch causing his gun to be fired. He was preparing for a hunt in Greenville County.

Issue of:
Thursday, January 18, 1877:
Married: On January 4, 1877 at the residence of the bride's father, Mr. W. W. Hamilton by Rev. H. N. Hays, Mr. John W. Harper and Miss Elizabeth Hamilton both of Oconee County.

Married: On January 14, 1877 by Rev. David F. Frierson, Mr. John E. Sadler and Mrs. Mary P. Sloan, both of Anderson Village.

Married: By Rev. F. G. Carpenter, at his residence on Sunday evening, 17th December last, Mr. Browning and Miss Rhodes, all of this County.

Married: By the Rev. F. G. Carpenter, on December 21st, Mr. J. E. Guyton and Miss Sallie Duckworth, all of Anderson County.

Married: By the Rev. F. G. Carpenter, on December 21st, Mr. Chesley M. Duckworth and Miss Sallie Guyton, all of Anderson County.

Issue of:
Thursday, January 25, 1877:
Married: January 16th, 1877 at the residence of the bride's father, J. D. Ferguson, near Pickens C. H., by Rev. W. F. Pearson of Due West. Mr. W. A. McFall of Anderson and Mrs. Sarah Griffin.

Obituary: Died, near Cleburn, Johnson County, Texas on 12th December, 1876, in the 77th year of her age, Miss Betsy Alexander, a native and until 1870 a resident of this County in the vicinity of Craytonville. The deceased was from early life a consistent member of the Presbyterian Church. "Thus star by star declines/ Till all have passed away,/ As morning high and higher shines/ To pure and perfect day;/ Nor sink those stars in empty night,/ But hide themselves in Heaven's own light." A Friend

Issue of:
Thursday, February 1, 1877:
Married: At the residence of the bride's father, James Carpenter Esq., in Polk County, N. C., on the 7th December 1876, by Rev. J. B. Carpenter, Mr. John D. Sitton of Anderson County, S. C. and Miss Emma E. Carpenter.

Married: On the 24th January 1877, by Rev. J. B. Carpenter, at the residence of the bride's father, James Carpenter Esq., in Polk County, N. C., Mr. Samuel W. Sitton of Anderson County, S. C. and Miss A. C. Carpenter.

Married: On January 28th, 1877 by Rev. E. F. Hyde, Mr. J. G. Sears and Miss Mary C., daughter of John T. Martin, all of Anderson County.

Married: On Sunday, 21st of January, by Rev. John Attaway, at the residence of the bride's father, Mr. M. P. Werner and Miss Emma Ingram, all of Anderson County.

Obituary: Mr. Michael Clancy, a native of Ireland, who has been a resident of this County for a number of years, died very suddenly on last Tuesday morning. He had been blasting upon the farm of Mrs. Adaline Martin. It is supposed that heart disease produced his death.

Issue of:
Thursday, February 8, 1877:
Obituary: We regret to announce the death of John Caminade which occurred on the 26th of January, after a protracted illness. He was a native of Savannah, belonged to a French family which refugeed to San Domingo about seventy years ago

and afterwards came to this country. The family removed to
Charleston when he was quite young and about forty years ago
Mr. Caminade came to Pendleton where he has since resided,
possessing the esteem and confidence of his neighbors. He
leaves five daughters, all married except one. He was about
68 years of age.

Issue of:
Thursday, February 15, 1877:
Obituary: Mr. James Stewart, an aged and respectable citizen
of this County, died on Tuesday last.

Obituary: The Abbeville papers record the death of Mr. Arthur
Erwin, an old and respectable citizen, who died on the 3rd
inst., at the residence of his son, Mr. Malcolm Erwin, on
Saluda River. Mr. Erwin, was a native of County Antrim,
Ireland and emigrated to this country in 1848, since which time
he has lived in Abbeville County, respected for his industry
and strict integrity and faithful in all the relations of life.
He was father-in-law to our fellow citizen, Mr. Ephraim
Buchanan of Centreville.

Married: On the morning of the 1st of February by Rev. W. M.
Wingate, D.D., William D. Trantham Esq., editor of the Camden
Journal and Miss Nannie E., eldest daughter of Prof. W. G.
Simmons of Wake Forest College, N. C. Our congratulations are
extended to the handsome groom upon this event. Members of
the Press Association have been expecting his entrance into
matrimony since that ardent woman right's speech he made in
Charleston two years ago.

Married: On the 24th of January by Rev. F. G. Carpenter, Mr.
J. Robert Thompson and Miss F. Maggie Williams, all of
Anderson County.

Married: By Rev. W. P. Martin, Feb. 11, 1877 at the residence
of the bride's father, Mr. George A. Bigby and Miss Emma V.
Robertson, daughter of Mr. E. H. Robertson, all of Anderson
County.

Issue of:
Thursday, February 22, 1877:
Sudden Death: Mrs. Rebecca Acker died very suddenly at the
residence of her mother, Mrs. Hester Rogers, on last Saturday
night. She had been in usual health and retired on the
night of her death withou any symptoms of disease. The next
morning she was found dead and there was no evidence of the
slightest convulsion or struggle in the hour of her death.
Coroner H. O. Herrick was notified on the next day and summoned
a jury of inquest, which, after receiving the testimony of
the family and also of Dr. M. L. Sharpe, the jury's physician,
rendered a verdict that the deceased came to her death from
heart disease.

Married: On the Feb. 15, 1877 at the residence of the bride's
mother, by Rev. W. Cuttino Smith, Mr. Baylis Whitten and Miss
Alice Pike.

Married: On the 14th instant, at the residence of the bride's

father, by Rev. H. M. Barton, Mr. J. Ben Abbott of Walhalla
and Miss Lizzie Isbell of Fair Play.

<u>Issue of</u>:
Thursday, March 1, 1877:
Married: At the residence of the bride's father on Thursday
evening, February 22nd, by Rev. D. E. Frierson, Mr. George W.
Garreckt and Miss Cornelia Langston, all of Anderson, S. C.

Married: By Rev. W. P. Martin, February 25th, at his own
residence, Mr. N. Harvey Welborn of Pickens County and Miss
Syntha Moore of Anderson County, S. C.

Married: At the residence of the bride's father by Rev. G. H.
Cartledge, Mr. W. J. Wilson and Miss Mittie E. Erskine, all of
Banks County, Ga.

Married: On the 7th of February by Rev. J. B. Earle, at the
residence of the bride's mother, Dr. James P. Duckett of
Newberry and Miss Eugenia Watson of Anderson.

Married: On the 21st of February at the residence of the
bride's grandfather, Mr. Thomas Dickson, by Rev. W. Cuttino
Smith, Mr. John L. Gilkerson of Laurens to Miss Nettie McElroy
of Anderson.

<u>Issue of</u>:
Thursday, March 8, 1877:
Obituary: Mr. William Manly, an aged and respected citizen
in the vicinity of Pendleton, died on the 23rd of February.

Obituary: Mr. Jeremiah Moore, an aged and respectable citizen
of this County, died at his home near Clinkscales Mill on the
28th ult.

Obituary: The death of Ezekiel S. Norris Esq. occurred at his
residence on Wednesday night, 28th February, in the 84th year
of his age. Mr. Norris was a hale, vigorous man and he was
ill only a few hours before death took place. He was a quiet,
unobtrusive citizen, greatly esteemed by a large circle of
friends and acquaintances. His remains were buried at Robert's
Church on Sunday last, the services being conducted by Rev.
Dr. Adger of Pendleton.

<u>Issue of</u>:
Thursday, March 15, 1877:
Obituary: Ezekiel S. Norris departed this life at his
residence on Mountain Creek on the 28th February, 1877 at the
age of 83 years and nine days. He spent his long life in
rural pursuits and "like a sheaf of corn fully ripe he has
been gathered into the garner of the Lord." His last sickness
was short but he leaves ample evidence that he was ready to
depart and be with the Lord. Early in life he professed
Christ as the only hope of salvation and exemplified the
sincerety of that profession by a consistent christian walk
through life. He was social, yet modest and retiring, respect-
ful, but firm in matured conviction. Industry, truth, justice,
charity, gentleness, kindness and benevolence were illustrated
in his daily action and conversation. He leaves three children
and a disconsolate widow, with many warm friends to mourn his

loss. Four children have proceded him to the grave to welcome
his ad-ent at the gate of Heaven. For many years he was an
acceptable Ruling Elder in the Roberts Presbyterian Church,
where he delighted to worship. "He sleeps in Jesus and is
blest."

Fatal Accident: On Friday afternoon, during the severe gale
which prevailed for several hours, a frightful accident
occurred upon the plantation of Mrs. D. M. Watson, resulting in
the sudden death of Mr. Thomas Stacks, who was crushed beneath
a falling tree in the open field. It appears that Mr. Stacks
was engaged in cutting briars along a ditch and had returned to
his work in the afternoon, where it was evident that he had
been diligently engaged and the amount of work done by him
produces the impression that he was killed towards night. Not
coming home at the usual hour, it was supposed that he had
gone to a neighbors to get medicine for one of the children
and it was late in the night before the family were alarmed at
his protracted absence, when a search was instituted, which
resulted in finding the body at the place designated, about
3 o'clock Sunday morning. He was found in such a position as
to make it plain that the tree struck him on the head and right
shoulder and then upon his left knee, which was dislocated.
The tree was limbless and decayed and the only one in a large
field. Coroner Herrick held an inquest over the body on
Saturday morning, when the jury rendered a verdict "that the
deceased came to his death by a blow from a falling tree."
Mr. Stacks was an industrious, hard working man, with a large
family of small children dependent upon his labor for support.
This sad affliction leaves them destitute, indeed.

Death of Maj. George Seaborn: The death of this estimable
gentleman occurred at his residence near Pendleton on Tuesday
last in the 81st year of his age. Maj. Seaborn was widely
known as a public-spirited citizen and was always foremost
in the advocacy of whatever tended to the advancement and
improvement of this section. He was for many years editor and
proprietor of the Farmer and Planter, which was published at
Pendleton until 1859 and through its pages he became known
as an agricultural writer of great proficiency and practical
knowledge. He was always the promoter and advocate of agricultural organizations and was President of the Pendleton
Farmers Society for a nubmer of years, an active and influential member of the old State Agricultural Society and for the
past ten years an honorary member of the Anderson Farmers and
Mechanics Association. He was a zealous Mason and one of the
oldest members of the craft in this portion of the State.
Thirty years ago he assisted to organize the Masonic Lodge
at this place and was its first Master. His services to the
brethen are held in grateful rememberance. Maj. Seaborn held
important and responsible positions at various times in his
life and we would be glad to receive a sketch of his career
from some of his earlier friends, who possess the requisite
information. The remains of the deceased were buried at the
Episcopal Church in Pendleton yesterday morning with the
ceremonies of the Masonic order.

Issue of:
Thursday, March 22, 1877:
Married: At the residence of the bride's mother, Mrs. Lucinda

Chamblee on Sunday 18th inst. by Rev. M. McGee, Mr. R. A.
Sullivan and Miss Mary Francis Chamblee. All of Anderson
County.

Issue of:
Thursday, March 29, 1877:
Obituary: Died, in Greenwood, Abbeville County, S. C. on the
night of the 14th inst., Mrs. Sarah Ann Millwee, wife of Dr.
W. B. Millwee, in the 46th year of her age. Her death was
sudden and unexpected. Her health, which for several years
past had been feeble, was regarded by her husband as much
better for some months past. For a number of years she had
been a member of the Presbyterian Church, first in Williamston
and then in Greenwood. In the later place she united with the
ladies of the Rock Church in the formation of a society to
raise funds to assist in the completion of a new house of worship. A short time ago she was chosen by the ladies as President of their Society. They were encouraged, from the increased
interest which was soon developed that they would succeed in
doing much to aid the Church in her straitened circumstances.
Her invention of certain Charts for cutting and fitting
ladies and childrens dresses on scientific principles evinced
uncommon genius which was further confirmed by her success in
relieving several children of hernia by cushioned models of
her own devising. The poor, the sick and the destitute were
often the objects of her kind attention and many who had
shared her liberality while she lived, entered her chamber
after her death and as with tears they gazed upon her faded
form, they spoke of her many acts of kindness to them in by-
gone days. But in her death we see the uncertainty of life.
She appeared as well as usual on the eveing of the 14th
inst. She retired at her usual hour but after a short time
she spoke to her husband and said that she was strangely
affected and that she was spitting blood; she was also coughing,
which was something she rarely ever did. He prepared some
antidote which he hastily administered to her. Three other
physicians living close by were hurridly called in; but alas!
even before they reached her room it was the chamber of death.
Early the next morning the whole town was surprised and saddened with grief to hear of her hasty departure into the world
of spirits. On Friday, the 16th inst., at 3 o'clock p.m., her
funeral services in the Presbyterian Church were attended by
an unusually large concourse of people; some of her relatives
and friends being present from Greenville, from Anderson and
from Donaldsville. After the service her remains were interred
in Greenwood Cemetery. In the death of this excellant lady the
community, but especially her friends and relatives have
sustained an irreparable loss. They are cheered however with
the hope that death is gain to her and that now since the
earthly house of her tabernacle is dissolved, she has entered
"the building of God and dwells in that house not made with
hands, eternal in the heavens."   Pastor
(She was the third daughter of the late W. A. Williams, Esq.,
the founder of Williamston.)

Issue of:
Thursday, April 5, 1877
Married: By J. L. Bryan, Esq., April 1st, 1877 Mr. James M.
Cook of Anderson County and Miss M. J. Burton of Abbeville Co.

Obituary: Died, at her fathers, near Slabtown, on the morning
of March 26th, Miss Cora Lewis, youngest child of E. B. and
Matilda Lewis, aged eighteen years. How sad the thought, how
awful the warning that another has been called away while
blooming into womanhood.   Friend

Issue of:
Thursday, April 12, 1877:
Sudden Death: The community of Central greatly shocked on
last Saturday night about 11 o'clock in the consequence of
Mr. Joseph C. Eaton, one of the oldest and most respected
citizens of the town, being found dead upon the street. Mr.
Eaton had an attack of heart disease some two weeks previous
to his death but had recovered sufficiently to attend to his
business and on the night of his death eat a hearty supper and
at nine o'clock went to sleep in the house of a friend whose
family was away from home. About 11 o'clock a son of Mr.
Eaton and Mr. C. C. Cummings discovered his body within a few
feet of his door, dead, but still warm with the fire of life
which had just departed. It is supposed that after he retired,
Mr. Eaton had another attack of heart disease and attempted
to reach his house but fell at the steps of his store. He was
in his seventy fifty year. An inquest was held over the body
by Coroner B. B. Earle and a verdict rendered in accordance
with the above facts. Mr. Eaton has many relatives and friends
who mourn his death and he will be greatly missed by the
community in which he lived.

Obituary: Mrs. C. M. Kay departed this life very suddenly on
the evening of the 5th inst.

Obituary: (Honea Path News) Mr. Wm. R. Greer, a resident of
this place, died in Columbia on Saturday and was buried at
Greenville Church on Tuesday last.

Issue of:
Thursday, April 19, 1877:
Obituary: Died, at her residence near Honea Path, on the night
of the 5th inst., Mrs. Mary E. Kay, leaving a husband and five
little children, together with father, mother, brothers, sisters
and many relatives and friends to mourn her loss. Yet they
sorrow not as those without hope. She made a profession of
religion several years ago and united herself with the Barker's
Creek Baptist Church, which profession she ever adorned by a
godly and pious life. On the morning of the 6th, her remains
were carried to her Church where a large congregation of
neighbors and friends awaited. After services, which were
conducted by Elder R. W. Burts, her remains were interred in
the Church Cemetery, there to await the summons on the ressur-
rection morn. Sister, thou was dear to us but the Master
called and thou hast gone. "Yet again we hope to meet thee,/
When the day of life is fled;/ Then in Heaven with joy to
greet thee/ Where no farewell tears is shed."   A Sister

Married: (Sandy Springs News) Last Sabbeth, Miss Carrie
Stribling and Mr. James Brown, of Greenville.

Issue of:
Thursday, April 26, 1877:
Married: On the 12th of April, 1877 at the residence of
Dr. George Eberhart, the bride's father, by Rev. W. P. Smith,
Mr. John H. McGill and Miss Laura L. Eberhart,allofHartwell, Ga.

Married: By Rev. W. P. Martin, at his residence, April 15, 1877, Mr. Amos N. Eskew of Greenville County and Miss Mary Jane Moore, daughter of Grant A. Moore of Anderson County.

Obituary: Mr. John Major, son of Mr. Wesley Major, who lives near Sandy Springs, died on Monday, 16th instant. The funeral services were conducted by Rev. J. T. Attaway on the following afternoon at Sandy Springs Church, after which the body was returned to mother earth. The young man, we believe, was a mute. The mourning relatives and friends of the deceased have our warmest sympathies in their bereavement.

Issue of:
Thursday, May 3, 1877:
Married: (Fork Township News) On Sunday 22nd ultimo, Mr. Lawrence Richardson and Miss Prudence Victoria Palmer, all of this township.

Issue of:
Thursday, May 10, 1877:
Obituary: William Henry, youngest child of Mr. William Clarke, died on last Saturday after a short and violent illness. Aged seventeen months.

Issue of:
Thursday, May 17, 1877:
Married: By Rev. W. E. Walters at the residence of the bride's father, on May 7, 1877, Mr. Joel H. Reed and Miss Anna M., daughter of Mr. Samuel Emerson, all of Anderson County.

Married: On Sunday evening, 13th of May 1877 by Rev. H. N. Hays, Mr. Lawrence Bruce and Miss Martha Hays, both of Oconee County, S. C.

Obituary: Died, near Williamston, S. C. on Saturday May 12th, 1877, L. Preston Cox, after a lingering disease for several months. In the death of our young friend we are called upon to record many commendable traits of character. He was always social, genial and honorable in the transactions of life. For the past seven years he had been engaged in mercantile pursuits at Williamston.

Issue of:
Thursday, May 24, 1877:
Married: At the residence of the bride's father on the 16th inst. by the Rev. T. E. Wannamaker, Mr. James M. Sullivan of Anderson and Miss Mary Alice, daughter of Capt. J. G. Wannamaker of Orangeburg, S. C.

Married: On the 10th inst. at Grange Academy by Rev. E. Z. Brown, Mr. George W. Busby and Miss Amanda Harvin. All of this County.

Issue of:
Thursday, May 31, 1877:
Obituary: Departed this life near Pendleton, by a painful accident, on the 14th inst., Mrs. Caroline Virginia, wife of Dr. H. C. Miller and youngest daughter of Zacharias Taliaferro, of Amherst and his wife, Margaret Chew Carter, of Caroline County, Virginia. Grim death has visited a once happy home -

a ghastly chasm has been made in the family circle and its
brightest ornament summoned to the silence of the tomb. It
has inflicted wounds upon the hearts of those who have been
left behind to mourn her loss which time alone can heal.
Their sorrows are the common lot of pure humanity and if they
should seem almost too painful to be endured, they should find
some comfort in the fact, that they are shared by their
relations and friends who deeply sympathize with them in their
melancholy bereavement. All who knew her acknowledge her
virtues as a woman, a wife, a mother and a friend. God has
in no manner more signalized his mercy to us than in so con-
stituting our natures that we can not always suffer from His
afflictions with the same intensity as when they first come
upon us. He has thus pointed out to us that our only true and
lasting comfort must be derived from a religious submission to
His holy will.   Relation.

Issue of:
Thursday, June 21, 1877:
Death of An Excellant Lady: It is with deep regret that we
perform the sad duty of chroncling [sic] the death of Mrs.
John E. Breazeale, formerly Miss Bellotte of Pendleton, which
occurred at the residence of her husband in this place after
an illness of little more than one week. Mrs. Breazeale
was an estimable lady, possessed of all those gentle and noble
traits which endear a true woman to her relations and friends.
In all the relations of life she attracted by her quiet grace
and domestic virtues the friendship and admiration of those
with whom she was associated. A devoted wife, a fond and
conscientious mother and a true friend, she leaves by her death
a vacant seat around the hearthstone which husband and
children, relatives and friends will sadly mourn. Mrs.
Breazeale at the time of her death was in the morning of her
womanhood, with bright prospects of life before her; but the
reaper came and the happy home has been left desolate. It
must, however, be a source of consolation to those who mourn
her death to have the assurance that they weep not as those
without hope, for the deceased was a pure, christian woman,
whose death was calm and composed. A member of the Baptist
Church, she was a conscientious and devoted christian, whose
faith gave her power to bid adieu to her loved ones and to
meet death with a smile as remoreseless and beautiful as that
which invokes slumber as a rest for physical fatigue. The
funeral services will take place at the Baptist Church today,
where many of the friends and acquaintances of the deceased
will assemble to pay the saddest of earth's tributes to a
departed friend.

Obituary: Our Townville correspondent announces the death of
Dr. W. L. Broyles, a prominent and influential citizen of this
County, residing in the Fork township. Dr. Broyles was a
thorough going, upright and intelligent gentleman, possessed
of a large degree of public spirit and devoted to the advancement of all reforms, whether they be moral, social, political
or agricultural. He was a younger brother of our former townsman, Maj. A. R. Broyles and his death will be lamented by a
very extensive circle of relatives and friends.

Issue of:
Thursday, June 28, 1877:
Obituary: Capt. A. A. Dickson, an aged and respectable citizen

of Anderson County, departed this life after a brief illness on last Friday. Capt. Dickson was about seventy years old and though his health was at times feeble, he retained to the last of his life more than the usual vigor for men of his years. He was one of the old teachers of the County and years ago, in his younger days, he was noted for the precision and thoroughness with which he trained the youthful mind. He ranked especially high as a mathematician among his fellow teachers. Capt. Dickson leaves numerous scholars who, with relatives and friends, cherish his memory and regret his decease.

Obituary: We regret to record the death of Mrs. Elizabeth, wife of the late Col. Herbert Hammond, who was ordinary of this County for twenty eight years previous to his death. Mrs. Hammond was one of the oldest ladies of our County, being at the time of her death, which occurred on last Thursday morning, in the 78th year of her age. She was a very excellant woman, having been attached to the Methodist faith for more than forty years. She was the oldest member of that Church in Anderson and bore witness to the sincerety of her professions by along and upright life, which terminated in a calm and happy death. The funeral services were conducted by her pastor, Rev. H. F. Crietsberg, in the Methodist Church on last Friday afternoon and her remains placed to rest beside those of her husband who had gone before.

Married: On Thursday the 21st inst. at the residence of Col. T. J. Roberts, the bride's father, by Rev. W. H. Strickland, Mr. C. W. Moore and Miss Nora Roberts, all of Anderson County.

Issue of:
Thursday, July 5, 1877:
Obituary: Departed this life June 25, 1877, Mrs. Frances Hanna, wife of Mr. C. B. Hanna, aged about seventy years. "Asleep in Jesus, blessed sleep/ From which no mortal wakes to weep." M.

Obituary: We regret to announce the death of little Rosa May daughter of Mr. William M. Osborne, which occurred on last Sunday morning. A bright child of fifteen months she was the idol of her father's household, but earth was not her home and death transplanted the little flower to bloom forever more in Heaven.

Issue of:
Thursday, July 12, 1877:
Obituary: Died, little Herbert Hurd Cromer on June 30, 1877. Aged one year, nine months and three days. Little Herbert was the son of Mr. and Mrs. Adam Cromer, formerly of Newberry County. Although the babe was an afflicted child, yet they loved it as they did the other children. The dear little boy died with a heavenly smile on his face. The Lord has taken him. We sympathize with the family and pray God's blessing upon them.
T. P. P.

Married: On the 26th of June at the residence of the bride's father, Dr. W. C. Brown, by Rev. Mr. Lawton, Mr. A. C. Latimer of Lowndesville and Miss Alice S. Brown of Belton.

Issue of:
Thursday, July 19, 1877:
Obituary: We regret to announce the death of little Della, infant daughter of Mr. and Mrs. Jeptha F. Wilson, of Anderson

which occurred on last Saturday afternnon. She was sick only
a short time until death claimed the young spirit and left
fond parents to mourn the death of a loved little daughter.

Issue of:
Thursday, July 26, 1877:
Obituary: We regret to announce the death of Mrs. Elizabeth
Robinson which occurred at the residence of her son-in-law,
Mr. Claudius S. Beaty, of Toccoa City, Ga. Mrs. Robinson was
originally an inhabitant of Abbeville County but the last
fifteen years she has lived with her son-in-law in this County
until she removed with his family to Toccoa City. She was an
excellant lady and died at the ripe old age of seventy five
years, much beloved by a large circle of relatives and friends.
Her remains were brought to Anderson on last Monday and
placed to rest in Good Hope Church yard where many of relatives
who had gone before sleep.

Obituary: Fork Township News - Mrs. Sallie Freeman died at her
home at the old Sloan's Ferry place on the morning of last
Friday after a very short illness. She was the youngest
daughter of Mr. Wm. Sears, being about twenty three years of
age. A year ago she married Mr. Edward Freeman and leave an
infant not yet two weeks old.

Issue of:
Thursday, August 2, 1877:
Obituary: We regret to announce the death of Mrs. Nancy, wife
of William Holmes, an old and respected citizen of Anderson
County which occurred at the residence of her husband, some
four miles east of Anderson on last Tuesday the 31st ult. after
a lon- and painful illness from consumption. Mrs. Holmes was
a Christian woman having been a member of the Belton Baptist
Church from its formation. She was a kind neighbor and a
faithful and devoted woman in her family relations. Her
decease will be mourned by many relatives and friends.

Obituary: Honea Path News - Wm. J. Hunt died on Saturday night
last, after a long and painful suffering.

Issue of:
Thursday, August 16, 1877:
Obituary: We regret to announce the death of little Bertrice,
daughter of Mr. W. A. Fant, which occurred at the residence
of her father in Anderson on Friday the 4th inst. Her remains
were interred on the following day in the Presbyterian Church
at this place.

Obituary: Mr. James Todd, formerly a citizen of this County
and a ruling Elder of the Midway Presbyterian Church, died at
his home in Texas on the 27th of July last. He was in the 78th
year of his age and was to the last a consistent member of the
Presbyterian faith.

Obituary: We regret to announce the death of Mrs. Elizabeth,
wife of the late David Morris, an old and respected citizen of
this County which occurred at her residence on last Tuesday
morning, after a long and painful illness from heart disease.
The deceased at the time of her death was in the 78th year of
her age. She was a Christian woman, having been a member of
the Baptist Church for more than thirty five years.

Thursday, August 23, 1877:
Married: At the residence of Mr. Henry Garrison on the 18th
inst. by Rev. Thos. F. Gadsden, Mr. W. F. Whitten and Miss
Josephine Collins, all of Anderson County.

Obituary: Died, on 31st July last, in Pickens County near
Pendleton of typhoid fever, Miss Nancy A. Dodd, daughter of
Dennis S. and L. Dodd, in the 18th year of her age. Her remains
were interred in Mount Tabor Baptist Churchyard to which Church
she connected herself in early life. A short time before her
death she confessed her willingness to meet her Saviour.
She leaves a large circle of relatives and friends to mourn their
loss and society an active member.

Obituary: We regret to announce the death of little Minnie,
only child of Mr. Jesse J. Dobbins of this town, which occurred
on the 15th inst. Her remains were interred in Providence
Church yard some eight miles southwest of Anderson on the
following day.

Obituary: We regret to announce the death of Mr. Leroy Barr
which occurred at his residence near Easley Station in Pickens
County on last Sunday the 19th inst. after a short illness from
paralysis. Mr. Barr was highly respected by all who knew him
and lived to a ripe old age, being in the 74th year of his age
at the time he died. He was for a number of years a citizen
of this County and was one of the first residents of Anderson
and now has a son, Mr. W. F. Barr, in business here. A number
of years ago, however, he removed to Pickens County and settled
at the residence occupied by him at the time of his death. On
Monday afternoon his remains were interred in St. Paul's
churchyard in this County.

Issue of:
Thursday, August 30, 1877:
Obituary: Death of Rev. J. L. Kennedy - The announcement of
the death of Rev. J. L. Kennedy which occurred at his residence in Williamston on Sunday the 19th inst., after a brief
illness, has been received with deep regret throughout this
County and the entire State. Mr. Kennedy, though an unassuming gentleman, was a fine scholar and has left a reputation as a teacher excelled by none and equalled by few.
The impress of his mind has been left upon more young pupils
than that of any man in Anderson County, if not more than any
man in South Carolina. For many years he was principal of
Slabtown Academy, which was a most prosperous and useful
institution and the success in life of the pupils who went out
to College and to business from it are the highest testimonials
to the worth and attainments of the faithful teacher, who is
now no more forever. Besides his scholastic duties, Mr.
Kennedy was a faithful and useful devine of prominence in the
Presbyterian Church and along with the duties of the schoolroom he performed the more solemn office of pastor and even
after health and strength failed him in the schoolroom, he
continued his services in the ministry and at the time of his
death, although about sixty six years of age, he was pastor of
the Presbyterian Church at Williamston. Mr. Kennedy was an
agreeable, courteous and intelligent gentleman who impressed
all who knew him best loved him most. Although he has gone

from earth he still lives in the memory of an extensive circle of friends and acquaintances.

Married: At Sandy Springs, on the 2d of September inst. by Rev. J. Attaway, Mr. James G. Riley and Miss Sallie A., daughter of Mr. T. L. Reid, all of Anderson County.

Obituary: Mrs. Margaret Cox, wife of the late Capt. Wm. Cox, died at the residence of her son, Maj. Geo. W. Cox, on last Saturday morning from the effects of the paralytic stroke of which we spoke last week. Mrs. Cox was over seventy years of age and had been a devoted christian and useful woman for many years. The funeral services were performed in the Belton Baptist Church by Rev. W. E. Walters on last Sunday in the presence of a very large audience of relatives and friends of the deceased. The occasion was very solemn and impressive.

Obituary: We regret to announce the death of Mrs. John A. Emerson, which occurred at the residence of her husband in this County on last Thursday evening after a short illness. Mrs. Emerson was highly respected and beloved by her neighbors and numerous acquaintances for the many noble christian virtues she possessed and illustrated in her daily life. Her untimely death which bereaves a devoted husband and three little children will be felt outside of the stricken family for it has removed a useful member of society who was highly appreciated in life and will be long mourned by those she has left behind. Her remains were interred at Ebenezer Churchyard on Friday after solemn services attended by a large congregation of sorrowing relatives and friends.

Married: At the residence of the bride's father, September 17th, 1877 by Rev. T. J. Jenkins, W. Jehu Thomas and Emma C. McCurry, all of Anderson County.

Obituary: Hopewell Township News - Since our last communication death has smitten one of our best citizens to the ground. Mr. Chesley Martin is no more. He died on the 12th inst. in the sixty sixth year of his age. He was an humble, retired and unassuming but, nevertheless, great man. In him centred those characteristics which constitute the true gentleman and upright citizen. A perfect paragon of honesty, veracity and firmness washe. Strange to say, he died without an enemy. He conducted his business on a strictly cash system, ever living within that moral injuction, "Owe no man anything, but to love him." On the day following his death his remains were followed by a long train of afflicted friends to Hopewell Church, where the last honors were paid them. The funeral services were conducted by Rev. F. G. Carpenter in a sermon well adapted to the occasion. He was then interred beside his wife who had preceded him four years. While we cease to call his name let us cherish his many virtues.

Obituary: Died, in this Town on the 4th inst., M. Maud, infant daughter of Warren D. and Docia Maroney, about two years of age. "Suffer little children to come unto me and forbid them not, for such is the kingdom of heaven."

Married: On September 12, 1877 by Rev. R. C. Ligon, Mr. W. C.
Sherard of Anderson County and Miss Lizzie Clinkscales, daughter
of Mr. Albert Clinkscales of Abbeville County.

Issue of:
Thursday, September 27, 1877:
Obituary: Mr. James McLees, a respected citizen of Rock Mills
township, died at his residence in this County on Wednesday
the 13th inst. He leaves a large circle of relatives and
friends to mourn his death.

Issue of:
Thursday, October 4, 1877:
Married: At the residence of the officiating clergyman on
Thursday, 27th of September by Rev. M. McGee, Mr. Prue B.
Gentry and Miss B. Ella Keys, daughter of Robert A. Keys, Esq.,
all of Anderson County.

Obituary: Died, on the 10th of August at his father's resi-
dence in Labaina, John Lewis Gibson, oldest son of Walter
Murray Gibson. The deceased was born near Pendleton, South
Carolina and was 34 years of age.

Death of John Lewis Gibson: We regret to announce the death
of John, the eldest son of Walter M. Gibson, which took place
at Labaina, on the 10th of August. The deceased has enjoyed
invariably good health during a residence of fourteen years
on the Island of Lanai, but owing to a fall from his horse he
received a severe contusion which resulted in a fatal congestion
of the kidneys. The departure of this young man is a severe
blow to his father and surviving brother and sister and his
loss is greatly mourned by all the native inhabitants of Lanai.
- From the Hawaiian Gazette, (Sandwich Island) August 22, 1877.

Obituary: Died, in Charleston, S. C. on Wednesday, September
12, 1877, Susan Taylor, wife of Edward L. Parker. She has borne
great suffering with exemplary fortitude and meekly prayed to
"touch the hem of her Saviour's garment." She has done so and
is whole. "Rest after toil/ Port after stormy seas/ Death
after life/ Doth greatly please."

Obituary: Honea Path News - Capt. S. M. Tribble died on Friday
night last and was buried on Saturday afternoon at Little
River Church. In his death the community at large sustains a
loss.

Obituary: Little Ella, daughter of C. E. Harper, died on
Saturday evening last, of diphtheria.

Issue of:
Thursday, October 11, 1877:
Obituary: Mr. Alfred Moore who was for many years of this
place, died at his residence in Pickens County last week in the
90th year of his age.

Issue of:
Thursday, October 18, 1877:
Obituary: Capt. James Adams, an old citizen of the South-
eastern portion of this County, died after a lingering illness
of some months on last Monday afternoon the 15th inst. He

was about sixty eight years of age and had many friends throughout the County. His remains were interred at Mt. Bethel Church on Tuesday last in the presence of a large concourse of his friends and acquaintances.

Obituary: Capt. Frank Ro-ertson, an old and respected citizen of this County, died at his residence on last Monday the 15th inst. after a long illness. He was about eighty seven years of age and leaves several sons and daughters, with a host of friends, to mourn his death. He was an upright and hightoned citizen and on Tuesday a large attendance gathered at Honea Path to pay the last tribute of earth to the departed one whose remains were interred in the church yard there.

A Smitten Family: During the past four days Mr. John C. Shaw has lost three interesting little children from dipptheria and membranous croup, the oldest of which was about five years of age. On last Sunday two - Olden and Golden - died and on Tuesday their little bodies were placed to rest in a single grave in Mt. Bethel Church Yard. On Wednesday morning the little infant daughter, Minneola, was gathered by the reaper from earth and today her body will be interred by the side of those who had so shortly preceded her. The afflicted family have the sympathy of the entire community in their very sore bereavement.

Obituary: Sandy Springs News - Mrs. B. F. Wilson departed this life on the afternoon of the 9th inst. She was ill for four months, a victim of consumption. The funeral services were conducted the following afternoon at Sandy Springs by Rev. J. T. Attaway after which the body was returned to mother earth. The relatives of the deceased have the sympathy of the entire community in their sore bereavement.

Issue of:
Thursday, October 25, 1877:
Obituary: Mr. Hezekiah McGee, familiarly known to the people of the upper part of the State on account of mental afflictions, which made him a very peculiar person, died in Greenville County on last Thurday in the 51st year of his age. Just before he died he was asked if he knew where he was going and replied, "Where all good folks go", and hence, we trust, his life, which was aimless and desolate here, has been exchanged for a better one beyond.

Issue of:
Thursday, November 1, 1877:
Married: In the Village Church, Huntersville, N. C. on the 25th inst. at 6½ p.m. by Rev. A. Ranson, D.D., assisted by Rev. R. G. Miller, of South Carolina, Mr. R. M. Ranson, formerly of Anderson, S. C. and Miss Agnes Sample of Huntersville.

Married: In the Baptist Church in Anderson by the Rev. W. H. Strickland, on Wednesday October 31st, at 4 o'clock p.m. Mr. William H. Lyles of Columbia, S. C. and Miss M. Mays Sloan of Anderson, S. C.

Issue of:
Thursday, November 8, 1877:
Obituary: Mrs. Elizabeth Rice, wife of Mr. A. E. Rice,

departed this life on last Saturday morning after a lingering illness from consumption. Mrs. Rice was an excellant lady with many warm and devoted friends who lament her untimely death and mingle their sincerest sympathies with the husband and children who survive her. On Sunday last her remains were placed to rest in First Creek Church Yard in the presence of a large and sorrowing audience.

Married: By the Rev. W. P. Martin, November 1st, 1877 at his own residence, Mr. J. B. Ellison and Miss J. J. Broom, daughter of the late Capt. W. J. Broom, all of Anderson County, S. C.

Issue of:
Thursday, November 15, 1877:
Obituary: Mr. Stephen Hanks of Martin township, died on Sunday October 28. He leaves many relatives and friends to mourn their loss.

Obituary: We regret to announce the death of Mr. Waller S. Norris, of this County on Tuesday last in the forty fifth year of his age. Mr. Norris, for the last eight or ten years was a great sufferer from a cancerous affliction which baffled the skill of his physicians. The family in their affliction have the sympathy of the community.

Issue of:
Thursday, November 22, 1877:
Married: By Rev. M. McGee, on Sunday evening 18th inst., at the residence of W. G. Watson, Mr. Azel Kelly to Miss Mary McConnell, all of Anderson County.

Married: On Wednesday 14th inst. at the residence of the bride's father, in this County, by the Rev. F. G. Carpenter, Mr. Benjamin Parson to Miss Savannah Hutchison.

Married: On the 15th of November at the residence of the bride's father, by Rev. W. T. M. Brock, Mr. F. P. Mize to Miss Susan J. Erskine, all of Banks County, Georgia.

Married: At the residence of the bride's father, Capt. Hugh Robinson, on the night of the 20th inst., by Rev. Wm. Henry Strickland, Mr. Wm. Cowan Armstrong and Miss Essie Robinson, all of Abbeville County.

Obituary: Sandy Springs News - The community was very much pained on Saturday evening, the 17th, on receiving a telegram that Mrs. D. A. Smith of Walhalla, was a corpse. Mr. W. G. Smith and lady went to Walhalla the same evening to pay last tribute of respect to the one they esteemed so highly. Mr. D. A. Smith and family have the warmest sympathies of the entire community in his sore Providential dispensation.

Issue of:
Thursday, November 29, 1877:
Married: At Robert's Church, November 18th, 1877, by Rev. W. A. Hodges, Mr. William H. Simpson and Miss Julia Allen, all of Anderson County, S. C.

Married: At the residence of the bride's father, by Rev. W. A. Hodges, November 22nd, 1877, Mr. Samuel A. Pickens and Miss Fannie E. Whitaker, all of Anderson County.

Married: At the residence of the bride's father, Mr. L. D.
Stringer, November 15th 1877 by Rev. D. E. Frierson, Mr. W.
Barr Erskine and Miss Emma Camilla Stringer, all of Anderson
County.

Married: On Tuesday, 20th inst. by Rev. Baxter Hays, Mr.
J. T. Dove of Mattison County, Georgia and Miss M. J. Tate
of Anderson County, S. C.

Married: On Monday 12th inst. by Rev. Baxter Hays, Mr. S. O.
Driver and Miss Nancy Williams, all of Anderson County.

Obituary: Departed this life after several months illness,
on the 13th of November inst., Nancy Harper, escort of W. C.
Harper, aged sixty eight years. She was an affectionate wife
and kind mother.   F. S. R.

Obituary: Died, of diphtheria, near Belton, S. C. on the 14th
of November, Wm. Riley Harper, only child of J. M. and M. J.
Harper, aged twenty months and 20 days. He was too precious
a jewel to linger in this world of sin. He was a grandson
of Wm. Riley.   F. S. R.

Issue of:
Thursday, December 6, 1877:
Married: November 22, 1877 by Rev. W. P. Martin, at the
residence of the bride's mother, Mr. D. B. Brooks and Miss
Sallie W. Broom, daughter of the late Capt. W. J. Broom. All
of Anderson County, S. C.

Married: At the residence of Mr. Hugh Mahaffey, November 29th
1877 by Rev. W. P. Martin, Mr. C. S. Thompson and Miss R. M.
Poore, daughter of Mrs. Nira Poore, all of Anderson County, S.C.

Obituary: Mrs. E. A. Banister died at the residence of her
husband, Mr. Alexander Banister, in this County on Saturday the
17th of November after an illness of several days. She leaves
a husband and several small children to mourn the early death
of one so dear to them.

Obituary: We regret to announce the death of Mr. Marion Davis
which occurred at his residence in the northern portion of
Anderson County on Tuesday the 27th of November last from an
attack of measles. Mr. Davis was a son-in-law of Mr. Joseph
L. Byrum and in his early death leaves a wife and two little
children to mourn the irreparable loss of a husband and
father.

Issue of:
Thursday, December 13, 1877:
Married: On the 4th December,1877 by Rev. R. H. Reid, Mr.
John D. Smith of Spartanburg, S. C. and Miss Ida N. Anderson,
eldest daughter of R. H. Anderson, of Anderson County, S. C.

Married: On the 4th of December instant by Rev. W. P. Martin,
at his residence, Mr. N. C. Dacus and Miss C. E. Rogers,
daughter of Jacob Rogers. All of Anderson County.

Obituary: Capt. Wm. W. Towns was born in Greenville County
near Grove Station, September 4th, 1800 and died at his home
about four miles south of Belton, October 25th, 1877. He
removed to Anderson County about the year 1826 and lived with

his parents in the upper portion of it until 1832, when he was married to Miss Chloe Clinkscales and took up his residence at the home where he died. Capt. Towns was gifted with a peculiarly happy disposition which ever endeared him to his neighbors and friends and rendered him popular with his associates. He was a kind and devoted husband and father. Some of his children had preceded to "that bourne from whence no traveler has ever yet returned" and although Captain Towns had never connected himself with the Church, he died in the possession of a sweet hope of meeting his loved ones in a better land beyond the skies. During his last illness he more than once expressed his willingness to meet death and seemed perfectly resigned to the will of God. He leaves a widow to mourn the loss of a dear husband a son and daughter grieve for a departed father. But they bow in meek submission to the will of the Almighty Father, humbly waiting for the reunion in that Home above.

Issue of:
Thursday, December 20, 1877:
Married: At the residence of the bride's father, Col. J. Jamison, on Tuesday December 4th by Rev. D. Weston Hiatt, Mr. J. J. Moseley and Miss M. J. Jamison. All of Anderson County.

Married: At the residence of the bride's father, Capt. James Welborn, on the morning of the 16th inst. by Rev. B. Hays, Mr. S. J. Newton and Miss A. E. Welborn. All of Anderson County.

Married: By Rev. A. Rice at the residence of the bride's father, on Wednesday morning the 19th inst. Mr. A. Meek of East Tennessee and Miss Ida E. Rice of Anderson County, S. C.

Obituary: We regret to announce the death of Mr. James Allen of Lowndesville which occurred on Wednesday morning the 12th inst. from a combined attack of paralysis and heart disease. Mr. Allen had been in feeble health for some time past, having suffered from a previous paralytic stroke. He was a gentleman of high character and was much esteemed and respected in the community in which he has always lived. He leaves behind him a wife and several children who mourn his death and together with numerous relatives and friends will fondly cherish his memory.

Obituary: Death of Dr. J. M. Sloan - Dr. James M. Sloan, of Walhalla, departed this life at 2 o'clock on last Monday morning after a short illness superinduced by the effects of a wound received in the Confederate service. Dr. Sloan was a very able physician and surgeon and has enjoyed a very extensive and successful practice in his profession since the war. He was a genial gentleman and possessed a host of friends who will long regret his death and retain pleasant memories of him throughout their lives. Dr. Sloan was severely wounded in one of the battles of our late war, the ball passing through his face and inflicting a very severe and dangerous wound, wihch has frequently given him trouble and pain. This, together with the fatigue and exposure incident to his profession has at last done its work and though the clash of war has long been hushed another of its victims has fallen. Dr. Sloan was in the prime of life and in his death leaves a wife and two little children, together with many relatives and an extensive circle of friends who weep for the loss of

one so dear to them. A very large congregation assembled
at the Baptist Church in Pendleton on Wednesday morning to
attend the funeral services, which were conducted by Rev. J.
S. Murray, after which the remains of the deceased were
interred in the adjacent church yard.

Issue of:
Thursday, December 27, 1877:
Obituary: Death of Dr. Reynolds - Rev. James Lawrence Reynolds
D. D., Professor of Latin and Roman Literature in Furman
University departed this life on last Wednesday morning after
a brief illness from neuralgia of the heart. Dr.Reynolds
was one of the purest gentleman, as well as one of the most
accomplished scholars of our State and his sudden demise has
been heard with sincere regret throughout our whole State. A
native of South Carolina he has shared the honors we well as
the trials of our commonwealth and has contributed much to its
literature and learning. Dr. Reynolds was a son of George N.
Reynolds, Esq. of Charleston and was born March 17th, 1812.
He graduated at the Charleston College and afterwards at
Newton Theological Seminary and returned to the State as pastor
of the Columbia Baptist Church. He was afterwards President
of the Georgetown College in Kentucky, of which Rev. B.
Manly Jr. is now the presiding officer. Dr. Reynolds afterwards filled several Professorships in our State University
and remained in this work as one of the most efficient members
of the faculty until the University went down by the course-
pursued by the Readicals, upon which he resigned and accepted
a Professorship in Furman University. As an orator Dr.
Reynolds was forcible, elegant and eloquent; as a writer he
was calssical, clear and pleasant; as a scholar he was pro-
foundly erudite and as a gentleman he had no superior. A
useful life has been terminated and it will be difficult to
fully supply the important sphere that has been made vacant.

Issue of:
Thursday, January 3, 1878:
Married: On December 26th by the Rev. Baxter Hays, Mr. H. C.
Latham and Miss S. A. Pearman, all of Anderson County.

Married: On December 19, 1877 by Rev. W. P. Martin, at the
residence of the bride's father, Mr. C. J. B. Lewis and Miss
F. C. Cooley, daughter of Mr. Wm. M. Cooley, all of Anderson
County.

Married: At the residence of the bride's father, in Walhalla,
S. C. December 25th 1877, by Rev. S. L. Morris, Mr. John E.
Breazeale of Anderson, S. C. and Miss Ida R. Johnson of Wal-
halla, S. C.

Obituary. We regret to announce the death of Mr. D. J. Tucker
Sr., a respected citizen of this County, which occurred at
his residence some eighteen miles south of this place on
Saturday the 29th of December last. Mr. Tucker had been in
feeble health for some years past and was at the time of his
death in the 84th year of his age. His remains were interred
in First Creek Church Yard after appropriate and solemn funeral
services in the presence of a large concourse of relatives and
friends of the deceased. Mr. Tucker was for many years a
member of the Rocky River Baptist Church and up to the time of
his failure in health was prominent in the affairs of his

church and a useful citizen to the community in which he lived. He leaves behind him a number of relatives, who, with many friends will long cherish his memory.

Issue of:
Thursday, January 10, 1878:
Married: By J. L. Bryan Esq. on the 10th of December 1877, Mr. C. A. Burton and Miss J. A. Simpson.

Married: By J. L. Bryan Esq., on the 27th December, 1877 at the bride's fathers, Mr. T. W. Seigler and Miss Emma J. Burton.

Married: By J. L. Bryan Esq., on the 27th ultimo, Mr. A. S. Burton and Miss Julia V. Dixon.

Married: By J. L. Bryan Esq., at the residence of G. F. Burdett on the 27th ultimo, Mr. J. R. Burton and Miss M. Smith.

Obituary: We regret to announce the death of Mr. William McGill, formerly a citizen of this place, which occurred at his residence ten miles above Walhalla on last Wednesday morning after a short illness from heart disease. Mr. McGill had many friends in this section who will regret to learn of his death.

Obituary: We regret to learn that Dr. J. T. Norris, a former resident of this place, who has a number of relatives and a great many friends in this County, died at his residence in Newberry County, whither he removed about 1860, on Sunday the 4th instant of consumption, with which he has been a sufferer for a long time. Dr. Norris was a pleasant and intelligent gentleman who made friends wherever he went. The announcement of his death will carry sorrow and regret to many of our readers.

Obituary: Col. James Long, a well known citizen of the upper portion of Anderson County, died at his residence on last Thursday night after an illness of a few hours. During the day of Thursday he had been up and going about and wrote several letters and felt as well as usual, with the exception of a very bad cough, which, it is supposed, caused the eruption of some blood vessel internally, thereby causing his sudden death. His remains were interred in the burying ground connected with Mt. Pisgah Church in the presence of a large number of persons who had assembled to pay earth's last tribute to their departed neighbor.

Issue of:
Thursday, January 17, 1878:
Married: January 10th, 1878 by Rev. W. P. Martin, at his residence, Mr. W. H. Broom and Miss J. E. Brooks. All of Anderson County.

Obituary: Mr. Daniel G. Finley, a former resident of this place, was thrown from a horse and killed near his residence about eighteen miles from Spartanburg on Wednesday the 9th inst. Mr. Finley was the father-in-law of Mr. John C. Whitfield of this place and was well known throughout this section of country for years previous to the war as the popular landlord of the hotel on the north of the public square, now known as the Waverly House. He was 62 years old at the time of his death and retained the full possession of his mental and physical powers up to the time of his sudden death.

222

Issue of:
Thursday, January 24, 1878:
Married: At the house of the bride's father on the morning of
the 13th of January, 1878 by Elder E. R. Carswell, Mr. Thomas
M. Welborn and Miss Lizzie C. Harper, all of Anderson County.

Married: At the house of the bride's father on the morning
of January 16, by Elder E. R. Carswell, Mr. E. Calhoun Pruiett
and Miss Annie D. Long, all of Anderson County.

Married: At the residence of the bride's father on the 8th
instant by Rev. Andrew McGuffin, Mr. W. L. Dobbins and Miss
Mattie King.

Issue of:
Thursday, January 31, 1878:
Married: On Wednesday the 23rd instant at the residence of
the bride's father in this County, by Rev. J. S. Murray, Mr.
Anderson P. Warnock and Miss Mary J. Geer.

Married: On Sunday the 23rd December 1877 by A. N. Thomas
Esq., Mr. C. B. Caldwell and Miss Caldonia Bagwell, both
of Gwinnette County, Georgia.

Married: On the 17th inst. at the residence of Mrs. Martha
Powell, by Rev. W. A. Fariss, Mr. Joseph G. White of Anderson
County and Miss Amanda R. Powell of Hart County, Georgia.

Issue of:
Thursday, February 14, 1878:
Married: On the 31st January, 1878 at the residence of the
bride's father in Abbeville County, S. C. by Rev. Benjamin
Thornton, Mr. John M. Presnell of Hartwell and Miss Nannie J.
Tucker.

Married: On the 7th inst. at 8 o'clock a.m. by the Rev. R. W.
Pratt at the residence of Col. T. C. Perrin in Abbeville,
Col. F. E. Harrison of Andersonville, S. C. and Miss Lizzie
Cothran of Abbeville, S. C.

Married: On the 7th inst. at the residence of Mrs. Nancy
Bolt by Rev. E. Z. Brown, Mr. Benjamin Hamby and Miss Mary
L. C. Bolt, all of Anderson County.

Issue of:
Thursday, February 21, 1878:
Married: On the 12th instant at the residence of Joseph Rose
Esq., 217 W. 38th Street, New York, Mr. S. A. Arnstein of
Anderson, S. C. and Miss Minnie Leopold, daughter of Nathan
Leopold.

Married: By Rev. W. P. Martin on February 14th at his residence, Mr. W. L. Gambrell and Miss Mary Alice Ballentine, all
of Anderson County.

Obituary: Died, in DeKalb County, Alabama on the 4th February
1878 Mrs. Sallie Masters, widow of G. W. Masters, formerly of
South Carolina, aged seventy five years. The deceased was a
devoted Christian, a tender, gentle and loving wife, an
affectionate mother, a warm and ardent friend. Her work on
earth is done and we await only a short time to meet again on
the other shore.   M. C. E.

Obituary: Mr. Jesse C. Morris, an aged and respected citizen of this County, died at his residence in Rock Mills township on Tuesday 12th inst. His remains were interred in the grave yard at Robert's Church with Masonic honors.

Obituary: We regret to announce the death of Mrs. J. W. Dacus which occurred at the residence of her husband in Williamston on last Wednesday from pneumonia. Mrs. Dacus had been married but little more than a year and was in the very morning of life with bright prospects of life and happiness before her. Death, however, has claimed the young, the beautiful and the good and her vacant place is mourned by her husband and many admiring friends.

Issue of:
Thursday, February 28, 1878:
Married: On the 21st instant at the residence of Mrs. Mitchell by Rev. Elias Z. Brown, Mr. William Morgan Holland and Miss Teresa L. Stacks, all of Anderson County.

Married: On Sunday the 24th inst., at 4 o'clock p.m. by Rev. J. S. Murray, at the residence of the bride's father, Mr. J. A. Pruiett and Miss Ida N. Riley, daughter of William Riley Esq., all of Anderson County.

Obituary: Died, at his residence near Williamston, S. C. January 23rd, 1878 of pneumonia, after five days illness, in the 35th year of his age, Mr. James Franklin Allen, son of Capt. Willis Allen. He was a soldier in the late war, was a good citizen and neighbor, joined the Baptist Church at Big Creek a number of years ago, was married June 3, 1866 to Miss Henrietta J. Gurley, sister of Dr. J. W. Gurley of Atlanta, Georgia, was a kind husband, and an affectionate father. The deceased leaves an affectionate wife and five children, a kind father and many relatives and friends to mourn his death. But they sorrow not as those without hope, but trust their loss in his infinite gain. He was buried in the grave yard at Big Creek meetinghouse where he waits in hope of a glorious resurrection from the dead.   W. P. M.

Obituary: The reaper Death has been in our midst again. All classes and conditions of society are subject to the inevitable and irresistable power of the grim monster. The young may die and the old must die and the wisest knoweth not how soon. We regret to announce the death of Mrs. Jamison which occurred at the residence of her husband, Mr. Samuel Jamison, of this County, on the 21st of February. She was about 35 years of age. Husband, children and many friends are left to mourn her death.

Tribute: Tribute of respect from Barnett Lodge No. 106, A.F.M., to Thomas E. Boggs, who died on December 2, 1877.

Issue of:
Thursday, March 7, 1878:
Obituary: Departed this life after a short illness on February the 15th, 1878, Mrs. Tecorah W. Gambrell, consort of J. E. Gambrell, aged 17 years and 9 months. She leaves many relatives and friends to mourn her early death.

Obituary: Mr. Josiah King died near Belton on last Monday of
cancer, from which he had suffered for a long time. He was
78 years old at the time of his death. He was buried in the
Belton Baptist cemetery on Tuesday. A useful citizen and a
good man has gone to his last reward, leaving a number of
children, relatives and friends to mourn their loss.

Issue of:
Thursday, March 14, 1878:
Married: On Thursday afternoon March 7th, 1878 at the Baptist
Church by Rev. J. S. Murray, Mr. John E. Peoples and Miss
Stella Josphine, daughter of S. Bleckley Esq., all of Anderson.

Married: On Wednesday the 6th inst. by Rev. T. P. Phillips,
Mr. W. T. McElroy and Miss Rosa N. Hammond, daughter of Geo.
W. Hammond Esq., all of Anderson County, S. C.

Married: At Trimity Church, Columbia, S. C. on Tuesday evening
March 5th, 1878 by Rev. Dr.Stringfellow, Mr. D. Taylor Bacot
of Greenville, S. C. and Miss Florence N. Norton of the former
place.

Obituary: Mr. Martin Bird, an old and respected citizen of
Martin township, fell dead while ploughing in a field near
his residence on last Friday morning. He seemed as well as
usual at breakfast and ploughed about three rounds after going
to the field. It is supposed that heart disease was the cause
of his sudden death. He leaves a wife to mourn his death.

Obituary: We regret to chronicle the death of Mr. Moses Dean
which occurred at his residence about seven miles south of
this place on last Tuesday morning, after a long and painful
illness. Mr. Dean was one of the oldest citizens in Anderson
County, being at the time of his death about eighty five years
of age and throughout his whole life was distinguished for
high character, honesty and integrity of purpose. Up to within
a few years back he was remarkably active and industrious but
his failing health had rendered him unfit for active labor
or exercise for the last four or five years. He leaves an
aged wife and a large family of children, grandchildren and
great grandchildren, together with a large circle of other
relatives and friends to mourn his death. His remains were
interred in the Cross Roads cemetery on Wednesday evening.

Married: Honea Path News - On the evening of the 10th inst.
at the residence of the bride's father, by Rev. W. A. Clarke,
Miss Agnes Wilson and Mr. George M. Greer.

Issue of:
Thursday, March 28, 1878:
Married: On Sunday March 17th by Rev. W. H. Strickland at
the residence of the officiating minister, Mr. J. C. Vandiver
and Miss Kate Hammond, all of Anderson County.

Obituary: Death of Col. R. S. Hill - We regret to announce
the death of Col. Richard S. Hill which occurred at his residence in this town on last Sunday after a long and painful
illness. His death, though long looked-for, brings sorrow
and grief to many households in Anderson County, Col. Hill
was a genial gentleman, affable disposition and pleasant
manners and gathered around him many friends wherever he went.

He was born on the 16th of December, 1822 near Andersonville
in this County. In early life his father removed to near
Craft's Ferry where he remained until his first marriage,
when he removed to Montevideo, Hart County, Ga. and lived
there until after the late war, when he removed to Anderson,
S. C. where he has since resided. He received his principal
education in the town of Anderson from the late Wesley Leverett.
Among his classmates and students were Ex-Governor Brown of
Georgia and the late Hon. James L. Orr. He was a member of
the Georgia Convention and advocated the ordinance of suces-
sion. At the commencement of the war he was appointed aid-
de-camp to the Governor and rendered valuable services to
Gov. Brown in the organization of the militia of the State.
He entered the active service in opposing Gen. Sherman's march
through the State and was engaged in many battles. He became
a member of the Methodist Church in early life and continued
so until his death. The funeral services were performed by
Revs. H. F. Chrietzberg and D. E. Frierson at Robert's Church
on Monday morning after which the solemn burial service of the
Masonic fraternity was performed and the remains of the
deceased interred in that Church yard which contains the tombs
of a large number of his family who have died before him.

Issue of:
Thursday, April 4, 1878:
Married: On Tuesday 26th March by Rev. T. P. Phillips, John C.
Gantt Esq. and Mrs. Matilda J. King, all of Anderson County.

Obituary: We regret to announce the death of Mrs. Brown, the
wife of Dr. W. G. Browne, which occurred in Atlanta, Ga. on
Tuesday last after a prolonged and lingering illness. During
the residence of Dr. and Mrs. Browne in our midst, they formed
many friendships and it is with sorrow that the death of the
departed wife is heard by our people. On Wednesday morning
the remains were brought to Anderson by railroad and carried
for interment to Ebenezer Church, where many relatives have
been placed to rest. The bereaved husband has the sincerest
sympathy of this community in his sore affliction.

Obituary: We regret to announce the death of Mr. John Hastie,
an old citizen of Pendleton, which occurred in that town on
last Thursday after a long illness. Mr. Hastie was a native
of New York but removed to Pendleton many years ago and has
since been a resident of that place. Mr. Hastie was a gentleman of quiet and unobtrusive nature and possessed many generous
and amiable qualities. His remains were interred in the
Episcopal Church Yard at Pendleton on last Friday in the presence
of a number of citizens of Pendleton, who assembled to pay
this last mark of respect to the departed one.

Issue of:
Thursday, April 18, 1878:
Married: On the morning of the 14th inst. at the residence
of the bride's father by Dr. Jones, Mr. Mathias B. Richardson
and Miss Sarah R. Newton, all of Anderson County.

Married: On the 11th inst. at the residence of the bride's
father by J. L. Bryan Esq., Mr. John Beck of Rabun, Georgia
and Miss Amanda Dunlap of Anderson County.

Issue of:
April 25, 1878:
Obituary: Rev. Benjamin Thornton, an aged minister of the
Baptist denomination in Hart County, Ga. died of apoplexy
on Friday the 12th inst. in the 77th year of his age. The
Hartwell Sun says, "he was beloved and respected by all
denominations and classes of people. His descendants number
near two hun dred and all are useful and respectable citizens."

Suicide: We learn that on Friday last a Mrs. Mauldin, residing
a short distance this side of Smyrna Church in Abbeville
County, committed suicide by hanging herself. She was left
alone at home by her husband when he returned found her
hanging by the neck to one of the joist of the house. We have
not been informed as to the cause of this sad event.

Obituary: We regret to announce the death of Mr. Elbert
Burriss at Goliad, Texas on Sunday morning the 14th instant.
Mr. Burriss died of typhoid fever after an illness of about
ten days, leaving six children to mourn their loss. Mr.
Burriss removed from this County to Texas some twenty five or
thirty years ago, where he settled and remained until his
death. He has a large family connection in this County who
commingle their sympathy with that of the bereaved ones in
their far off home.

Obituary: Teh Abbeville Medium notices the death of Mrs.
Addie V., wife of William Wakefield, formerly of this County,
which occurred at the residence of her husband in Abbeville
County on the 27th of March last after a long and painful
illness with chronic bronchitis. Mrs. Wakefield was 29 years
of age at the time of her death and leaves a fond husband and
a little child to mourn her death. She has been a consistent
member of the Baptist Church for years and died in the full
hope of a blessed immortality.

Issue of:
Thursday, May 2, 1878:
Married: At the residence of Mr. C. E. Horton, the bride's
father, in Williamston, on May 1st, 1878 by Rev. J. C. Furman,
Mr. C. C. Simpson of Anderson County and Miss Fannie Horton.

Obituary: Departed this life April 20th, 1878, Lee Augustus
Howard, son of George Howard, aged 13 years, 11 months and 20
days. "Life is a span, a fleeting hour,/ How soon the vapor
flies;/ Man is a tender, transient flower,/ That e'en in
blooming dies."   M.

Mrs. E. E. Gibson of Rockport, Texas arrived in Anderson on
yesterday morning and will spend several months in visiting
relatives and friends in this County. Mrs. Gibson is a native
of this County and removed with her husband to the Loan [sic]
Star State several years before the war.

Correction: We were misinformed last week as to the name
of the lady who committed suicide near Lowndesville in Abbeville
County, notice of which was made in our last issue. It was a
Mrs. Prince instead of a Mrs. Mauldin and when the act was
committed the unfortunate lady was in a state of demency.

Obituary: We regret to announce the death of Mr. L. A. Howard
which occurred in this County on the 20th of April. The funeral

services were conducted at Cross Roads Church on the following
day by Rev. W. A. Hodges and were attended by a large concourse
of relatives and friends who mourn the death of the departed
one.

Issue of:
Thursday, May 9, 1878:
Fatal Accident: We regret to chronicle a sad and fatal accident which occurred at the saw mill of Mr. L. Reid Watson on
last Monday evening about sunset resulting in the death of
Mr. William Alexander who had been employed only the morning
before to assist in running the mill. Mr. Alexander was bearing
of plank from the saw when one accidently struck it which
threw him in front of it and before he was able to recover and
rescue himself, had one of his legs cut off with the exception
of a small piece of flesh and the other badly broken. Medical
aid was immediately summoned and every possible effort was
made to save the unfortunate mans life but all to no purpose
as he died that night about 1 o'clock after the most intense
suffering. Mr. Alexander hailed from Greenville but his
parents reside in Pickens County. He was about twenty five
years of age. His remains were interred in Concord graveyard
on Tuesday afternoon.

Issue of:
Thursday, May 16, 1878:
Death of Aged Citizens: Mr. David Geer, an aged and highly
respected citizen of Anderson County departed this life on
last Monday afternoon at the residence of his son, Mr. Solomon
Geer, after an illness of several months. Mr. David Geer,
the subject of this sketch, was the son of Mr. Solomon Geer,
who was originally a citizen of North Carolina but removed
to this State about seventy five years ago and settled the
plantation owned by Maj. J. N. Vandiver. He was the oldest
son in a family of nine children, all of whom were raised to
be useful and worthy citizens and several of them are now
living in this County. Mr. David Geer was married at the age
of 18 years to Miss Nancy Taylor and immediately located at
the place where he resided ever afterwards until his last
illness, during which he was removed to his son's in order
that he might receive the attention and care which his declining
age required. Mr. Geer raised six sons and two daughters. He
was a gentleman of fine memory and more than ordinary intelligence and influence over his neighborhood and acquaintances.
History was his favorite reading and his knowledge of it
through all ages and countries was remarkably minute and
accurate. Though an energetic and influential man, he was
exceedingly modest and diffident so that he never south
public position or notoriety which he could have acquired
had he been ambitious of them. He always felt and manifested
a most active interest in the public welfare and in 1868,
although feeble and quite an old man served as president of
Neal's Creek Democratic Club. He was constantly willing to
work for the party whose principles he exposed and no man was
more sincerely gratified at the redemption of our State than
he. He was a skillful and industrious farmer and before the
war broke out he had acquired a large property, a considerable
portion of which, however, he lost by result of the war. He
was a kind, upright and conscientious man who had the confidence and respect of his neighbors and acquaintances. During
the latter part of last year, Mr. Geer was stricken with

paralysis, from which he never recovered and the angel of
death came to him as an messenger of mercy, to relieve him
from suffering. He had been a member of Broadway Division,
Sons of Temperance, since its formation and on last Tuesday
afternoon his remains were deposited to rest in Neal's Creek
Church cemetery with the funeral rites of the Temperance Order,
after a solemn discourse from Rev. W. H. King. A useful
citizen has departed and his aged widow, together with his
children and friends have the sympathy of the entire community
in their loss.

We regret to announce the death of Mrs. Martha A. Webb, relict
of the late Dr. Edmund Webb of this place, which occurred
at her residence on last Monday morning. Mrs. Webb was one
of the oldest ladies in Anderson, having been born on the 25th
of August 1803. She was a meek and unobtrusive lady of
amiable temper who spent her life in the performance of those
duties which devolve upon a wife and mother and in acts of
human kindness and general benevolence. For some time past
she has been quite feeble in health and entirely deprived of
sight but she bore these afflictions with patience and humilty,
waiting for the summons which has at last called her from the
sufferings of this world to her eternal reward. As her life
has been quiet and serene, so her death was peaceful and calm.
The remains of the deceased were placed to rest by the side of
her husband in the Baptist Church yard on Wednesday morning
after impressive and appropriate funeral services, conducted
by Rev. J. S. Murray. Her relatives have the sympathies of
numerous friends and acquaintances in their bereavement.

Obituary: Mrs. Sallie Kay, widow of the late Strother Kay,
deceased, died at the residence of her son, Mr. Nimrod Kay,
in this County at two o'clock on Tuesday last after a short
illness. Mrs. Kay was an aged and respected lady whose death
is regretted by all who knew her. She was a pious and excellant woman and in her death she has passed to reap the reward
of a faithful life.

Obituary: We regret to announce the death of Mr. Peter Rogers
which occurred at his residence in the Fork township of this
County on last Monday after an illness from rheumatism and
other complicated diseases for more than a year. Mr. Rogers
was at the time of his death about sixty or sixty five years
of age. He had been an industrious, upright and honorable
citizen whose death will be regretted by all who knew him.

Issue of:
Thursday, May 23, 1878:
Married: On the 16th inst. by Warren D. Wilkes Esq. at the
residence of the bride's father in Greenville County, Mr.
George Lafayette Cooley and Miss Ella Lugenia, daughter of
Mr. James E. Holliday.

Obituary: Dr. and Mrs.JT. McFall have the sympathy of our
community in the loss of their infant child, Wade, a handsome
little boy of 18 months, who died on last Saturday from the
effects of measles. Beautiful and solemn funeral services were
performed on Sunday by Revs. J. S. Murray and D. E. Frierson
after which the remains of the little child were interred in
the Baptist Church Yard.

Obituary: Death of Mr. Langston - Our readers will regret to learn that Mr. Samuel H. Langston of our town died on Friday morning the 18th inst. from the effect of the paralytic stroke from which he had been suffering for more than twenty one months. Mr. Langston had been identified with the town of Anderson for forty years, having come here when only fifteen years old. During the time of his residence here he was an extensive and skilled contractor and builder and the monuments of his work not only stand in Anderson but also throughout the whole upper Carolina. He filled the office of Town Councilman in Anderson for a number of terms and exercised a strong influence in town matters. In 1848 he became a member of the Masonic Order and took much interest in the craft. He served once or twice as Master of Hiram Lodge at this place. He was a charter member of the first Pemperance Division formed in Anderson and was at the time of his death a member of this Order, in which he held various positions. Mr. Langston served through the Confederate war. At first he was in the regular service but later in the war was appointed purchasing agent for the commissary department of the government and as such was an efficient and valuable officer. He was a member of the Anderson Baptist Church for many years before his death and was a modest, upright and faithful citizen and christian. Having been stricken with paralysis on the 6th day of August, 1876 and being confined to his bed most of the time since, his death was not unexpected but came to him as a deliver from pain, when he was ready to go hence with the calmness which marks the death of the righteous. The funeral services were performed in the Presbyterian Church in the presence of a large congregation by Revs. J. L. Murray and D. E. Frierson on Saturday. Mr. Langston leaves a wife and several children who have the sympathy of our entire community in their bereavement.

Issue of:
Thursday, May 30, 1878:
Married: At the Methodist Parsonage, Anderson, S. C. May 23rd, 1878 by Rev. H. F. Chrietzberg, Mr. Jas. P. Bailey to Miss Levonia Hammond, all of Anderson County.

Obituary: We are pained to announce that Rev. Nathaniel Gaines, of this County, died of bilious fever at his home near Honea Path on Friday morning 24th inst. He was born in Abbeville County on the 24th February, 1798 and was in his 81st year. In early manhood he entered the ministry of the Baptist denomination and remained through his long life a consistent, able and correct expounder of Christianity. Always independent in his mode of thinking, he used his office for the good of his race. As a citizen, his intercourse with men was well nigh blameless. He was frugal and energetic in business matters and acquired a moderate possession of property which he retained and increased in his old age. His rule was to "owe no man anything but goodwill". He reared a large family which has contributed strong members to the State. The recent reforms in the State and County contributed much to the solid joy of this aged son of Carolina. It may truthfully be said in reference to him, "Mark the perfect man and behold the upright for the end of that man is peace". The funeral services were performed at Shady Grove Church, in this County, by Rev. W. P. Martin in the presence of a large and sorrowing congregation after which his remains were placed to rest in the adjoining church-yard.

Obituary: Mr. James Armstrong died on the 23rd inst. at his
residence near Honea Path at the advanced age of 83 years. He
was the last of the numerous sons of a father who was one of
the earliest settlers of the County. He was uninterruptedly
healthy until a short time before his death and it may be said
he died of old age. Though the deceased was not, in common
acceptation, a man of learning, yet having the strongest
common sense, his information was ain accord with his years and
it was a treat to hear him narrate the events of the past. No
man was ever more temperate in his habits and by frugality and
industry he accummulated a good estate, part of which he most
kindly used in rearing some orphan children. To his friends he
was ever profusly hospitable and the poor he never turned
away empty. He was a lover of his country and ever seemed
interested in his neighborhood, County and State. Mr. Armstrong, like the class of men reared in his time, possessed
traits of character so strongly marked that they cannot be
forgotten and though dead he will continue to speak to those he
has left behind him.

Obituary: We regret to announce the death of Mr. M. L. Kennedy,
the senior member of the firm of Kennedy Bros. of this place
which occurred on last Thursday after an illness of several
months, by which he had been confined to his house and much
of the time to his bed. Mr. Kennedy was originally a citizen
of Lowndesville in Abbeville County but removed to Anderson
six or eight years ago and has since been engaged in the mercantile business. He was an upright, conscientious and
retiring man who had the confidence of the community and leaves
many friends who with our entire community sympathize with his
wife and little children in their sore bereavement. At the
funeral hour on Friday the stores of the town were closed as
a mark of respect and a large congregation repaired to the
Presbyterian Church to pay earth's last tribute to the departed.
The solemn funeral services were conducted by Rev. D. E.
Frierson.

Obituary: We regret to announce the death of Mrs. Martha
Bronston, an aged and respected lady, which occurred at the
residence of her son, Mr. Jesse P. McGee in this County, on
last Friday after a short illness. Mrs. Bronston was born in
1805 and first married the late Michael McGee who resided
near Belton in this County and died many years before the
late war. His widow afterwards married Mr. Bronston and in
1858 removed to Tennessee where Mr. Bronston died several
years ago and three weeks before her death Mrs. Bronston
returned to this County to spend her remaining days with her
son. She was an excellant lady and was greatly beloved by
many of the older people of the County who were well acquainted
with her exemplary life. Her remains were interred at First
Creek on last Saturday after solemn and appropriate funeral
services conducted by Rev. A. Rice in the presence of a
large number of sorrowing relatives and friends.

Obituary: Again death has visited our midst and claimed the
little child of one year as its victim. On last Sunday the
little daughter of Mr. and Mrs. A. L. Welch of our town,
died of the effects of measles after an illness of about two
weeks. Teh funeral services were conducted by Rev. D. E.
Frierson in the Presbyterian Church on last Monday morning
and the remains of the little one were placed to rest in the

adjoining church-yard. The bereaved parents have the sympathy of our community in their affliction.

Issue of:
Thursday, June 6, 1878:
Married: On Tuesday evening May 28, 1878 at the residence of the bride's father by Rev. Dr. Pressley, Mr. M. B. Clinkscales and Miss Kitty, daughter of Robert Haddon Esq. all of Due West, S. C.

Obituary: We regret to announce the death of Mrs. Ann Rogers, widow of the late John P. Rogers, which occurred at her residence near Williamston on last Friday the 31st of May. Mrs. Rogers was sick but a short time having been taken ill only on the Wednesday preceding her death. She was highly esteemed by those who knew her and her death is mourned by a number of relatives and friends.

Obituary: We regret to announce the death of Dr. J. L. Crumley which occurred at his residence in Anderson on Friday the 31st day of May last. Dr. Crumley was born on the 30th of May, 1804 in Buncombe County, N. C. but when quite small his parents removed to Kentucky in which State he studied and practiced medicine. In 1837 he professed religion and studied for the ministry, acquainting himself thoroughly with the Scriptures and participating in the proclamation of the Gospel. A severe throat and lung affection however, prevented his making the ministry or medicine his profession and he was compelled, on account of his health, to enter other pursuits. In 1843 he married and two years later removed to this State and lived here until 1853 when he went to Asheville, N. C. and lived there until 1860 when he returned to this County to spend the remainder of his years. For a number of years after the war, until his health completely failed, he was United States Commissioner for this County. During the past six or eight years he has been confined to his house most of the time and to his bed for a very large part of the time. He was patient throughout his entire illness and though he suffered immenseley, he died peacefully in the faith which had been strong for more than forty years. He was an upright and conscientious man whose death will be regretted by many relatives and friends. On Saturday morning his remains were interred in the Presbyterian Church Yard after a beautiful tribute to the deceased from Rev. D. E. Frierson.

Obituary: Mr. Conrad Wakefield died at his residence in Abbeville County last week after an illness of several months. He was formerly a citizen of Anderson County and his many friends and acquaintances in it who will hear with deep regret of his demise. Mr. Wakefield lived to be an old man and throughout his life he sustained a reputation for amiability and integrity. He possessed the confidence of all who knew him and in his death his neighborhood has lost a good and valuable citizen. His remains were interred in the Churchyard of the First Creek Baptist Church of which the deceased had been long a member.

Obituary: We regret to announce the death of Mr. Lemuel Hall, an aged and respected citizen of this County which occurred at his residence some thirteen miles from Anderson about the middle of last week. Mr. Hall was in his ninetieth year and had been enjoying good health for a man of his years almost up to the very time of his death which was sudden and unexpected. He was an honorable and upright man who through a long life had won for himself the confidence and respect of his neighbors. He was interred near his residence by the side of the grave of his wife who had preceded him about two years.

Obituary: Rev. V. Young died suddenly at his residence near Liberty, in Pickens County, on last Monday. He was a minister of the Baptist Church and for many years resided in Abbeville County until his removal to Pickens County a few years since. He was well known to the people of Anderson County and was highly respected by all of his acquaintances. He was an upright, earnest and consistent man whose death is regretted by a very large number of friends and acquaintances.

Issue of:
Thursday, June 13, 1878:
Obituary: Freddie, son of P. K. and Margaret J. McCully, died on the 9th of May 1878, aged two years and five months. "And this is the darling's portion,/ In Heaven, where he has fled,/ By angels securely guarded,/ By angels securely led./ Brooding in sorrowful silence/ Over the empty nest,/ Can you not see through the shadows,/ Why it is all for the best?/ Better the heavenly kingdom/ Than riches of earthly crown,/ Better the early morning flight,/ Than one when the sun is down;/ Better an empty casket,/ Than jewels besmirched with sin;/ Safer than these without the fold,/ Are those that have entered in."   M.

Obituary: Departed this life on May 30, 1878, near Storeville in Anderson County, Mr. Lemuel Hall, one of the oldest and most respected citizens of the community. He was born on Rocky River near Lee's Shoals on the 7th day of May, 1789 and has lived within a few miles of the place of his birth until he passed to the spirit-land. He may truly have been recognized as an honest, upright, generous and noble man. He neither sought nor claimed in his business associations with the world, only that which was truly and legitimately his own and he was ever ready to accord to others that which he claimed for himself. His noble and generous heart, as exhibited in the charities which he dispensed, furnish us living evidences of the nobility and goodness of his character. The appeal of the hungry and suffering were never presented to him in vain and his deeds of benevolence will be tenderly remembered by many who knew him. Of him it may truly be said, "that his left hand knew not what his right hand done." Early in life he realized the importance of preparation for eternity and sought most sincerely Jesus, the only hope of man's redemption. He was for a number of years a consistent member of the Baptist Church and more than twenty five years ago he united himself to that body of believers known as "Christians or Disciples," and continued steadfast in the faith until the day of his death. Tho' denied the pleasure of attending the meetings of any local organization of "Christians", his faith in their doctrines never wavered. He was a constant and faithful reader of the Bible and especially the New Testament Scriptures and always demanded a "thus saith the Lord" for every demand of faith and practice. God's Word was his constant companion and guide. For many years he looked forward to the summons of the Master which should call him home. It was a

subject upon which he delighted to talk to all who were about
him, always expressing his readiness "to depart and be with
Jesus". Several years ago he made preparation for his burial
having the necessary clothing, made and selecting and marking
the place for his grave. On Thursday, May 30, 1878 he occupied
his usual place at the dinner table; in the afternoon entertained his friends who had called to see him and even when
night began to throw its mantle upon earth, he talked long
and pleasantly to a great grand-daughter who lingered beside
him. But ere nine o'clock had come, the mantle of death had
been thrown around him, his body was gathered in its dark
folds and his spirit had passed to its Redeemer. Without
one complaint, without one struggle, life's last moments were
passed, the contest over and the soul gathered with the
ransomed. His wife and two children had preceded him and he
leaves one son, with many relatives and a host of friends to
mourn their sad and irreparable loss. But why weep? For
him it is far better to be with God. "He is not dead, but
sleepth"; "Asleep in Jesus! blessed sleep,/ From which none
ever wake to weep." A Friend

Obituary: We regret to announce the death of Mrs. S. A. Smith
of Ninety Six, which occurred on last Saturday after a short
illness. Mrs. Smith was a sister of Mrs. J. H. Bewley of this
place and had many friends in Anderson who will regret to
learn of her death.

Obituary: The many relatives and friends of Mr. Franklin
Burriss of California, formerly of this County, will regret
to learn of his death which occurred in his adopted State
on the 20th of May last from the falling of a bridge. Mr.
Burriss left this County about twenty five years ago and first
settled in Texas but subsequently moved to California. He was
51 years old and was a brother of Mr. Newton Burriss of this
County.

Issue of:
Thursday, June 27, 1878:
Obituary: The only child of Mr. J. W. Dacus, of Williamston
township, died on Sunday morning, 16th inst.

Obituary: Nancy O. Tate, wife of William P. Tate of Walker
County, Georgia, died 13th day of June after a long and painful illness. The deceased was a daughter of the late Samuel
Smith of this County. She leaves a husband and several children
to mourn for her.

Obituary: On Tuesday afternoon, Mr. A. McC. Brown of the firm
of J. E. Adger & Co., Charleston, died at 5 o'clock at Pendleton. Mr. Brown was visiting Pendleton to improve his health
which had been poor for some time. His remains were taken to
Charleston the following morning.

Obituary: Wade H., son of Dr. J. T. and Mrs. McFall, died on
the 18th of May, 1878 aged eighteen months. "Another darling
lies sweetly sleeping,/ Little loved one early blest,/ Free
from care and pain and sorrow,/ We should rejoice he is at
rest./ His dark eyes, like angels beaming,/ Never more will
meet our own;/ Oh, his absence makes most dreary/ Our once
cheerful, happy home./ Vainly do we try to find him,/ Vacant
is his little crib,/ Our precious darling in the churchyard,/

Low is laid thy little head./ Side by side in Heaven's bright
region,/ Three little angels sing and soar,/ Welcomed by the
Lord of heaven,/ There they live forever more."

Issue of:
Thursday, July 4, 1878:
Obituary: We regret to announce the death of Mrs. Jefferson
King which occurred at the residence of her husband in Brushy
Creek township on Wednesday the 26th of June after an illness
of a few days from an attack of fever. Mrs. King leaves a
husband and several children together with many friends to
mourn her loss. She was an excellant and useful member of
the community in which she lived.

Obituary: We are pained to announce the death of Mr. G. O.
Hammond of Vermont, which occurred on last Saturday in Horse
Shoe Cove whither he had gone in quest of health. Some months
since Mr. Hammond came to Anderson in the last stages of
consumption and after his arrival his health improved very
much so that about ten days ago he left for a mountain trip
during the summer. It is thought the variable temperature of
the mountains hastened his death. Although he came into our
midst a perfect stranger he formed many acquaintances and
by his gentlemanly deportment made friends who have heard of
his early death with unfeigned regret.

Obituary: "Death from Hydrophobia": Spartanburg - W. J.
"Asa" Pool, son of Col. R. C. Pool, about 45 years old, died
after being bitten by a rabid dog in a field. He had no
family and lived with his father.

Issue of:
Thursday, July 11, 1878:
Married: By Rev. W. P. Martin, June 18, 1878 at his residence.
Mr. Anderson Brock and Miss Lula Hawley, all of Anderson County.

Obituary: As we go to press we regret to hear of the death
of Mrs. Polly Watson, mother of our townsman Mr. John B.
Watson. Mrs. Watson was an aged christian lady and leaves
a very large circle of mourning relatives and friends.

Obituary: We regret to announce the death of Mrs. A. E. Harris
which occurred in Anderson on Saturday morning the 6th inst.
after a lingering illness of several weeks. Mrs. Harris was
born in Laurens County on the 18th of January 1819 and married
Mr. A. W. Harris of Greenville, where she lived until the death
of her husband, after which she removed about twenty years
ago to the town of Anderson where she has since resided. Mrs.
Harris had been a member of the Baptist Church for thirty
years before her death and was an excellant Christian lady.
Her disposition was unostentatious and retiring and her life
a quiet one. During her residence in Anderson she formed
many friendships and the whole community unite in sympathy
with her children in their bereavement. On Sabbath morning
her remains were placed to rest in the Baptist Church Yard
after the performance of solemn funeral services by Rev.
W. H. Strickland.

Thursday, July 18, 1878:

Obituary: Death has robbed us of one in the bud of youth;
one who knew no sin; whose innocence of character disclosed
traits sweeter than the perfumes of flowers and his soul
has winged its flight from this world of woe to bloom in
heaven. These words, which would be unmeaning praise of most
humans, are but a just tribute to the memory of little Hallie,
only child of Mr. and Mrs. D. Richardson, who was born in
Hart County, Georgia, September 14, 1876 and died in Anderson
County, S. C. June 25, 1878.   M.

Obituary: We are pained to announce the death of Mrs. Mary
Caroline Clinkscales, an excellant lady of this County, which
occurred at the residence of her husband, Mr. T. L. Clinkscales, near Storeville, on last Tuesday morning at 9 o'clock
after a lingering and painful illness from consumption. She
was a Christian lady and exemplified in practice the profession she made. Her death has brought sorrow to a husband
and four children who have the sincere sympathy of the community
in their bereavement.

Obituary: Mrs. Martha Melton died very suddenly on Tuesday
the 9th inst. at the residence of her husband, Mr. David
Melton, in Garvin township of this County. Mrs. Melton had
been quite sick for several days and on Tuesday she appeared
to become more free from pain and to go to sleep but on some
of the family going to her it was ascertained that her sleep
was the lasting sleep of death. Her bereaved husband and
family have the sympathy of many friends and acquaintances
in this sad affliction.

Obituary: It is our sad duty to record the death of Miss
Zulia O. Watson which occurred at the residence of her
father, Mr. William B. Watson, near this place on last Saturday after an illness of little more than two weeks from
typhoid fever. Miss Zulia was a little more than sixteen
years of age and was universally beloved by all who knew her.
As a daughter she was dutiful, as a companion she was pleasant
and amiable, as a scholar she was studious and bright. To
these much-to-be admired qualities she added that greatest
adnorment of life, true piety, and for more than a year had
been a devoted member of the Baptist Church. Death came for
her in the morning of life and removed her from loving relations and admiring friends who will ever cherish her memory
with a sweet, sad pleasure. On last Sunday her remains were
placed to rest in Generostee Church Yard, where several other
members of her family repose.

Obituary: Death of Mrs. Mary Watson - This excellant lady, of
whose death we made a brief mention last week, was one of
the oldest ladies in this portion of the State and her useful
and exemplary life demands more than the short notice we were
able to give at that time. Mrs. Watson was born on the 4th
of June, 1792 near Brush River Baptist Church in Newberry
County, in this State and removed with her parents to this
(then Pendleton) County about 1800. In 1810 she married
Mr. David Watson and she with her husband joined the Baptist
Church at Mountain Creek in 1830. In August 1843 Mr. Watson
died and she has since that time lived at the old homestead.

Mrs. Watson raised eight children, all of whom were upright, intelligent and useful gentlemen and ladies. Four of her children, with some thirty grandchildren, now survive her and mourn the departure of their aged relative. Mrs. Watson was a pious lady and always devoted much of her time and attention to her domestic relations and her influence may be traced in the lives of her children. As a neighbor she was kind and considerate of those around, though for several years past her health has been too feeble for her to get about so as to enjoy company. Her memory will long be cherished by a host of relatives and friends.

Issue of:
Thursday, July 25, 1878:
Obituary: Death of Mr. A. E. Reed - We are pained to record the death of Mr. Alfred Elkin Reed which occurred at his residence in this County on last Sunday the 21st inst. from the effects of a stroke of paralysis in September last and although he recovered in a great measure from this attack he has suffered greatly and almost constantly from Brights disease of the kidneys, though for several weeks past he had appeared to improve rapidly and it was hoped his health would in a great measure be restored. But on last Saturday at three o'clock he was stricken a second time with paralysis and although every effort that medical skill and attention could make was tried to arrest the effects of this attack, it availed nothing and just twelve hours later he died. Mr. Reed was born near Honea Path on the 19th of September, 1813 and has always resided in this county, having settled on Bear Creek, in Martin township, in 1841 in the residence occupied by him at the time of his death. He was an upright, industrious and honorable citizen, having, as he said himself, for forty five years labored actively in the work of agriculture. He was a very successful farmer and during the whole time he did not buy for his own use a pound of bacon, flour or meal as he was a great believer in the independence of the farmer, if he would only raise his own provisions. During his life he accummulated a good property and has left an example worthy of imitation. Mr. Reed was a kind and amiable neighbor who had the respect and friendship fo all who knew him and whose departure will be mourned by a host of relatives and friends. His remains were placed to rest in Ebenezer Church Yard on Monday the 22nd inst. after solemn and appropriate funeral services which were attended by a large crowd of his neighbors and acquaintances who assembled to pay their last tribute to the memory of one whose death they lament.

Issue of:
Thursday, August 8, 1878:
Married: On Tuesday July 30th by Rev. R. P. Franks, Mr. R. Lewis Moorhead of Anderson and Mrs. M. E. Black of Abbeville County, S. C.

Obituary: Mr. Andrew McLees, the oldest citizen of the County, died at his residence on Sadler's Creek on the 25th ult. in the 92nd year of his age. Mr. McLees was born in Newberry District in 1787 but removed to this County in 1804. Mr. McLees was not only our oldest but one of our best citizens. In his death not only his family but the entire community has sustained a great loss.

Obituary: Death of Rev. A. Rice - It is with sincere regret
that we announce the death of the Rev. A. Rice in the 81st
year of his age. He was born in this County on the 20th day
of June A.D. 1798 and died on the 31st day of July A.D.
1878 after a brief illness of three days. He received in early
life as good an education as could be obtained in the common
County schools of the day and completed his academic course
in the Academy at Varrennes when in his nineteenth year. Soon
after this he entered as clerk in the store of his father and
Mr. Christopher Orr at Craytonville where he had inculcated
and imbibed those strict business principles which subsequently contributed to his own success in life and enable him
to discharge faithfully the many trusts afterwards committed
to him without the imputation of a strain upon any of his
transactions. On the 16th of March, 1820 he was married to
Miss Sallie Thompson who was for 48 years the faithful partner
of his joys and sorrows. About this time he was elected
Colonel of one of the militia regiments and the year 1826 or
1828 was elected a member of the Legislature and continued
to represent the people of Pendleton District in the Legislature for six years. As a representative he faithfully
represented his constituency and it was his privilege to cast
his vote in favor of granting a charter to the first railroad
company in this country and the longest one at that time in
the world. About this time Col. Rice connected himself with
the Baptist Church and in 1836 or 1837 was at the request of
the Neal's Creek Church, ordained to the work of the ministry.
For upwards of forty years he was a faithful preacher of
the Gospel. He sought not wealthy Churches but being himself
a man of wealth, it was his delight to preach in poor Churches
and in destitute places. He was a leader in the Saluda
Association and much of the prominence of that Association is
due to his judgement and labors. His last days were as calm
and bright as his life had been pure and devoted and faithful
to all thr bright trusts committed to his charge. The funeral
services were conducted by Rev. J. S. Murray and his remains
interred in the family burial ground. The very large attendance at his burial attest the high estimation in which he was
held in the community. We commingle our sympathies with the
bereaved family in the great loss which they and the community
have sustained in the death of one of our oldest and best
citizens.

Issue of:
Thursday, August 22, 1878:
Married: On the 28th July 1878 by J. L. Bryan Esq., Mr. Jas.
M. Stewart and Miss Elizabeth J. Taylor, all of Anderson County.

Married: At the residence of the bride's father, Mr. Kenon
Pepper, Thursday 8th of August 1878 by Rev. R. N. Hays, Mr.
Joseph Thomas and Miss Sally Pepper, all of Anderson County.

Obituary: We regret to announce the death of Mrs. Elizabeth
Moore, wife of Mr. Bruce Moore of Hopewell Township, which
occurred on last Sunday after an illness of several weeks
from fever. Her remains were interred at Hopewell on Monday
in the presence of many friends and relatives who mourn the
departed one.

Drowning: The citizens of Rock Mills township and of the

surrounding country were greatly shocked on last Tuesday to
learn that Henry, a little son of Mr. Joseph A. McLeskey about
twelve years of age, had been accidently drowned in Seneca
River. Henry and a younger brother were engaged in pulling
fodder in a field near the river and about 10 o'clock he went
bathing by himself. He remained so long that his brother went
to look for him and upon arriving at the river bank found
his clothes but could see nothing of Henry, where-upon the alarm
was given and upon the assemblage of a number of the neighbors
the river was searched and the body found some fifty yards
below the bathing place. When found he had been drowned for
more than three hours so that resuscitation was impossible.
This occurrence is an exceedingly sad one and is greatly
lamented by the whole community. Henry McLeskey was a bright
and energetic lad who was much beloved by his friends. His
parents have the warmest sympathies of the entire community
in this sudden and sad bereavement.

Obituary: Once more the reaper has been in our midst and
removed from life a most excellant and pious young lady.
Miss Hattie, daughter of Mr. E. F. Murrah, died on last Sunday
morning after a long and tedious illness during which she
received every care and attention which it was possible for
medical skill or devoted parents to render. It was, however,
impossible to arrest the course of the destroyer and after
suffering for months she passed from a world of anguish and
sorrow with a peace and resignation which render even death
beautiful and point to a happy state beyond. Miss Murrah was
an intelligent, christian lady and had for several years been
a consistent member of the Methodist Church at this place.
She was affable toward those she met and was greatly beloved
by her friends. Her early death is lamented by many friends
and acquaintances who sympathize most sincerely with her
bereaved parents in their sorrow. Her remains were placed to
rest in the Presbyterian Church yard on last Monday after very
solemn, beautiful and aporopriate funeral services which were
conducted by Revs. H. F. Chrietzberg and D. E. Frierson.

Issue of:
Thursday, September 5, 1878:
Obituary: We regret to announce the death of Lilian, a little
daughter of Mr. J. L. Nance of Hall township, which occurred
from an infection of the throat supposed to be diptheria,
on Sunday 25th of August, after an illness of a few days. The
little girl was but three years of age and the fond parents have
the sympathy of the community in their bereavement at her untimely death just as she was entering the years of interesting
childhood.

Obituary: It is with sorrow that we announce the death of
Paul, a little son of Mr. Mike Nicely of Belton, which occurred
on last Monday morning after a short illness from diphtheria.
He had just passed five summers when the destroyer claimed him
as not of this world and transferred his little spirit to a
better ahd happier world. The remains were brought to Anderson by a special train on Tuesday and interred in the Presbyterian Church Yard after appropriate funeral services. The
community sympathize with the stricken family in their loss.

Obituary: We regret to announce the death of Mrs. J. C. Allen
which occurred at the residence of her husband in the Corner

township of this County on last Sunday morning after a lingering illness. Mrs. Allen was a sister of Rev. W. A. Hodges
and was an excellant lady in all of the relations of life.
She was an affectionate wife, a fond mother and a genial
companion and has gone to the grave lamented by friends and
acquaintances who sympathize with her family in this sore
affliction. On Monday her remains were placed to rest in
Roberts' Churchyard where many of her family who have preceded
her in death sleep that sleep which knows no waking until the
final day of all things come.

Issue of:
Thursday, September 12, 1878:
Obituary: Died, the evening of the 28th of August 1878 after
an illness with fever of four days at the Parsonage of Williamsburg Church near Kingstree, S. C., Mary Manning, aged 6 years
and 8 months, eldest child of Rev. W. Cuttino and Martha M.
Smith.

Obituary: Lillian Toccoa, only daughter of John L. and Lulie
Nance, died on Sabbeth morning 25th August 1878, in her third
year. With many a heartpang and many a sorrow we consigned
her little corpse to the folds of the tomb. E. T. W.

Issue of:
Thursday, September 19, 1878:
Obituary: Mr. David D. Spearman, of Brushy Creek township,
died on Monday 9th inst. in the 73rd year of his age. He was
born and raised and has always lived within a half mile of
where he died and throughout his entire life has possessed
the confidence and good will of his neighbors and acquaintances.
He had been a consistent member of the Methodist Church for
more than fifty years and in his death his church, family,
community and County sustain a serious loss. His remains
were interred in the graveyard at Shiloh (Methodist) Church
on the 11th inst.

Issue of:
Thursday, September 26, 1878:
Married: On Thursday 12th inst. at the residence of the bride's
father by Rev. D. W. Hiatt, Mr. John T. Richey of Anderson
County and Miss D. J. D. Nally of Pickens County.

Obituary: The many friends of Mr. David A. Woodson will
regret to learn of his death which occurred last week in
Salisbury, N. C. in the sixty ninth year of his age. Mr.
Woodson came to Anderson more than thirty years ago where he
married and settled. After the death of his wife a few
years ago, he sold his property here and returned to his
native town, Salisbury, that he might spend his last days
among his kindred and the scenes of his youth. During his
residence in our midst he made many friends, all of whom
will sympathize with his rereaved relatives. He was a printer
by trade and for many years a faithful compositer in this
office.

Obituary: We are pained to announce the death of little Cora
Wilhite, daughter of Mr. and Mrs. W. F. Baker of Atlanta,
Georgia and grand-daughter of Dr. P. A. Wilhite of Anderson.
The little girl was a bright child aged twelve months and was

attacked at the residence of Mr. Baker in Atlanta on last
Friday night with brain fever which terminated fatally on the
following day. Those who mourn the early termination of a
sweet and interesting infant's life weep not as those without
hope for the tender bud which the touch of death has withered
here, has but been wafted to a purer and happier sphere where,
free from sorrow and pain and suffering, the little spirit has
already been transformed into a more perfect and beautiful
life which shall know no ending.

Obituary: Death of Rev. A. Acker - We regret to record the
death of Rev. A. Acker, an excellant and useful citizen of
Greenville County who was well known and much beloved by many
persons in this County. Mr. Acker was born on the 11th day
of August 1803 in Anderson County and died on the evening of
Wednesday the 18th inst. at his residence after a short
illness, having attained the advanced age of a little more
than seventy five years. He was married in 1824 to Miss
Mourning Garrison of Greenville County and daughter of Capt.
Charles Garrison and soon afterward removed to Greenville
County within a mile of his fathers residence in this County
and has remained at the same place ever since. He joined
the Baptist Church in 1832 and was ordained to the ministry
in 1836 and has been an influential and useful servant of the
Gospel. He was a meek, amiable and intelligent gentleman of
great charity and benevolence towards the needy and with the
uttermost liberality and brotherly kindness towards all denominations and was therefore justly popular and beloved by
all with whom he came in contact. His family has the sincerest
sympathy of friends and acquaintances in their bereavement.

Issue of:
Thursday, October 3, 1878:
Married: On the afternoon of the 25th September 1878 at the
residence of the bride's grandfather, Z. Hall Esq., by Rev.
D. E. Frierson D.D., Rev. Roderick A. Henderson of Canada and
Miss Juliet A. Hall of Anderson County, South Carolina.

Obituary: It is with sad feelings that we announce the death
of Mr. Samuel R. Earle, at Deep Creek, on Thursday of last
week. Mr. Earle on the evening preceding was cautioning a
new hand against the danger of cleaning out the gin while in
motion and raising the breast of the gin instructed him not
to permit his arm in a certain position to come too near the
saws, he at the time assuming the position, when his arm was
caught by the saws and terribly lacerated. He died the next
morning. The funeral services were performed on Friday by
Rev. J. S. Murray and his remains deposited in the family
burial ground. He leaves a wife and two children with a large
circle of relatives and friends to mourn their loss. Mr.
Earle was a young gentleman of industry, energy and promise
and had entered life with every promise of future success and
usefulness. The family have the sympathy of the entire
community in their sudden and sad bereavement.

Obituary: We regret to announce the death of little Charlie
F. Stringer, son of Mr. and Mrs. A. J. Stringer of Belton,
which occurred on Tuesday the 24th of September from a relapse
of diphtheria. The little boy, though only eighteen months
old, was a bright and interesting child whose untimely death

has caused sorrow among many outside of the stricken parents. Death, however, claimed his young spirit as a thing to pure and bright for earth and neither the tender years of childhood nor the devotion of fond parents was able to retain the loved one here. In their sorrow, however, there is left to those who loved him the hope which consoled David of old, that though the child may not return to them, they can go to him in a world where sorrow and parting will never again give grief and pain.

Obituary: Another of our aged and respected citizens has been removed from us by the hand of death. Mr. Luke Haynie died on last Tuesday morning in the 87th year of his age. He was born in the County and in the neighborhood of his nativity spent a long and respected life. A large family connection mourn the loss of this patriarch of the home circle and in their grief have the synpathies of the community in which the deceased lived for so many years.

Obituary: Mr. William Wilson took an ounce of laudanum on last Friday evening and as soon as its effects were discovered, several physicians were summoned to his relief, but all of their skill was unable to revive him and on Saturday morning he died. It is thought that he was not of his right mind at the time he took the fatal dose. His family have the sympathy of the entire community in this bereavement, which is a sad one and is greatly regretted.

Issue of:
Thursday, October 10, 1878:
Family Background: A sketch of Hon. (Gen.) Matthew Calbraith Butler....

Issue of:
Thursday, October 17, 1878:
Obituary: A very sad accident occurred on last Friday morning at the gin house of Mr. B. F. Hammond about four miles east of this place resulting in the death of a little son about nine years old of Mr. Lewis Smith of Broadway township, who had carried a load of cotton to the gin, taking his little boy with him. It was the childs first visit to a gin house and as might have been expected, the most attractive feature about the place to him was the horses and machinery underneath the gin. He had been there about half an hour when he got upon the shaft under the cog wheel and while riding around was caught by the neck between an arm of the cog wheel and a gallows which supported the band wheel. The space through which his neck was forced was about two inches. He lived until next morning when he died, medical aid failing to prolong his life.

Issue of:
Thursday, October 24, 1878:
Obituary: We regret to chronicle the death of another of Andersons aged and respected citizens, Mr. Jacob Mouchet of Savannah township, which occurred on last Friday, 18th inst., in the 83rd year of his age. Mr. Mouchet was born and raised in Abbeville County and removed to Anderson County about the year 1832 where he has since resided. He was an honest, upright citizen, attended strictly to his own business and had the respect and confidence of all who came in contact with

him. He was a faithful soldier in the war of 1812 and has
long been a consistent member of the Methodist Church. An
aged wife and three children mourn his death.

Married: On Tuesday October 22nd, 1878 at the residence of
Mrs. H. T. Brown, Townville, S. C. by Rev. W. H. Strickland,
Mr. J. L. Tribble and Miss Emma E. Feaster.

Issue of:
Thursday, October 31, 1878:
Obituary: We regret to record the death of Mrs. David
Simmons, wife of Rev. David Simmons, who died after an illness of several weeks in Lynden, Cass County, Texas on the
13th day of September last. Rev. David Simmons removed from
this county to Texas some ten or twelve years ago. Mrs.
Simmons was an aged mother is Israel and died in the hope of
a blessed immortality. The bereaved ones, in their far off
home, have the sympathy of a large circle of relatives and
friends in this County in their sad bereavement.

Issue of:
Thursday, November 7, 1878:
Married: At the residence of the bride's father on Sunday
morning October 27th by Rev. J. B. Griffin, Mr. Thomas J.
Burdine and Miss Eleanor A. Grambrell.

Married: On October 24th at the residence of the officiating
minister, Rev. W. P. Martin, Mr. John W. Harper and Miss Susan
E. Major.

Married: At the residence of the bride's grandmother, Mrs.
Eliza Robinson, on Thursday evening Nov. 7th by Rev. D. E.
Frierson D.D., Mr. Louis Sharpe and Miss Lizzie Partlow, all
of Anderson C.H.

Obituary: The remains of an infant of Mr. C. S. Davis were
interred in the Baptist graveyard on Sunday afternoon.

Issue of:
Thursday, November 14, 1878:
Married: By Rev. M. McGee on the 7th November at 3 p.m., at
the residence of the bride's father, Mr. M. Scott Holland and
Miss Fannie Williamson, daughter of James Williamson, all of
Anderson County.

Married: By Rev. M. McGee on the 7th November at 6 p.m. at
the residence of the bride's father, Mr. T. L. Clinkscales Jr.
and Miss Emma Harris, daughter of Mr. Ezekiel Harris, all of
Anderson County.

Obituary: We regret to announce the death of Mr. Daniel
Campbell which occurred at his home near Belton one day last
week in the 95th year of his age from general debility and old
age. Mr. Campbell was a remarkably active and industrious
man and has reared a large and respectable family of children,
grandchildren and great grandchildren who mourn his death.
Throughout his long life he was distinguished for honesty
and integrity of purpose and leaves behind him a name and
character untarnished.

Obituary: Mrs. Peggy Leavell, wife of Rev. John Leavell, who

resides near Belton in this County, died at the residence
of her husband on last Friday night after a lingering illness
of many months. Mrs. Leavell was an aged woman, who by a
pious life, had commanded the respect of all acquaintances
and her husband has the sincere sympathy of the community in
this bereavement, which takes from him in old age the partner
of his life for near half a century past. The remains of the
deceased were interred in the Baptist church-yard at Belton
on last Sunday morning after a very impressive funeral service
by the venerable Rev. W. P. Martin.

Obituary: Mr. William Smith, of Broadway township, died suddenly from an attack of appoplexy on last Monday morning in the
seventy eighth year of his age. He was born on the 1st day of
January 1801 and during his long life he has uniformly maintained the reputation of an upright and industrious citizen and
as such has been respected and liked by his neighbors and
acquaintances. He has always been engaged in agriculture and
never grew too feeble or too indifferent to his occupation to
give up active labor until the day of his death. A shower of
rain compelled him and his sons, who were with him, to leave
the cotton field and repair to the house, where he conversed
on the piazza for a few moments. He then went into the house
to warm and upon reaching the fire he fell, so that but for
his aged wife, who was near enough to catch him, he would have
fallen into the fire. Every possible attention was paid him
in the hopes of producing a revival but it availed nothing.
He never spoke again and in a short time his spirit had
flown. Mr. Smith had eleven children, all of whom are grown
and now living. About two years ago he united with the Dor-
chester Baptist Church and has been a consistent member since.
His remains were interred at Neal's Creek on last Tuesday after
a very solemn funeral service, which was attended by a large
concourse of persons who were present as a last token of
respect for the deceased.

Obituary: Maj. Joseph M. Adams of Oconee County, died on last
Friday morning after a long and distressing illness. He was
an excellant gentleman and an accomplished scholar. For some
years previous to the war he was the principal of the flourishing male academy in Anderson and was a thorough and successful
instructor. After the war Maj. Adams was admitted to the Bar
and practiced law as the partner of Gen. S. McGowan at old
Pickens Court House until he decided to follow agricultural
pursuits and accordingly removed to his plantation near Perryville, in Oconee County. For the past two years he has been
declining in health so that his death was not altogether
unexpected. On Friday last his remains were interred in the
family burying ground at Deep Creek, in this County, after
solemn funeral services conducted by Rev. J. S. Murray. His
family have the sympathy of this community in their bereavement.

Issue of:
Thursday, November 21, 1878:
Married: Thursday morning November 14, 1878 at the residence
of the bride's sister in Columbia, S. C. by Rev. P. J. Shand,
Mr. E. W. Taylor of Anderson and Miss Annie C. Bacot of
Columbia.

Married: At the residence of the bride's father in Belton on
Tuesday 19th inst. by Rev. J. S. Murray, Mr. C. S. McCullough

of Darlington, formerly of Anderson and Miss Emma H. McGee, daughter of Mr. G. W. McGee.

Obituary: We regret to announce the death of Mr. Jordan Burns, a respected citizen of the Fork township of this County, which occurred at his residence on last Friday night from dropsy of the heart, resulting from an attack of pleurisy, which has confined him to his bed for several weeks. Mr. Burns was, at the time of his death, sixty seven years of age and his upright and genial conduct through life had established himself in the friendships and esteem of his neighbors and acquaintances who sympathize with his family in the bereavement they are called upon to bear. On Sunday afternoon the deceased was interred in the Townville Baptist Church yard after appropriate and feeling funeral services. Mr. Burns was a good man and in his death a kind neighbor and useful citizen has been removed from earth.

Obituary: Death of Col. F. E. Harrison: The readers of the Intelligencer will read the announcement of the death of Col. F. E. Harrison, of Andersonville, with profound regret. The announcement last week that this estimable gentleman was hopelessly ill has proved to be sadly true and on last Saturday night about eleven o'clock his spirit was released from the toils of life to enter upon the rewards of the faithful. Col. Harrison was about fifty three years of age and was a native of Anderson County. Since his father's death he has owned and resided upon the old family homestead at Andersonville, which has long been noted as the abode of culture, hospitality and refinement. There may have been men as kind and gentle as Col. Harrison, but there certainly have been one to excel him in these enviable traits and thousands of deeds of charity and acts of benevolence to the poor and needy will secure for his memory a love and respect from hundreds of those who have received assistance from him who is gone. He was a pure, christian and noble gentleman whose intellectual culture and refinement were hightened by those qualities of the heart which so greatly assist to make up the perfect man. He was for many years a devoted member of the Presbyterian Church and was one of the leading lay members in the upcountry, helping to sustain and propagate his religion both by his example and by a liberal contribution of his means. Col. Harrison was a progressive man and did much to improve the condition of the country, taking a lively and beneficial interest in agriculture, manufacturing and railroads. In his death the County has lost a valuable and excellant citizen and the sympathy of all our people is extended to the smitten family in their sore bereavement. On Sunday afternoon a large concourse of friends assembled at the residence of the deceased in Andersonville to witness the sad funeral rites which were most solemnly beautiful and touching, the Rev. John B. Adger preaching the sermon, after which the remains were interred in the family grave yard at Andersonville, there to await the resurrection to life eternal.

Obituary: Townville News - Mrs. Nancy Cromer, relict of the late Jacob Cromer, died at her home near Brown's muster ground on the 10th inst., aged about 80 years.

Married: Thursday evening 7th inst. by Rev. Prof. Riley of

Adger College, Walhalla, Mr. J. Lafayette Farmer and Miss
Lula A. Hunter, both of this town.

Issue of:
Thursday, November 28, 1878:
Married: In the Roman Catholic Cathedral, Baltimore, Md.
on the 6th November by the Rev. Father Curtis, Mr. John B.
Harrison, formerly of Anderson and Miss Imogen Baugher of
Baltimore.

Married: At Lowndesville on the 14th inst. by the Rev. R. C.
Ligon, Mr. J. F. Seawright of Donnaldsville and Miss J. L.
Hall of Anderson County.

Married: At Six and Twenty Church Sunday night 10th inst. by
Rev. J. S. Simmons, Mr. J. D. Cartee and Miss Josephine
Riley.

Married: At the residence of Mr. John Browning Sunday night
17th inst. by Rev. J. S. Simmons, Mr. Stephen McAlister and
Miss Mary A. Smith.

Married: On the 21st inst. by Rev. B. Hays, Mr. W. W. Melton
and Miss E. A. King.

Married: On the 20th inst. by Rev. B. Hays, Mr. Thomas M. King
and Miss Alice E. Jolly.

Married: On October 17th, by Rev. T. P. Cleveland, Mr.
J. N. Telford of Banks County, Ga. and Miss L. K. West of
Habersham County, Ga.

Married: On October 20th by Rev. G. H. Cartledge, Mr. L. M.
Turk of Homer, Ga. and Miss C. I. Telford, youngest daughter
of G. B. Telford, Esq. of Banks County, Ga.

Married: At the residence of the bride's mother, Sunday
evening 24th inst. by Rev. B. Hays, Mr. F. W. Moss of Franklin
County, Ga. and Miss E. A. Stephenson of Anderson County, S. C.

Issue of:
Thursday, December 5, 1878:
Married: At the residence of the bride's father on the 14th
ultimo by Rev. W. A. Hodges, Mr. W. H. Cox and Miss Heppie H.
Campbell.

Married: At Asbury Church on Sunday evening last, 1st inst.
by Rev. J. T. Attaway, Mr. Arthur Buchanan and Miss Mary Jane
Bolt, daughter of Wm. Bolt.

Obituary: Mr. Wm. E. Pagett, formerly of this County, but a
citizen of Ellis County, Texas since the fall of 1871, died on
the 19th ult. of pulmonary consumption in the 50th year of
his age. Mr. Pagett was well known in this County, having
been born and raised within its limits and the news of his
death will be received by many with sadness.

Issue of:
Thursday, December 12, 1878:
Married: At the residence of the bride's father, Rev. James

McMullan in Hart County, Ga. December 5th, 1878 by Rev. H. F.
Chrietzberg, Mr. Rufus S. Hill of Anderson C.H., S. C. and
Miss Emma H. McMullan of Hart Co., Ga.

Married: December 4th, by Rev. W. A. Hodges, Mr. M. J. Evans
and Miss E. J. Webb.

Issue of:
Thursday, December 19, 1878:
Married: On the 5th inst. at the residence of the bride's
father by Rev. Thomas Dawson, Mr. James McCorkle and Miss Mary
Smith.

Married: On 3rd November by Rev. G. M. Rogers, Mr. H. M. Stone
of Abbeville and Miss Syvilla Wiginton, daughter of Mr. Elisha
Wiginton, of Anderson County.

Married: On the 11th inst. by Rev. M. McGee at the residence
of the bride's mother, Mr. Preston B. Acker and Miss Mattie
Glenn, daughter of Mrs. Martha Glenn.

Married: On the 12th inst. by Rev. M. McGee at the residence
of the bride's mother, Mr. C. L. Tucker of Abbeville County and
Miss Sallie E. Gentry, daughter of Mrs. Nancy Gentry of Anderson County.

Obituary: Townville News - Mrs. Maria Milford, the young wife
of Mr. Samuel Milford, died on the 14th inst. at the residence
of her father, Mr. Thomas B. Palmer of this township. Her
remains were interred on Monday at Cedar Grove graveyard.

Married: In this town on Sunday the 8th inst. by Rev. J. R.
Riley, Mr. John J. McCarley and Miss Hortie Simmons, both of
this place.

                    ****

Issue of:
Thursday, July 27, 1882:
Married: On the evening of the 20th inst. at the Methodist
Church, Hartwell, Ga., Miss Maud P. Cater and Mr. Albert F.
Brown, Rev. R. A. Seale officiating.

Obituary: An infant son of Mr. James M. and Mrs. Mary Sullivan
died Saturday afternoon last of Cholera infantum after an
illness of only about 24 hours. The remains were interred in
the Baptist cemetery Sunday afternoon. Many friends sympathize
with the bereaved parents in their affliction.

Obituary: Mrs. Emma Stone died on last Thursday night at the
residence of her husband, Mr. J. F. Stone, in Brushy Creek
township, after a short illness. She was highly respected
and beloved in her neighborhood. The remains were placed to
rest in Shiloh Churchyard on Saturday after funeral services
conducted by Rev. W. A. Hodges.

Issue of:
Thursday, August 3, 1882:
Obituary: The infant daughter of Maj. and Mrs. J. [?] Moore
died Tuesday night.

Obituary: Died, July 17, 1882, Mrs. F. M. Anderson, widow of the late Micajah Anderson in Rock Mills township, aged 76 years.

Accident: One of the most heart-rending accidents occurred in our city last Saturday afternoon that it has ever been our duty to record. Two little boys, Berry and John Wilson, aged respectively about seven and five years and sons of Messrs. J. F. and S. P. Wilson, were sent by the latter to his fathers brick yard to get a pair of shoes and upon reaching the brick yard the little boys climbed upon a heavy slab that was lying across the heads of two hogsheads and indismouting it is supposed that Berry jumped down first, which caused the slab to fall to the ground, one end of it stricking little John on the back of his head and crushing his skull. His little companion hurried to Mr. Wilson and told him that John was hurt and Mr. W. went immediately to him and found him in an unconscious condition. He took him to the residence of Mr. J. F. Wilson, where he died in a few minutes. The afflicted parents have the sympathies of all our people in their sad bereavement. The remains were interred in the Presbyterian graveyard Sunday morning.

Issue of:
Thursday, August 10, 1882:
Obituary: Miss Carrie Lester, second daughter of Mr. George Lester, living below Prosperity, who was formerly a citizen of this County, was seriously burned by fire while igniting the same from a kerosene can last Monday evening. She lingered in great pain until 4 o'clock Tuesday afternoon when she was released by death. Miss Lester was about seventeen and an amiable and lovely young lady.

Lynching: The Hartwell Sun says that Pinckney Hewin, who lived not far from the Savannah River, on the Carolina side, in this County, was lynched in Texas recently. It seems that he was working a contract on a railroad in that State, had gotten into a row with a man and killed him in self defence, was arrested and put in jail, but a mob took him therefrom and lynched him. Mr. Hewin was extensively known in this County.

Obituary: Mrs. Lovey Gentry, wife of Mr. John Gentry of Centreville township died on last Saturday morning at the advanced age of 72 years. Mrs. Gentry had been a sufferer from rheumatism and erysipelas for the past thirty eight years and had been confined to her bed for that length of time. She bore her sufferings with enduring patience and was ready when the Master made his summons. Her remains were interred in the Baptist Cemetery in this city on last Sunday morning, Rev. Baxter Hays conducting the funeral services.

Issue of:
Thursday, August 17, 1882:
Obituary: Miss Julia Glenn, third daughter of Mrs. M. A. Glenn, died at the residence of her mother, in Rock Mills township, on Wednesday evening 9th inst. after an illness of three weeks from typhoid fever, aged 23 years. Miss Glenn was a most estimable young lady and was much beloved by all who knew her. She was a consistent member of Flat Rock Church at which place she was buried on last Thursday in the presence of a large circle of relatives and friends.

Issue of:
Thursday, August 24, 1882:
Married: Walter S. Fant, formerly of this city, was married
to Miss Fannie Murphy in [...], Texas on Thursday morning
[.....]

Accident and Death of Mr. T. J. Sutherland: We have received
through friends at Belton, S. C. the following particulars of
the fatal accident, which occurred on the 8th inst. to Mr.
Thos. J. Sutherland, a young man formerly of this County,
which resulted in his death on the 10th inst. Mr. Sutherland
was in the act of boarding a passing train at White Oak
station, on the Little Rock and Fort Smith Railroad in Arkansas
and missing the step, fell between the cars at the station
platform in such a manner as to be caught by the moving train
and rolled the entire length of the car, from which he sustained such severe injuries as to cause his death two days
afterwards. He received every attention after his injuries
that could have been bestowed upon him by the many friends he
had made during his residence there. After death his remains
were taken in charge by the Masons and interred with the burial
rites of that ancient order at Mulberry on the L. R. and Ft.
S. R. R. Mr. Sutherland was a young man about 31 years of age
and had lived in the neighborhood of Belton, S. C. from boyhood. He leaves a wife and two small children, both girls,
together with many other relatives and friends in this community
who mourn his untimely death.

Issue of:
Thursday, September 7, 1882:
Obituary: Little Annie, daughter of Col. R. B. A. Robinson
of Martin township, died on Wednesday morning from diphtheria,
aged six years. Her remains will be interred in the Ebenezer
graveyard today. Our sympathies are with the bereaved parents
in their sore affliction.

Married: On Sunday morning 3rd inst. by Rev. W. H. King, Mr.
Josiah Burgess and Miss Fannie Kay, daughter of Mr. M. Kay.

Married: On Sunday 3rd inst. by Rev. W. H. King, Mr. John A.
Hayes and Miss C. E. Whittaker, daughter of Mr. S. A. Whittaker,
all of this County.

Issue of:
Thursday, September 14, 1882:
Married: On Wednesday evening September 6, at the residence
of the bride's [....] Mr. J. Monroe Smith by Rev. A. P.
[...dson], Dr. L. G. Clayton of Central, Pickens County, S. C.
and Miss Addie [......] of Anderson County.

Obituary: Death of An Excellant Young Man - On last Friday
morning our community was saddened by the announcement of the
death of one of our most promising young men, J. A. McSwain
Carlisle. Mr. Carlisle was born June 8th, 1860. About five
years ago he joined the Methodist Church in this place ...
Buried Presbyterian burial ground.

Issue of:
Thursday, September 21, 1882:
Obituary: Mr. T. C. Kilbourne, outside manager of the Piedmont
Mills, died at Piedmont on last Monday afternoon. Mr. Kil-
bourne was 56 years of age and a native of Maine, having come

to this State in 1859. He leaves a wife and one child.

Obituary: Miss Mattie Russell, youngest daughter of Maj. Thos. H. Russell, died at the residence of her father in Brushy Creek township in this County on last Sunday afternoon after an illness of two weeks from typhoid fever. Miss Russell was in her twentieth year and a most attractive and estimable young lady, whose death is regretted by very many friends. She was a member of Mt. Carmel Presbyterian Church and was buried in the cemetery connected with the church, after solemn and appropriate funeral services on Monday afternoon.

Issue of:
Thursday, September 28, 1882:
Married: On the 13th inst. by Rev. M. McGee, at his own residence, Mr. J. W. [...nie] and Miss Mary Shaw, all of Anderson County.

Obituary: Little Sylvester Bleckley, son of Mr. and Mrs. J. J. Fretwell, age 3, died last Monday evening, after a short illness from pneumonia. Buried in the Baptist Cemetery.

Issue of:
Thursday, October 5, 1882:
Obituary: Mr. Patrick J. O'Donnell, a brother of Mr. John D'Donnell of this city, died of pneumonia in Sumter on last Saturday after a short illness. Mr. O'Donnell was a native of Ireland but had been in America a number of years.

Issue of:
Thursday, October 12, 1882:
Married: On the 24th of September at the residence of the bride's father by Rev. D. [.....iott], Mr. J. H. Brown and Miss Mary McCord, all of Pickens.

Issue of:
Thursday, November 1, 1860:
A write up on Wm. Lowndes Yancey of Abbeville.

Issue of:
October 19, 1871:
Married: On Thursday afternoon, October 12th, 1871, by Rev.
W. A. Hodges, Mr. James E. Payne and Miss Cora Crawford, all
of Anderson.

Issue of:
Thursday, January 7, 1875:
Married: On Tuesday, Dec. 22, by Rev. John Johnson, Mr. James
L. Dean of Spartanburg and Miss Martha C., eldest daughter of
P. J. Holland of Charleston.

Married: On the 22nd of December, 1874, by Rev. D. L. Whitaker,
Mr. J. H. Rainey and Miss Katie R. Hall, all of Anderson County.

Married: On Tuesday morning, January 5, 1875, by Rev. D. E.
Frierson, Capt. S. M. Pegg and Miss C. C. Daniels, all of
Anderson.

Obituary: Col. N. J. Walker, a former resident of Barnwell
County and who was distinguished for gallant services in the
Mexican war, died at his residence at Peori, Hill Co., Texas
on the 11th ult.

Issue of:
Thursday, January 14, 1875:
Married: December 22, 1874, by the Rev. W. P. Martin, at the
residence of the bride's grandfather, Mr. Aaron Hall, Mr.
Pinckney L. Tate and Miss Carra E. Arnold, all of Anderson
County.

Obituary: Rev. G. C. Grimes, of Laurens, after a protracted
and painful illness of several months, died at his residence
in that village on the 14th inst. Mr. Grimes was for many years
connected with the ministry of the Baptist denomination and
his death will be regretted by a large circle of acquaintances
and friends.

Issue of:
Thursdya, January 21, 1875:
Married: By the Rev. G. H. Cartlege, on Thursday, December 31st.
Mr. R. D. Owen and Miss Mary A. Telford, eldest daughter of
G. B. Telford, all of Banks County, Ga.

Married: On the 6th of January, 1875 by Rev. E. F. Hyde, Mr.
S. N. Brown and Miss M. A., daughter of Mr. W. J. Bowen, all
of Anderson County.

Married: On Thursday evening, December 24th, 1874 by Rev. W. E.
Walters, Mr. W. C. Andrew and Miss Kate Harris, all of Anderson.

Married: At the residence of F. L. Sitton, on the 18th
December, 1874, by Rev. W. C. Smith, Mr. Thomas E. Dickson of
Anderson and Miss Ella Jones of Oconee County.

Married: On the 31st December, 1874, at the residence of the
bride's father, by Rev. S. Isbell, Mr. S. Newton Browne and
Miss Maria E. Dobbins, all of Anderson County.

251

Issue of: Continued
Thursday, January 21, 1875:
Married: On January 12th at the residence of the bride's
brother, Dr. N. J. Newell, by Rev. E. F. Hyde, Mr. John L.
Moore and Miss J. R. Newell, all of Anderson County.